Freedom and Development | Uhuru na Maendeleo

Other Books by the Author

Freedom and Unity/Uhuru na Umoja
(A selection from writings and speeches 1952-1965)

Freedom and Socialism/Uhuru na Ujamaa
(A selection from writings and speeches 1965-1967)

Nyerere on Socialism
(The collected Introductions to the above two works)

Ujamaa — Essays on Socialism
(A selection from *Freedom and Socialism | Uhuru na Ujamaa*)

Ujamaa
(The Swahili version of *Ujamaa | Essays on Socialism*)

Man and Development
(A selection from *Freedom and Development | Uhuru na Maendeleo*)

Mwanaadamu na Maendeleo
(The Swahili version of *Man and Development*)

Swahili Translations

Juliasi Kaizari
(Shakespeare's *Julius Caesar*)

Mabepari wa Venisi
(Shakespeare's *The Merchant of Venice*)

President Julius K. Nyerere

TO

THE PEOPLE

FREEDOM UHURU
AND NA
DEVELOPMENT MAENDELEO

A Selection from Writings and Speeches
1968-1973

JULIUS K. NYERERE

OXFORD UNIVERSITY PRESS
London   Oxford   New York

OXFORD UNIVERSITY PRESS

London   Oxford   New York
Glasgow   Toronto   Melbourne   Wellington
Cape Town   Ibadan   Nairobi   Dar es Salaam   Lusaka   Addis Ababa
Delhi   Bombay   Calcutta   Madras   Karachi   Lahore   Dacca
Kuala Lumpur   Singapore   Hong Kong   Tokyo

Printed in the United States of America

Contents

Illustrations

President Julius K. Nyerere (Photo: Adarsh Nayar).

1   Chairman Mao and the President meet again in Peking in 1968 (T.I.S.).

2   In Moscow, during October 1969, the President had long official talks with his hosts. But there were also social meetings —as in this photograph taken at a lunch party in the House of Receptions. The President is with Prime Minister Kosygin, President Podgorny, and Mr. Mazurov, Deputy Prime Minister (Copyright: A.S.P., London).

3   During his State Visit to Hungary in October 1969 the President visited the publicly owned 'Ikarus' Bus Factory at Budapest—and was given a bus fitted out as a mobile dispensary. Hungarian President Pal Losonczi is fourth from the left (front row) in this photograph (Copyright: Interfoto Mti).

4   King Frederick IX of Denmark and the President in interested conversation at State House, Dar es Salaam, during the State Visit of the Danish King and Queen, January 1970 (T.I.S.).

5   President Tito and Madame Broz of Yugoslavia pictured with the President at State House, Dar es Salaam in January 1970 (T.I.S.).

6   President Obote of Uganda, and President Nyerere, leave Dar es Salaam for the Non-Aligned Conference in Lusaka, September 1970 (Adarsh Nayar).

7   The President delivered his speech 'Church and Society' to the Maryknoll Sisters' Conference on 16 October 1970 at their Headquarters outside New York, USA (T.I.S.).

8   The President and his party with Pope Paul when the President was returning from the United Nations in October 1970 (T.I.S.).

9   The old search for water is still much too common—this photograph comes from Shinyanga District (T.I.S.).

10   In the same District, the villagers of Mwamalasa Ujamaa

Village have clean tap water—provided by a combination of self-help work and Government finance (T.I.S.).

11   The President discussing design work for *vitenge* with a worker at the Friendship Textile Mill, Dar es Salaam (*Daily News*).

12   In October 1970 work on the Tanzania/Zambia railway was formally started at a ceremony attended by President Kaunda and President Nyerere as well as a visiting Chinese Minister. This photograph shows the two Presidents examining a map of the railroad (T.I.S.).

13   The Presidential, Parliamentary, and Local Elections were all held simultaneously in October 1970. This photograph was taken at a polling station in Mtoni, near Dar es Salaam (T.I.S.).

14   In January 1971 the President paid a State Visit to India. He is seen here with (r. to l.) Prime Minister Mrs. Gandhi, President V. Giri, and the Indian Vice-President Mr. G. S. Pathak (T.I.S.).

15   The Mass Literacy Campaign now covers the whole of Tanzania—this class is in Monduli District (T.I.S.).

16   The President's interest in adult education is reflected as he visits this class in Ruvu during 1971 (T.I.S.).

17   The President enjoys a joke made by the retiring Chief Justice Georges when replying to the President's speech at a Dinner given in his honour in March 1971 (T.I.S.).

18   The President spent some weeks in Dodoma District in 1971, helping the people in their move into ujamaa villages. Here he is mixing mud for brick-making (T.I.S.).

19   The Prime Minister of Sweden, Mr. Olof Palme, was a guest at the TANU National Conference in September 1971 (Adarsh Nayar).

20   On his return from a visit to President Kenyatta at Nakuru, President Nyerere was greeted by the First Vice-President of the United Republic, Sheikh Aboud Jumbe, and the Second Vice-President and Prime Minister, Mr. Rashidi Kawawa (T.I.S.).

21   A large Buffet Dinner was given on 9 December 1971 in honour of the 10th Anniversary of Tanganyika's independence. Traditional Tanzanian dishes were cooked for the occasion by members of Umoja wa Wanawake (the national women's

organization). With the President in this photograph are (l. to r.), Lady Seretse Khama, President Barre of Somalia, President Micombero of Burundi, and President Seretse Khama (T.I.S.).

Contents List by Subject

Preface

This third Preface that I have written for collections of my speeches and writings published by Oxford University Press can say nothing that is not a repetition of what was said on the two previous occasions. The purpose of the book is that people who find my ideas and explanations useful can have them readily available, and those who wish to check up on what I have been saying may easily do so. But it is important to remember that this book is not a description of what exists in Tanzania, or Africa, except when the words specifically say so. Generally, it is a description of what we in Tanzania are aiming at, not what we are. For although Tanzania is engaged in building a socialist society, it certainly is not one at present; and although Africa is aiming at unity, it is not yet united. If the ideas expressed in this book, and the book itself, make some small contribution towards the achievement of those goals, then they will have done all that is expected of them.

Once again, however, particular individuals have made possible the preparation of this book. Miss Esther Mwinyimvua did the larger part of the typing, after taking over from Mrs. Betty Karstead as my Personal Secretary. And for the third time I want to express appreciation for the assistance of Miss Joan E. Wicken, my Personal Assistant, who has done all the other donkey work involved, both for the book and for the selections included in it.

Finally, I wish to acknowledge with thanks the work of the photographers of the Tanzania Information Services, of the *Daily News*, and of other Agencies—some of whose results provide relief from the mass of type presented in this book.

July 1973   J.K.N.

xvii

1

A Peaceful New Year

At the beginning of every year, President Nyerere gives a reception at State House for the diplomats accredited to the United Republic of Tanzania. On 1 January 1968, his speech was longer and more serious than is normally the case.

... It is a sad reflection on the state of the world in recent decades that the wish for a 'Happy New Year'—which we used to extend to each other—has been amended, so that we now more usually wish each other a 'Happy and Peaceful New Year'. Historians tell us that this simply indicates the development of communications, because there has always been conflict somewhere in the world—only we did not know about it. I suspect that is true; but it is unfortunately also true that peace elsewhere can no longer be a matter of indifference to us—even from the point of view of our own security. 'Peace on Earth' is no longer a matter of academic or humane interest only; we are all too involved in one another for us to be indifferent to its breakdown, even thousands of miles from our borders. Peace everywhere is now something which matters to us all; our own human happiness, and our own economic and social progress are involved in it.

Yet peace by itself is not enough for the human spirit if it means just an absence of violent conflict. For that could merely become an excuse for the kind of social stagnation which deprives many human beings of their humanity. The world is not yet so perfect in its social relations that any of us could really call for peace at any price within nations. There may even be times when international action against inhumanity by one nation is called for—although all of us can see the dangers of this concept and the necessity for long and earnest consideration before we embark upon anything of the kind. Yet would it not have been better for the world if the League of Nations had been able to intervene in the mid-1930s to destroy the Nazi racialism which finally led to six million Jews being murdered? Was peace at that time the kind of peace which human beings should support?

Your Excellencies will, I hope, believe me when I say that I am not advocating violence as a means of solving social problems, nor would I support any one nation attacking another because of a belief that it is cruel and inhumane in its internal or external policies. Indeed I do not believe that any one nation should ever attack another. All that I am trying to say is that peace and human justice are inter-linked, and should be inter-linked. In our international endeavours for peace we must involve ourselves in international endeavours for justice.

There is a continuing need for an extension of human rights throughout the world; that surely is incontrovertible. We cannot rest where we are because some of us are comfortable or content. Those of us who are free to develop ourselves and our nation have no right to demand that the oppressed, the victims of discrimination, the starving, and the persecuted, should acquiesce in their present condition. If we do make such a demand we are ourselves becoming their persecutors and their oppressors. The peace which exists while such human conditions prevail is neither secure nor justifiable. We have no right to be patient with the wrongs suffered by others.

Yet peace is of vital importance to us all; social change and the improvement of the human condition must, therefore be made possible by other means—means which do not involve killing and destruction. For we do have a right to demand of our fellow human beings that they should secure change by peaceful means if these are open to them. We do have a right to demand that those who seek change should use every opportunity which exists for peaceful change, even if this appears to mean the slower progress of adapting the society in which they live rather than the excitement of pulling it down upon the bodies of all—including themselves. We must insist upon this. But if every avenue of peaceful change has been closed; if people are made outcasts in their own society, and denied any possibility of securing change through participation—do we then have any right to demand our peace at the price of their slavery?

Surely peace under such circumstances is neither to be expected, nor to be justified?

This recognition of the ultimate paramountcy of human rights is not a justification for national interventionism, nor a call for some peoples to attempt to free other peoples. No nation has the right to make decisions for another nation; no people for another people. Some of us, like Tanzania, may fervently believe in a socialist organization of our society as being both morally right and economically practicable. Others may believe equally fervently in capitalism, or in communism. But none of us could, or should, assume that what we have decided to be right for ourselves must automatically be right for others. For the truth is that it is what a people want for themselves at a particular time which is right for them; no one else is justified in trying to impose a different way of life.

And equally, it is impossible for one people to free another people, or even to defend the freedom of another people. Freedom won for a people by outsiders is lost to those outsiders, however good their intentions, or however much the outsiders had desired to free their oppressed brothers. That is the nature of freedom; it has to be won, and protected, by those who desire it.

Of course others can help a people who are struggling for freedom; they can give refuge, facilities for action, and they can give moral and diplomatic support to an oppressed people. But no group or nation—however powerful—can make another group or another nation free. The struggle must be waged by those who expect to benefit from it. If the persecuted and the oppressed have really been denied their human rights, and if there really is no peaceful means of progress available to them, then they have the right to demand of the rest of us that we should support their struggle—and not join their oppressors on the grounds of maintaining peace. But we cannot replace their struggle, and we should not try. For if we do so we are not trying to free our brothers; we are simply trying to replace one oppression by a different one. It may be less harsh, it may take different forms; but it will not mean freedom for those who now lack it.

Your Excellencies, I have spoken for longer than is my custom at these gatherings, and I have been trying to express in a few words concepts which are extremely complex and terrifyingly difficult—and which philosophers have written many books about. But what it really amounts to is a very simple statement. It is that as we, the peoples of the earth, extend human justice so we are furthering the cause of peace; and that every moment of peace is a moment stolen unless it is used to further justice between men and between nations.

We in Tanzania will continue with our endeavours to live up to that belief during 1968, and we look forward to the co-operation of yourselves and the peoples you represent.

2
Implementation of Rural Socialism

On 1 January 1968, the President opened the TANU Youth League (University Branch) Seminar on the policy paper 'Socialism and Rural Development'. In this speech he stressed the importance of self-government by the ujamaa villages, and discussed the function of leaders in relation to them.

I am extremely pleased that the University Branch of the TANU Youth League has selected the policy paper 'Socialism and Rural Development' for serious study. For in some ways this policy is a problem; it is very difficult to get it organized and implemented. The new education policy outlined in 'Education for Self-Reliance' can be—and is being—worked out in some detail by the Ministry of Education; they can organize its introduction, and supervise the action being taken on it. Of course, a very great deal still depends upon the teachers and principals in schools throughout the country—upon their initiative and understanding. But in this field you do have a recognizable group, all of whom are public employees, to whom the new policy can be explained; you can direct your guidance and assistance easily to the right places, and you can supervise developments almost as they occur.

The policy paper we are talking about today is very different. It is directed at all the people of Tanzania—or at least all of those who live in the rural areas. It is an outline of a policy of inter-linked, self-governing village communities which are *of* the people, and which therefore cannot be created for them or imposed on them. The paper, therefore, calls for leadership, but not for orders to be given; it directs the people along the socialist path, but excludes any attempt to whip them into it—saying clearly that you cannot force people to lead socialist lives.

This inevitably creates a difficulty, for it leaves open the question of how the Government can actively promote ujamaa villages on a healthy basis. Instead, there are two opposing dangers at the outset; on the one hand there is a danger that enthusiastic TANU members, and others, might rush out and bully people into artificial communities which will collapse with the first breath of adversity, and on the other there is a danger that nothing will happen at all.

... The first problem which must be faced is the one I have already referred to: how do we get started? The policy is there, with the goals clearly stated. The document suggests that any Tanzanian can take the initiative. Fine! But how do we move from the fact that any Tanzanian may and can take the initiative to the fact of his doing so?

In considering this question it is absolutely essential that the crucial point about an ujamaa village or farm should not be forgotten. The community must own, control, and run its own activities. They must be democratic and socialist working and living communities, in which the members are jointly responsible to themselves. Does this mean that they must therefore be started by the members without outside initiative or participation? In considering this question we have to remember that the vast majority of our people are still illiterate; they could not read and study this policy document even if it were easily available to them. . . .

How then do we get moving? Government and TANU leaders could certainly encourage, explain, and teach about these ideas; but is this enough? Would it really help very much if every person in this seminar simply talked about the policy in his home area during the vacation, and then came back to the towns? What of the idea that more educated people should join in the practical work of initiating an ujamaa village, and become a founder member of it? Is it likely that we should have any volunteers for such work, when it is realized how hard, and how materially unrewarding, it will be in comparison with the opportunities open to educated people—even after Arusha?

I am putting these questions frankly, because I think they must be answered. The fact that I pose them should not be taken to imply that I think there is no answer, or that it is necessarily a discouraging one! My own experience suggests that our people in the rural areas are prepared to work together for their common good; in many places they have never stopped this traditional custom, and would take quite easily to an extension of it. The problem is not the principle; the problem is that of getting people to adopt practices which retain the central idea at the same time as they allow for development and growth. For we are not just trying to go backwards into the traditional past; we are trying to retain the traditional values of human equality and dignity while taking advantage of modern knowledge about the advantages of scale and improved tools. But inevitably this requires some adaptation in traditional social organization; it requires a conscious working together for the common good, and a conscious effort to utilize the strength of united activity for social purposes. In the past we worked together because that was the custom; now we have to do it deliberately, and do it in such a manner that modern knowledge can be utilized for the common good.

One thing is certainly known; nothing succeeds like success! If we can get a few of these village communities working in every area, their success will lead to others also being started. The essential thing therefore is to begin. It is for this reason that the paper suggests that anyone can take the initiative, and suggests also that a small handful of people—the members of a ten-house cell or an even smaller number—could begin. Of course, such a small unit would not be able to achieve very much; but it can grow. The present twelve ujamaa villages in the Ruvuma Development Association have grown out of a beginning made by ten individuals, and the fact that after a complete crop failure in the first year, three of those ten were prepared to try again the following year.

There is, in fact, an advantage in starting very small, in that the members will know each other well and be able to work together to overcome the inevitable difficulties without taking refuge in blaming others. Because there are only a few of them they will be able to discuss their problems together, and make decisions together for which they all feel equally responsible. Yet there obviously comes a point below which you cannot fall and still have an ujamaa village. What is the ideal size? Will it vary very much in different conditions? And how can you determine what the optimum figure is—and reach it?

In all this discussion we must realize the central fact; that an ujamaa village must be governed by the members themselves, equally. I have already stated this, but I make no apology for saying it again; it is the essence of rural socialism. Members must jointly make their own decisions on everything which is of exclusive concern to the village—where to plant, what to plant, how to share the work, how to share the returns, what to invest in the future development, and so on. Obviously the communities, and their members, must obey the laws of the land; they cannot be exempt from taxation or other national responsibilities. But the decisions about the way they run their farm and their village—the amount of private farming and ownership they allow, etc.—must be made by them, and not by others.

There will, in fact, probably be no shortage of people who come to a new embryonic village and tell the members what to do. Indeed, I hope the Agricultural Field Workers and other skilled and trained people will be offering their advice freely, and doing all they can to encourage ujamaa villages to adopt modern methods from the start. But the decisions must be made by the members, not by anyone else—even Area Commissioners or visiting Presidents.

Yet we must be clear what we are saying here; for we have a real dilemma. It may easily happen that a visiting political or government leader knows that the people are making a mistake which could prove fatal to their ambition, either in organization, in their selection of their leader, or in their methods. The temptation to intervene must surely be very great indeed under these circumstances; part of the visitor's job is to help these communities. Obviously he should explain his point, illustrate his argument by pointing to experience elsewhere, and discuss the whole question with the members. But suppose the members still insist on their own decision? It is at that point that we have to go back to the essence of these villages; people must be allowed to make their own decisions, and therefore their own mistakes. Only if we accept this are we really accepting the philosophy of Socialism and Rural Development. If we prevent people making their own mistakes we are preventing the establishment of ujamaa villages; we can advise and warn, but if we try to run them we are destroying them. We may have to pay a price in failures and disappointments as a result, but it cannot be avoided. And in any case obstinate local people can sometimes prove all previous experience, and all skilled advice, to be wrong! The fact that a man is employed by Government, or elected in TANU—or even educated at University College—does not make him infallible!

In one sense all that I have been saying so far is a call for leadership. We need people to lead others into an understanding of the concept of ujamaa villages, to lead the members in the villages, to promote good methods of husbandry and practical methods of organization; we need people to rally the members when they get discouraged, show them the way out of their difficulties, and so on. Progress in socialist rural development does in fact depend almost entirely on leadership at all levels; it needs leadership to get the groups started, and it needs leadership to maintain them and have them grow.

Let me emphasize that this leadership I am now talking about does not imply control, any more than it implies bullying or intimidating people. A good leader will explain, teach, and inspire. In an ujamaa village he will do more; he will lead by doing. He is in the front of the people, showing them what can be done, guiding them, and encouraging them. But he is with them. You do not lead people by being so far in front or so theoretical in your teaching that the people cannot see what you are doing or saying. You do not lead people by yapping at their heels like a dog herding cattle. You can lead the people only by being one of them, by just being more active as well as more thoughtful, and more willing to teach as well as more willing to learn—from them and others.

The members of an ujamaa village must control their own affairs—I say it again! But the role of a leader is crucial and good leadership will make all the difference to the socialist success and the material success of such a community.

Let me give one example of the kind of leadership which is needed. Suppose a group of families have decided to start a co-operative farm and village, and are discussing where to build their houses. The problem is whether to build on a hill or down in the valley; and the argument is about the ease of getting water versus the danger of flooding. A good leader who is a member of this group may argue that it is better to build on the hill and face the drudgery of carrying the water until they can afford a pump and pipes; but let us suppose that despite all his efforts the general opinion is to build near the water's edge. What should he do? The answer is clear: he must play a very full part in the work of building the village in the valley. Having done that he must also think out plans for action if his fears are proved well-founded. He might persuade the members to build some of their stores on the hill so as to have a reserve in case of trouble; he might persuade them to keep a reserve of poles and thatching material on the hill which can then be used wherever and whenever it is necessary; and he will certainly work out in his own mind a plan for rescue and shelter on higher ground so that he at least knows what must be done in case of emergency.

But this kind of leadership is only one of many different kinds which will be needed. There is the same problem of management— although on a different scale—for an ujamaa farm as for a capitalist farm which employs many people. Work has still to be organized, the crops harvested and sold, etc. This will require some delegation, by the members, of their power over themselves—for you cannot have a members' meeting every day in order to decide whether to weed the beans or the tobacco! The selection of the right person as the 'farm manager' or as the 'farm treasurer' can be of vital importance; how then can the members be helped to choose the best man from among their number? And if they do make a mistake, how can they be sure of effecting a change, without having so much daily 'democracy' in the running of the farm that no work gets done because of the time spent in talking?

These are practical questions. The little experience we have so far in Tanzania shows the importance of the village leaders. It is clear they must be strong men, yet humble; they must be capable of ensuring that everyone does a fair share of the work—including themselves—and at the same time they must be willing to accept group decisions on basic issues. For example, they must be able to convince the members that everyone will have to work for eight hours a day in order to get through all the jobs; able to accept a group decision that this will be done from 6.0 a.m. until 2.0 p.m.; and then able to allocate different members to different jobs in rotation—and see that they are done.

This brings me to the final problem which I intend to refer to today—the problem of incentives. For it is all very well to say that members will 'live together and work together for the common good'; it is all very well to say a leader's job is to see that everyone does his fair share. But we are not all angels, and it is not unknown for everyone to do a fair share on a communal project just because everyone does as much as the laziest member, and no more! What kind of organization, or what kind of rules about distribution of returns, should be recommended to groups setting up together, so as to ensure that between them they produce the maximum? For if there is no difference in return, is it not likely that the good and fast worker may get tired of putting his best efforts forward while another member merely does the bare minimum which keeps him in the scheme? In an ideal world he might shrug his shoulders and carry on; in the world as it is he might decide to do less himself too!

Is it enough, therefore, to rely upon every member understanding the benefit to himself of everyone putting forward his maximum effort? Is it enough to rely upon social sanctions as a discipline against those who slack, with explusion as the only and final weapon against them? Or would such groups be advised to work out some system of division according to the amount of work done, or the number of hours spent on the communal projects? If you do this, are you breaking the socialist principle of equality—for it will lead to some differences in income between the members? And if you do not do it, are you allowing the poor workers, or the lazy ones, to exploit the others? But again, if you do advocate payment by work done, what about those people who work to the best of their ability, but who are sick, or weak, or just not very capable?

Mr. Chairman, there are many other problems I could raise—some of which may be raised by other speakers. . . .

. . . For the policy outlined in 'Socialism and Rural Development' is not the work of a month or a year; it is the work for ten or twenty years ahead. What we have to do now is start; and the more people who understand the objectives, and who are willing to join in, the greater—and the quicker—will be our success.

3

Unity Must Incorporate
Differences

On a state visit to West Africa, President Nyerere's speech at a banquet in the Ivory Coast, on 26 February 1968, stressed that African unity must accommodate African diversity, and argued that unity should take priority over ideological differences.

... We are all separate and sovereign states. No African state has the right to interfere in the internal affairs of the others. And each state has the power, and the duty, to determine its own path forward. But we can, and must, still work together.

Thus, for example, we in Tanzania have adopted the principles of socialism as our creed; we are deliberately trying to build a socialist state on the foundations of our traditional communalism. We are proud of the progress we have made so far, although we recognize that we have only just begun the work we have set ourselves. The political philosophy of the Ivory Coast, on the other hand, has been defined by you, Mr. President, as 'evolution within freedom'. But these different choices do not mean that there has to be hostility, or even suspicion, between our two countries. These different decisions do not preclude constructive co-operation within the limits laid down by our geographical separation. Our different philosophies may affect the institutional arrangements we make for our mutual benefit; but they do not affect our African brotherhood, nor provide us with an escape from Africa's need for unity. And what is true between Tanzania and the Ivory Coast is true for each of us in relation to other and nearer African states.

The fact is that free Africa is made up of 38 sovereign states, every one of which is different from all the others. Those countries which have shown a preference for socialist policies differ among themselves in their political and economic organization; those which

prefer capitalism—and all the others which defy such categorization
—also differ among themselves. And we shall all continue to differ
as we develop out of the present which we are even now creating.
The differences are there. The only way forward for us is to accept
them. The different philosophies and organizations in Africa are
as much part of the Africa which has to be united as are the common
cultural heritage and the almost universal experience of colonialism.
It is no use our waiting for differences of approach, or of political
belief, to disappear before we think of working for unity in Africa.
They will not disappear. If we are ever to unite, the differences
must be accommodated within our growing unity, and our growing
unity must be shaped in a manner which allows for the existing
differences.

Of course this will not be easy. We shall not be able to make
ourselves into a neat and logical parcel—at least at the beginning.
International co-operation, even between nations which have the
same kind of political system, is not without its difficulties, as we
can see if we look around the world! But our task is not impossible.
There are only three basic things we all have to accept if we are to
move through co-operation to unity, or through unity to co-operation. The first thing is that each people, and each nation, must
have the right to choose their own economic and political institutions
and systems, in relation to matters which are of exclusive concern
to them. The second thing is that, when we are working out arrangements for inter-African co-operation, we have to recognize that no
one of us will be able to have things just as we would like them;
all of us will have to compromise with the needs and desires of
others. And thirdly, all of us have to accept the paramountcy of
Africa, and brotherhood and co-operation within Africa, over all
outside relationships.

These basic requirements for the growth of unity are, of course,
easy to state; in practice they will cause argument and some difficulty. But if we can hold fast to them we can make progress in
Africa, and it will be a progress which will be to the benefit of every
one of us.

There is only one other thing I would like to stress in connection
with the movement for African unity. That is, that it does not have
to imply hostility to other parts of the world. To be a member
of a tribe does not automatically mean hostility to the nation of

which one is a member; to be a citizen of a sovereign nation in Africa does not preclude a loyalty to Africa and its growing unity. Similarly, the movement towards unity in Africa does not have to mean hostility to Europe, or Asia, or to America. For every individual is a member of many communities; he is a member sometimes of his clan, and also of his tribe. He is now a citizen of his nation, and linked with the other nations of Africa through the Organization of African Unity; and he is also a citizen of the world. Our individual membership of all these groups is a fact, whether we are conscious of it or not. And all these groups continue within one another, and interact upon one another.

To say that one's loyalty to Africa must predominate over loyalty to any single non-African relationship, therefore, no more implies hostility to outside groups than the predominant loyalty of brothers to each other implies hostility to other members of the village community. Brothers in a family stand together, and work together for their common good, in preference to working with outsiders, when a choice has to be made between the two. In case of conflict with other members of the society, brothers stand together. And when there are family quarrels they settle them among themselves, fiercely resenting the intervention of others. Let us African states organize ourselves as members of the one family we in fact are, and then, as one group, we shall be able to work easily and on equal terms with the rest of the world.

This work we have already started. All free African states are members of the Organization of African Unity, and despite its inevitable difficulties and growing pains, I believe that our organization will in the future be of great service to us all. It is true that when we had established the OAU we tried to go too fast, and to give it work which was beyond its strength, because we had not yet built up confidence between ourselves. But I believe that Africa has now learned that lesson. We have learned that the OAU represents only the first plank of wood across the chasm of disunity; we must guard that plank, but we must gradually strengthen it before we put too much weight upon it. This strengthening we can do by our various arrangements for regional and technical co-operation. But we must never forget the final goal, nor allow our regional arrangements to damage, or preclude, the attainment of our final continental unity. . . .

4

Unity Must be Worked For

On 28 January 1968, President Nyerere spoke to the Liberian Parliament on the subject of African unity. This same theme was at the centre of most of his speeches during his West African tour.

... Liberia and Tanzania must be interested in each other, for we are each involved in the development of the other. We are involved because we are all involved in the well-being and the development of Africa—our continent. Whether we like it or not, and despite our separate sovereignties, the outside world is interested in Africa much more than it is interested in Liberia, Tanzania, or any other African country separately. The powers of Europe, Asia and America will use us separately, but their objective is not control of this state or that, but the domination of the whole of Africa. And when each of us struggles for our independence from outside control, we are struggling as Africans for the independence of Africa.

These things we all know, and have all accepted. It is because we realize our inter-dependence that we have talked so much, and for so long, about African unity. It is because we have realized that instability, poverty, disease—and even development—in one country affects the rest of Africa, that we have taken some steps towards African unity.

In fact I believe the vague idea that 'African unity is a good thing' is accepted in our continent to almost a dangerous degree. And I believe that it is dangerous because we all say we support unity, and our unanimity in this leads us to assume that everything is agreed and there is nothing more to be done about it.

But if unity in Africa is ever to be achieved, steps towards it should be almost the most important aspect of policy in every single

African state. For it is certainly the most difficult aspect of policy. The experiences of the last few years have demonstrated that fact without any possibility of argument. And if we in Africa, in our separate sovereign states, were giving serious consideration to the advance towards unity, the arguments between us might be very fierce indeed. For on any important issue people must feel strongly. Of course, we would not have to quarrel on the issue, but we should certainly disagree on many facets of it. (The fact that we disagreed without quarrelling would, in truth, be evidence of our determination to achieve unity!) The real danger, Mr. Speaker, is not such disagreements, but such a fear of them that we take refuge in vague statements of support for unity and do not tackle the problems at all.

It is for this reason that I propose to use the opportunity of your kind invitation to address you today, to examine the question of African unity, our progress towards it, and the steps which we have to take to achieve it.

Ultimately, Mr. Speaker, African unity must mean a union of African states—a transfer of some sovereignty from our national units to a new single unit of which we are all part. It means the existence of some kind of federal government, to which all the state governments have surrendered some of their separate powers.

If African unity is to be a reality there is no alternative. There must be one government which can speak for Africa to the outside world. There must be one organ which is responsible for the defence of Africa against attack or subversion from outside. There must be one representative body which can co-ordinate and facilitate the economic development of Africa as a whole in such a manner as to ensure the well-being of every part of our continent; this means there must be one currency, one tariff system, and so on, as well as other institutions to promote economic growth.

Simply to spell out this shows both the importance of unity, and the distance we have to travel to reach it. But only when we have reached that position can Africa begin to stand on equal terms with the rest of the world and play our proper part in its councils. For what happens now? Africa has 38 representatives in the General Assembly of the United Nations; a good part of the time we divide our votes and cancel each other out. The rest of the time we form a bloc which might determine whether a resolution is passed or not.

But having passed it we are too weak, or too divided, to see that it is implemented. When great events happen in the world, which need a common African stand, we cannot provide it. There cannot be meetings of Heads of States immediately on every such occasion, nor all-African Ministers' meetings. And even if there were, our separate sovereignty means that the joint decisions cannot be enforced if any one country is too weak to carry them out.

In economics, too, Africa suffers for its present division into sovereign states. Each of us separately competes with the others for the favours of the richer nations—for more capital investment, more aid, or for the sale of our exports. I am not criticizing anyone for this; it is inevitable because every government in Africa must at the present time look after the exclusive interests of its own people. But the net result is that we are all in a weak bargaining position with our wealthy trade partners; separately and collectively we suffer from the resultant poor terms of trade, from expensive outside capital, and so on. Only as a single unit could we hope to overcome this weakness. Whatever efforts we make for co-operation between our sovereign states, our condition is such that each separate country will be sorely tempted—and may even be forced by economic circumstances—to try to buy favours from outside, even at the expense of other African nations.

But this is not all, Mr. Speaker. No African state is large enough to become economically viable and independent at any high level, regardless of the efforts and sacrifices it makes It is no accident, nor is it a tribute to any special racial characteristic, that the really wealthy nations of the modern world are the United States of America and the Soviet Union. Neither is it through lack of inter-state suspicion and traditional hostility that the states of Europe are coming together—and that Britain is so anxious to join them. It is because a high standard of living demands a large market free movement of capital and people, and so on. It is true that the European Community does not yet have a single government responsible to all its people; but does anyone, Mr. Speaker, doubt that this is where it is going to? Until Africa is one economic unit, it will remain the plaything of the great powers of the world; and the only way for a people to keep control of one economic unit is to have one representative political power covering the whole area.

This, Mr. Speaker, is, in our opinion, what we have to attain: this is what Africa must become. But we shall not have solved our problems when we have established one United States of Africa, one Federation, or Confederation of Africa—and by simply listing these alternative names I indicate the important questions which have to be settled. Whether we achieve this kind of unity next week, or in a hundred years, the consolidation and the operation of a united Africa would still be difficult. The creation of unity will not solve the problems of Africa; it will only enable them to be solved by Africa. By the act of union we shall have down-graded certain African problems—problems of border conflicts, for example—but we shall have made others, such as the siting of major industries, more pressing. Yet the new problems, and the ones which become more obvious with unity, are the problems of construction. Too many of the others are the problems of avoiding destruction.

Union between sovereign states, or even between areas separately administered, is never easy. There will be conflicts of interest between the different areas; there will be problems arising from the sheer size of the unit; there will be problems arising out of our ignorance of each other, and perhaps even out of personal ambitions. There will be problems of adjustment, and of confusion as to who has power in what field. All these and many more will exist. But they have existed, and still exist, in the United States of America. They exist in the USSR. They even exist within many of our separate nations now. Is there anyone who doubts the justification for the American federation because of the difficulties it is experiencing? Is there anyone who believes that because some American states are reactionary in particular fields, and others progressive, it would be better if the United States again split up into its component parts? Africa, too, must face its destiny. Africa, too, must face up to the real problems of development.

Yet to state the objective, and demonstrate its importance, does not solve our problems now. How shall we attain that unity?

Three things we know. God is not going to descend from heaven and say, 'Let there be Unity' in the way He once said, 'Let there be Light'. Nor would any African state agree to the creation of unity by conquest, by the force of a stronger African state—much less the force of an outside power. If there is to be unity it must be created by us, by our own determined effort, and by our own free will. Unity in Africa must be the unity of free, and freely-consenting, peoples who have decided to take up the challenge together.

Yet there are now 38 sovereign nations in free Africa. We are used to our sovereignty; we have developed—or in some cases are developing—a national pride. Indeed, every day that passes takes us further along the road to a nationalism which ignores our African-ness. We all salute our national flags, teach our children about our own countries, and their institutions, and create new symbols of national loyalty. And there is no comparable symbol of the loyalty we must feel to Africa, if we are ever to attain the unity we need.

Each of our states is grappling with difficult internal problems; sometimes problems of unification, sometimes of administration, sometimes of economics—and sometimes all of them simultaneously. What time have governments and legislators to devote to the problems of unity? What priority can we give to them when we are all exclusively responsible to the electors in a particular part of Africa?

To state these difficulties in the way of achieving unity is simply to recognize the facts as they are. But it is no reason for surrendering the goal. Nor is it any reason for despondency. On the contrary, the double recognition of the need for unity, and of the difficulty of achieving it, is a necessary pre-condition for success.

There are two basic methods by which we can ensure that we are always moving forward; they must be used concurrently.

First, we have to hold on to the objective of total African unity and try to avoid any action which might complicate its later attainment.

We have to keep the concept of Africa, as one unit, before our people all the time. In our schools we must teach our children that they are Africans as well as Liberians or Tanzanians. Through our newspapers and radios we must extend knowledge of other parts of our continent, and ensure that all our people know how much they have in common with each other. We must share our dances and our songs, our literature and our music. In short, we must help our people to get to know each other, and understand each other's history and development.

Then on the political front, we must all try to strengthen—or at least not to weaken—the Organization of African Unity. This is our Organization; we created it. It is ours to use for our own African purposes. In the past we, the African nations, have damaged—at one time almost destroyed—the OAU; some through impatience or verbosity, and others through a reluctance to make the smallest effort. We used the OAU to talk big, as if we imagined that the enemies of free Africa would be frightened by our big words. But we could not follow up that big talk by even small action, so we harmed and discredited the thing that we had created. But the OAU does exist, and now that we have learned to be realistic about its strength we can begin to use it properly—that is, for the slow, careful work of promoting understanding and co-ordination. Then, when its muscles have developed, we can again try to put more weight upon it in the drive forward to real unity.

For we must continue to obtain united African action whenever this is possible, whether this be in political, economic, or technical matters. Improved telecommunications, transport, or trade between African states can all contribute to our coming together. The kind of discussions we held at Algeria prior to the UNCTAD Conference now going on in New Delhi; the regular discussions our representatives hold in the United Nations; all these things help to avoid a public display of disunity, and help to prevent the kind of inter-African suspicions which others can use to drive a wedge between us. We must have more all-African discussions; we must try to see what agreement we can get for common action in any and every field. For the more we act as one, the easier it will be finally to become actually one.

In this connection it is, of course, particularly important that African leaders should always refrain from public displays of disunity. Our quarrels—if we have any—should be conducted privately! But I think this lesson has been learned; we now realize that by public attacks on each other—and even more by organizing subversion against each other—we are serving neither our own states nor Africa. We have, in fact, learned the practical importance of the principles enunciated in Article III of the OAU Charter.

Yet it remains true that, however hard we try, advance towards unity on an all-African basis is going to be slow and hardly won. The larger any group, the more difficult it is to get unanimous agreement—and while sovereignty is retained by our separate states, the unanimity rule is unavoidable.

Secondly, Mr. Speaker, therefore, we have—at the same time as we work for all-African advance—to try to achieve greater regional unity. Provided this is always done under the umbrella of the OAU, and never includes provisions which will block total unity in the future, regional co-operation can only help us. And this regional co-operation too, can be of any kind, in any field.

Sometimes it will be possible for two or more separate states to merge into one union or federation. By so doing they are reducing the number of sovereign states in Africa and, to that extent, reducing the ultimate problem. At the same time they are strengthening the position of one part of Africa, and enabling the people there to co-operate among themselves without reservation.

More often, however, regional co-operation will take the form of reducing economic or bureaucratic barriers between states, or of increasing joint functional activities. It is in this field that there have been advances during the past twelve months or so. A number of customs unions or agreements to reduce tariffs between two or more states have been established, and others are being negotiated. The successful inauguration of the East African Community, with its common services and common market, is another example. This kind of work demands great and patient attention to detail, and long and arduous negotiations, if it is to succeed in laying a foundation for further advance in African well-being. And—from experience—I can assure you that the negotiations are not always easy. They demand a willingness to compromise on the part of all participants; an understanding of what is essential, and an acceptance of the fact that no one country can hope to get everything it wants.

But however hard, and however unexciting, such negotiations may be, they are the kind of thing which is involved in African unity—whether they are done before or after the political decision to unite has been taken. Let me give another example from East African experience. When Tanganyika and Zanzibar decided to form the present United Republic of Tanzania, only the most basic questions of principle were settled between the two Governments. The detailed negotiations about unification of tariffs, the division of tax revenues, etc., were carried out later—and in some respects are still unfinished. But in the case of the East African Community, all these detailed discussions have taken place without a decision for political unity; we have settled for something less than federation because we were not all equally ready to make the merger. My point is that the same work has to be done through whichever road unity is approached; there is no short cut. Sometimes one route may be better and easier, at other times the other.

There is only one qualification I would make about unification measures which do not include all African states. That is that they should be made on a regional basis, not on an ideological one. There are in Africa 38 sovereign states, and 38 different internal policies. Some of us call ourselves socialists, some don't; some have sympathy with the policies being pursued in one country, others with a different one. But if we fall into the trap of establishing 'socialist blocs' and 'non-socialist blocs', we shall be doing very great harm to our cause of unity.

Naturally, countries which have great sympathy with each other's declared policies or practices will tend to be particularly friendly; they may send delegations to each other's Party Conferences and share experiences. But this must never be allowed to develop into an ideological grouping, or into a clique which combines to the exclusion of others. It is geography which must be the basis of co-operation, not ideology. Where the two factors coincide, progress may be easier; but, where they do not, we have always to remember that it is at the neighbourhood level that conflicts grow and at the neighbourhood level that real co-operation must be developed. . . .

In1963, after the formation of the Organization of African Unity, we in Africa rejoiced too much. We acted as though we had reached the end of the road. By 1966 we despaired too much; we reacted as though setbacks represented a final defeat. Now Africa has recovered its balance. In a spirit of realism and determination we are picking our way foward. It may be that we shall suffer further setbacks; it may be that our progress will be slow. But, if we use the vision of all African unity as our guiding star, we shall not lose our way. . . .

5

The Intellectual Needs Society

President Nyerere's address to the University of Liberia on 29 February 1968, dealt with the responsibility of intellectuals to their society and their own need for that society.

... There is, in fact, only one reason why underdeveloped societies like ours establish and maintain universities. We do so as an investment in our future. We are spending large and disproportionate amounts of money on a few individuals so that they should, in the future, make a disproportionate return to the society. We are investing in a man's brain in just the same way as we invest in a tractor; and just as we expect the tractor to do many times as much work for us as a hand-hoe, so we expect the student we have trained to make many times as great a contribution to our well-being as the man who has not had this good fortune. We are giving to the student while he is at the university, so that we may receive more from him afterwards. There is nothing altruistic about it; poor people cannot afford financial altruism. We have a right to expect things from university graduates and others who have had higher education of any kind; we do not just have a hope, but an expectation.

This, Mr. President, is not an unusual position, nor a peculiar demand made on Africans by Africans which is not made in other places. You know better than I do that two thousand years ago, Jesus said: 'For unto whomsoever much is given, of him shall be much required; and to whom men have committed much, of him they shall ask the more'.

What is it, then, that we require of those in our societies who have education? We require service to the community—and service in geometric progression according to the amount they have received.

There is no doubt, of course, that the knowledge which has been acquired at schools and higher educational institutions can be used almost exclusively for personal gain, with benefit to the society being a mere by-product. Indeed, it sometimes seems that we have organized our societies on this basis, as the temptation of the highest wages is so often connected with the least socially useful occupations. But even in the most needed positions, highly educated and skilled people can at present often abuse their trust if they have a mind to do so. It is not unknown for people to demand higher and higher wages, or better and better conditions, for using the training and the skill they have acquired at the expense of the society. Instead of accepting that they have a debt of service to repay, these individuals demand greater and greater differentials between them and the unskilled labourer, on the grounds that they are 'key workers' —that without an engineer no bridge can be built, etc.

Whether or not it is right, in any abstract terms, that an engineer should get more than a technician, and a technician more than a labourer—or even a President more than the people he represents— is not my concern today.

. . . But how far are we educated people going to take the demand for a higher reward, which we have already established? It is true that the bridge cannot be built without the engineer; but it cannot be built without the labourers either. Shall we always compare our wages and salaries with those higher ones that other people are getting—perhaps in the wealthy societies of America and Europe? Or shall we begin to compare them with the people who get much less for working as hard, although differently? Shall we, in other words, use the skills which society has enabled us to acquire, in order to hold that same society to ransom?

If we stop to think about our position in our society I do not think we shall do this. For the fact is that, as well as having special responsibilities because of the investment which was made in us, we also have special opportunities—a fact which is being increasingly realized. Africa today is an exciting place to live in; African development is an exciting challenge, and we have the opportunity to shape and to lead the response to that challenge. For, going back to my example of the bridge, carrying bags of cement, working in water, and so on, without any vision of what it is all about—which is the labourer's fate—is not much fun. It is very exciting, however, to take part in the designing of a bridge and participate in its building according to the plan you have drawn up.

Graduates in the developed societies do not have such opportunities as we have in Africa, and such social satisfactions as we can have. A young man or woman there can certainly participate in raising the standard of living of his country; but he may well find that this means the difference between a coloured and a black-and-white television service—which is hardly calculated to give one mental or emotional stimulus! But here in Africa we can, by the use of our skills, help people to transform their lives from abject poverty—that is, from fear of hunger and always endless drudgery—to decency and simple comfort. We can help to relieve the women of the burden of carrying water on their heads for miles; we can help to bring light and hope to small children otherwise condemned to malnutrition and disease. We can make our own homes—that is, the homes where the masses of our people live—into decent comfortable places, where all the inhabitants can live in dignity.

But there is one essential qualification we have to fulfil if we are to receive this kind of satisfaction of a job well done. We have to be part of the society which we are changing; we have to work from within it, and not try to descend like ancient gods, do something, and disappear again. A country, or a village, or a community, cannot *be* developed; it can only develop itself. For real development means the development, the growth, of people. Every country in Africa can show examples of modern facilities which have been provided for the people—and which are now rotting unused. We have schools, irrigation works, expensive markets, and so on—things by which someone came and tried to 'bring development to the people'. If real development is to take place, the people have to be involved. Educated people can give a lead—and should do so. They can show what can be done, and how. But they can only succeed in effecting changes in the society if they work from a position within the society. Educated people, in other words, can only be effective when they are full members of the society they are trying to change, involved in its good and bad fortune, and committed to it whatever happens.

In order to do this the educated people of Africa have to identify themselves with the uneducated, and do so without reservation.

Otherwise their best efforts will be wasted. We have found this out by experience in Tanzania. We have found that, if you want to introduce changes in a village most quickly, you do not necessarily go to the most educated person—or even to the Party or Government official. You go to the person whom the people of that village respect and look to for leadership. When this 'natural leader' is the most educated man, progress is easier and better, for he has won the hearts as well as the minds of the people, and they feel that he is 'one of them'. The next best thing is if the most educated person has a good relationship with the natural leader of that particular society; he can then influence development indirectly. But if the educated man is so arrogant in his knowledge, or so superior in his living standards, that the people are fearful of him, or hold him in contempt—in this case he would be better not there; for he will be a brake, not an accelerator, on development.

Of course, this does not mean that to be useful and successful in the work of national development, the university graduate, or the teacher, must always live in a traditional manner without using his greater knowledge for his own comfort. Nor does it mean that he must always conform to the majority views on everything. But his divergences from his community must be—and must be seen to be—adaptations of something people already understand. They must not be allowed to indicate a contempt for the majority or their way of life; they must include a recognizable basis of loyalty to the community. And when the educated person has reasons for his different way of life which arise out of his greater knowledge then he must be willing to explain this difference to those among whom he lives and works, that is, to his equals. If, for example, he always boils the water he drinks, and people can see the better health of his child, he must explain the connection between the two things when people ask, or as the occasion arises. And he must do this knowing that people may be disbelieving at first, and without appearing to have the attitude that they are stupid fellows who cannot even look after their own children.

For this acceptance of equality regardless of education is essential. And really we would be betraying our own ignorance if we imagined that only modern technology, and modern knowledge, is of any value, or that it somehow bequeaths to us a superiority over our fellows who are not as lucky as we are. Africa's traditional respect for the aged was not—and is not—stupid. It arose out of their accumulated opportunity to learn from experience of life and its problems. The assumption that uneducated local elders know nothing can lead to disastrous results. In Tanganyika, for example, £36 million was spent by our colonial masters on what was called the Groundnut Scheme—and now we import peanut butter! One of the contributory reasons for this expensive failure was that the 'experts'—that is to say, the educated fellows—found the average rainfall over a ten-year period in the relevant area, and planned accordingly. They assumed that, because the local farmers were illiterate, they could give no information about the regularity of the rains, year by year, or month by month. They assumed, too, that it was simple indolence which made people reluctant to cut down all the trees when planting a shamba. So large areas were cleared—and few nuts grew, but erosion began!

I did not give this example in any spirit of criticism of expatriate experts. Other examples could be given when local educated people are involved. I simply use it because it is the most expensive mistake we have experienced in Tanzania—or are likely to—and it makes one realize the importance of recognizing that we can learn from everyone. Knowledge does not only come out of books, or lecturers—or visiting Presidents! We have wisdom in our own past, and in those who still carry the traditional knowledge accumulated in that tribal past. And in particular, we should remember that, although traditional Africa was backward technologically, it cannot be described as having been backward in the harmonization it had achieved between man and his society. We would be stupid indeed if we allowed the development of our economies to destroy the human and social values which African societies had built up over centuries. Yet if we are to save these, we cannot afford the arrogance which our technical superiority tempts us to assume.

Mr. President, what I am trying to say is that we are all, educated and uneducated alike, members of one society, and equal human beings in that society. We can try to cut ourselves off from our fellows on the basis of the education we have had; we can try to carve out for ourselves an unfair share of the wealth of the society. But the cost to us, as well as to our fellow citizens, will be very high. It will be high not only in terms of satisfactions forgone, but also in terms of our own security and well-being.

But this means that university studies, and the university itself, are only justified in Africa if they—and it—are geared to the satisfaction of the needs of the society, the majority of whose members do not have any education. Work at the university must, therefore, be so organized that it enables the students, upon graduation, to become effective servants. For servants they must be. And servants have no rights which are superior to those of their masters; they have more duties, but no more privileges or rights. And the masters of us educated people are, and must be, the masses of the people.

For saying things like this in East Africa, and making demands upon our intellectuals which are consistent with these words, I have been accused of turning on my own kind—of being a kind of intellectual cannibal! It has been said that my education and my nature make me an intellectual, but now I am anti-intellectuals. If this is the case, I can only say that I have much company, for there are now many people—many 'intellectuals'—who adopt the same position as myself!

But in fact I believe such accusations are only made by those who have basically misunderstood the points I have been trying to make. And I certainly hope that this is not the impression I am leaving with you today. It is true that I reject the proposition that intellectuals are a special breed of men and women, by their very existence deserving privileges and rewards denied to others. But I do accept that intellectuals have a special contribution to make to the development of our nations, and to Africa. And I am asking that their knowledge, and the greater understanding that they should possess, should be used for the benefit of the society of which we are all members.

For we are all members of one another. Educated and uneducated are all citizens of one nation, one continent, and one world. Our future is inextricably linked, and intellectuals above all are dependent upon the society of which they are members. For the peasant can eke out a living on his own; he can grow his own food, make his own clothes, and shelter. The intellectual can do no more—and indeed may find it difficult now to do even that. And certainly without society he will not find much opportunity to use his intellectual abilities! It is for his own interests, therefore, as much as anything else, that the intellectual must use his abilities in the service of the health and well-being of society.

There is one final point I wish to make. I have been appealing to African universities and African university students—as well as to others receiving higher education—to be committed members of their society, and to design all their work for its service. I do not believe that this is at all inconsistent with the traditional function of a university, which is often defined as the search for truth. For I believe that society is served by truth. I believe that we need the universities, and their products, to stand up for truth as they see it, regardless of the personal consequences to themselves. Neither leaders nor masses are infallible; it may be that we are wrong—either through ignorance, or through malice. It is part of the task of those who are not burdened with day-to-day responsibilities to help us, and the people, to the best of their ability. And this may sometimes involve saying unpopular things if you believe them to be true.

But you will have noticed that I said the truth as it is seen should be spoken regardless of personal consequences. It would be sheer arrogance to speak the truth as you see it regardless of the consequences for society. The man who shouts 'Fire' in a crowded schoolroom may be responsible for more deaths through panic than if he had said nothing—and certainly more than if he had quietly organized an evacuation. For the whole truth is known to none of us; we may have found out a new part of it, but we must not assume more.

Universities in Africa must try to deal objectively with the problems they investigate; they should analyse and describe them in a scientific manner; and from their accumulated knowledge they should suggest methods of dealing with them. But objectivity does not mean working in a vacuum. The university, whether it likes it or not, is part of the society. Both in the selection of the problems to be examined, and in the manner of dealing with them, this fact must be taken into account. It is part of that essential truth which a university has to promote.

Africa needs objectivity from its universities. We are dealing with new problems; we need all the light thrown on them that can be obtained. But the universities must be committed institutions too; committed to the growth and the development of our societies. They must promote committed service—and therefore honest, truthful and selfless service.

Mr. President: thank you.

6

The Party Must Speak
for the People

On 7 June 1968, President Nyerere, as President of TANU, conveyed fraternal greetings to the Uganda People's Congress Conference—just as President Obote had spoken at the TANU Conference in Mwanza in 1967. President Nyerere used the opportunity to discuss the function of political parties in post-independent Africa.

Tanzania and Uganda and Kenya once had a dream—or a vision—that we would all become part of one larger unit. Some of us still hold to that dream, and believe it can be made into a reality. We have simply accepted a change in the timing for its implementation, and adopted a more gradualistic approach to it, for we know that federations can only survive when they are based on the whole-hearted enthusiasm of all the people involved.

For the present, therefore, your country and mine are still separate sovereign states. TANU and UPC are separate political parties. But our states are partners in a tripartite economic community; our governments are close friends who consult and co-operate together on all matters of common interest. And our Parties, too, are brother organizations. For the truth is that our separateness is not, and cannot be, complete. We are all part of one movement, which is greater than any of us. We are part of an African movement. We are part of the movement for the real freedom, the unity, and the progress of the people of Africa.

It is in that spirit that I bring greetings to the Uganda People's Congress from TANU and the Afro-Shirazi Party. We watch your progress with great interest; we rejoice in your successes, and sympathize with your difficulties. For our relationship, and our friendship, is not a new thing. Indeed, it goes back to the beginning

of UPC—and before! Our Parties were both members of
PAFMECA. Our struggles for independence were the struggles
of friends and allies forced into separate organizations by the needs
of the colonial situation in which we found ourselves. Our current
struggle to maintain the political independence we have won, and
to attain the economic independence and prosperity which we need,
is also part of a common African struggle.

The tactics adopted by our different countries are different now
as they were different before we each achieved our first goal. We each
take account of our own circumstances. But I do not believe there
is any difference in the objectives of our Parties. We are all aiming
at building societies in which the people control their own destiny
and work for their own benefit as they see it. We are all concerned
to exclude external interference in our affairs, and to secure national
control of our economies. Each of our Parties has adopted the basic
principle of human equality, and all of us know that equality and
dignity is a matter of economics as well as of law and politics.

We all know these things. And yet we have sometimes acted as
if the work of the Party is finished once we have a nationalist government—once we have independence. Nothing could be further
from the truth. Whether we have a one-party system, or a multi-
party system, the objectives of our nationalist movements can only
be fulfilled on one condition. Our peoples' governments must be
backed up by strong political parties, deeply rooted in the people,
and capable of providing a living link between the people and the
governments which the people have elected to serve them.

. . . Mr. President, ladies and gentlemen: government is a complicated business in the modern world. There may have been a time
when the job of a government was simply to ensure that all citizens
lived in peace together, and were jointly capable of withstanding
an invasion by outside armies. But nowadays that is only the
beginning of a government's work, and a government's problems.
An African government in the year 1968, which wishes to act in
accordance with the aspirations of its people, must take an active
part in the economy of the country; it must organize institutions of
trade, commerce, manufacturing. A modern government has to
help the people to modernize their agriculture; it has to help them
to get clean water supplies. It has to organize and provide education
and health services—and so on.

In the midst of all these responsibilities, governments can lose their way—they can forget what is the purpose of all their activity! Seeking for the most efficient agricultural system, it is very easy to forget that the purpose of that efficiency is the service of the people. Seeking for development, they can forget that the people may have some things they are not willing to sacrifice for material benefit. And even if neither the elected government, nor its civil service, ever forgets that the purpose of its activity is the people, they can still get so immersed in the problems of giving good service that they lose touch with the people. And if that happens, the people can misunderstand what is being done, and can sabotage their own purposes by a failure to understand what co-operation is needed from them, and why they should give it.

Let me give a very simple example of what I mean. Our people want a higher standard of living for themselves and their children. They expect their government to work for this. But in an agricultural country a higher standard of living means that there must be increased agricultural output—which requires harder work and more modern methods. Suppose, then, that the government taxes the people so as to be able to provide trained agricultural extension workers, and to subsidize fertilizers. The people will be better off as a result—if they use these services! But if the people fail to learn from the experts, and do not use the fertilizers, then they will be worse off than ever before. They will be worse off because they pay more taxes and do not benefit from the services those taxes are providing. In effect, the government will be trying to serve the people, but the people will be sabotaging their own development. Worse still, they may become hostile to their government because of this misunderstanding; they may then allow themselves to be used against their own government by people who wish to use the people's power for personal advantage.

The job of a strong political party is to act as a bridge linking the people to the government they have elected, and the government to the people it wishes to serve. The Party has to help the people to understand what the government is doing and why; it has to help the people to co-operate with their government, in a combined effort to overcome the poverty which still holds us in thrall. But the Party has also to ensure that the government stays in close touch with the feelings, the difficulties and the aspirations of the people.

It has to speak for the people. And it has to educate the people and help them to see what the government's actions mean in terms of their own future security and their own future opportunities.

Mr. President, the job of our political parties is much more difficult now than it was when we were struggling for independence. Then we called mass meetings: we shouted 'Uhuru'; we abused the colonialists—who, I may add, richly deserved it! But now we are building nations. If we have mass meetings we cannot abuse the government—for we are the government, and the people are the government. Our job now is to educate, to explain, and to build. We have to lead the people in the constructive work of development, we have to listen to them, co-operate with them, and work with them. And we have to speak for them to our instrument—the Government.

For the truth is that it is not the Party which is the instrument of the Government. It is the Government which is the instrument through which the Party tries to implement the wishes of the people and serve their interests. And the Party has therefore to determine the basic principles on which Government should act; it has to determine the policies its government will follow. Of course, the Party cannot replace the Government; it cannot do the detailed legislative and executive work which governments have to do. But only a Party which is rooted in the hearts of the people, which has its devoted workers in the villages and the towns throughout the country—only such a Party can tell the Government what are the people's purposes, and whether these are being carried out effectively. Only the existence of such a Party can ensure that Government and people work together for the people's purposes.

It is for this reason that the Party Conference is the most important event in a country's political calender. Parliament is important—Members of Parliament are important. But Members of Parliament are able to represent the people only if they are supported by a strong Party consisting of thousands upon thousands of active, intelligent and selfless men and women. Presidents, Ministers, Members of Parliament, and so on, may get their names written in the newspapers, they may appear on television. But if they are good, they are good largely because they are backed up by a strong Party, which knows and understands the people's needs and the people's feelings. And if such leaders are abusing their position, or getting out of touch with the people, then it is in large part because the

Party is failing to speak up for the people, and to act as the people's watchdogs.

Mr. President, it is a little odd to come to your Party Conference and talk about the importance of the Party. Every delegate present today must be here because he knows the Party is important! Yet we Party workers do sometimes suffer from a sense of inferiority. We know that Government has executive power and the Party does not have it. We know that the President and Parliament make laws, and the Party Conference does not. And some of us then begin to think that members of these bodies are therefore more important, and we begin to lose interest in our Party job. From Tanzanian experience it would appear that some of us do not make that mistake; but instead we try to convince others of our importance by throwing our weight around and trying to intimidate people! Yet the truth is that the Party is the foundation of democratic government if it is working properly. And the Party worker is the most important person in our towns and villages, if he is doing his job properly— that is, if he is working with the people, earning their confidence and their trust as the one of themselves whom they go to in cases of difficulty, or with ideas, or when they do not understand something. If you doubt the truth of these words, look around Africa— indeed, around the world—and see what has happened in those states where political parties failed to be, or ceased to be, active representatives of, and the spokesmen for, the people. . . .

7

The Supremacy of the People

During his second state visit to China, President Nyerere spoke at a state banquet in Peking on 18 June 1968. This speech, which was delivered in Swahili, is produced in full.

It is only just over three years since my previous visit to this great country, but there have been many important developments since then, both in China and in Tanzania. In this country you have been carrying through the Cultural Revolution, which I hope to learn more about in the next few days. We in Tanzania, on the other hand, have introduced a new democratic One-Party State Constitution, and have also defined the meaning and the method of socialism as it will be applied in our country.

These recent developments in China and Tanzania are very different in many respects. The constitutions, and the economies, of our nations are also different—as indeed are the size and the history of China and Tanzania. But I do not believe there is very much difference in the purposes of our different activities. All of the major changes Tanzania has introduced have been intended to secure, or at least to further, the supremacy of the people. As I understand it, that was also the purpose of the Cultural Revolution.

Mr. Premier, the sovereignty of the people is the most important of all our aspirations, and in many ways the most difficult to achieve. It is the most important because the good of the people is the only legitimate purpose of all national activities, and only the people themselves can say what is to their good. There is a saying in English: 'Only the wearer knows where the shoe pinches'. The sovereignty of the people means that they themselves control their own economic activities, decide for themselves the laws they will have, the customs they will follow, and the political institutions through which they will govern themselves. And these things can only be done by the people if they are free from any external control, free from exploitation, from petty tyranny, and from the threat of hunger, or the lethargy of debilitating diseases.

Unfortunately, this is easier said than done! To achieve the freedom from hunger, the educational advance, and the healthy bodies which we all desire, men and women must work together—sometimes in very large-scale undertakings. There is greater productivity in agriculture if people work as a group, using modern methods and more sophisticated machinery. Schools require trained teachers, and need to be backed up by research, and by universities. Good health requires knowledge, and also the services of doctors and hospitals. And all of these things themselves demand a fairly elaborate organization, as well as complex communications systems, and so on. In other words, if people are to have real freedom, they must work co-operatively and they must agree to a communal discipline for the implementation of communal tasks. For if their sovereignty is to be maintained, the people must be able to determine for themselves the disciplines they will accept; they must be able to decide the balance which shall exist in their society between economic, social and political satisfactions. The problem then becomes one of the people's control over the instruments which they create for their service.

Socialism ensures that decisions about priorities do not result from the manipulation of the masses by exploiters. It ensures that the organization necessary for co-operative tasks is undertaken by the people's representatives, and it prevents some individuals from making large profits out of the people's needs. But the inevitable complexity of modern social and economic organization introduces a new danger—that the people's servants will become a bureaucracy which is out of touch with the masses, and which is slothful, inefficient or complacent in its own comfort.

On the other hand, there is the danger that in an effort to avoid the pitfalls of bureaucracy, skilled jobs will be undertaken without the necessary knowledge or preparation, or that skilled workers will be frustrated by limitations on their power to make necessary decisions. In these cases the people will not receive any benefits from the efforts they have made, so that their sovereignty is, in practice, once again nullified.

It is not easy to keep the balance between these contrasting dangers, and to find that middle position where the people are really able to secure control of their own destiny and still achieve the communal objectives they have set themselves. Indeed, I think it fair to say that nowhere in the world have we yet found the answer to this problem. Chairman Mao has many times called for the 'Red Expert'—the skilled man who is devoted to the political creed of China. We in Tanzania search for the 'committed expert'. Both of us are really trying to find the kind of expert, whether he be skilled in scientific subjects, in administration, or in any of the other many jobs we need, who seeks only to use his knowledge and abilities for the service of the people—and service as the people themselves define it. Such people do exist, but the temptations for anyone in a position of power are very great. For although none of us like to be exploited, most of us are happy to exploit others—at least to a small extent!

There are, of course, various organizational techniques which we use to try and keep power in the people's hands. The self-governing communities, the systems of local government, the devolution of administrative authority—all these and many other devices have the purpose of keeping government under the control of the people, and identified with their needs and aspirations. Our political parties, also, have the vital function of speaking for the people as well as leading them.

Yet I wonder if there is any country in the world where it can be truly said that no citizen is ever humiliated by the agents of his government, and no injustice is ever perpetrated against the people? I certainly could not make such a claim for Tanzania. In fact, I believe that all of us, everywhere, have to wage a constant struggle to support the supremacy of the people. We have to be constantly vigilant to ensure that the people are not used by the individuals to whom they have entrusted power, and are neither stifled by bureaucracy and inefficiency, nor misled by their own ignorance.

The history of China since the revolution has shown the determination of the leaders of the People's Republic in this matter. Time and again, campaigns have been waged against leaders who are believed to have abused their responsibilities, or to have become alienated from the people. But at the same time, there has remained a consciousness that leadership does not always mean immediate and unanimous popularity. For the fact is that discipline is essential to the service of the people. A manager who is unable to ensure that all his workers do a full day's duty is not serving the people—even though the lazy workers might abuse him if he tried to do his job properly.

Mr. Premier, that was an extremely bad example for me to use in this country as an illustration of my point. For the thing which impressed me most of all when I was in China in 1965—and the thing which most impresses Tanzanians about the Chinese workers who are now in our country—is their hard work. I suppose there are lazy Chinese people, just as there are lazy people of every other nationality. But they certainly seem to be very exceptional!

Yet the point I was trying to illustrate remains valid. The adoption of socialism is essential to getting rid of capitalist exploitation. But it is only the first thing we have to do. Once we have organized our society to prevent capitalist exploitation, we then have to establish the people's instruments for positive progress. At the same time we have to prevent new forms of exploitation arising out of dishonesty, inefficiency, laziness or the abuse of office.

China and Tanzania have both declared themselves to be dedicated to the building of socialism. We have adopted different methods—if you like, we use different bricks and a different ground plan in the building of our people's societies. But by methods which seem to the peoples of our respective countries to be appropriate to their own needs, China and Tanzania are, I believe, working for the same objectives—the sovereignty of the people, and their freedom from exploitation.

It is my hope that during our few days in the People's Republic of China my colleagues and I will have an opportunity to learn something of your experience in tackling this problem. For although ideas and institutions cannot simply be transplanted from one country to another, we believe that there are certain principles of growth underlying all human experience, and that we in Tanzania should learn from the endeavours and experience of all other nations. And of course, we are especially interested in those countries which are struggling against an inheritance of poverty and which are—like ourselves—committed to the uplifting of the masses.

In all these matters the People's Republic of China has made tremendous strides forward in recent years. It has shown what a determined people can do, however great the obstacles in front of them. We in Tanzania salute the efforts of the Chinese people under the leadership of Chairman Mao Tse Tung, and desire to express our hopes for continued progress along the road to socialism and the supremacy of the people.

Mr. Premier, ladies and gentlemen, I ask you to join with me in a toast to: the People's Republic of China, and the leadership of Chairman Mao Tse Tung.

8

Equality in Sovereign Relationships

At the return banquet which he gave to the Chinese Premier Chou en Lai on 21 June 1968, President Nyerere spoke about Tanzania's attitude to the Nuclear Non-Proliferation Treaty, as well as questions of friendship between 'unequal equals'. Once again, he spoke in Swahili.

The friendship between Tanzania and the People's Republic of China is a friendship between most unequal equals. Perhaps for that reason some other nations of the world find it hard to understand: they are always trying to suggest that Tanzania is a satellite of China, or—alternatively—that our friendship is about to break up. This is probably an expression of wishful thinking, or else it is a misunderstanding of the nature of friendship and an assumption that friendship is exclusive—that you cannot be friends with many nations if these are not themselves close friends.

I admit that in the modern world real friendship between very big nations and very small nations is a comparatively rare thing. For friendship in these circumstances means a recognition on both sides that the differences in size, wealth, and power, are irrelevant to the equality which exists between sovereign nations. It means that both sides recognize the differences, but treat them as facts which have relevance only when the friendship itself needs them, or can benefit from them.

Mr. Premier, the friendship between China and Tanzania is based on these principles of respect and equality. It is not an exclusive thing, and we do not interfere in each other's affairs. When we feel able to co-operate, we do so; if either of us feels reluctant, then we move on to some other matter. I can state quite categorically that Tanzania is enriched by this friendship, and we value it. No outside nation will be able to interfere with it; only we ourselves, by our own actions to one another, could destroy it. I have, therefore, no reason to believe that friendship between Tanzania and China will not continue indefinitely, and grow stronger as time passes.

Having said that, I would like to say further, Mr. Prime Minister, that my colleagues and I have not come to China to ask China to place a protective nuclear umbrella over Tanzania. Colonialism in Africa passed under many labels. Some of our countries were called colonies, others protectorates, some provinces, and yet others trust territories. In fact they were all colonies, and all of them rightly rejected their colonial status. If, therefore, I had come to ask China to declare Tanzania to be her nuclear protectorate, the people of Tanzania would have every right to denounce me as a lackey of nuclear neo-colonialism.

The relation we seek between ourselves and the rest of the world is a relation of equality. It is mainly for that reason that Tanzania has opposed the Treaty against the spread of nuclear weapons. We regard it as a most unequal treaty. It asks non-nuclear nations, including potential nuclear states, to denounce the right to make or possess nuclear weapons, but it does not ask the nuclear powers themselves to stop making any more nuclear weapons; it does not ask the nuclear powers to destroy the weapons they already possess. And, worst of all, it does not ask the nuclear powers to pledge that they will neither use nor threaten to use nuclear weapons against states which agree to sign the treaty. Instead, the nuclear powers, on their own, simply declare that they will protect non-nuclear signatories against nuclear attack. Under this Treaty, if a nation could swear on the Bible, or the Holy Qur'an, that it wanted to develop nuclear explosives purely for peaceful purposes, it would not be allowed to do so. It must buy such explosives from the nuclear powers. This is the first time in history that a tremendous and far-reaching human discovery is made the monopoly of a few.

We have opposed this treaty not because we want to reserve our right to make or receive nuclear weapons. We have neither the ability nor the wish to do so. We have opposed it because it is an unequal treaty, which cannot even contribute to the cause of peace. A monopoly of weapons cannot produce real peace. It could only produce so-called peace, like *Pax Romana* or *Pax Britannica*.

Mr. Prime Minister, your country is a nuclear power; mine is not. For the time being we happen to hold similar views on this particular matter. Of course, this does not mean that China and Tanzania will always adopt the same policies, and will always have the same priorities of action. China is an Asian power; we are a part of Africa. Both of us are interested in international peace, and in human justice, but our immediate pre-occupations will be different, and our difficulties will be of a different kind.

Thus, for example, colonialism of the traditional kind has now been virtually defeated in Asia. Political independence has been won everywhere. The struggle which remains is a struggle to make that independence meaningful—to make it the independence of the people and not a mere matter of flags, and Presidents, and protocol, while the masses continue to be exploited either by their old masters or by new ones.

In Africa we do have this struggle against neo-colonialism. But we also still have a struggle against foreign occupation, and racialist minority oppression. We still have to face the fact that Tanzania's southern neighbour is governed by Portugal, and that 60,000 Portuguese troops are trying to maintain that European rule against the wishes of the people of Mozambique.

Nor is that an isolated case. Angola, Portuguese Guinea and South West Africa are all still occupied territories held in thrall by colonialists who are determined to continue their direct exploitation of African people. And, on top of that, there are in South Africa, and in Rhodesia, racialist minority governments engaged in a systematic attempt to maintain their power and economic privilege by denying the humanity of those who are non-white.

Mr. Premier, ladies and gentlemen, my country is free. It is because of that freedom that I am able to come here on behalf of my countrymen to cement the friendship which exists between our two peoples. Yet at the same time my country feels that it is not free, because Africa is not free. My countrymen know that they are insulted because the blackness of our brothers is being insulted in Africa. And my country, with the other independent nations of Africa, is determined that this situation will be changed. Africa will be free. Africans will be respected in Africa. For Africa will liberate Africa. The struggle before us may be a long one; the machinations of neo-colonialism may sometimes cause us to stumble in our progress to liberation. But the Organization of African Unity will succeed in both its objectives. It will lead Africa to freedom and human dignity, and it will lead Africa to unity.

For the unity of free Africa is our ultimate objective. I look forward to the day when I cannot come to China as President of the United Republic of Tanzania, because to the outside world there is no Tanzania—only Africa. My ambition is that the President of a United States of Africa goes on state visits—to China and to other countries. (Let me hasten to add that this does not mean a reluctance on my part ever to come to China again! It only means that I want to be in a position where I come as a citizen of Africa who is renewing old friendships!)

This ambition of ours is a very large one, and we do not expect it soon to be fulfilled. But we shall not surrender the goal because we cannot see it clearly, any more than you surrendered because you could not see the China of today from the caves of Yenan. Most of all, we shall never compromise on our determination to rid Africa of imperialism. The people of Africa have now taken up arms in Mozambique, in Angola, in Portuguese Guinea, and in Rhodesia. Sooner or later these fighters will triumph; which means that Africa will triumph, and therefore Tanzania will triumph. We shall succeed, because we are fighting for our freedom, our own homes, and the future of our children. To no one will we surrender our birthright. Africa will be governed by Africans, and Africans of all colours, races, and languages, will one day be equal citizens in their homeland.

I believe that the people of China understand this determination of ours—this determination of Tanzania, and of Africa. I believe that you sympathize with us in our struggle, just as we sympathize with the Chinese people's determination to defend their own country and build it according to their own desires. We do not ask for more. For we know that no one else can make a people free; freedom must be won and maintained by the people who expect to enjoy it.

Finally, Mr. Prime Minister, I want to repeat that I have come to China to learn. In particular, I wanted to see something of your country after the Cultural Revolution. The last three days have once again confirmed my conviction that we have a lot to learn from China. First, we should reject the proposition that peace will be served by isolating China. This is very silly. You cannot isolate 700 million human beings, unless they go to sleep. Secondly, there is a danger in Africa for some of us to believe that independence is enough. If we really want to move from national independence to the real independence of the people of Africa, and if we really want to make sure that the African Revolution will ever move forward and not degenerate into neo-colonialism, then I say that we should learn from you. Indeed, from what I had seen of China in 1965, I must say that if you found it necessary to begin a Cultural Revolution in order to make sure that the new generation would carry forward the banner of your Revolution, then certainly we need one. We have seen in Tanzania how easy it is to pay lip service to the importance of socialism and the people, while in fact we behave like capitalists and petty dictators!

On my first visit I said in Shanghai, after I had witnessed the revolutionary spirit of your people, that I wished all the people could come to China and witness for themselves what a determined people can do. Today, after the Cultural Revolution, the spirit of the people of China is even greater than before. One of the sayings of Christianity is that faith can move mountains. You Chinese people have great faith; nor is it blind faith. You believe in the creative power of the people; you believe in your great leader, Chairman Mao Tse Tung; you believe in the spirit of self-reliance and self-criticism; and you believe in the oneness of the oppressed peoples of the world. But you do more than believe. You are showing us that it is not enough to believe: one must practise what one believes.

With this immense spiritual strength, always very great in China but now renewed and deepened by the Cultural Revolution, and under the guidance of the great leader, Chairman Mao Tse Tung, I am sure you will move from victory to victory, and I do wish you well It has been a great pleasure for my colleagues and me to re-visit the People's Republic of China. You have received us with great warmth, and great hospitality. Our stay has been both enjoyable and useful.

9

Rice Means Socialism

President Nyerere went from China to Korea and, at a return banquet given by him on 24 June 1968, he spoke about Tanzania's development priorities and the meaning of socialism in the context of the people's welfare.

. . . Despite the great destruction suffered during the war, the people of North Korea have greatly increased their output of both industrial and agricultural products. Coming as I do from a country where we are only now beginning to establish an industrial sector of the economy, and where the general living standard of the people is very low, your achievements are of very great interest. In pursuit of our policy of self-reliance—which I notice is paralleled in Korea—we have to build our economy by concentrating first on agricultural development. That is the industry we have, and which can be expanded with our existing resources of capital and man-power. It is from the surplus we create in the agricultural industry that we shall develop our industrial sector. Of course, this does not mean that we are uninterested in industrial growth, for agricultural development itself demands not only processing plants, but also the manufacture of simple tools, and of fertilizers, etc. It is a question of emphasis and of priorities. All that I am saying is that, in our circumstances, agriculture and rural development is of prime importance.

Our immediate interest is, therefore, in your great advances in this field. Before we came to Korea I had been very impressed by a short saying of yours Mr. Kim Il Sung. You are reported to have said: 'Fertilizers mean rice and rice means socialism'. I was very struck by the truth and profundity of this statement. Now I have seen that Korea has demonstrated in practice what it means. For this is a small country compared with Tanzania—at least in area. Yet I understand that you produce 1,200,000 tons of fertilizer a year—to say nothing of having electrified 98 per cent of all the farm villages, and 86 per cent of the farm houses in the country. Knowing that, it is not surprising to me that agricultural production in Korea has doubled over the past 20 years, with consequent benefit both to the individual citizens and to the economy as a whole.

But the point of your statement, Mr. Premier, was not only that fertilizers would enable increased agricultural output. It was that this, in turn, means socialism. Of course, you were not implying that socialism follows increased output in the same scientific manner that greater yields follow the application of the right fertilizer. But increased wealth in the hands of the people, used by them for their own development and for their own betterment, and used in a spirit of co-operation and human equality—this is almost a definition of socialism in itself. For socialism is not something abstract, a thing which is good in any idealistic sense. Socialism is good because it is an organization of society by all the people of the society, and for their common benefit. Socialism is good, in other words, because it is people-centred. The service of the people is the object of socialist organization; complete identification with his fellow men, and a desire to serve their interests as they see them, is the motive of a socialist. And service of the people means, at its very lowest, that all shall have sufficient food, clothing and shelter, and in particular that no member of the society shall have more than these basic needs while others continue without them.

Mr. Premier, it almost seems as if I am trying to explain the simple truth which you have summed up in the statement I quoted. That is not my intention. My purpose is simply to pay tribute to the efforts of the people of North Korea, under the leadership of your Government, in putting this truth into practice. Korea, like other countries which are building socialism, has a long way to go yet before its people can relax. But your progress has been astonishing and we from Tanzania can learn a great deal from it.

Let me conclude, therefore, by saying once again how much my colleagues and I have appreciated the kindness that has been shown to us by all the people of this country. Let me also express our good wishes for your continued progress in peace towards the socialist goals you have set yourselves. . . .

10

Work Targets

When he opened the Friendship Textile Mill on 6 July 1968, President Nyerere used the opportunity to explain again that aid can help self-reliance. He then went on to suggest that production 'targets' should be worked out for all parts of this and other factories.

A large crowd was present at this ceremony, which was conducted in Swahili.

... The Friendship Textile Mill is a demonstration that our struggle for self-reliance does not mean hostility to the people of other countries, nor a rejection of the help they are willing to give us when that help enables us to become more self-reliant in the long run. Indeed, the phrase 'the right kind of assistance' can be defined as 'assistance which helps us to become more self-reliant in the long run'.

This textile mill belongs to Tanzania. It is our property, and our responsibility. But it exists today because of the assistance we have received from the People's Republic of China. The people of that country have helped us by the provision of large amounts of credit, and also by providing the services of Chinese technicians. These Chinese workers have helped in the establishment of the factory, and are actively training Tanzanians to take over from them. I should add that they have set an example to us all by their hard work and their dedication.

... What is the opportunity created by this textile mill? How does it contribute to our aim of self-reliance when it was built mostly with Chinese money, and with the help of Chinese technicians?

... This textile mill is a new tool; it is a means of increasing our output of goods. By using it we shall be able to increase the amount of wealth we produce in Tanzania, in just the same way as a farmer can increase the amount of land he cultivates if he obtains a plough instead of having to depend upon his hoe. But just as the farmer's plough has to be used and looked after if he is to get any benefit from it, so this mill has to be used and looked after if Tanzania is to receive the full benefit from its existence. The Chinese people have helped us to create this tool; we now have to use it properly.

In the past, our farmers grew cotton and we exported the cotton lint and some cotton-seed oil. People in other countries converted our cotton lint into cotton cloth—and we bought that cloth from them. What we were in fact doing was paying wages and profit to people in other countries for processing our cotton. The existence of this mill, and the others which are now coming into production in Tanzania, means that we shall not have to do this in future. By the end of this year we shall spin, weave, dye and print almost as much of our raw cotton as is needed to provide the people of Tanzania with cloth—with khangas, *vitenge*, and many other kinds of material.

In other words, the existence of this and the other new textile factories means that Tanzania will not have to depend upon any other country for its cotton cloth. Instead of paying wages to the spinners and weavers of Europe, we shall be paying wages to the spinners and weavers of Tanzania. Instead of allowing foreign firms to make a profit out of the cotton they buy from us, and then sell back to us in a processed form, we shall ourselves receive any profit which is made. Indeed, in the case of the Friendship Textile Mill, the people as a whole will receive any profit which is made because this factory is entirely publicly owned.

. . . The question of efficiency is vital. Our new textile mills have to produce good cloth, with attractive designs too, at a price which our people can afford to buy. Only an efficient Tanzanian factory is a service to the people of Tanzania. This means that our management must be good, and our workers must be careful, hard-working and disciplined. Every person who works in this factory, or who has anything to do with finding markets for its produce, or with transporting goods to and from it, has a responsibility to Tanzania.

The workers on the factory floor have to work hard throughout their shift; they must attend on time, and leave only after the day's work is finished. They must look after these machines—they are ours, and if they are damaged through carelessness, then the people of Tanzania will have less money to spend on the things we want, because we shall have to spend money on replacements or repairs. Workers must ensure that they do not allow mistakes to pass them— no one wants to buy faulty cloth. They must take a pride in the fact that they are working in the Friendship Textile Mill; which is, among other things, the first factory in East Africa to be able to print cotton. And, in return, the workers can demand respect, reasonable wages and reasonable conditions.

Let me emphasize, however, that the respect which the workers can rightly demand does not involve indiscipline. Whenever people work together in a team, discipline is essential. It should be self-discipline—the workers together recognizing the kind of actions which cannot be allowed if maximum production is to be achieved. But if that fails, then there must be hard industrial discipline imposed by management. It seems that some people in this country have taken the emphasis on people in the Arusha Declaration to mean that there can be slackness in work, and that people in supervisory positions should do nothing about it. Nothing can be further from the truth. The Arusha Declaration demands more discipline, not less. It demands that the workers should not be exploited; it demands that all the fruits of our labour should be received by the people who work. But that means that we have to accept the responsibility too. When ten men get together to lift a heavy log, they all have to exert their strength together, and at the same moment. If any one of the ten is late, or doesn't really push properly, then one of two things happens. Either the other nine have to do more than their fair share of pushing—in which case the benefit of lifting should be divided between nine men and not between ten—or the log will not be lifted at all—in which case the efforts of the nine have been wasted and none benefits. Disciplined work is essential, and here once again our Chinese technicians have set us a great example.

Good, hard and disciplined work on the factory floor, however, is not very much good on its own. It has to be backed upby good management, at all levels. The management has to ensure that everything runs smoothly, that cotton of the right type is available when needed; that movement from one process to another is easy, and that there is co-ordination of all the different tasks so that no worker sits idle waiting for another to finish his part of the job.

Management has to see to the buying of the raw materials and the sale of the finished product; it has to ensure that wages are paid on time, that accounts are properly kept, that maintenance work is done, and a thousand other things. The efficient carrying out of these tasks is just as vital to the success of the factory as the efforts to prevent broken threads or faulty weaving.

Management is also responsible for planning the output of the factory—indeed, until it has done this it can hardly do all its other jobs. On this there are two things I want to say.

First, by the end of this year we in Tanzania will be able to produce something like 90 million square yards of cloth a year—or even more. If this cloth is of the right kind, the right price and the right quality, we should be able to sell all of it within Tanzania very easily. But it is no use each mill producing the same kind of cloth; for example, we don't want 90 million square yards of khanga cloth and no *vitenge* or household cotton. Our total production must be rationalized; we must produce the kind of cotton goods which our people will need, and in the right quantities. And we can only do this without waste if there is some co-ordinated planning between the different factories. This is a job where the National Development Corporation (which has an ownership interest in the two largest textile mills) should take the initiative. Together with the different managements of the factories, and in consultation with the leaders of the workers in those factories, it should plan for the kind of goods to be produced, bearing in mind the current purchasing pattern and that which might reasonably be expected in the future as our other economic plans advance. This is important. If we are to make the best use of our new factories, we must plan their work as a whole, not have four or five different plans which do not add up to a sensible arrangement for our country.

But once these plans are worked out we should stop treating them as if they were deep secrets. My second point, therefore, is that each of our new factories—and indeed our old ones—should have a target for production, which is known to every worker involved.

We ask people to work hard, yet in modern factories each man and woman is doing only a very small part of the whole process of production. How can he really go on year in and year out, taking a pride in that one job? The imaginative people can do it, but for the majority it is very hard to relate one simple task to the total output of the factory. Often the worker doesn't even know where his task fits into the total scheme of things; he doesn't know what the factory as a whole is aiming at; and he doesn't know what progress they are making towards their combined aims. It is not sensible to expect people to be enthusiastic about their job under these circumstances.

Let us therefore have targets for each factory, worked out on the basis of what can be sold—and where. Let these targets be known to each worker; let them be placarded in big letters on the walls. And don't stop there; let each separate workshop, or process, or group of work-people, also have its target, per year, per month, per day. And then—having got the target clear—let it be equally clear what was actually achieved in the past year, month, or day.

I believe that, when our people have a clear target in front of them, and when they can see how far they have exceeded, or how far they fall short of it, they will respond to this challenge as they have responded to so many challenges in our recent history. They will want to beat the target; they will take pride in their factory exceeding its target with good quality output. And they will realize that, as they do their work, they are making a positive contribution to the success of Tanzania's target—which can only be made up of all the different targets of our factories, farms, and offices. . . .

11

The Tazama Pipeline

After the oil embargo had been placed on Rhodesia, Zambia turned north for her supplies, which had to be carried from Dar es Salaam port in heavy lorries over a road not built for that kind and quantity of traffic. The joint Zambia/Tanzania decision to build an oil pipeline was taken soon after the emergency arrangements had been instituted, and in less than a year building started. The opening of the Pipeline was done at two ceremonies. First, President Kaunda visited Dar es Salaam and turned on the oil flow; then on 2 September 1968, President Nyerere spoke at Ndola where the oil was arriving.

For all of us, this is a very happy occasion. It is a happy day for Tanzania, and for Zambia. And it is also a happy day for all those who support the fight against colonialism and racialism. For we are celebrating the successful result of a 'convention'—or treaty—between two independent African states. We are celebrating the completion of a joint undertaking, which is for our mutual benefit, and which strengthens the fight for our real independence and self-reliance.

The oil coming out of this pipeline today was put into the eight-inch diameter pipe on 29 July, at Dar es Salaam. It has travelled 1,058 miles, at an approximate speed of $1\frac{1}{2}$ miles per hour. It has gone up and down hills, crossed rivers, through populated areas, and across undeveloped bushland. Slowly but surely the oil has moved forward through this pipeline to Ndola. Now it has arrived, and Zambia's oil supply is assured; Mr. President, her nightmare of stringency and worry about this commodity is over. . . .

Tanzania and Zambia are separate sovereign states. We do not interfere in each other's affairs. We do not accept the strange doctrine that international friendship gives one country the right to tell the other what policy it shall pursue, either internally or externally. But in fact, our two countries are united by a number of common purposes.

In both Zambia and Tanzania, the Governments and peoples are determined to develop the economy for the good of all the people. Both countries have accepted a philosophy which is man-centred. And both realize that in very many fields we shall all benefit from joint action.

Both Tanzania and Zambia accept, and most fiercely uphold, a belief in the equality of all men, regardless of race, tribe, religion, or anything else. And both of our countries accept the full implications of this belief, for ourselves, and for Africa.

Zambia and Tanzania both believe in, and work for, the unity and freedom of Africa. We know that our own development, and our own freedom, is linked up with this.

But the first priority for both Zambia and Tanzania is to survive in freedom. It is possible for nations to survive as entities which are legally independent, but which really have no freedom to determine their own policies. In such cases the protocol of independence continues: flags fly, Presidents are received with guards of honour, and so on. A country which accepts such a position can, in fact, even make short-term economic gains through its subservience. It may receive large amounts of external aid and foreign investment, which enable it to carry out desirable projects. It may be set up as an example of good, realistic government, which is bringing employment to its people—and so on.

We in Africa should not be so easily trapped. From our own history we know that a destitute man can sometimes get a good meal, clothes and shelter by selling himself into slavery. But once he is in the power of the master, these good things may, or may not, continue. Once he is a slave, he will receive just those things which it is in the interests of the master to give him. He will receive nothing else.

It is the same with countries. Once a nation has sold its freedom for economic assistance, or once it has accepted the domination of external forces, that nation is lost. It will be exploited, and its people oppressed whenever it is in the interests of its master that these things should happen. Development will be incidental to the needs and desires of the master. The real progress of the people will be regarded as irrelevant. And all the time the people will suffer from the knowledge that theirs is not really a free country, and that therefore they are not really a free people able to determine their own destiny without external interference.

I think we in Africa have to be quite realistic about this. For it is our problem now When our countries achieved independence, it was a great triumph. Yet to some extent that independence was a paper independence. Our peoples were poor, our nat ions undeveloped economically, and we had almost no skilled and educated citizens. In so far as we did have some developed economic resources and institutions, they were almost always foreign-owned and foreign-run. We achieved political power, and the trappings of sovereignty; but our real power was much more limited than sovereign independence normally implies.

Our job has been—and still is—to convert that situation into one of real independence. This means achieving the practical power to implement the theoretical freedom we possess. This is neither easy nor quick. It is not a matter of 'defeating an enemy'; it is not a matter of military fighting, nor of destroying the power of others. It is a matter of building, and of educating; both things which take hard work, persistence and time.

What is needed in our situation is the kind of courage which recognizes the situation as it is, and uses it to achieve the kind of change we desire. This is the most difficult kind of courage, for it means recognizing limitations and accepting them while you deliberately build up the power and capacity to overcome them. And this must be a courage, and persistence, possessed by all the people; it is the courage to work and wait (for they also serve who only stand and wait), and then to accept the moment for action when it comes.

This kind of deliberate planning for future creative independence demands good leadership. Its success depends upon unity behind that leadership despite attempts to divide the nation along tribal, regional, religious, or other grounds. And it demands a patience which does not forget, or lose sight of, the ultimate objective in the midst of the compromises on method which are required. Most of all, it demands a national willingness to sacrifice present comfort, and present satisfactions, in order to gain the real freedom which can only come with an ability to be fully self-reliant.

Tanzania—and, Mr. President, I believe Zambia also—is now engaged in this task of creating the kind of independence which need not fear interference from outside. We are engaged in building our economies, training our skilled men, educating our people, and designing the kind of future that we ourselves want. But our efforts in these matters are threatened even as we undertake them. The great powers of the world are thousands of miles from our borders, and it is unlikely that they will send occupying forces to invade us. But on the borders of Zambia and Tanzania are states whose philosophy of existence is incompatible with our objective of freedom on the basis of human equality.

The racialist government of South Africa, and the racialist ruling clique in Rhodesia, deny both our ability, and our right, to develop in our own way and in freedom. The Portuguese colonial administrations will be able to continue only as long as the reality of the idea of freedom does not take a real hold among the peoples of those territories. To all these neighbours of ours, our success in the struggle for real independence therefore constitutes a threat. Most importantly, it will prove their philosophy wrong, and be an inspiration to our fellow believers in human equality who live in their own territories. And, in addition, an expression of our greater power must be greater reality in our commitment to the cause of African freedom and human equality. These things are known; we are not dealing with fools. So these racialists and colonialists will try to prevent our success; they will destroy our struggle for development if they can. They will seek to divide and to weaken us by every conceivable means—ranging from the spreading of false rumours, to sabotage, to using economic power against us, and perhaps even to direct attacks on us.

We cannot answer these nations by mounting military attacks on them. Even if such aggression were consistent with our own philosophy—which it is not—we do not have the power. We know, and they know, that the idea of our attacking the countries to the south is ridiculous. They talk of it only to find excuses for their own threats against us.

There is only one way in which we threaten them—and we do threaten them. That is by our successes in building our nations on the basis of human equality, freedom and self-reliance. And even then, the threat comes not from any action of ours, but simply because such success undermines their oppression. Tyrannies everywhere are never secure; oppressors everywhere are always fearful of the spirit of freedom. Effective freedom in Zambia and Tanzania—that is, the freedom which comes from self-reliant economic strength—will act like a bush fire: it will sweep the racialists and colonialists out of control as it ignites the spirit of the oppressed peoples.

Knowing these facts, and knowing that the racialists of Southern Africa will sabotage our efforts if they can, what can we do? Their armies are more numerous, and better equipped than anything which we could produce. A frontal attack by them would force us back however brave our soldiers and airmen. If this happens, we have recently been provided with an example of a different kind of national resistance—the determined non-military resistance of a united people who refuse to be controlled by an occupying power, however powerful. What the Czechoslovak people can do, the people of Zambia and Tanzania could do too.

But, in fact, this is not the most likely form of attack on our freedom and our progress. We are more likely to experience attempts at economic strangulation, at sabotage of our new institutions, and—most probable of all—attempts to divide us among ourselves. And against these things we can defend ourselves if we have the courage and the selflessness to refuse to be used by the enemies of Africa. Vigilance, unity, and a dogged determination to work together, whatever the difficulties and disagreements, are the people's effective defence against those who wish to destroy us and take away our freedom. Those same qualities are the essential ingredients of our attack against the poverty, ignorance and disease which now oppress us. And there is not one single citizen of Zambia or Tanzania who is exempted from this battle on two fronts. A worker who does not do his job with care and efficiency can destroy the creation of thousands of people, and thus weaken us in relation to the racialists of Southern Africa. A politician who seeks to exploit the people's real difficulties in order to divide our nations, is laying open to slavery the very people whom he pretends to be helping. And any citizen who fails to join in the struggle for human equality regardless of human differences, and regardless of his own short-term pocket-book interests, is serving the interests of the same fascists and colonialists—who would laugh while they grind his African face in the dirt of Africa.

Mr. President, these things which I have been saying are not irrelevant to the successful inauguration of this oil pipeline. For this pipeline is a small example of our serious intent to work together on these hard, practical jobs which will help our nations to develop on the basis of freedom and self-reliance. We can be happy today because for this one commodity Zambia is no longer in jeopardy. For the past $2\frac{1}{2}$ years, priority on the Great North Road to the ports of Tanzania has had to be given to petroleum products. Now only a very small quantity of special fuels will have to travel by these difficult routes. And, because of this, Zambia and Tanzania will be able to co-operate on relieving the people of this country from the necessity to use southern routes for some other products—routes which are always subject to the decisions of Africa's enemies.

Zambia's freedom is enlarged a little bit by this pipeline, and therefore Tanzania's freedom is enlarged a little bit. The friendship and co-operation between our two independent and equal sovereign states is further strengthened by this long line linking the cities of Dar es Salaam and Ndola.

To all the peoples of Tanzania and Zambia, therefore, my message is this: *Guard this pipeline, and guard it well.*

If you work on it, do your job carefully and efficiently. But whether you work on it, live near it, or are simply a citizen or friend of our countries, help us to guard it against the sabotage of those to whom this day of our rejoicing is a day of anger. This pipeline is a weapon in the struggle for African freedom and unity; it is a shield against threats to our own progress. May it be the first of many such joint Zambian/Tanzanian and Zambian/East African activities for the greater well-being of all our peoples.

Mr. President, as a symbol of the unity of our two countries, let us go forward together and jointly turn the tap which will make this oil—Zambia's oil—flow freely from Dar es Salaam.

12

Freedom and Development

This Paper was published by President Nyerere on 16 October 1968, and was distributed at the TANU National Executive Committee Meeting in Tanga later that month. It was accepted as a TANU Policy Document, but it made much less popular impact than earlier policy papers. This can be attributed in part to the fact that some highly controversial questions of immediate political impact were discussed at the same meeting.

Freedom and development are as completely linked together as are chickens and eggs! Without chickens you get no eggs; and without eggs you soon have no chickens. Similarly, without freedom you get no development, and without development you very soon lose your freedom.

FREEDOM DEPENDS ON DEVELOPMENT

For what do we mean when we talk of freedom? First, there is national freedom; that is, the ability of the citizens of Tanzania to determine their own future, and to govern themselves without interference from non-Tanzanians. Second, there is freedom from hunger, disease, and poverty. And third, there is personal freedom for the individual; that is, his right to live in dignity and equality with all others, his right to freedom of speech, freedom to participate in the making of all decisions which affect his life, and freedom from arbitrary arrest because he happens to annoy someone in authority—and so on. All these things are aspects of freedom, and the citizens of Tanzania cannot be said to be truly free until all of them are assured.

Yet it is obvious that these things depend on economic and social development. To the extent that our country remains poor, and its people illiterate and without understanding or strength, then our national freedom can be endangered by any foreign power which is better equipped. This is not simply a question of military armaments —although if these are necessary they have to be paid for out of the wealth of the community. It is a question of consciousness among all the people of the nation that they are free men who have something to defend, whether the appropriate means of defence be by force of arms or by more subtle methods.

Equally obvious is the fact that freedom from hunger, sickness and poverty depends upon an increase in the wealth and the knowledge available in the community; for a group of people can only consume and use the wealth they have already produced. And even personal freedom becomes more real if it is buttressed by development. A man can defend his rights effectively only when he understands what they are, and knows how to use the constitutional machinery which exists for the defence of those rights—and knowledge of this kind is part of development.

For the truth is that development means the development of *people*. Roads, buildings, the increases of crop output, and other things of this nature, are not development; they are only tools of development. A new road extends a man's freedom only if he travels upon it. An increase in the number of school buildings is development only if those buildings can be, and are being, used to develop the minds and the understanding of people. An increase in the output of wheat, maize, or beans, is only development if it leads to the better nutrition of people. An expansion of the cotton, coffee, or sisal crop is development only if these things can be sold, and the money used for other things which improve the health, comfort, and understanding of the people. Development which is not development of people may be of interest to historians in the year 3,000; it is irrelevant to the kind of future which is created. Thus, for example, the pyramids of Egypt, and the Roman roads of Europe, were material developments which still excite our amazement. But because they were only buildings, and the people of those times were not developed, the empires, and the cultures, of which they were a part have long ago collapsed. The Egyptian culture of those days—with all the knowledge and wisdom which it possessed—was quickly overthrown by foreign invasion, because it was a culture of a few; the masses were slaves who simply suffered because of the demands of this material development, and did not benefit from it. Equally, when the Roman Empire was attacked, and its legionnaires retreated to their homeland, the fine roads and buildings were left to rot because they were irrelevant to the people of the occupied areas. Further, it is doubtful whether either the Egyytian pyramids, or the Roman roads have made the slightest difference to the histories of the countries concerned, or the lives of their peoples.

Development brings freedom, provided it is development *of people*. But people cannot be developed; they can only develop themselves. For while it is possible for an outsider to build a man's house, an outsider cannot give the man pride and self-confidence in himself as a human being. Those things a man has to create in himself by his own actions. He develops himself by what he does; he develops himself by making his own decisions, by increasing his understanding of what he is doing, and why; by increasing his own knowledge and ability, and by his own full participation—as an equal—in the life of the community he lives in. Thus, for example, a man is developing himself when he grows, or earns, enough to provide decent conditions for himself and his family; he is not being developed if someone gives him these things. A man is developing himself when he improves his education—whatever he learns about; he is not being developed if he simply carries out orders from someone better educated than himself without understanding why those orders have been given. A man develops himself by joining in free discussion of a new venture, and participating in the subsequent decision; he is not being developed if he is herded like an animal into the new venture. Development of a man can, in fact, only be effected by that man; development of the people can only be effected *by the people*.

Finally, if development is to increase people's freedom, it must be development *for the people*. It must serve them, and their interests. Every proposal must be judged by the criterion of whether it serves the purpose of development—and the purpose of development is the people. Yet if a proposal contributes to the development of people, and if it is being carried out by the people of their own free will, it will automatically be for the people's interests, provided three conditions are fulfilled. First, if the people understand their own needs; second, if they understand how these needs can be met; and third, if they have the freedom to make their own decisions, and to carry them into effect.

DEVELOPMENT DEPENDS UPON FREEDOM

If the purpose of development is the greater freedom and well-being of the people, it cannot result from force. For the proverb tells the truth in this matter: you can drive a donkey to water, but you cannot make it drink. By orders, or even by slavery, you can build pyramids and magnificent roads, you can achieve expanded acreages of cultivation, and increases in the quantity of goods produced in your factories. All these things, and many more, can be achieved through the use of force; but none of them result in the development of people. Force, and deceitful promises can, in fact, only achieve short-term material goals. They cannot bring strength to a nation or a community, and they cannot provide a basis for the freedom of the people, or security for any individual or group of persons.

There is only one way in which you can cause people to undertake their own development. That is by education and leadership. Through these means—and no other—people can be helped to understand both their own needs, and the things which they can do to satisfy these needs. This is the kind of leadership which TANU and Government officials should be giving the people; this is the way in which we can bring development to Tanzania. But, although we must give this leadership, the decisions must come from the people themselves, and they themselves must carry out the programmes they have decided upon.

There are thus two factors which are essential in the development of people. The first is leadership through education, and the second is democracy 'n decision-making. For leadership does not mean shouting at people; it does not mean abusing individuals or groups of people you disagree with; even less does it mean ordering people to do this or that. Leadership means talking and discussing with the people, explaining and persuading. It means making constructive suggestions, and working with the people to show by actions what it is that you are urging them to do. It means being one of the people, and recognizing your equality with them.

In particular, at this stage in our history we should not be trying to blame particular groups or individuals for things which are not to our liking, or not to the liking of the people. The exploiters,who are now apparently so beloved by our leaders that they spend all their time talking about them, are a negligible factor in our development now. Those few who remain can most effectively be dealt with by constructive development work on the part of the people and their leaders; it is certainly absurd that we leaders should spend all our time abusing exploiters—especially as some of us do not understand the work which is being done by some of the individuals we abuse. Instead we should be providing creative and positive leadership. We should have taken the trouble to understand the development policies our Party is trying to pursue, and we should be explaining these policies to the people. When we have convinced the people that TANU's policies are good and sound, then we should be working with them to create a society in which exploiters will find no opportunities for their evil doing.

But giving leadership does not mean usurping the role of the people. The people must make the decisions about their own future through democratic procedures. Leadership cannot replace democracy; it must be part of democracy. If the decision relates to national affairs, then the people make it through the National Executive Committee, and Parliament, and through the National Conference of TANU. If it is a decision about district affairs, the people make it through the District Committee and District Council. If it is a question of purely local interest—for example whether to undertake a particular self-help scheme—then the people directly concerned must make the decision following a free debate. There is no other way in which real development can take place. For just as real freedom for the people requires development, so real development of the people requires freedom.

TWO ESSENTIALS OF DEMOCRACY

There are, however, two essential elements of democracy without which it cannot work. First, is that everyone must be allowed to speak freely, and everyone must be listened to. It does not matter how unpopular a man's ideas, or how mistaken the majority think him. It does not make any difference whether he is liked or disliked for his personal qualities. Every Tanzanian, every member of a community, every member of a District Council, every Member of Parliament, and so on, must have the freedom to speak without fear of intimidation—either inside or outside the meeting place. The minority in any debate must have the right to speak without fear of persecution; it must be defeated in argument, not by threat of force. The debates leading to a decision must be free debates. And even after a decision has been made, free discussion about it should be allowed to continue. For the minority must know that if it has a good case, and if it argues properly and correctly, it will be able to convert the majority. Similarly, the majority must be willing to maintain the argument until the minority has been convinced of the correctness of the decision which has been made. Free debate must continue. It is an essential element of personal freedom.

But the necessity for continued freedom in discussion must not be allowed to prevent decisions from being made. There comes a point where action must follow discussion, or else we shall do nothing but talk. When there has been adequate discussion of a question, and every point of view has been expressed, then the decision must be reached, and the majority must be allowed to prevail. For just as the minority on any question have a right to be heard, so the majority have the right to be obeyed. Once a decision is reached, it must be accepted as the decision of all. And everyone—including those who were in opposition—have to co-operate in carrying out that decision. Thus, for example, once a law has been passed it must be obeyed by everyone, including those who spoke against it and have not been convinced by the arguments put forward in its support. More than that, once a law has been passed, it must be actively supported by everyone. It should not be merely a matter of acquiescence. It is not enough that a citizen should himself refrain from stealing; he must co-operate with the police in upholding the law, and must give over to the police those who transgress it.

For democratic decision-making must be followed by discipline in carrying out the decisions. The minority must be allowed to campaign for a change in the law or the decision. But until they have succeeded in getting majority support for a change, they must obey the law or the rule which has been laid down. Without this kind of discipline no development of any kind is possible

DISCIPLINE MUST FOLLOW DECISION

Discipline must exist in every aspect of our lives. And it must be willingly accepted discipline. For it is an essential part of both freedom and development. The greater freedom which comes from working together, and achieving things by co-operation which none of us could achieve alone, is only possible if there is disciplined acceptance of joint decisions. And this involves the acceptance of lawfully constituted authority. It means that if we work in a factory, we have to accept the discipline of that factory. Whether the factory is privately or publicly owned makes no difference; its rules must be adhered to, and the people who are in charge of particular operations must be obeyed. Similarly, in hospitals, schools, offices, and so on. If the doctor orders certain treatment for the patient, it must be carried out by the nurse without argument, and without carelessness. If the matron lays down rules designed to ensure the smooth operation of the hospital, every nurse must obey these rules. If there are difficulties, representations can be made, but in the meantime the hospital discipline must be maintained or the person must accept dismissal. The same thing is true in our villages and rural communities. Once a community has democratically decided upon a particular self-help scheme everyone must co-operate in carrying out that decision, or pay the penalty which the village agrees upon.

Yet provided decisions are made after free and friendly discussion, and by majority will, the essential discipline should be freely accepted, and should in fact. be largely self-discipline. For if our people want freedom for themselves, and if they want development, then they will accept the need for disciplined action. Indeed, the acceptance of community discipline is only a problem in Tanzania when our people do not understand the implications of the changes which we have already effected in our lives. In traditional society we had discipline—often very severe. It was accepted by everyone, and everyone co-operated in imposing it. Our problem now comes not from the discipline itself, but from a lack of understanding about the machinery which is necessary for discipline in a modern state, and from a failure to realize that different kinds of discipline are needed in the organizations of a modern society. Thus, for example, theft was dealt with directly by the community when each village looked after its own peace and security. Now it is essential that suspected thieves should be handed over to the police, and not mishandled by the people themselves. Or again, the simple rules of an isolated village are not enough for the running of a modern factory. In the village it rarely mattered whether a man carried out his task at daybreak or at noon; in a factory hundreds of other people can be made idle just because one man does not do his job at the right time.

These new kinds of discipline must be accepted by our people, and by all our leaders. And if anyone is unwilling to accept his responsibilities in this matter, then he must accept the penalties of his failure. If he disobeys the law, then the courts must punish him. If he fails to observe discipline in his work, then he must be dismissed. For we have to accept that the people in authority in Tanzania now are the agents of the people of Tanzania. If they do their job badly, or if they fail to respect the humanity of every human being, then the Government will replace them, or at an election the people will replace them. But in the meantime they must be upheld while they are carrying out the law, or issuing orders which are in conformity with the law. We must ourselves stop abusing people who are trying to ensure discipline; we must stop calling a man a *mkoloni* when he demands strict observance of the rules in an office, a factory, a hospital, a school, or any other institution.

If we are to live our lives in peace and harmony, and if we are to achieve our ambitions of improving the conditions under which we live, we must have both freedom and discipline. For freedom without discipline is anarchy; discipline without freedom is tyranny.

Discipline, however, must be a means of implementing decisions. Only in the very limited sense of orderly debate is discipline involved in the making of decisions. And discipline is not another word for force. A meeting must be disciplined if every member is to have an opportunity to be heard, but a disciplined meeting is not one where everyone automatically says 'yes' to whatever is suggested. A disciplined meeting is one where the rules which have been accepted as fair are observed by everyone—for example, where every member speaks through the chairman, and where each person is allowed to make his point without being shouted down or abused. For discipline allows the orderly conduct of affairs; it is the means by which decisions are implemented—not the way they are made.

UJAMAA VILLAGES

It is particularly important that we should now understand the connection between freedom, development, and discipline, because our national policy of creating socialist villages throughout the rural areas depends upon it. For we have known for a very long time that development had to go on in the rural areas, and that this required co-operative activities by the people. Ever since 1959, therefore, TANU has encouraged people to go in groups to farm in the rural areas, and our TANU Government has initiated settlement schemes of many kinds. But we can now see that we have committed many mistakes, and it is important that we should learn the right lessons from them.

When we tried to promote rural development in the past, we sometimes spent huge sums of money on establishing a settlement, and supplying it with modern equipment, and social services, as well as often providing it with a management hierarchy. In other cases, we just encouraged young men to leave the towns for a particular rural area and then left them to their own devices. We did these things because we recognized that the land is important to our economic future, but we acted on the assumption that there was a short cut to development in these rural areas. All too often, therefore, we persuaded people to go to new settlements by promising them that they could quickly grow rich there, or that Government would give them services and equipment which they could not hope to receive either in the towns or in their traditional farming places. In very few cases was any ideology involved; we thought and talked in terms of greatly increased output, and of things being provided for the settlers.

What we were doing, in fact, was thinking of development in terms of things, and not of people. Further, we thought in terms of monetary investment in order to achieve the increases in output we were aiming at. In effect, we said that capital equipment, or other forms of investment, would lead to increased output, and this would lead to a transformation in the lives of the people involved. The people were secondary; the first priority was the output. As a result, there have been very many cases where heavy capital investment has resulted in no increase in output—where the investment has been wasted. And in most of the officially sponsored or supported schemes, the majority of the people who went to settle lost their enthusiasm, and either left the scheme altogether, or failed to carry out the orders of the outsiders who were put in charge—and who were not themselves involved in the success or failure of the project.

It is important, therefore, to realize that the policy of *Ujamaa Vijijini* is not intended to be merely a revival of the old settlement schemes under another name. The ujamaa village is a new conception, based on the post-Arusha Declaration understanding that what we need to develop is people, not things, and that people can only develop themselves. The policy is, in fact, the result of learning from the failures which we have had, and from the successes of those small groups which began and grew on a different basis.

Ujamaa villages are intended to be socialist organizations created by the people, and governed by those who live and work in them. They cannot be created from outside, nor governed from outside. No one can be forced into an ujamaa village, and no official—at any level—can go and tell the members of an ujamaa village what they should do together, and what they should continue to do as individual farmers. No official of the Government or Party can go to an ujamaa village and tell the members what they must grow. No non-member of the village can go and tell the members to use a tractor, or not to use a tractor. For if these things happen—that is, if an outsider gives such instructions and enforces them—then it will no longer be an ujamaa village!

An ujamaa village is a voluntary association of people who decide of their own free will to live together and work together for their common good. They, and no one else, will decide how much of their land they will cultivate together from the beginning, and how much they will cultivate individually. They, and no one else, will decide how to use the money they earn jointly—whether to buy an ox-plough, install water, or do something else. They, and no one else, will make all the decisions about their working and living arrangements.

It is important that these things should be thoroughly understood. It is also important that the people should not be persuaded to start an ujamaa village by promises of the things which will be given to them if they do so. A group of people must decide to start an ujamaa village because they have understood that only through this method can they live and develop in dignity and freedom, receiving the full benefits of their co-operative endeavour. They must understand that there will be difficulties, and that the sheer coming together will not bring them prosperity. They must understand that coming together enables their work to be more productive in the long run, but is not a replacement for that work.

Unless the purpose and socialist ideology of an ujamaa village is understood by the members from the beginning—at least to some extent—it will not survive the early difficulties. For no one can guarantee that there will not be a crop failure in the first or second year—there might be a drought, or floods. And the greater self-discipline which is necessary when working in a community will only be forthcoming if the people understand what they are doing and why. Yet if the purposes, and the potential, are understood and accepted, then the members of an ujamaa village will be able to surmount such difficulties, and use them to strengthen their organization and determination. The difficulties will help to speed up their development to socialism. But the people have to realize that ujamaa living does not cause miracles; it only allows them to improve their own lives.

The fact that people cannot be forced into ujamaa villages, nor told how to run them, does not mean that Government and TANU have just to sit back and hope that people will be inspired to create them on their own. To get ujamaa villages established, and to help them to succeed, education and leadership are required. These are the things which TANU has to provide. It is our job to explain what an ujamaa village is, and to keep explaining it until the people understand. But the decision to start must be made by the people themselves—and it must be made by each individual. For if a group of 20 people discuss the idea and only 7 decide to go ahead, then that ujamaa village will consist of 7 people at the beginning. If 15 decide to start, then it will begin with 15 members—others will join as they are ready. There is no other way forward, because by joining a man has committed himself to a particular kind of life, and five who come in unwillingly can destroy the efforts of the 15 who want to work out a new pattern for themselves.

The decision to join with others in creating an ujamaa village is an individual one. But once that decision is made, then normal democratic rules will apply to all members. Thus, for example, the 15 people will sit down together and discuss whether to cultivate all their crops together, or whether to begin by jointly cultivating only the cash crops, leaving food crops for individual activity. If they can, they will talk until they agree; but if they cannot come to a unanimous agreement before it is time for work to begin, then they will decide by majority rule. Once this decision has been taken for the forthcoming season, all the members have to accept the discipline of the work which has been made necessary by the majority decision—even if they voted against it. While working hard the minority can continue to try to persuade the other members to make a change next year, but their talk must not lead to a reduction of the effort they make in carrying out the majority decision.

In fact, once an ujamaa village is created, it is a democracy at work. For it provides an example of free discussion among equals, leading to their own decision-making; it shows that when discussion has to give way to action, then the majority will prevails; and it demonstrates the need for discipline by all members in the implementation of the decisions which the group has made. And in this very process, the people will have begun to develop themselves as dignified and confident human beings, in a way which is impossible if they simply take orders from someone else. The fact that the orders of an 'expert' may have led to greater output of a crop if they were fully carried out, does not affect this issue. By debating this matter and then deciding for themselves, the people will be doing real development of themselves. Achieving greater output will come later as they learn from their own experience, and as they are convinced that it would be a good idea to try a new method. Progress may appear to be slower in the sense that statistics of crop output will not increase very fast at the beginning. We should remember, however, that those people who marched hundreds of miles in support of the Arusha Declaration did not break speed records. They plodded steadily on until they reached their objective, suiting both their speed, and their hours of walking, to what they felt they could maintain.

Yet Government and TANU leaders can and should help these ujamaa villages and their members. Leaders should help people to understand the arguments for and against different methods of organization. We should help a group which decides to start by making sure that they can get adequate land in a convenient parcel. We should help to explain the advantages of working a communal farm, and how the problems can be overcome. We should make sure that the members have agricultural and other advice available tothem when they are making their decisions.

Further, Government and Party leaders must make sure that ujamaa villages get priority in service to back up their own efforts and their own decisions. For example, if the members of an ujamaa village decide that they have a priority need for water, and that they can dig the ditches and buy the pipes but not the pump, then Government and Party should help them by providing a pump rather than laying on water to some other area. But there must be no question of Government assistance replacing the efforts of the members of an ujamaa village. Advice must be given, but the decisions must be those of the members themselves; help must be given when possible, but it must be help for something the people are already doing for themselves. These villages must start, and must grow, on the basis of self-reliance. For self-reliance is the means by which people develop.

TANZANIA IS ALL THE PEOPLE

By developing the people of Tanzania, we are developing Tanzania. For Tanzania is the people; and the people means everyone. (*Tanzania ni ya Watanzania; na Watanzania ni wote.*) No one person has the right to say, 'I am the people'. No Tanzanian has the right to say 'I know what is good for Tanzania and the others must do it'.

All Tanzanians have to make the decisions for Tanzania; all have to work together, and all of us have to accept the discipline we impose upon ourselves. It must be joint discipline—applying to us all equally. But in accepting this discipline we must remain free men, implementing our own decisions. The group involved in any particular decision, and any particular discipline, will vary. Some decisions are national, and the discipline is that of law which we must all obey. Some decisions affect only those who live in a particular town or district, and the discipline is that of by-laws. Some decisions arise out of our own free decision to participate in a particular group—to work in a factory, to live in an ujamaa village, etc.; and the discipline then applies to us because of our membership of that group. But all of us are Tanzanians. Together we are the people. Our development is our affair; and it is to the development of ourselves as people that we must dedicate ourselves.

13

Things We Must Correct

On 9 December 1968, President Nyerere used the occasion of his Republic Day Broadcast to 'talk about the things we have not done so well, and which will continue to go badly unless we correct ourselves'. He began by discussing some disappointments about agricultural production, analysing the reasons for them, and urging the peasants to follow the advice of agricultural officers about methods of production. He then went on to deal with the questions of administration and unity.

... The second thing I want to talk about is our Administration. One thing which makes me very happy is to see how our young men and women in positions of responsibility in government and parastatal organizations improve their work year by year. Sometimes I am afraid when I see how these young people are working, because it seems to me that they are in danger of damaging their physical or mental health by the amount and the intensity of the work they try to do. Indeed, very often I have to insist that they take some leave and have a rest. But, as I say, I am very happy to see the way most of these people are working and contributing to our progress by their effort. And I believe that our country has the right to be proud of these young men and women, and also has cause to be grateful to these servants.

But unfortunately things are not going so well as regards Local Government. At first we thought that the reason was the shortage of good and experienced local government employees, and in the last few years we have made great efforts to send more educated and better quality people into the Local Government Service. This has reduced the problem. But in some places good Local Government workers are unable to do their work properly because of interference

and intrigue by the Councillors. For these reasons the troubles
in Local Government are continuing even in those places which
have good employees.

At present there are very few Councils which are able to prepare
proper yearly estimates of revenue and expenditure. And there are
even fewer Local Councils which follow up their estimates by
collecting the money they have estimated and using it in accordance
with the approved estimates. As a result, many Councils do not
even have enough money to carry on their normal and essential
business. For a long time many Councils have just been doing
educational work; they have given up almost everything else. But
now, some of them are even proving incapable of looking after
primary education. The greater part of the money for teachers'
wages is paid by the Central Government, but instead of setting this
money on one side to pay the teachers their money as it becomes due,
many Councils are spending this money on other things. Many
primary school teachers are therefore left without the money they
have earned, and which they need to keep themselves and their
families. I am grateful to these teachers that they have not gone on
strike; but I would not have been surprised had they done so,
because to leave your servants without pay is asking for trouble. It is
certainly no way to run any sort of government.

Again, in the new constitutions of Local Councils, the President
is given power to nominate a certain number of Councillors. Many
of those who were chosen are experienced in different fields, and
they were appointed in order that they should help their fellow
Councillors on matters of planning and development. Often I have
had complaints that some of these nominated people do not attend
the Council Meetings. But, when I investigate, the answer is very
often that their reluctance to attend stems from the fact that Council
Meetings are not relevant to development, but that the time is
spent on political intrigue, in discussing allowances, or in abusing
the Local Government workers. I am now asking, with great
seriousness, that those in charge of Local Councils should make
an effort to change these habits. We cannot allow this kind of
practice to continue, because the people who suffer are the citizens
of Tanzania.

UNITY

The last thing I want to talk about today is unity. Our country is one of those in Africa which is highly praised for its unity. We have no tribalism, no religious quarrelling, no colour discrimination, and we oppose discrimination and oppression on grounds of tribe, religion, or colour, wherever it exists. Those who know us are not surprised to see that we oppose the Portuguese and the South Africans. They are not surprised at seeing us criticize America for its part in the Vietnam war, and for the colour discrimination which exists within America itself. Nor are such people surprised when we oppose people like Enoch Powell of England, and the massacres of the Ibo people of Biafra. They are not surprised because they know that we believe in the fundamental equality of man, and that our purpose is the human justice which is inextricably linked with human equality. The most basic belief of our Party is about the equality of man, and its first canon is a statement of our humanity and our African-ness. TANU believes that all men are equal; and every TANU member, of his own free will, accepts the statement: 'All men are my brothers, and Africa is one'.

It is true, therefore, that we deserve this reputation. What I want to say today, my brothers, is that I beg you, and I also plead to God, to see that we continue to deserve it.

Why do I say this today? I do so because I have begun to hear whispers, and more than whispers, which I wish to bring out into the open so that we can forestall the dangers they bring.

TRIBALISM

First, I have begun to hear whispers about tribalism. Just after independence we got complaints that people were being appointed to government work on the basis of tribalism, and we immediately appointed a Commission to look into these allegations. The Commission proved without any doubt that there was no tribalism in the allocation of jobs in government. But just recently I began to hear this complaint again. I did not treat this grumbling lightly. We called some of these people who were saying that there is tribalism, and told them to give their evidence either to me or to

Chief Mang'enya. We promised to investigate it immediately. But they have not given us one shred of evidence.

There are two things I want to say. The first is to ask any citizen who has some evidence of tribalism, to pass that evidence in confidence to anyone whom he trusts and who will be able to get the information either to me, to the First or Second Vice-President, or to Chief Mang'enya. I promise you that we shall deal with anyone who practises tribalism.

But the second thing, and more important, is that the man who talks about tribalism being practised without having any evidence for his statement is often a man who wants to stir up tribalism. Even if that is not his purpose, the result can be just the same. People will begin to think that there is tribalism and, once people begin to think in these terms, then tribalism has begun to enter into our society.

My purpose in bringing this matter out into the open is so that you may all be on your guard against people who want to stir up tribalism here. The work of civil servants is different from that of politicians. In order to be a political leader, a man does not have to have any particular educational qualifications. But the work of the civil servants and people in the parastatal organizations does require education—indeed, year after year we spend large amounts of money on education just so that later on our young people will be able to do the work of government and public institutions. For the time being we use foreign experts and those few Tanzanians who had the good fortune to go to school during the colonial times.

It so happened that the Tanzanians who had the opportunity for higher education under the colonialists were mostly Wahaya, Wachagga and Wanyakyusa. And because most of the education was provided by missionaries, most of these people are also Christians. That was our inheritance. These conditions will change, but they have not changed yet. And for these reasons, when we get rid of the Europeans who were doing responsible jobs, and give these jobs to Tanzanians, the people who get them come mostly from one or other of these three tribes.

Therefore, if you ask me why Wahaya, Wachagga and Wanyakyusa have most of the jobs which require higher education, the answer is very obvious. They were the ones who received higher education during colonial times. I'd say: investigate the position in politics, where a man is not asked about his educational qualifications. Look at the Parliament, the National Executive and Central Committee of TANU, and at the Cabinet. How many Wanyakyusa, Wahaya or Wachagga are members? You will find that perhaps there aren't any, or there are one or two. This is the truth.

Anyone who refuses to accept a very obvious truth like this, and says that the reason is tribalism, must provide us with the evidence for his statement. If he cannot provide any evidence, we must conclude either that he is a fool, or that he is stirring up tribalism deliberately. He is the sort of person who begs work on a tribal basis, and when he is refused because he does not have the capabilities, he pretends he was refused on tribal grounds.

It is the job of Government to help, and even to favour, the more backward parts of the country, especially as regards education. We are doing this and will continue. But if a Mchagga, a Mhaya or a Mnyakyusa young man were refused work simply because of his tribe—when he is capable and there is no other Tanzanian with the qualifications—then we would be practising a very stupid and very evil kind of tribalism such as that which caused the establishment of Biafra. I beg you, my brothers, avoid anything which could bring our country into this kind of disgrace.

RACIAL DISCRIMINATION

Secondly, I want to talk about discrimination on the basis of colour. There are now whispers, and sometimes more than whispers, indicating a hatred or suspicion of people because of their colour.

I myself have said many times, and I shall go on saying, that self-government means self-reliance. Our country cannot claim to be really independent if it continues to depend on other countries; and Africans cannot say that they are truly free if they are the shadows, puppets, or the stooges, of other countries. Freedom is equality, and the first step is for us ourselves to recognize our equality with other countries.

But when I say this, I am not saying that we are better than the Europeans, the Asians, or the Chinese. I have never said this, and I shall not say it, because it would be a lie. And when I say these things, I am not saying that the people of other countries dislike us or wish us ill. I have never said this, and I shall not say it, because it is not true. There are those who dislike us; there are those who have no reason either to like us or to dislike us; and there are others who like us very much and who like our policies of socialism and self-reliance.

When I say that independence means self-reliance, I am not saying that we shall not co-operate with people of goodwill from different countries, who are willing to work with us for the furtherance of our policies of socialism and self-reliance.

But unfortunately there are these whispers. Some of our people have ill-will towards Europeans or Asians, not because of any sin these people have committed, but just because they are Europeans or Asians. My brothers, do not pay any heed to these whisperers. Treat people according to their own actions, as individuals, not according to their colour.

Take, for example, the Asians here. A socialist country usually divides people into two categories. The first are the exploiters—the capitalists and feudalists—and the second are those who are exploited—the workers and peasants. Those whom a socialist country abhors are the capitalists and feudalists, but the thing which socialists attack is their exploitation, not the people themselves. It is absolutely taboo for a socialist country to divide people according to their colour and afterwards to persecute them because of their colour, even if they are peasants or workers. Yet to listen to some of our people talking you would think that exploitation is a matter of colour. One person says: 'In our village there is no exploitation and all the shopkeepers are Africans.' If you ask him whether the shops are co-operatives, he says: 'No, but there is no exploitation because the shops are not owned by Asians.'! Others of our people believe that all Indians are exploiters. But this is not in the least true. Very few of the Indians are capitalists. Most of them are just workers, and many of them are exploited like any other worker. And very often the people we harass are not the capitalists themselves, but other workers.

Last year, when we nationalized the banks, the capitalists thought we would fail to keep them running because they knew that there were no Africans with the knowledge necessary to run a bank properly. And immediately the big banks withdrew all their managers, because they knew that if the banks failed to work, our entire economy would collapse, and therefore the Arusha Declaration would fail.

But although there were no Africans who had the knowledge to keep these banks running properly, fortunately there were Asians who had this knowledge. So we immediately appointed the best qualified Asians to be managers. Then, instead of collapsing, the banks continued to operate, and work went ahead very well. And after a few weeks we began to reduce the salaries and perquisites of the civil servants and workers in nationalized industries. Immediately I was warned that it would be very dangerous to touch the wages or perquisites of the bank workers, because they were all Asians and they would sabotage our work and the banks would fail after all. I did not agree, so I called the bank managers and I discovered that it was true that they were nearly all Asians. There was one European, and one African—who unfortunately has since died. I told these managers that those who were not Tanzanian citizens were not affected, but those who were Tanzanians would be treated in exactly the same way as a Msukuma or a Mnyamwezi. They told me right there and then that they did not want to be treated any differently from other Tanzanians, and that it was absolutely untrue that they did not agree with the Government's plans to implement the Arusha Declaration.

In fact, these people deserve the gratitude of our country, because together with other Tanzanians they enabled us to support the Arusha Declaration with deeds. Yet now, a Mzanaki goes to the bank to borrow money: he is refused a loan because he does not have any security or for some other good reason. And afterwards he comes running to me or to the Chairman of TANU, saying that the Asians favour each other and that we should make Wazanaki managers of the banks. Countrymen, I beg you to beware of this kind of thinking. I am absolutely certain that, if we distinguish between the Asians who are exploiters and those who are exploited, and if we resolve to treat the exploited in the same way as other workers, they will help us to implement our policies of socialism and self-reliance. Even if we did not believe that all men are our brothers, there is a Swahili saying: 'Better an unbeliever who helps than a Muslim who is no good.' But, in any case, we are socialists.

Look at all the different countries of the world and ask yourself which countries practise racial discrimination. You will find that they are all capitalist or feudalist countries. There is not a socialist country, or one which calls itself socialist, which practises racial discrimination. It is possible that not all socialist countries in the world believe as we do that all men are our brothers; but all socialists, and all who call themselves socialists, believe that all workers are brothers regardless of their colour, religion or citizenship. We cannot claim to be socialists and at the same time distinguish between people on the grounds of colour. Socialism and racialism are like water and oil; they never mix. Look at the disturbances caused by students in different countries recently. You will see that one thing all the students agree upon is opposition to racial discrimination and oppression in the world. My hope is that all Tanzanians, and especially our young people, will also oppose racialism; and, if they see any trace of racial discrimination here in Tanzania, I hope they will not be afraid to organize a procession of protest about it.

If we have really accepted the principle that all men are our brothers, and that Africa is one, we will also believe—and more easily—that all Tanzanians are brothers and that Tanzania is one.

14

To Plan is to Choose

When the Second Five-Year Economic Development Plan was prepared
it was decided that it should be submitted for general approval to
TANU before being submitted to Parliament for consideration. At the
TANU National Conference held in Dar es Salaam, on 28 May 1969,
the President therefore introduced the Plan to the delegates (in
Swahili), stressing the difficult choices which had had to be made
in its preparation.

The President began by welcoming President Obote, President
Kaunda, and President Mobutu, who had all come to bring fraternal
greetings to TANU. He then proceeded directly to giving an ex-
planation of the task of the Conference, and to outlining the major
aspects of the Plan. His theme throughout was that planning means
choosing.

. . . During this week and the week following you will have an
opportunity to listen to each Minister explaining the Plan as it
relates to his own Ministry. Therefore it is not my purpose to explain
the Plan for each Ministry. My purpose this morning is to emphasize
certain matters which I believe need emphasizing—and particularly
those which are not so pleasing.

Such a large body as this cannot usefully discuss the details of
the two-volume Five-Year Development Plan which has been
prepared by Government. What it can do, and should do, is to
discuss the general strategy laid down in the Plan. For the task of
TANU is to determine general policy; Parliament has to look at
Government's proposals in more detail and within the framework
of the policy laid down by the Party. I shall therefore try to make three
things clear in my speech this morning: to explain in broad outline
the problems we encountered during the First Five-Year Plan

period; the lessons we have learned; and the decisions which the Government has made about the priorities for the next five years.

These priorities have been decided upon in the light of our objectives, which are: firstly, providing an adequate and balanced diet for all our people—which means healthy bodies; secondly, providing sufficient good, and if possible attractive, clothing for all our people; thirdly, providing decent housing for all our people; and fourthly, providing educational opportunities for all the people.

There is, of course, a very important sense in which our Party has already made the basic decisions underlying the Second Five-Year Plan. By the resolutions of the Arusha Declaration we have decided that our Government and our people must work for economic growth in a manner *which will bring benefit to all;* and we have decided on the policy of *Socialism and Self-Reliance.* It is in the light of these accepted objectives that the Government has examined the achievements and failures during the First Plan period, and used the accumulated experience in drawing up the Second Plan.

PROBLEMS AND LESSONS OF THE FIRST PLAN

It is not yet possible to give a full assessment of how far we achieved First Plan targets, because information about our achievements during 1968/69 will not become available until next year. The best we can do for this final year is to estimate. Even then, it will not be very much use trying to compare what we actually achieved with the target figures set out in the First Plan document; we made adjustments and amendments to the Plan as experience showed that we were making mistakes or as the circumstances changed. Thus, for example, the failure of Cosata to give good service to our people meant that it was wound up and its international trade functions taken over by Intrata—itself absorbed in the State Trading Corporation at a later date. The drastic fall in the price of sisal also required a radical change in the output plans for this crop, at the same time as it affected the whole financing expectations of the Plan. In addition, the Rhodesian minority declaration of independence in 1965 required an emphasis on communications with Zambia which had not been planned for.

Real changes in outside circumstances were not the only problem.

Another problem was the lack of adequate statistical information about our country. Thus, whereas we worked on the assumption that our population was growing at a rate of 2.2 per cent per annum the census revealed that there were many more Tanzanians than we had imagined, and that the number was increasing at a rate of 2.7 per cent per annum.

Making assumptions about things outside domestic control, and working on the basis of inadequate statistics, are both inevitable for any underdeveloped country which is preparing an economic development plan. Tanzania is taking steps to improve the quantity and quality of the information at our command; the full analysis of the population census, the agricultural census which will be taken shortly, and the continuous attempts to collect better industrial and commercial information, are all part of this work. But for the time being, both of these problems remain, and have to be taken into account. . . .

THE ARUSHA DECLARATION

There is another factor which makes it extremely difficult to assess our achievements over the past five years by comparing what we have actually done with the figures presented in the First Plan document. In 1964 we had not worked out at all clearly the implications of our socialist belief. As a result, we were simply trying to attract investment of any type, and the role of public enterprise appeared to be that of filling in gaps left by private investment. Indeed, it is worth remembering that the National Development Corporation was not created until 1965, and its functions as a promoter of socialist large-scale production was spelt out even later.

All this changed in 1967 when the Arusha Declaration was adopted; the NDC was then given its very heavy new responsibilities, and other parastatal organizations were created. A similar change affected agriculture. In the First Plan we talked only in terms of increased production and our efforts were directed at encouraging greater output, even when this meant helping individual peasants to become employers of labour. The policy of *Ujamaa Vijijini* which was adopted by the Party in October 1967, meant the beginning of a change: gradually we are moving towards a programme of integrated rural development which leads in the direction of the kind of socialist society we are trying to create. This changed policy is fully reflected in the new Plan, which has socialist rural development at its very core.

For all these reasons the Second Plan document is very different from the First. It is much more a statement of strategy and its projections into the future are not always as precise. . . .

PLANNING MEANS CHOOSING

But although this Second Plan is an improvement on the First, planning is always the same in one important respect. It involves making decisions about the allocation of scarce resources; it means choosing between many desirable activities, because not everything can be done at once. It is vital that this should be clearly understood. There are many things which are urgently needed in Tanzania and which the Plan does not provide for. Every delegate to this Conference will be able to provide a list of things in his district, or in his village, which will not be done in the next five years even if every project mentioned in the Plan is carried through. We have to accept that. To a greater or lesser extent every country in the world has a limit to its resources and the more it spends on one thing, the less it can spend on another. This is true even in a rich country like the United States of America, where it is frequently stated that the plans for tackling the internal problem of poverty were destroyed by the costs of the Vietnam war to which it gave priority.

This problem of choice is very much greater for Tanzania. The publication of a five-year plan does not create more resources; all it does is to enable the nation to allocate the resources it possesses in a manner which will bring the people as quickly as possible towards the goals they have set themselves. The less your resources, the greater the number of difficult choices which have to be made. For just as a poor worker has to decide whether to spend less on food in order to buy himself a new shirt, so a poor nation has to decide whether to provide schools or hospitals; new houses or new water supplies; to make an attack on the ignorance which causes people to suffer from preventable diseases, or to build roads which will enable peasants to market the goods they produce. Indeed, before it can make any of these choices between alternative investments, a poor nation has to decide what proportion of its wealth it is willing to devote to any kind of investment because every shilling spent on investment means that one shilling less is available for current consumption. That is our position now, just as it was in 1964. In this respect the two Plans do not differ. We have to make choices between good things, not between good things and bad things: to plan means to choose.

THE FINANCIAL ACHIEVEMENT

The fact that difficult choices remain does not mean that we have made no progress during the first five years, or that the First Plan was a bad one. On the contrary, we have laid a firm foundation for future growth. It is not my intention this morning to list our numerous successes; the Ministers will do that as they address the Conference. Nor is a post-mortem called for! It is true that, after making allowances for changed prices, our real investment achievement was only about 75 per cent of the target set out in the Plan, and that we achieved an economic growth rate of nearer 5 per cent than 6.7 per cent. However, if we take into consideration the problems with which we started, and that this was our first Plan, our achievement is not a small one; for our progress compares reasonably well with that made by most other developing countries. A large part of our shortfall arose because we were not adequately prepared to begin work immediately the Plan period opened, and because we were relying too heavily on external or private investment.

As time went on we realized these faults and we took corrective action which, in relation to the financing of the Plan, was a great success. We forecast that about 22 per cent of the Central Government expenditure and about 48 per cent of the total investment expenditure would come from local sources; for the rest, we were relying on external assistance. In fact, however, out of a total expenditure only slightly smaller in money terms than that planned, more than 65 per cent of the Central Government capital expenditure was financed from domestic sources, and something like 70 per cent of the total investment spending came from within Tanzania. The

Minister for Finance will give more details of this magnificent achievement—with some warnings about the future! I will only say that these figures show both the sacrifices our people are making for the development of their country, and an example of first-class financial management on the part of our Minister and his officials. The Ministry of Finance is always unpopular with other Ministries of Government, and I would be the last to suggest that improvements in administration are not both necessary and possible. But when results like this have been achieved, I think those responsible for imposing the necessary financial discipline deserve our thanks. The Ministry of Finance, and the people themselves, deserve congratulations for our great success in self-reliance.

EDUCATION

Just as the meaning of our success in the field of finance was that we were able to go ahead with planned and essential development work, so the cost was that all of us had somewhat less in our pocket for private expenditure than we would have liked. In the other area where we fulfilled Plan targets—that of education—the cost of our success was met by our younger children. Let me explain.

At the beginning of the last Plan we took a very definite decision to give priority to the expansion of secondary education, teacher training and the University. Because to plan is to choose, that meant that we had very little money available to devote to expanding the primary school system. And we carried out that decision. More than 7,100 children will enter Form I of the secondary school this year as against 5,250 in 1964. The number of young people entering Form V is more than twice as great this year as it was at the beginning of the First Plan. And the number of young men and women who are beginning a Grade A teacher training course in 1969 will be nearly four times as great as the number who did so in 1964—that is, 1,200 this year as against 320 in 1964. These achievements will contribute greatly to our aim of becoming self-sufficient in high-level manpower by 1980; in overall terms, and with an exception I shall refer to later, we have achieved what we set out to achieve.

The effect of this has been, however, that expansion in the number of primary school places has been held back. We have done very little more than expand at the same rate as the number of Tanzanian children was increasing because of the population growth. Indeed, the census has revealed that the chances of a 7-year-old Tanzanian going to school are worse now than we thought they were when we drew up the First Plan. At that time we used to say that about 50 per cent of our children went to school. The much larger population of the country which was revealed in the census figures showed us that the actual percentage in 1964 was nearer 46 per cent, and even now, at the end of the Plan period, only about 47 per cent of our children can find a primary school place.

This state of affairs must be unacceptable to a country which claims to be building socialism. Obviously the emphasis in the new Plan must be shifted to primary education. But the amount of money which we can devote to education is still limited, and the census could not reveal an increase in the number of trained teachers because we already knew exactly how many teachers had been trained! The Government has therefore been forced to think of priorities even within the primary school sector. For the truth is that many of our children who do go to primary school have to leave after Standard IV. Over much of the country, therefore, we are still wasting money and effort by giving children four years' education, and then abandoning them at an age when they are very likely to forget even that little which they have learned. Government has therefore been forced to choose between an all-out attack on the numbers of children entering primary Standard I on the one hand, or removing this iniquitous and absurd Standard IV examination on the other. For to plan is to choose. Our resources do not allow us to do both at the same time. The decision which Government has taken is that we should concentrate our efforts on getting rid of the necessity for selection at Standard IV. This means that, instead of greatly expanding the number of Standard I classes, we have rapidly to increase the number of classes at Standards V, VI and VII, in order that every child who enters primary school should get a full seven years' education.

We have made this decision because we believe it is better that money should be spent on providing one child with a 7-year education which may help him or her to become a useful member of society, rather than divide that same amount of money and staff between two children, neither of whom is likely to get any permanent benefit. For the justification of spending money on education in our present economic situation is that this is an investment in our future. Giving a large number of children only four years' education, means merely that we have forgone the present satisfaction of other needs without gaining anything in the future. It is rather as if we spent our money on putting up the walls of two factories knowing that we had insufficient money to put a machine in either, instead of building one factory properly so that it could begin to produce the goods we need.

The effect of giving priority to eliminating the Standard IV examination is that by the end of the Second Plan we will still only have places for about 52 per cent of our eligible children in Standard I. But no child who enters primary school this year—1969—or afterwards will have to take that examination; they will go straight through to Standard VII. It will, however, now be 1989 before we are able to introduce universal primary education in Tanzania.

Before I leave this question of primary school education for our children, I want to discuss one other thing which is related to it. I have already pointed out that when we took the census we discovered that our population was increasing at a faster rate than we had assumed when we prepared the First Plan. We had worked on the assumption that the total population of Tanzania was about 10 million, but the census showed that in fact it was $12\frac{1}{4}$ million. We had also thought that the annual rate of increase was 22 for every thousand people; we discovered that the annual rate of increase was 27 for every thousand people. And that means that in the coming five years our population will increase by 350,000 people every year.

The thing I want to say is this. It is very good to increase our population, because our country is large and there is plenty of unused land. But it is necessary to remember that these 350,000 extra people every year will be babies in arms, not workers. They will have to be fed, clothed, given medical attention, schooling, and many other services for very many years before they will be able to contribute to the economy of the country through their work. This is right and proper and is in accordance with the teachings of the Arusha Declaration. But it is obvious that just as the number of our children is increasing, so the burden on the adults—the workers—is also increasing. Giving birth is something in which mankind and animals are equal, but rearing the young, and especially educating them for many years, is something which is a unique gift and responsibility of men. It is for this reason that it is important for human beings to put emphasis on caring for children and the ability to look after them properly, rather than thinking only about the numbers of children and the ability to give birth. For it often happens that men's ability to give birth is greater than their ability to bring up the children in a proper manner.

There is one other aspect of our educational work over the past five years which I must mention. We have recognized that, in order to meet the requirements of high-level manpower by 1980, we have to achieve a drastic increase in the number of university science graduates. But we are not achieving that necessary increase. The failures in science at both higher school certificate and at university degree level are such that, unless some improvement can be made quickly, we shall miss our 1980 target in this important field by as much as 30 per cent. It is no use lowering our standards; that would be merely hiding the problem under pieces of paper. Building roads, bridges, electric appliances, or running factories, agricultural research, and so on, are matters of knowledge not of certificates.

Quite clearly some investigation and corrective action has to be taken on this matter; and this must begin as a matter of urgency. Are our students failing because of the teaching, of the facilities available, of the curriculum at lower levels which leaves our pupils unfamiliar with scientific concepts, or is there some other reason for this experience? These things we must know, for Tanzania is involved in a world based on technology, and we shall remain backward and dependent upon others until we are able to produce our own people with scientific skills.

INDUSTRIALIZATION

Let me now turn to the implication for the Second Five-Year Plan of our recent successes and failures in the field of processing and manufactured goods. . . .

It is true that we doubled the value of the capital goods—that is, the machines in factories, the buildings, the industrial equipment, and so on—being used for productive purposes. But this meant that we were expanding our industrial production at a rate of only 10 per cent per annum instead of the 14.8 per cent per annum which was our target. Industry therefore now accounts for about 7 per cent of our gross domestic product, which is slightly less than we had hoped for.

Nonetheless, the number of Tanzanian manufactures now on sale in our shops demonstrates that we did make considerable progress in the production of goods which we used to import. We shall continue to expand simple manufacturing, the processing of primary commodities, and the provision of basic construction materials; but we have now reached the stage where we must think seriously about the next and more difficult phase of industrialization. For it is comparatively easy to produce your own textiles, cement, and similar goods; beginning to produce your own capital goods, and goods which are used only in the production of other things, is a more complex operation and demands a more sophisticated degree of economic planning. Yet such a move is essential for long-term growth; an important task which will be undertaken early in the Second Plan period is the preparation of a long-term industrialization plan, taking into account the possibilities of the East African Common Market and of exports. The aim is that we should be ready to embark on this kind of work at the very beginning of the Third Plan.

Let me just add one further point. Although mass production is the best and cheapest way of meeting the needs of our people for certain types of goods, there are many others where the needs can be best met by labour-intensive, small-scale industries and craft workshops. Obvious examples of this are furniture, which can be made locally from local materials without the problem of transportation over long distances; ready-made clothes; and local food preservation. It is vital that we should increase our efforts in this matter, for such activities have the further advantage that they require very little capital investment, and they can be carried on in the villages and small towns of our country, thus improving the quality and variety of life in the rural areas.

The details of this and other parts of the Plan will be presented to you by the Minister. I would, however, like to draw your attention to the fact that most investment in industry will take place in the parastatal sector, in accordance with the Arusha Declaration.

Only about 16 per cent of the total industrial investment will be undertaken by the private sector, and it is expected that a large element of this will be these small-scale projects where only a small number of people are employed. It is also expected that the workers and co-operative organizations will play a part in expanding the industrial sector of our economy; we are relying upon them for something like 7 per cent of the total increase in industrial potential.

AGRICULTURE

Industrialization, however, was not the central element in the First Plan any more than it is in the Second. We did then, as we do now, recognize that the basis for our development in the near future must be agriculture. Unfortunately we made two decisions in 1964 which events have proved wrong. The first of these was in relation to sisal.

In 1964 we produced almost 230,000 tons of sisal and the average price actually received by the producer—taking all grades together—was in the region of Shs. 1,700/- per ton. The target we set ourselves for 1970 was a production of 270,000 tons and we anticipated that our export price would have dropped a little. In the event, the export price dropped catastrophically as early as 1965, and low prices continued, until in 1968 the average price received by the producer was only Shs. 765/- per ton. Consequently, our target for this crop had to be radically revised, because many estates became uneconomic to run; the amount actually produced last year was therefore less than 194,000 tons. This caused a very great change in many sectors of the Plan. The amount of employment in the sisal industry dropped from 96,400 in 1964 to 41,668 in 1968; and the foreign exchange earned by the industry—which was badly needed for capital imports—dropped from Shs. 434 million in 1964 to less than Shs. 187 million in 1968. The question as regards sisal now is not the rate at which we can expand the industry, but how slowly, and to what extent, we should contract it and shift our resources on to the production of other more profitable crops or of livestock.

The other aspect of the First Plan which proved to be mistaken was our emphasis on what we called transformation approach—the opening of new Government-financed settlement schemes of a highly mechanized nature. There is no need for me to discuss this now;

I did so when we recognized that this policy was too expensive in money and mistaken in its estimates of economic and psychological results. All the settlement schemes which were started and which still survive will now be gradually converted into ujamaa villages.

The production of many other crops has been in accordance with the Plan targets, although in general the prices we receive are slightly lower than those prevailing in 1964. But the crucial thing for us to realize is that the increases in output were almost everywhere realized without any change in the method of production.

Our farmers have expanded the acreage they cultivate; they have worked harder. But almost everywhere they are still using the hoe, *jembe* and *shoka*. They have not yet changed the tools they work with. The expansion possible with these tools is very limited; we have probably reached the maximum in many areas. Yet we have done much too little to encourage our farmers to change over to ox-ploughs and other ox-drawn implements for weeding, sowing, and spreading fertilizer. In the whole country we still have only four ox-training centres, with another five due to be opened soon; our farmers still have to buy ox-ploughs from abroad unless local carpenters have the knowledge and initiative to get a model from the Machinery Testing Unit at Arusha, which they could copy. Further, our women still carry the crops to market on their heads; ox-carts or donkey-carts are still so rare as to attract attention despite the large number of animals which are eating our fodder.

This situation must be changed—and the Plan includes provision for a big expansion of oxen-plough training. The Ministry must act rapidly to make improved tools available, and the farmers must press forward into using new methods—which will often involve working co-operatively and not continuing as individual peasant farmers. There is no alternative if we are to improve our standard of living. For a higher standard of living does not mean just having money to spend on clothes, roads, and so on, although of course it includes these things. It also means not having to act as a beast of burden, not having to walk miles for clean water, having plenty of good and nutritious food. All these things we could do easily. To use people instead of an ox or a donkey, when we have both oxen and donkeys, is not sensible. We are holding back our own development. Firstly, we cultivate shambas which are too small; secondly, we reduce the time available for other development work and for educating ourselves. I hope that during the period of the coming Plan, both TANU and Government leaders will exert every effort to persuade the people in our rural areas to change their methods of work, and will help them to obtain the new tools.

FOOD

Although we emphasize cash crops in our agricultural policy, today I want to discuss the question of our food—for, as we said earlier, our first aim is to provide sufficient and better food for everyone. Anyone travelling in this country sees poor and undernourished children, some of them sitting listlessly—lacking even the energy to play—and others easily exhausted. Also, those who have seen the Chinese working on the railway survey, or the Americans building the road to Zambia, will have noticed how our people get tired very quickly in comparison with the Chinese and Americans. The reason is not that our people are lazy. It is that they do not get enough meat, eggs, fish, and milk, or other protein foods even to feed their bodies properly. But although this is well known, if you suggest to our citizens that they should keep chickens they will ask: 'Where shall we sell them?' Or: 'Where shall we sell the eggs?' These are very stupid questions. Those who buy chickens or eggs do so to have food. Similarly, those who keep chickens should do so for the purpose of providing their food and that of their children.

Why is there a single family in our rural areas which does not keep decent chickens? They could be fed on the scraps from the farm: it is only if you are trying to sell eggs to the tourist hotels that you need to spend money on expensive special foodstuffs. Or who is there in our rural areas who would be unable to keep ducks or rabbits in order to improve the feeding of his family—if he wanted to do so? Yet we do not do it; meat remains a luxury to many of our people!

And it is not only meat; the production of groundnuts has gone down because the price is unattractive. But is every farmer in the possible areas growing some groundnuts for the feeding of his family? Nuts, beans, and vegetables, are good nutritious food which build up the body and mind; and at least one green vegetable, one type of nut, and one type of bean can be grown in almost every part of Tanzania.

And what of fruit? We act as if fruit is only good for Europeans or for children, and even for our children we rely upon the accidental growth of a self-seeded tree somewhere in the vicinity. Surely the time has come when the Ministry of Agriculture, Food and Co-operatives should be preparing nurseries of fruit trees in each District, so that our farmers could plant a selection of different fruit trees around their own homesteads. Pawpaw, mangoes, oranges, limes, etc., provide essential vitamins which are important for the health of every human being and should be a regular part of our diet. As I have said before, a handful of nuts and a slice of pawpaw every day could protect many of our children from vitamin deficiency blindness, as well as give their bodies a defence against many other diseases. Yet at present in our rural areas we waste the fruit which is available. We do not try to preserve it for use in the out-of-season period—we neither dry it, make chutney, jams or anything else. And in Dar es Salaam we sometimes see children knocking down unripe mangoes and cashew apples from the trees. Surely we can line our streets with fruit trees, so that eventually the citizens and children of this city can always get what they want, and we can have shade from the hot sun. Further, if the Ministry of Agriculture, Food and Co-operatives prepares nurseries in this Region, it should be possible for every family in the new housing estates of Dar es Salaam to grow one or two different trees in its garden. This would provide fruit at different times of the year and at the same time beautify our city.

Our present attitude to food is the result of ignorance, indifference and indolence. Many of our people do not realize what they can do, or why it is important that they should; and they find it easier to carry on in the old fashioned way than to make the effort to change the condition of their life—partly, of course, because they are them-selves suffering from the effect of long-term bad feeding. It is essential that Government and Party officials at all levels should intervene actively. We must spread knowledge—through the Health Education Units, Community Development workers, and the Agricultural Field Officers, all working as a team to show why and how improvements in diet can be made. But it is also necessary for Central Government and parastatal organizations to bear our health problems in mind. The mills which process sugar, flour, and rice, must consider the health of our people more than the appearance of the product; they must not think just of filling our stomachs without worrying about the nutritive value of the food.

I have talked at length about this question of food because the foundation of development is people. A hungry person cannot bring progress. He is weak of body and also weak of mind. This must always be remembered, especially in relation to children. When a child is not well fed he will not grow properly—he will be deformed, and his intelligence will be affected also; he will not reach to his full potential. The question of sufficient food, and good food, is absolutely vital to the development of our people, in both towns and villages.

The priority given to rural development has very wide implications. Certainly increased production of both cash crops and food crops is essential. In particular, we must expand our production of cotton, cashews, tobacco, and wheat; we must use our cattle, sheep and goats more productively. Plans for all these things are laid out in the documents, and the targets must be broken down into Regional, District, and even village targets so that our people understand the challenge which is before them and can rise to the opportunities it presents.

This matter of understanding our plan is very important. For we make a big mistake if we try to force people to produce certain amounts or even to cultivate certain acreages of cash crops. Political officers who have tried this in the past find that the people cultivate the required area for the first year but that the crop is surprisingly small, and then when the second year comes along the peasants have moved further into the bush to get away from the officers of Government! This is contrary to all our long-term interests. Persuasion may appear slower than force, but it is more effective.

UJAMAA VIJIJINI

Increases in output and in the amount of wealth produced is, however, only one aspect of the socialist rural development we are aiming at. It is not necessary for me to repeat at length what I have said many times about the need for the development of ujamaa villages and co-operative production units. Our policy is firm; and we have now organized Government and Party so as to enable maximum help and encouragement to be given to all these socialist communities. The only point I wish to stress is the decision to start ujamaa villages, big and small, throughout the country.

We have rejected the idea that we should concentrate all Government assistance on the development of ujamaa villages in certain Regions or Districts, and have decided that we must make a widespread frontal attack on this problem. All Departments of Government will be involved in this task. Training of agricultural officers, of co-operative officers, of Party workers and of rural health workers, etc., will all include discussion of how they can assist the implementation of the policy of *Ujamaa Vijijini*. Ujamaa villages and groups of villages will be given priority in the services of these trained people, as well as in the location of new schools, dispensaries, local water supplies, and so on. Groups of people working together in socialist or co-operative units must also get priority in the allocation of regional development funds. In other words, all Government activities in the rural areas will be directed towards helping the sound, economic development of socialist rural production and socialist living.

It is perhaps necessary to add a word of warning. Our resources do not suddenly increase because of this policy. We can give priority to ujamaa villages but we cannot help them if the resources are not available. The basis of ujamaa village organization is, and must be, self-help and self-reliance. It would be absurd and very wrong for TANU or Government officers to persuade people to start or to join an ujamaa village through promises of outside help. People must join together in this way because they understand that their own efforts will be more productive, and their lives made more secure and more enjoyable, because of their mutual responsibility for each other. But life in ujamaa villages must include modern development. The Government must help the members to make progress as quickly as possible away from the hoe, the sickle, and the need to carry everything on their heads.

THE WIDER IMPLICATIONS OF PRIORITY
TO THE RURAL AREAS

The decision to give top priority to rural development does not only affect what is done in the rural areas; it also has implications for every other aspect of the Development Plan. Thus, for example, it means that there is less money and less manpower which can be devoted to improving conditions in the urban areas. In this Second Plan period it is therefore necessary to put a limit of Shs. 250 million on urban infra-structure expenditure—that is, on the provision of roads, sewerage, lighting, etc. This still means that for every person who now lives in an urban area, there will be just under Shs. 60/- spent every year on building roads and everything else. It sounds a lot, but you cannot lay many inches of a tarmac road for Shs. 60/-! This urban expenditure will be concentrated on the areas where the less highly paid workers live, but even so, it is quite obvious that very little new development will be possible unless there is a great increase in the amount of self-help work done in towns.

This need for self-reliance and frugality is reflected also in the new plans for houses to be built with Government or parastatal loans. Further attempts will be made to build decent houses at a still lower cost for renting purposes. Where house purchase is involved, there will be a new development—'site and service facilities' —which will mean that only the very basic work will be done by the National Housing Corporation, and the rest will be left for the owner to do as and when he can add to his house in accordance with approved plans.

But despite our shortage of money, we have decided to make a special effort in order to expand certain of our towns. We have made this decision for two reasons. Firstly, people are attracted away from the villages in search of work and other services which are available in the towns, and at present the great attraction is Dar es Salaam itself. As a result there are now in this city many people who came to look for work, but who cannot find any, and many others who have no houses to live in. It would be better to spread to other parts of the country the attraction which is now concentrated in one place.

Secondly, there is the fact that progress begets more progress, and a developing town helps the development of nearby rural areas.

For it must be recognized that the more factories which exist in any one place, the cheaper and easier it is to build a new factory there. For example, in a town where there are 5,000 workers employed, there is a ready market of about 25,000 people, all of whom need to buy food, clothes, and other consumer goods. Their presence justifies expenditure on building, let us say, a modern bakery, a small plant for making cooking pots, and so on—each of which will employ more people. And the fact that roads, water supplies, power supplies, etc., have already been provided for some factories makes it convenient to site new factories in the same place. This is to say nothing of the fact that a large urban centre provides opportunities for local farmers to sell vegetables, fruit and other foodstuffs without great transportation costs. It is therefore Government's intention to try to build up 10 urban growth centres by diverting suitable new factories and employment opportunities to selected towns. The aim is to help each of these growth centres reach the point where it is in itself an attraction to industry without special Government intervention.

It is obvious that certain towns will be very disappointed to find that they have not been designated as urban growth centres in this Second Five-Year Plan. I can only say that we have more than 10 towns and some disappointment is therefore inevitable—to plan is to choose. If we tried to spread our efforts over more than 10 towns in this next period, we should find that we do not have urban growth centres at all; we should just have what we have now—a number of small towns none of which has got sufficient industry and public services to make it an attractive economic proposition for the siting of new factories. By concentrating our attention on the towns selected, at least two or three should be able to stand on their own by the end of this Plan period. In the Third Five-Year Plan we shall then be able to add other towns to this classification.

COMMERCE AND TRADE

The underlying meaning of all these Plans is that we are trying gradually to transform our economy so that it is no longer export dominated but is directed to the creation and service of a rising local market. Up to now the patterns of trade have been such that it is often easier to sell Mwanza goods in London than it is to sell them in Mtwara. Some progress has been made in correcting this situation over the past five years, but further effort is needed to improve our internal marketing and credit arrangements. This does not mean, and must not mean, a decrease in our exports; we need the foreign exchange they earn in order to pay for essential development goods. But we cannot continue to rely upon imported consumer goods and simple manufactures. In fact, in order to leave us with sufficient foreign exchange to buy the machines and other things we need for our new factories, it is necessary that the total value of consumer goods imported should be held constant over the next five years. As people earn more money from increased efforts, they will have to buy locally produced goods—and it is the responsibility of Government and parastatal organizations to ensure that the things required are available at the places where they are needed. Of course this does mean a restriction of consumer choice. For example, we are now producing instant coffee; it would be stupid for us to continue importing other brands of instant coffee just so that people can have a choice. Let them buy instant coffee produced in Tanzania or perhaps in East Africa. Similarly with cotton cloth: instead of being able to select from a choice of luxury cloth produced in all parts of the world, we have to learn to use the cloth we produce ourselves. It is either that and the success of our factories, or continuing to import and allowing our factories to go bankrupt. To plan is to choose! We are nearly self-sufficient in the production of textiles and we cannot continue to indulge our stupid preference for imported cloth. What we cannot produce in Tanzania we should buy from East Africa—or, if the things are not essential, we should do without.

This restriction of choice is necessary and inevitable. But it must not be allowed to lead to inefficiency in production; our Tanzanian citizens must not be forced into buying poor stuff just because it is produced in Tanzania. Our local products need not be so handsomely wrapped, or so sophisticated in concept, as those produced in London, Bonn, Washington, or Peking, and the variety of patterns will naturally be reduced. But matches must light, flour must be free from weevils, cloth be hard wearing and of fast colour, and so on. I know that not all our products are yet as good as they should be, but many are already of very good quality. I know, for example, that our cloth is very good, yet there are some stupid people who continue to prefer imported cloth.

In all these questions of quality in production, care in storage, and speed and efficiency of distribution, the parastatal organizations and the co-operative movement have a prime responsibility. The workers in these organizations must have initiative and drive; they must go out and seek new opportunities for service and they must be aware of developing demands. For these publicly-owned organizations not only constitute the largest element in the productive sector; over this Plan period and that following, they will become increasingly responsible for wholesale and retail trade. It is intended that the State Trading Corporation shall take on an increasing share of the wholesale trade, as well as most responsibility for imports and exports. Further, locally-based co-operative retail shops will get every encouragement from Government and after they have proved their ability to serve our people so co-operatives will gradually take over the larger part of retail trading.

COMMUNICATIONS

The only other specific sector of our economy to which I intend to refer today is that of communications. Once again we are faced with hard choices. Do we improve existing heavily used roads so that traffic is less liable to be held up by washaways or floods? Or do we build better roads in areas where traffic is not yet very dense, in the hope that good communications will encourage development where at present there is none?

The fact is that the cost of all the road works and the aerodrome construction which is now economically justified would be Shs.1,182 million—or 47 per cent of the total Second Plan Government Investment Budget! Obviously we cannot make this kind of allocation to communications. We have to select the most urgent and most important schemes, leaving the others to be done later—for to plan is to choose. Government's decision is that first priority must be given to the bitumenization of the full length of the Tanzania/Zambia highway, with all improvements necessary to ensure that this road remains open at all times. I do not think I need to justify that choice to this Conference. But we must accept its implications.

Very little other major road works can be begun until the fourth year of the present Plan; and only a small amount of work relative to the need can be done on the feeder road systems. Fortunately the construction of the Kilimanjaro International Airport makes a different kind of demand on our resources, and we expect to be able to go ahead with it. By doing so we shall put ourselves in a position to take full advantage of the tourist potential of Northern Tanzania.

The other communications project with which we expect to make headway is the Tanzania/Zambia railway. There are many enemies of this project; indeed, the world has never seen such a profusion of railway projects in Southern Africa as those which are now being canvassed—and all of them are designed to try and stop this railway from being built. I do not believe that these efforts at sabotage will have any success at all. I am confident that the railway connecting the Zambia system with the East African rail system through Dar es Salaam will be constructed. We have therefore allocated Shs. 305 million over the Five-Year Plan period for the local costs of building the TanZam railway.

OVERALL TARGETS

In the First Plan we had a target rate of growth of 6.7 per cent per annum—in other words, we hoped to increase our wealth by more than 6 per cent every year. As I have already said, our achievement was a growth rate of about 5 per cent. At this rate, and because our population is increasing by 2.7 per cent every year, it would take us 30 years to double the average income per head in Tanzania. We must do better than that, even if we cannot achieve the 1980 target we set ourselves in 1964.

The Second Plan aims to achieve a growth rate of 6.5 per cent in real terms—that is, after allowing for price changes. This is now a realistic target because of the work we did during the First Plan period. But it will not be easy; to achieve it we have to increase still further the proportion of our wealth that we devote to investment. We have already done quite well. Whereas in 1964 only about 15 per cent of the wealth we produced was put aside for investment work, the comparable figure in 1967 was 22.9 per cent. That is a very big increase; we can be proud of it. But we must do still better.

The target set in the Plan, therefore, is that by 1974 we should be devoting to investment 25 per cent of the wealth we produce in any one year. This is not quite as hard as it sounds; by then the total value of the wealth we are producing will be larger than it is now, for we shall be feeling the benefit of some of the investments we have already made. . . .

The total value of our planned investments in the next five years is Shs. 8,085 million. Of this, Government expenditure will be Shs. 3,055 million; the parastatals and co-operatives are expected to invest Shs. 2,300 million; and the East African Community is expected, in accordance with its plans, to invest about Shs. 580 million in Tanzania. These are our targets. Of this amount, it is anticipated that about 60 per cent of Government expenditure will be financed from within Tanzania; between 60 per cent and 65 per cent of parastatal investment will also come from within the United Republic. In fact, during this Plan period something like 30 per cent of the investment needs of the parastatal organizations will have to be financed from Government sources, but as time goes on they will gradually be expected to be increasingly self-reliant— that is why they will be aiming at making profits now. Out of these profits they will make future investments.

Yet to talk as though development were simply a matter of investment is a big mistake. After all, if that were the case, a country which invested all its available resources in building a big palace of gold and marble could claim to be developing. What matters is not just the quantity of investment, but also its effectiveness in increasing wealth. A textile mill must produce good quality and attractive cloth; it is no use if it does not do so. And it is no use clearing a large farm and cultivating huge areas of groundnuts if no one is going to buy groundnuts. Research into the best way of spending the money available for investment, and checks on the efficiency of investments which have already been made, are very important indeed.

To poor people, what is called 'cost effectiveness' is absolutely vital. That means that we need to assess how big will be the reward for spending money on one investment as against another, for it is essential that we should get the best possible return from our efforts. For, I repeat; to plan is to choose. Also, once a factory or farm is established, we need to ensure that it is giving the best possible service. Sometimes this can be measured by profits; for example, if there are two factories which cost exactly the same to construct and both of which produce cotton cloth, then their comparative profits will give an indication of whether they are equally efficient in producing the things our people want. But in a socialist developing society, profits can never be the only measure of success. We have to take into account things like whether a factory uses a lot of scarce resources, such as highly skilled manpower, and whether it is sited in an area where there is a shortage of employment opportunities. Of course, our room for flexibility in this matter is not unlimited; we cannot afford permanently to subsidize new factories or industries. Yet it is still true that we cannot depend only on profits as a measurement of investment efficiency. We are not a company seeking profits; we are a country seeking development. What a private company would not undertake because it would not make a profit may be necessary for our development.

This Five-Year Plan therefore provides for the working out of new checks on the practical impact of investments. This will involve research of many different kinds in industry, agriculture, commerce and administration; consequently I hope that we shall all abandon the idea that research is the same as spying, or that a researcher is really a person who is contributing nothing to our economy. Properly directed research can ensure that our money is properly spent, that our plans are really being carried out, and that we get the maximum benefit from the efforts we make and the policies we pursue.

At the same time we have to make extra efforts to improve the efficiency of our administrative services in Government, parastatal organizations, co-operatives, and workers' organizations. At the moment many of our public services leave very much to be desired in this respe t; and I think the position has got worse rather than better in recent years. It takes longer for letters to be dealt with, people are kept waiting in offices, an attitude of indifference is sometimes adopted towards our people who are seeking help or advice, equipment is not serviced properly, and so on. This is partly a matter of training and leadership, and further efforts will be made during the next five years to increase the training and educational facilities available for our public servants. But it is also a matter of work discipline.

It is sometimes said that Tanzanians are too kind to be willing to impose discipline on others and too casual to impose it upon themselves. Those who say this are not trying to praise us, but to criticize us. But it is our responsibility to make sure that we do not deserve these comments. For if we fail we shall have to give up any expectation of becoming self-reliant participants in the modern technological world. Those who want the benefits of modern life have to accept the discipline of modern life ni factories, offices, hospitals, schools, workshops, etc. This means self-discipline for service in the first place, and then leadership in the second place. It means knowing what standards of work and behaviour are required, and then observing them.

Another matter of great importance for the success of this Plan is that there should be an improvement in planning and administration at Regional and local levels. The development of Tanzania cannot be effected from Dar es Salaam; local initiative, local co-ordination of plans, and local democratic control over decisions are also necessary. Some re-allocation of financial and administrative responsibilities between the centre and the districts is included in this Second Five-Year Plan, and consideration is being given to the possibilities of further decentralization. But whatever the form of organization, it is essential that every Party and Government official, at both local and national level, should regard it as his duty to encourage socialist developments which spring out of the people's initiatives. We must not be hide-bound by plan documents, but must recognize that if people are willing to make an extra effort and do not need to call upon national resources for success, then they must be encouraged.

For the truth is that the people of this country are the real developers of Tanzania, as well as being the purpose of Tanzanian development. Even large-scale projects like mass production factories, tourist hotels, state farms, etc., are undertaken only to further the well-being of Tanzanian citizens; it is vital that we should always remember that. For sometimes these big projects, which are of benefit to the nation as a whole, require a big change in the lives of particular groups of people, and this group may well be more conscious of the direct problems they are experiencing than the very indirect benefits they will later receive. It is therefore not good enough for the responsible officials just to go to the location of the project and start digging the foundations. At the very least the people in the immediate vicinity should be told in advance what is being planned, why, and when work will start. Then they can begin to make their own plans accordingly, and in the process they should receive all possible help and co-operation from TANU and Government officials.

Running right through our development activities must be this kind of consideration for people. No one who ignores the feelings of people can be a socialist, for socialism is about people. And it is not good enough just to think of the 'masses' and how they will benefit from a particular project in the long run. The masses are the people considered together: if you do not care about a small group of people, it is at least open to doubt whether you really care about the large group. Of course, it is true that we have to proceed with nationally needed projects, even though they will cause inconvenience and difficulty for particular groups; we cannot stop building a railway because some people have their farms on the proposed route or object to the noise which the trains will make. But the question I am discussing is not whether the project goes ahead, but how this inconvenience and difficulty for a few people is handled. A socialist will care about them, as well as about the railway; a socialist leader will get their understanding and support for the railway, and will help them to take the opportunity of the move to organize their new lives on a basis which allows for socialist growth.

Friends; we have a lot to do. I hope that this week every delegate will work hard to understand the problems and opportunities before our people. We rely upon you to explain this Plan, and to co-operate with all your fellow citizens for its success. The people of Tanzania have shown what they can do despite great difficulties. Now that we have prepared our organization for further development, let us go forward to even greater efforts in the future.

To plan is to choose. Choose to go forward.

15

A Tribute to Canadian Attitudes

During his four-day stay in Canada, President Nyerere paid tribute to Canadian attitudes and aid in a speech delivered at a lunch given by Prime Minister Trudeau on 30 September 1969.

. . . Canada's world involvement is inevitably that of a fairly large and wealthy country—certainly in comparative terms. Yet small and poor countries like mine have warm respect for Canada; we do not find your comparative power intimidating, but rather a reassurance in world affairs.

The background to this attitude of ours is, of course, the general record of Canada in the post-1939/1945 war years. But I hope I will not be misunderstood in this democratic country, Mr. Prime Minister, when I say that for many of the new nations, Canada became personified in Mr. Lester Pearson, your distinguished predecessor. It was under his leadership that Canada first demonstrated its understanding of the emerging Third World. Without always agreeing with us, he expressed Canada's respect for the principles of national sovereignty, and for their application even to small and weak nations. He also showed Canada's acceptance of the principle of human equality and dignity. Thus, to mention only two instances, Mr. Pearson's peace-making work in the Suez crisis of 1956, and his understanding of Africa's position on Rhodesia and South Africa, have been very important for the world and also, I believe, for this country.

It is against this background of reciprocal respect that Tanzania appealed to Canada in 1964, when it became necessary for us to ask for assistance in military training. The Canadian Government was reluctant to respond to this appeal because of the very understandable, and indeed very good, reason that this country did not wish even to appear to be involved in the military affairs of other nations. These scruples Tanzania respects, but I am glad to say that our two countries were able to agree on practical assistance which reduced this danger to the minimum. It was agreed that we should not have 'military advisers'; these are rather discredited in the modern world. But Canada did undertake to help us with the training of officers and with the establishment of an Air Transport Wing for the People's Defence Forces.

Mr. Prime Minister, I wish to take this opportunity to say that we appreciate that assistance. The work has been extremely well done, and the officers and men of the Canadian forces have been helpful and very correct. They have enhanced the reputation of this country as one which respects others even while helping them.

The fact that Tanzania has now given notice that we shall not ask for a renewal of this five-year contract is thus a tribute to Canada. It does not mark any deterioration in relations, nor the growth of any suspicions or hostilities between us. We are able to allow this agreement to come to its natural end because m ost of the things which were agreed upon will have been completed by the due date. Mr. Prime Minister—thanks to the work of Canadians in Tanzania and in this country—we believe that, for the most part, we shall be able to take over officer training ourselves next year. We shall also be able to maintain the Air Transport Wing which you have helped us to establish. We may ask Canada or other countries for help on particular occasions, such as the training of specialist officers; but we can now say: 'Thank you for completing the work we agreed upon'.

Yet although assistance in military training is coming to an end, we are extremely pleased that technical assistance in the economic and social sectors is increasing. The amount of Canadian money devoted to technical assistance for Tanzania has increased steadily over the last three years. I can assure you that this is a trend we appreciate; the people you send us have been of great help in our work. . . .

Finally, Mr. Prime Minister, let me say that we greatly appreciate the development loans which have been made available to us. In particular, the fact that they are long-term and without interest means that we are not expected to repay money used for infrastructural development—things like roads and surveys—before they have had an impact on our economy. . . .

Mr. Prime Minister, let me just close by saying that you will not find us becoming permanent beggars on your doorstep. Indeed, the reason we appreciate Canada's help is because it is directed at strengthening our own efforts and does not try to replace them. But the most important thing which I wish to make clear is that relations between our two countries are not dependent upon aid. They are good because we respect each other and are both trying to work for peace and justice in the world. I am confident that on this basis they will continue to give satisfaction to both our peoples.

16

Stability and Change in Africa

On 2 October 1969, President Nyerere was awarded an Honorary Doctorate of Law by the University of Toronto, Canada. At the special ceremony for this purpose the President addressed a large and enthusiastic crowd of staff, students, and members of the public on the challenge of the African freedom struggle.

This is my first visit to the University of Toronto but it is very far from being my first contact with it. People from this University have worked at our University College in Dar es Salaam and in many different sectors of our Government; they have made great contributions to our progress. We have many old and valued friends here; people to whom we are indebted for good service gladly rendered. . . .

This kind of technical assistance is very valuable to us. It also has a by-product which is, I believe, important to Canada as well. For not only have we learned something about Canada from these workers. As intelligent people who have lived with us and worked with us, they have learned something about us. When they return to this country, they are therefore frequently able to spread an understanding of what we are trying to do. They can tell of our successes and our failures; more important, they can also put our actions into the context of our circumstances and our motives. I believe this to be important to both countries. For Tanzania's policy of self-reliance does not imply that we dream of isolating ourselves. We recognize that we are involved in the world and that the world is involved in us.

Involvement without understanding, however, can be embarrassing and even dangerous. And while the involvement is inevitable, a lack of understanding about Africa is only too easy. Our very existence as nations is exotic. And now our voices on the international scene are strident: we complain about things which others take for granted; we make demands on other nations of the world, which appear unreasonable to more traditional habits of thought. The reaction is natural. Our actions and our demands are looked upon with all the suspicion which is normally directed towards upstarts. And everything we do is judged in the light of attitudes which grew out of the aftermath of the Second World War. In other words, every possible attempt is made to squeeze African events into the framework of the cold war or other big power conflicts. The big question is always: 'Is this or that African country pro-East or pro-West?'.

These kinds of question are understandable because of the recent history of Europe and America. But they are the wrong questions for anyone who wishes to understand what is happening in Africa. They are based on a very fundamental mistake—and, I would add, an unwarranted degree of arrogance! They imply that Africa has no ideas of its own and no interests of its own. They assume the exclusive validity of the international conflicts which existed when we achieved nationhood. They are based on the belief that African actions must inevitably be determined by reference to either the Western liberal tradition or to communist theory or practice.

In fact, I hope that Africa has learned, and will continue to learn, from total human experience—from peoples in the west, east, north and south, whether we use these compass points as political or geographical terms! But what we are, in fact, trying to do is to solve the problems of Africa—and in our case, of Tanzania—as we experience them. And we are making this attempt as Africans and as Tanzanians; as people who have been shaped by a history which goes back further than the century or so of colonialism. Further, we look at the world as people who believe that they have something to contribute to mankind, as well as something to gain from it.

OUR NEED FOR BOTH CHANGE AND STABILITY

Yet we are new nations. Like every other people in the world we have always had a desire to be our own masters. We lost our freedom through defeat by the technically superior forces of Europe. Our first concern was to regain it, and our first priority now is to guard that freedom and to make it a reality.

When we did regain our freedom, however, we gained control over a different structure. In Tanzania it was more than one hundred tribal units which lost their freedom; it was one nation which regained it. By the forces of history we have been brought politically into this twentieth century world; our new freedom can only be maintained if we adopt other aspects of twentieth century life as well.

Another fundamental change makes other demands upon the national government which were not made on the traditional tribal governments. The Tanzanian people now know that our poverty, our ignorance, and our diseases, are not an inevitable part of the human condition. Once we accepted these things as the will of God; now they are recognized as being within the control of man. Political freedom is therefore no longer enough for us.

We in Tanzania are thus conscious of two overwhelming needs. We are determined to maintain our mastery over our own destiny— to defend our national freedom. We are also determined to change the condition of our lives. It is to meet these two needs that we must have both change and stability. Somehow these two must be combined, because in the circumstances of Tanzania, and indeed of Africa, neither is possible without the other.

CHANGE TO MAKE FREEDOM A REALITY

For although political and social stability are necessary to any real national or personal freedom, so too is change in our circumstances. At present our national freedom often exists on paper only, for our country is so poor, and so weak, relative to other nations, that we do not play our rightful part in the human community. Decisions on matters which vitally concern us can be—and often are—made without any reference to us. And this is understandable. Even defending our national integrity against the intervention of foreign powers strains us to the utmost. A very great change in our economic well-being is necessary before we can meet these responsibilities of national freedom.

Nor is it only in national terms that real freedom is undermined by our poverty. What freedom has our subsistence farmer? He scratches a bare living from the soil provided the rains do not fail; his children work at his side without schooling, medical care, or even good feeding. Certainly he has freedom to vote and to speak as he wishes. But these freedoms are much less real to him than his freedom to be exploited. Only as his poverty is reduced will his existing political freedom become properly meaningful and his right to human dignity become a fact of human dignity.

This essential economic change will not, and cannot, take place in isolation. It depends upon, and it brings, social and political change. It is not even possible simply to expand the social and political organization which was introduced into the country by the colonial power. These were based on an individualistic philosophy which is contrary to both our traditions and our aspirations for human equality. And they were directed at the problems of imposing and maintaining an alien law and order, not at securing mobilization for that improvement in living conditions which our people now demand.

THE NEED FOR STABILITY

Yet stable government, and stability in the society, is also essential to our freedom. For without political stability African countries will remain the playthings of others. Without it, alien forces can influence our policies for their own benefit, and outside powers can wage their wars on our territories and with our peoples. It is perfectly true that many of us in Africa are in danger of getting a phobia about foreign plots, and of attributing to foreign machinations all the evils we suffer from. But although the original failures may be ours, no intelligent and knowledgeable person would deny that outside forces do take advantage of African division for their own benefit, or that they exacerbate our conflicts when this suits their purposes.

Quite apart from the defence of our national integrity, however, stability is also essential for economic development. We cannot increase agricultural production, organize markets for home-produced goods, meet export orders, or arrange for the supply of essential investment goods, unless there is stability and security in the country. An effective administration, secure communications, and personal safety, are prerequisites for any attack on the poverty which now oppresses us.

In brief, change causes disturbance and thus upsets stability, but positive change is impossible without stability. And stability is itself impossible in Africa without change. Africa's task is therefore to achieve a difficult balance between the conflicting and complementary needs for change and stability.

TANZANIA'S INTERNAL POLICIES

Tanzania is attempting to achieve change by deliberate policy, and to maintain stability by involving all the people in both the direction and the process of change. We are under no illusions about the difficulty of the task we have undertaken. With few socialists we are trying to build socialism; with few people conscious of the basic requirements of democracy we are trying to achieve change by democratic means; with few technicians we are trying to effect a fundamental transformation of our economy. And with an educational *élite* whose whole teaching encouraged motives of individualistic advancement, we are trying to create an egalitarian society!

It is not my intention to speak about these internal policies today. I will only say that so far we have retained our balance. But I am optimistic about our future, provided that factors outside our control do not prevent us from continuing with our efforts.

CHANGE AND STABILITY IN SOUTHERN AFRICA

For Tanzania is one small part of Africa, and our future is linked with that of the continent as a whole. Even if we wished, we could not be unaffected by what happens on this land mass. But in fact none of us in Africa has learned to think in exclusively nationalistic terms—we still think of ourselves as Africans. It is, of course, true that there are some conflicts between African states and within African states. Yet these are like the conflicts between the Provinces of Canada—important provided there is no overwhelming external challenge to the principles on which the existence of each state is based. Our part of Africa feels itself to be involved with all other parts. We are learning—indeed I think we have learned—that the people from one free state have no right or duty to intervene in the affairs of another free state. We recognize that each nation has to deal with the conflicting needs of stability and change in its own way. If we think other free peoples are wrong, or if they fail in their endeavours, we still have no choice but to adapt ourselves to deal with the problems that their policies create for us.

But the situation is very different in relation to Southern Africa and to the remaining Portuguese colonies in Africa. In Mozambique, Angola and Portuguese Guinea, the African peoples are being governed by an external power which categorically rejects the principle of self-determination. In Southern Rhodesia the colonial power claims to accept the principle of self-determination, but has utterly failed to assert its authority against a racialist minority which denies this principle. In South Africa the apartheid policy is imposed on the Africans and other non-white peoples, and maintained by the most ruthless suppression. And the United Nations has failed to take any effective steps to dislodge this same tyranny from South-West Africa. In all these cases, outside forces are suppressing Africans, and Africans are being humiliated and persecuted simply for being what they are—black or coloured Africans.

In relation to all these areas of our continent, therefore, Africa as a whole recognizes a challenge from external forces and from a racialism which denies our rights as human beings. We cannot be uninvolved. Just one African state does not have a recent experience of colonialism—and for many years that was independent in name only. We have all suffered from some degree of racial discrimination. If we accept the continuation of such conditions in Southern Africa, we are denying our own moral right to freedom and human equality, and are forced to justify our existence on the grounds of an economic and military strength which we do not, in fact, possess. We cannot adopt this attitude.

But in any case, whatever the emotions may be, the fact is that Tanzania's freedom is itself in jeopardy while colonialism and racialism remain dominant on our borders. As long as we insist on making a reality of our freedom, and pursuing policies which uphold the dignity of African people, our existence is a threat to the colonialist and racialist states of Southern Africa. They would inevitably take steps to reduce the effectiveness of our policies and to control our actions. For just as their policy of racialism makes it daily more difficult for us to build a state on the basis of non-racialism, so they cannot secure their slave systems while the rest of Africa uses its freedom for the benefit of its people. The principles of freedom and equality have no validity unless they are of universal validity; and the principle of racial supremacy is invalid unless it is universally valid. Conflict between these two conceptions of humanity is inevitable. Where they meet, the conflict will become an active one.

Tanzania's concern with the situation in South Africa is thus not something which is extraneous to our other policies. It is a matter affecting our security. It is central to everything we try to do. It is not that we are great altruists who love freedom so much that we will fight for it everywhere and anywhere. We know our limitations. We also know that people can only free themselves—no one else can prevent them from trying to win their freedom, and no one else can do it for them. But in the case of Southern Africa, we and the other free states are all involved. We are all Africans; we all need to work together for the real development of any of us; and a continuing freedom struggle in one part of the continent affects the security of all other parts. This involvement is acutely realized in Tanzania because we are a border state between free Africa and colonial Africa; but the same considerations apply to a greater or lesser extent to all free African states. Very little can be understood about Africa until this is understood.

Let me therefore try to sum up our position on this matter. The common objective of the African people is self-determination for the peoples of Southern Africa and the other Portuguese colonies, and an end to the official propagation and practice of racialism in our continent. That is all. We are not anti-white terrorists wishing to impose a reverse racialism; we wish to uphold human equality and to give human dignity and non-racialism a chance to grow in our lands.

As far as the free states of Africa are concerned, what comes after freedom is an affair of the peoples of those territories. It is not for us to decide what sort of government they will have or what sort of system they will adopt. Tanzania must support the struggle for freedom in these areas regardless of the political philosophy of those who are conducting the struggle. If they are capitalists, we must support them; if they are liberals, we must support them; if they are communists, we must support them; if they are socialists, we must support them. We support them as nationalists. Our own commitment to socialism in Tanzania is irrelevant to the right of the people of Mozambique (and the other areas) to choose their own government and their own political system. The right of a people to freedom from alien domination comes before socialism. The right of a man to stand upright as a human being in his own country comes before questions of the kind of society he will create once he has that right. Freedom is the only thing that matters until it is won. The support which is given to the freedom struggles by Tanzania and by other African states is neither a disguised form of new imperialism nor an evangelical mission for socialism or capitalism. It is a recognition of the oneness of Africa.

BY PEACE OR VIOLENCE?

Yet there remains a big question. Is the freedom struggle to be waged by peaceful methods or by violence? Is Africa to support the freedom movement regardless of the methods used, or could we make our support conditional?

There are some people who appear to believe that there is virtue in violence and that only if a freedom struggle is conducted by war and bloodshed can it lead to real liberation. I am not one of these people; the Government of Tanzania does not accept this doctrine, and nor do any of the other free African governments as far as I am aware. We know that war causes immense sufferings, that it is usually the most innocent who are the chief victims, and that the hatred and fear generated by war are dangerous to the very freedom and non-racialism it is our purpose to support. We have a deep desire for a peaceful transfer of power to the people. We believe that if a door is shut, attempts should be made to open it; if it is ajar, it should be pushed until it is open wide. In neither case should the door be blown up at the expense of those inside.

But if the door to freedom is locked and bolted, and the present guardians of the door have refused to turn the key or pull the bolts, the choice is very straightforward. Either you accept the lack of freedom or you break the door down.

That, unfortunately, is the present position in Southern Africa; and, unless there is some new outside influence which forces a reversal of policy on those now in power, that is the choice now before us.

Portugal has proclaimed that its colonies in Africa are part of the metropolitan country and that self-determination for the peoples of these territories is therefore not a matter for discussion. Political organization is prohibited, all attempts at peaceful protest are suppressed, and change by negotiation is ruled out. In Rhodesia, the people's organizations have been banned and the leaders imprisoned. Even the British Government's absurd suggestion that the white minority should promise to bring discrimination to an end gradually has been answered by a clear statement of determination to maintain perpetual white supremacy. To the South African Government, discrimination on racial grounds is a basic article of faith which admits no argument.

In all these areas the demand for freedom has been rejected in principle. The door to progress is shut, bolted and barred.

In such a situation the only way the people can get freedom is by force. A peaceful end to oppression is impossible. The only choice before the people is organized or unorganized violence. But chaos, not freedom, will result from spontaneous uprisings when the frustrations get too great to be borne, or when some fresh turn of the screw goads the people to madness. Indeed, spontaneous uprisings in a modern and ruthless state are little more than mass suicide; they only achieve the release of death for many, and increased suffering for the others. When every avenue of peaceful change is blocked, then the only way forward to positive change is by channelling and directing the people's fury—that is, by organized violence; by a people's war against their government.

When this happens, Tanzania cannot deny support, for to do so would be to deny the validity of African freedom and African dignity. We are naturally and inevitably allies of the freedom fighters. We may decide, as we have decided, that no Tanzanian will take part in these wars; we may recognize the fact that we cannot arm the freedom fighters. But we cannot call for freedom in Southern

Africa, and at the same time deny all assistance to those who are fighting for it, when we know, as well as they do, that every other means of achieving freedom has been excluded by those now in power.

THE INVOLVEMENT OF THE WEST

But it is not only African states which are inevitably involved in this conflict. All the traditional friends and allies of the powers concerned are also involved. Portugal is a member of NATO. To say the very least—much less than we believe to be the case!—the resulting military support allows Portugal to devote a greater proportion of her men and resources to the occupation of her African colonies than would otherwise be the case. Further, Portugal is a member of EFTA; it derives great benefit from selling to its Western allies goods which originate in the African colonies. Such economic links are another factor in the ability of the poorest state in Europe to spend something like 47 per cent of its budget on 'overseas defence'—which really means on the maintenance of colonialism in Africa.

About South Africa's position, I am sure it is unnecessary for me to say very much. It has great wealth and economic strength derived in part from past foreign investment. Its continuing economic development also owes much to new investment and re-investment by Western firms, and its international trade links with the West are very important to both sides. Indeed, the size of the Western involvement in South Africa's economy can be gauged by the indignation with which African demands for an economic boycott are met.

The illegality of the Southern Rhodesia régin e has led to an economic boycott being imposed on that country. Nonetheless, the refusal of the colonial power either to make the boycott a total and effective one, or to enforce its decisions by direct intervention, has a reason. It reflects a sense of involvement with that administration and the people it represents—in other words, the dominant minority.

But my real point is not the fact of the West's economic involvement with Southern Africa. My concern is with their ideological involvement. I am not accusing the Western powers of conscious racialism, but of a pre-occupation with conflicts which are at present irrelevant to the situation in Africa.

NATO is a Western military alliance against East European communism—perhaps against communism itself—and Portugal is a member of NATO. South Africa claims to be a bastion against communism in Africa. The régime in Rhodesia claims that it is defending its part of Africa against communist-inspired chaos. These states are all anxious that their struggle against the freedom movements should be interpreted in the West as part of a world-wide anti-communist struggle. The real danger which worries me is that the West will accept this interpretation, and that it will, in consequence, betray its own principles by supporting these Southern African régimes.

The principle of self-determination and of national freedom is part of the democratic ideal; it is enshrined in all the greatest philosophies and documents of the Western world. But will the West recognize that this is the question at issue in Southern Africa, or will it be confused by this talk of 'Western civilization' fighting 'Eastern communism'?

If the struggle in Southern Africa is seen as the freedom struggle which it in fact is, the policies of Western states—both governments and peoples—will be determined only by the degree of their willingness to sacrifice immediate economic interests to political principles. But if the West accepts the South African and Portuguese argument that they are fighting on behalf of the 'free world' against communism, then I believe that in time this interpretation will become defensible—at least as regards their enemies. For if the West supports these racialist and fascist states, the freedom struggle will in reality become a part of the world ideological conflict—as it is now wrongly alleged to be. Further, I believe that if this is allowed to happen, we are liable to finish up with an even more disastrous conflict—a conflict of the races. For Africa and the West will be on opposite sides of the barricades; and Africa will have the support of Asia and large parts of Latin America.

Let me explain my fears and what I believe can be done by countries of the Western bloc to avoid such catastrophes.

PRESSURE FOR PEACEFUL CHANGE

Africa is anxious for peace in Southern Africa. But the possibility of this depends upon the possibility of ending the present injustice without war. Neither free Africa nor the Western world has the right to ask the peoples of Souhern Africa to accept indefinitely the present humiliation, oppression and foreign domination; and in any case they would not pay heed to any such demands. The only chance for peace in Southern Africa is if change can be secured without violence. If this is possible, no one will be happier than the people of Africa. But we have tried peaceful methods and we have failed. The people of Southern Africa are therefore resorting to war, and the free African states are supporting them. The only chance for peace now is if the allies of the Southern African states are willing and able to exert the kind of pressure which brings change with the minimum of violence.

Do the Western powers have the ability to exert such pressure? I believe that they have a great deal of power if they are willing to use it for this purpose. Both South Africa and Portugal gain great benefit from their association with the Western nations; they will not wish to lose that benefit.

It is possible that South Africa would refuse to make any concessions to the democratic sensibilities of its allies, even at the cost of complete international isolation. I say this is possible because many people in South Africa believe in apartheid as a religion and will defend their faith until death. But there are other South Africans who rejoice in, and who support, the segregationist policies of that Government because of the material benefit and the position of privilege it gives them. I believe this is the majority. Such people give a support which is conditional to the extent that it is not based on fear; there is a limit to the degree of international isolation they would be willing to accept rather than accept an organized move towards individual human equality. At the very least, therefore, strong Western pressure on South Africa could introduce a new uncertainty and new insecurity among the dominant group. The police state machine would thus lose the virtually total white support which it at present enjoys. In that case, the violence may not be of such long duration or of such bitterness.

But whatever the situation in South Africa, it is quite certain that Portugal could not withstand real pressures for change exerted by its NATO allies. A nation can withstand pressures from outside when it is united in hostility to that pressure. But a poor nation cannot maintain its domination over territories twenty times its own size, and over populations 50 per cent greater than its own, unless it has the support of more powerful countries. In relation to the Portuguese colonies at least, members of the Western alliance do have the power to secure peace in Africa. They have the power to make a continuation of their support conditional upon Portugal's accepting the principle of self-determination.

Thus, in one case certainly, and in the other case possibly, it is the West which makes the choice between peace and war in Southern Africa. The question is not whether the Western powers are able to exert pressure on Portugal and on South Africa, but whether they are willing to do so. It is the implications of that question which I hope the people of this and other countries will carefully consider.

For I must stress that the choice before the free states of the world—which includes both Canada and Tanzania—is not between peaceful change and no change. The choice is between peaceful change and conflict. In the absence of peaceful change and real prospects of it continuing, the African people will fight for their rights. They will destroy stability rather than suffer under the stability of oppression. They have already begun to do so. We are not at the eleventh hour; we are past the twelfth. Already peace has to be re-established and confidence regained—both of which are harder things to do than to prevent war or to retain trust. So what is the alternative to a change in Southern Africa which is combined with stability?

THE IMPLICATIONS OF WAR

Portugal, South Africa and the régime in Southern Rhodesia are all heavily armed with modern weapons and they have access to more weapons. They even manufacture some. If the freedom fighters are to succeed in war, they too must have arms. Not even the most skilled guerilla movement can fight machine guns with bows and arrows, or dig elephant traps across surfaced roads. Africa cannot supply these arms; we do not make them, and we have no money to buy them.

But if the Western powers will not put pressure on their friends to secure peaceful change, is it likely that they will supply arms to those who in desperation have decided to get change by force? We all know the answer. The freedom movements will therefore get their arms from the communist powers. And these communist powers will be their exclusive suppliers.

In these circumstances it is no use anyone telling the freedom fighters—or telling the free states of Africa—about the evils of communism, or about the possibility that the supplying states may present a bill for their support. We all know of that possibility; we do not imagine that communism makes great powers less subject to the temptations of greatness. But we are much less concerned about possible future dangers—which may never develop—than we are with present facts. And those facts are that Africa is occupied by an alien power now; its people are suffering under minority domination now. We have to fight these things. So, we accept arms from communist states, and say 'thank you' for them.

On the same basis, the nationalists of Southern Africa get their training where they can and from whom they can. Sometimes free African states can help in this; sometimes they cannot. And when they cannot, it is again communist countries which offer to help. and again we accept with gratitude.

We know our own motives in these actions. We are not communists; we are nationalists desiring freedom. We recognize the possibility that those who are helping us may have different motives. That is what we are told and we have no proof that it is not so. But we do have proof of our existing need and of practical offers to help.

So the freedom fighters use communist arms and are trained in communist countries because they have no choice. This is happening now and it will continue. And then South Africa and Portugal will proclaim to their allies this 'proof' that they are fighting communism. They will show captured communist weapons and display some hapless prisoner-of-war (whom they will call a criminal) in order to persuade those opposed to communism to support their war against the freedom fighters. They will also show evidence of cruelties, and tell tales of fear and suffering experienced by noncombatants on their side. And they will argue that this is the kind of people their opponents are—communists and racialists. Some of this evidence will be forged, but some will be true. Wars are always ugly and brutal, and guerilla warfare is no exception.

In the face of this kind of psychological pressure, I am afraid that Western states would strengthen their support for the Southern African régimes. They would argue that for their own protection it was necessary to prevent Africa from falling into the hands of communists. They will therefore strengthen their economic support, and then agree to sell arms—or to give them—to the regimes of Southern Africa. Even the democratic and liberal people of the Western states will lose sympathy for the freedom movements, because they will come to believe that these have been captured by the communists. And gradually this conflict will become the ideological conflict which at present it is not.

At that point, because Africa does not look at things through cold war spectacles, the nature of the conflict may change again; it may become a confrontation between the poor, coloured world and the rich, white world. Only support for the freedom fighters from the Russian and East European communists would be breaking the colour pattern, and perhaps saving the world from this disaster. Indeed, it may be that the liberal humanitarians of Western Europe and North America may find themselves grateful to the white communists!

I am talking of what seems to me to be a terrifying series of events unless some effort is made to break the chain of logic in African and Western bloc relations. Of course, I have grossly simplified what would really happen; but we in Africa are not very sophisticated people, and indeed I do not believe the masses in any country are politically sophisticated. Therefore, I think that the pattern I have outlined is the way things might well look to us from our different sides. The people in the West would be seeing us as communists who wish them ill; we would be seeing them as supporters of racialism and of tyranny.

THE INEVITABLE CAN BE AVOIDED

These possibilities are real. If they develop, the effect on Africa could be terrible, and Africa's freedom struggle will bring great trouble to the world instead of releasing new energies for human growth—which is what we would like to think will happen. Yet knowing all that, we cannot draw back. For these are dangers and, however inevitable they may appear in logic, they are possibilities only. Our oppression is real and present.

Yet I believe that the dangers I have outlined can still be avoided, or at least very greatly reduced, if the Western powers look at the Southern African question in its proper framework, and if they now take the necessary action to de-fuse the situation. I know that it is not easy for the Western states to put pressure on their allies; all developed states are reluctant to interfere in what they regard as the internal affairs of another developed state. I know too that international trade is of mutual benefit, and that—as far as the Western states are concerned—their partners' gain from this trade is incidental to their own. I know that the West has heavy investments in Southern Africa which they wish to protect. But I do not believe that these facts necessarily determine the issue, for I do not believe that the only thing which the West cares about is economics. I am neither a Marxist nor a capitalist. I do not believe that every human value is, or need always be, sacrificed to economic interests. I believe that the basic philosophy of Western democracy has its own life and its own power, and that the people's concept of freedom can triumph over their materialism.

However, even if I did believe that economics was the only thing which mattered to the West, I would still ask myself whether short-term or long-term factors will determine the West's policies. For although South Africa may now be a bigger trading partner than all the rest of Africa put together—I do not know whether this is true for Canada—this will not always be the case. The population of South Africa is about 18 million; that of the rest of Africa is in the region of 250 million. However great the difference in wealth, these stark figures have their own logic—especially as the rest of us develop and become better markets because we are richer.

Further, the value of investments depends on their productivity. They are no use if the cost of protecting them is more than the return they give. And investments in areas of inevitable and fore-seeable instability are surely of less value than investments where instability is a present but passing danger. For Southern Africa is still fighting for the right to begin change. Except to the extent that the kind of change develops out of the nature of the struggle, the real problems of African development in these areas will remain to be settled when freedom is won.

CONCLUSION

Mr. President, when you asked me to speak at this university, it may be that you were expecting me to speak about the internal affairs of Tanzania or about the relevance of our experiment in socialism for other countries—though you were too kind to express your wishes. But I have chosen to talk of change as an essential element in the stability which we need, and to emphasize this in relation to Southern Africa. I have done this for a very particular reason.

This is a Canadian university, and we in Tanzania have very great respect and admiration for the people of Canada. We believe that this country has both the opportunity and the willingness to try to build bridges in the world, and in particular to build a bridge across the chasm of colour. I therefore chose to discuss this question with you because I believe you will understand what I am trying to say, and will care about these matters.

I know, of course, that Canada has its own problems of cultural conflict, of peoples with different languages and different backgrounds living together. I know that within your own society you are now trying to work out new modes of co-operation, which allow a full expression of democracy without jeopardizing the special cultural interests of any minority. These are real problems for you; indeed your efforts in this matter are of world-wide interest. It would therefore not be surprising if such questions pre-occupied the attention of the Canadian people. But the world is very small now. Canada's actions—or lack of them—in relation to Africa are also important to your future, as well as to ours. For the questions are there; and the threat to peace is there. They will not go away because this large, wealthy and peace-loving state wishes to concentrate on its internal problems. You cannot escape giving an answer to the challenge of the freedom movements in Africa— even if it is only an answer by default.

Let me make it quite clear that I am not promising peace, stability, democracy, humanity or an absence of oppression in Africa, provided Canada (either alone or with its allies) recognizes the freedom struggle in Southern Africa for what it is, and adopts attitudes in conformity with its own principles. Africa has too many problems for that kind of optimism. When national freedom exists all over Africa, and when racial minorities cease to dominate any part of our continent, we will still have daunting difficulties to face and few resources with which to tackle them. We may still fail to make good use of our opportunities; we may be as slow to develop real individual freedom from both economic and political oppression as the worst states in the world. But we are determined to gain the chance to try to deal with these problems. And we can only give top priority to these questions of developing individual freedom and individual dignity when the whole of Africa is free.

The questions remain. Will Canada at least understand that freedom means as much to us in Africa as it does to any other people? And, if Canada cannot support our struggle, will it at least be able to refrain from giving comfort and help to those who would deny freedom and dignity to us? For the sake of Tanzania and Africa most of all, but also for the sake of future relations between men of different colours and different creeds, I hope that Canadians will be able to give attention to these problems. I hope that universities like this one will help the people of this country to consider all the implications of their choice.

Mr. President, ladies and gentlemen: thank you.

17

Socialism and Rich Societies

In his capacity as President of TANU, President Nyerere addressed the Swedish Social Democratic Party Conference in Stockholm on 3 October 1969. He criticized Tanzania's reputation as a 'socialist country', and discussed the meaning of socialism and its challenge for the Swedish Party.

... It is not surprising that my Party should be anxious for me to represent them at your Conference while I am in this country. Relations between TANU and the Social Democratic Party have always been those of good friends, and TANU greatly values this link of sympathy with an older, but still committed, socialist movement. Between our two youth movements there has also been close co-operation, and in fact the TANU Youth League has received great assistance from the youth wing of your Party. Not only did young people of this movement contribute substantially to the cost of building TANU Youth League Headquarters in Dar es Salaam. More important, they have also sent out members to work with our youth movement and to participate in training and educational activities. Let me add that never once has any of this assistance, or any aspect of our friendship, been used as an excuse to interfere with our policies or our actions. You have given as one socialist gives to another—with trust and understanding. This is sufficiently rare, Mr. Chairman, to warrant comment from the recipient!

It is therefore with very great pleasure, Mr. Chairman, that I bring warm greetings to the socialist movement of Sweden from my Party and my country. This is a greeting from a country which is beginning to try to build socialism, to a country where many of the basic attitudes of socialism are fully accepted throughout the nation. It will therefore be clear to everyone that I do not come here to teach you socialism: I come to express comradeship.

For the truth is that I am a little embarrassed by the reputation of Tanzania as a socialist state. I am afraid that we receive more praise than the facts warrant—and that we might therefore at a later date receive a great deal of unwarranted blame for not being what people thought we were! People might even get disillusioned with the idea of socialism if they believe it exists in Tanzania now. For— look at the situation! In Tanzania poverty is endemic. . . .

To many of our people hunger is still something to be dreaded, not something which is inconceivable. The diseases resulting from malnutrition are widespread. Many of our people are inadequately clothed—even for our climate. Our public services are still few in number. And in large areas of the country life continues in very much the same poverty as it did a hundred years ago, the only difference being that people are now aware of it.

Mr. Chairman, there is nothing socialist about that. Socialism is not poverty. A country cannot claim to be socialist while its citizens live under the conditions which many of our people suffer.

Or again; our people are ignorant. The majority of the adults cannot even read and write in their own language; they know nothing of modern techniques of production and are thus unable to take the simple steps which could remedy their own most desperate poverty. Not even with our children have we overcome this problem. . . .

Mr. Chairman, this ignorance is not socialist. A socialist country is not one where most of the children do not go to school, and where people do not even know how to make their sweat serve their own best interests.

Even worse, Tanzania is still a country in which there are gross inequalities of income between different people. . . .

Mr. Chairman, this kind of inequality is not socialist. A socialist country does not allow such differentials between its citizens.

These are serious criticisms of my country, and I can assure you that I am saying nothing here that I do not say within Tanzania. For by recognizing the facts, we have acknowledged how far we have to go. And the one thing we can with justice claim is that we have decided on our goal and our direction. We have decided to attack the poverty which now oppresses us, and we have decided that we will build a socialist society. Thus there are certain things we know.

We know that the basic philosophy of socialism is human equality and human dignity, and that the achievement of this basic and equal human respect for all people is what socialism is about. . . . -

The political and economic organization of the society must be such that the people themselves can control their government, their administration, and the way they earn their living. Production must be organized to meet the needs of men. Its motive must be those needs, and it must be the needs of all—not the profit of a few. And these things mean that men must control the tools they use; their livelihood must not be at the mercy of another man's decisions. A peasant should own his own hoe, his own *panga*, and his own ox; when two men are needed to use a particular tool, they should own it jointly. When mass production techniques result in the development of huge factories, then all those involved—which means the whole community—must own the machines. But in that case care must be taken to ensure that this community ownership does not degenerate into a faceless tyranny; somehow the decisions about it must be under democratic control—that is, control by the people in whose service it is supposed to be operating.

These things we know. We know that the basis of socialism is human equality and that all the institutions of a socialist state should be directed at making a reality of that equality in social, political, and economic terms. We also know that these things are not easy to achieve. . . .

Sweden's success in building socialism is therefore important to Tanzania. This is not because you can build socialism for us. You cannot. We have to do this for ourselves. But the principles of equality and of social responsibility, which are the essence of socialism, cannot survive if they try to stop short at a national boundary. Socialism involves an affirmative reply to the question: 'Am I my brother's keeper?' It requires the answer: 'Yes, I am my brother's keeper and every human being is my brother.'

Yet, Mr. Chairman, it is comparatively easy for Tanzania to appear to be true to the socialist philosophy and to urge human equality and an end of exploitation internationally as well as nationally. We are among the poor and exploited. I venture to imagine that the position is not so easy for Sweden; you cannot say these things and believe that their fulfilment would directly benefit the Swedish people.

There used to be a slogan in socialist movements of Europe: 'Workers of the world unite; you have nothing to lose but your chains.' But that is not true in Sweden any more. The workers of this country have a great deal to lose. You may have some poverty in this country, but it is comparative poverty—comparative to a high standard of living which is enjoyed by the majority of your workers. So, can the socialists of Sweden still accept the doctrines of socialism in their hearts and in their actions? Can the policies of this Party—which are controlled by its members—show to the world that socialism is not just a question of envy by the have-nots? Can this socialist party go on from establishing socialist equality within Sweden to supporting the struggle for socialist equality in the world, and even across the colour line? Let me make it quite clear, Mr. Chairman, that these are difficult questions, and I do not believe that a clear answer can be obtained easily and unanimously. But that is what socialism must mean ultimately. It is indeed because the Swedish socialist movement has shown signs of giving the right answer that this country is held in such high regard in countries like mine.

But it is not only in economic terms that Swedish socialism has to answer a world challenge. Involved in socialism is human freedom, political as well as economic. We in Africa are still fighting for that freedom. We are fighting for an end to colonialism in the Portuguese-controlled territories. Will the Swedish socialist movement support the right of the African people to determine their own futures and to build their own socialism? Wars are now going on in Southern Africa—wars between guerillas and great powers. Will the workers of Sweden allow arms to be sold to these powers? Will Sweden trade with the oppressors of Africa and strengthen them while we fight them? . . . .

What has the socialist movement of Sweden got to say on these questions? . . . .

18

The Co-operative Movement

On 4 October 1969, the President addressed a large gathering of Swedish co-operators in Stockholm. He congratulated them on the important role played by the co-operative movement in Sweden. He then spoke of the function of co-operative societies and the history of co-operation in Tanzania, before paying tribute to the assistance which has been given to the Tanzania co-operative movement by Swedish co-operators.

. . . As I understand it, there are basically two economic benefits to be obtained from co-operation. Firstly, the community is able to benefit from the advantages of large-scale production and marketing. Secondly, it does this in a manner which precludes exploitation of the workers or farmers by any individual or group of individuals, and at the same time allows consumers to gain direct service at the lowest cost. In other words, both the increased production which is possible from joint effort, and the prevention of exploitation, are central to co-operative enterprise: from this it follows that the more widely co-operation is spread, and the more aspects of the economy which it covers, the more benefit the members of any particular co-operative will receive from their efforts.

Of course, effective co-operative activity requires both democracy and efficiency in operation. In each sector the requisite machinery has to be created which will achieve these two ends. The members must exercise effective control over policy and be able to supervise the management, but the individuals given the responsibility of running the enterprise must be able to use their initiative, and their special training, to best effect. This is a difficult combination to achieve—as we in Tanzania well know. It appears from the results that the Swedish co-operative movement has gone a long way towards achieving the necessary mixture.

But there is another important aspect of co-operation. It is based on the principle of human equality and human brotherhood. Every member of a co-operative is equal to every other member. He has accepted that, in order not to be exploited, he has to surrender his 'right' and power to exploit others. And he has accepted that his own advantage lies in co-operating with his fellows, not in trying to fight them or, if you prefer it, compete with them. Indeed, this is why I said earlier that the wider ranging and the larger is the co-operative sector, the better it is for every individual member. For theoretically it would be possible for a co-operative of producers to exploit the consumers: this danger is eliminated when both producers and consumers are in the co-operative movement. Further, in their dual capacity as co-operative makers and co-operative users, men can work towards that balance of life in which economic factors take their appropriate place, and do not dominate all other aspects of living as a full person. And when co-operation is the dominant mode in the economy, every co-operative society is able to carry out all its activities in accordance with its true nature—that is, in a spirit of brotherhood and common endeavour. . . .

Although the Government of Tanzania takes a very active part in encouraging and supervising the co-operative movement, this does not mean that our co-operatives are in some way creatures of a bureaucracy. Government is active for two reasons. Firstly, because we believe that only through co-operatives can the people defend themselves against exploitation at the same time as achieving modernization. And secondly because, in our circumstances, Government assistance is essential to the expansion of the movement and to ensure that the co-operative societies really do serve their members.

For co-operatives in Tanzania have many problems which do not face those in a developed nation like Sweden. One example of this is the illiteracy of the mass of people, their complete ignorance of commercial organization, and the absence of any capital resources among the people except for their own unskilled labour. Indeed it is true to say that many of the people in our rural areas are only now being introduced into the money economy at all: the ease with which they can be exploited, and the difficulty they experience in managing their own economic affairs in the larger society can therefore be easily imagined. Government activity in support of the co-operative movement is absolutely essential if progress is not to be delayed for generations, with widespread exploitation being suffered in the meantime.

Of course we realize the dangers of Government intervention— indeed some of them we now know through bitter experience! Thus, in the first flush of post-independence enthusiasm for the co-operative movement, we supported anything calling itself a co-operative, and there were some cases in which we gave a crop marketing monopoly to a few people—who then proceeded with great success to exploit their neighbours. We also made the mistake of trying to establish a consumers' movement working from the top downwards! I need not tell this meeting that these attempts failed or that we damaged the cause of co-operation by our over-enthusiasm! But we learned from these mistakes, and took corrective action. Each society was scrutinized as regards its membership and its system of control; some were de-registered. Others which were too small ever to be viable were encouraged to unite; one of the larger co-operatives was reorganized to increase effective membership control; and so on. This kind of work is continuing. . . .

19

Visit to the USSR

From Sweden, President Nyerere flew directly to Moscow, as the first stop on his state visit to the USSR. There were long private discussions, but only one public speech. This was delivered on 8 October 1969, in the Kremlin, at a large banquet given by President Podgorny in honour of his guest.

... I am extremely happy to be with you here today, fulfilling a long-standing ambition to visit the Union of Soviet Socialist Republics. It is my fervent hope that my visit will increase mutual understanding between our two countries.

Tanzania is a small country—only one-third the size of Kazakhstan, one of the constituent Republics of this Union, and with a population about the same size as that Republic. Tanganyika won her independence only in 1961 and Zanzibar three years later. Our Union came into existence only in 1964. This means that, at birth, we found the world divided in many ways. In particular, we immediately became aware of the division of nations into great power blocs, and the division of peoples between the competing ideologies of communism and capitalism.

These divisions have presented many problems to our young nation, and we have had to consider our own position in this divided world. Yet in fact our own circumstances made our choice almost inevitable. We had just achieved victory over colonialism in Tanzania; and we had had a purpose in our fight for freedom. We desired to use that freedom for our own progress. It is obvious, however, that having won freedom we have to maintain it. Our first priority has to be that of guarding the independence of our young nation against external aggression, against neo-colonialism, and against externally-promoted internal subversion. This will always be our paramount concern, for to us national independence is the foundation upon which everything else must be built. We are African nationalists first; all other aspects of our policy come after that.

But we have fully recognized that, if national independence is to be meaningful to our people, it must lead them to new freedoms in their daily lives. It must enable them to lift themselves out of poverty, and to free themselves from the pain of watching their children die through malnutrition. Our political freedom must give every one of our citizens an opportunity to increase his or her well-being as a dignified human being in the twentieth-century world. This means that political independence and democracy must be combined with economic independence, and economic development, of such a kind that it will increase the well-being of every citizen in our United Republic.

Our main pre-occupations are thus domestic ones. Every other aspect of world affairs has to be considered by us in relation to its impact upon our goals of political, economic, and social freedom. But we are not hostile to the world. On the contrary, we desire to be friends with all peoples and all nations which are willing to respect our independence and our human equality and dignity. Our policy is therefore one of friendship to all, but non-alignment in the great power conflicts, and non-involvement in world ideological conflicts which are irrelevant to Africa.

In standing outside these great conflicts, we are not trying to pretend that we have no interest in them. On the contrary, we wish to join with other peoples in the work of overcoming human injustice and human suffering. Our first international interest is therefore in the promotion of peace and justice. We desire to contribute to that world peace on which depends the future of every human being. But in order to do this effectively, we know that we must recognize both the limitations and the responsibilities of our size and youth. Therefore, we assert and maintain our independence and our right to be friends with all nations, allowing no one to choose our enemies for us. And we endeavour to decide each issue of world affairs on its own merits, in accordance with the principles of human equality and national sovereignty.

In other words, Tanzania is not linked militarily or politically with any other nation or group of nations. But we are working to promote that unity of Africa which could bring greater strength and greater well-being to all the people of our continent. Indeed in furtherance of African unity, we shall be willing to merge our sovereignty with that of other African countries to create a greater sovereign nation. For just as Tanzania is greater than the sum of Tanganyika and Zanzibar which are its constituent parts, so we believe that new voluntary associations of African states will strengthen all its parts—and make a new contribution to world peace and justice. In this ambition for African unity, I may add that we are inspired by the experience of countries like the USSR, whose power and strength is in no small measure due to the union of many different peoples, all working for the common purpose of their own well-being.

Yet while we pursue these foreign policy objectives of African unity and of non-alignment in world struggles, we have to develop our own country. For this purpose we have decided to build a socialist Tanzania, recognizing that only by this means can all the people of our country benefit from the freedom they fought for in equal measure. There are many people in the world who believe that Africa is not ready for socialism. But there are others in Africa who believe that Africa has no choice.

And in fact this choice of socialism out of the theoretical alternatives before us stems in large part from the communal traditions of Africa. It is on those traditions that we are building. We are trying to maintain the traditional equality of our people and to work out new forms of political and economic association which will enable us to increase our real wealth while completely eliminating both economic and social exploitation. In other words, we are trying to build socialism in a manner which is appropriate to our past, our circumstances, and our ambitions for human equality and human dignity in all spheres of life.

But although it is necessary and correct for us to work out our own path to socialism, we are of course very interested in the experience of other socialist countries. We recognize that we have a great deal to learn from the experience of other peoples who have made some progress along this path. There are therefore two reasons for my happiness in visiting the Union of Soviet Socialist Republics at this time. The first is that I am able to bring greetings to the Government and people of this great country from all the people of the United Republic of Tanzania. And the second is to learn more of your socialist experience so that we may see what of it is relevant to our circumstances and our needs.

20

Adult Education Year

In his New Year's Eve Broadcast, 31 December 1969, President Nyerere emphasized the importance of adult education, and announced that 1970 would be Adult Education Year for the whole country.

. . . One of the promises of a TANU member says: 'I shall educate myself to the best of my ability and use my education for the benefit of all.' For a long time we have been saying that 'we must educate the adults of Tanzania'. I myself have pointed out that we cannot wait until our educated children are grown up before we get economic and social development; it is the task of those who are already full-grown citizens of our country to begin this work. Yet although there has been a lot of talk about education for adults, and quite a lot of people have been working in this field, we have never yet really organized ourselves for a major attack on our ignorance. The Central Committee of TANU has decided that we must do this in 1970. The coming twelve months must be 'Adult Education Year', and we must give this work very high priority.

The importance of adult education, both for our country and for every individual, cannot be over-emphasized. We are poor, and backward; and too many of us just accept our present conditions as 'the will of God', and imagine that we can do nothing about them. . . .

The first job of adult education will therefore be to make us reject bad houses, bad *jembe*, and preventable diseases; it will make us recognize that we ourselves have the ability to obtain better houses, better tools, and better health.

Of course, many people already know this. What they need to learn is how they can effect improvements in their lives. They need to know such things as the fact that dirty water makes their children ill, and that they themselves can avoid those sicknesses by working together to bring clean water before drinking it. In other words, the second objective of adult education is learning *how* to improve our lives. We thus have to learn how to produce more on our farms or in our factories and offices. We have to learn about better food, what a balanced diet is and how it can be obtained by our own efforts. . . .

We need to learn about modern methods of hygiene, about making furniture for ourselves out of local materials, about how to work together to improve the conditions in our villages and streets, and so on.

But this is not enough. For we can only do these things if all members of the nation work together for our common good. The third objective of adult education must therefore be for everyone to understand our national policies of socialism and self-reliance. And we must learn about the plans for national economic advance, so that we can ensure that we all play our part in making them a success, and that we all benefit from them.

But what is adult education? Quite simply, it is learning—about anything at all which can help us to understand the environment we live in, and the manner in which we can change and use this environment in order to improve ourselves. Education is not just something which happens in classrooms. It is learning from others, and from our own experience of past successes or failures.

Education is learning from books, from the radio, from films, from discussions about matters which affect our lives, and especially from doing things. This question of learning by doing is very important. The best way to learn to sew is to sew; the best way to learn to farm is to cultivate; the best way to learn cooking is to cook; the best way to learn how to teach is to teach; and so on. . . .

The first education anyone ever gets is from his parents and his brothers and sisters as he grows out of babyhood into childhood. When our children go to school at the age of seven, they have already learned many things—starting from learning to walk, and including good manners, useful jobs around the house or farm, as well as many other things. This can be called 'basic education'. It is something everyone receives, without being conscious of it. Secondly there is formal education at school. . . .

Adult education is the third stage—and it can cover many of the subjects learned at school for those who never had such opportunity. It applies to every one of us, without exception. We can all learn more. Those who have never been to school, those who have just attended primary school, and those who have attended secondary school or university—all have many more things which they can learn about our work, and about areas of knowledge which they were not taught when they were at school.

I know that there are some of my literate fellow citizens who never read at all. Their purpose in going to school was to get a certificate which they could use to get work. After getting the certificate and using it to obtain employment, they just put the certificate on the wall so that everyone can see it. But they never use the knowledge of reading and writing; they never read at all. This is a big mistake which arises out of colonial attitudes of mind.

A very pleasant thing about adult education is that we can learn what we want to learn—what we feel would be useful to us in our lives. At school, children are taught the things which we adults decide they should be taught. But adults are not like children who sit in classrooms and are then taught history, or grammar, or a foreign language. As adults, we can try to learn these things if we wish; we do not have to do so. Instead, we can learn more about growing a particular crop, about the government, about house-building—about whatever interests us. We can build on the education we already have—using the tools of literacy or a foreign language, or an understanding of scientific principles. Or, if we never went to school, we can start by learning about the things of most immediate importance to us—better farming methods, better child care, better feeding. We do not even have to start by learning to read and write!

For literacy is just a tool; it is a means by which we can learn more, more easily. That is its importance. . . .

Education is very important to a country like Tanzania. We want to improve our lives, and to maintain our freedom; we shall only be able to do it if we apply ourselves to learning as much as possible and as quickly as possible. This is easily understandable. Thus, many of our farmers realize that a neighbour who does not keep his shamba clean is both a disgrace and a danger to the whole village. He and his children live in poverty and sickness, and sooner or later the other villagers get angry with him because the weeds and insects from his plot spread disease to their shambas. Let our country not be like that bad farmer who, by his laziness, antagonizes neighbours who are bigger and stronger than he is. For the rest of the world is advancing all the time. Other countries are using new methods of production, and are organizing themselves for their own benefit. They will not wait for us! Unless we determine to educate ourselves we shall get left behind again; we shall be at the mercy of other nations and peoples. Independence which is subject to the decisions of other peoples is not independence; it is an illusion.

We must ourselves change our conditions of life; and we can learn how to do this by educating ourselves. We must recognize that our poverty is not inevitable; and we must recognize that it is no use demanding that someone else should do something about it. Nor is it any use citizens simply sitting back and waiting for 'the Government', or 'the Party', to come and change their lives. The Government and the Party are simply organizations of citizens—a coming together of people for certain purposes. Neither the Government, nor TANU, can do anything apart from the citizens; nor could these organizations do everything which has to be done in our country. Every one of us, through improving his own education, can begin to make improvements in his own life—and therefore in the lives of us all. Through educating ourselves more, each one of us can help to make our country stronger, and our children's lives better.

This is the task to which we must give more emphasis in the coming year. Of course, quite a lot of adult education has been done here and there in the past. . . .

TANU and the Government are now preparing plans to give increased emphasis to adult education, and to make our efforts in this matter more effective. You will be hearing about these plans in the coming months.

But plans by Government and by TANU are not enough by themselves. If 1970 is really to be 'Adult Education Year', then all of us have to work together. We all have to be students; that is, we all have to be willing to learn, and anxious to use every method of learning that is available to us. We have to listen to the radio, learn from Government workers, from people who themselves have had an opportunity to learn more, and of course from books and magazines and newspapers. And, as I said at the beginning, we have to learn from doing.

But as well as all being students, we all have to be willing to be teachers. We have to be willing to teach whatever skills we have by whatever method we can—by demonstration and example, by discussion, by answering questions, or by formal classroom work. If we all play our part, both as students and teachers, we shall really make some progress.

That, then, is the message for 1970. To live is to learn; and to learn is to try to live better. Therefore, in the new year let us learn more things and better things so that we can live better and in harmony with one another. And let us ask God to help us to live so that we can learn more about his wonders in the world we live in, and really obtain its benefits for ourselves, our children, and our country.

21

Kibaha Nordic Centre

On 10 January 1970, in the presence of King Frederick IX and Queen Ingrid of Denmark, as well as official representatives of Sweden, Norway, and Finland, and other diplomats, President Nyerere formally received the Kibaha Centre on behalf of the Tanzania Government. The project, which had been built up over many years, was being officially handed over by the Nordic countries as an integrated unit.

After welcoming the King and Queen to Tanzania, the President explained the reasons for his long standing interest in the Kibaha project.

. . . This project is a combined operation of Tanzania and four other countries working together. Sweden, Denmark, Norway and Finland have been working as a unit in partnership with Tanzania. And this partnership has not quite been on terms of equality, for Tanzania—one country—has been accepted as one partner, and the four Nordic countries together have been accepted as the other partner.

It is true that these four countries have financed Kibaha. In addition to the capital expenditure, something like Shs. 40 million covering the recurrent expenditure until now, has been paid entirely by the Nordic countries. It has been a grant to us. We do not even have to consider its repayment at some time in the future. This we very much appreciate.

But despite this financial fact, the whole project has been regarded as a Tanzanian one. All the time the endeavour has been to meet our needs and our objectives. . . .

There is another factor which pleases me very much about this project. The four Nordic countries worked together as a co-ordinated group. We in Tanzania had no need to negotiate which people from which countries should do which job; we had no need to negotiate on matters of costing or purchasing. All these things were done by Sweden, Denmark, Norway and Finland, acting as one. This example of united action gives us great pleasure, for we like unity in the world—even when it is not our unity!

Is the Kibaha project then the result of pure altruism by the Nordic peoples? I do not know how one answers that question. It is, of course, true that many people from these countries have had an opportunity to do a job which was visibly worthwhile. This is pleasurable and rewarding to good men and women. Many people from those countries also had an opportunity to spend some time in Tanzania—and we at least think that our sun must be more enjoyable than the cold and dark of Nordic winters! It is also true that the Nordic people who have worked here have been able to contribute to a greater understanding in Tanzania of conditions and attitudes which exist in their homeland—they have been able in a sense to act as ambassadors for their countries. But these are side effects of the project. The real benefit has been Tanzania's. My own feeling, therefore, is that this Kibaha project marks a recognition by the Nordic peoples of the unity of man. It shows a practical recognition that the wealthier nations of the world have a responsibility to contribute to the development of the poorer nations, on terms which recognize human equality and human dignity. Certainly this is what has been done, and we appreciate this gesture of human brotherhood, both for its content and for the spirit in which it has been implemented.

The second reason for my great interest in this project is that it is a project of rural development. Certainly Kibaha is only 23 miles from Dar es Salaam and, looking at these buildings now, it is difficult for newcomers to realize just how rural this area is. Yet that is merely to say that a new Centre has opened up an area of bush land, where the inhabitants previously lived self-contained lives far too divorced from the development of the nation as a whole. Kibaha is a rural project, both in location and in impact. . . .

Finally, my interest in Kibaha arises from the fact that it is an integrated development which encourages balanced growth in many different fields, so that each aspect of change reinforces and encourages the others.

Thus, we have here a secondary school and two primary schools—

one of which is temporarily being used as a Nordic school so as not to interrupt the education of children from the four partner countries. The former, of course, does not just serve people from this locality; it is part of our national education system, and reflects the emphasis which was given to the expansion of secondary schools under the First Five-Year Plan. There are something like 590 pupils being educated in this school now—that is, in a school which did not exist in 1964. It is also worth mentioning that in the Fifth and Sixth Forms, there are two Science streams and one stream for Arts, thus reflecting the educational emphasis which is necessary for the rapid development of our nation. The magnificent facilities here have, of course, made this emphasis possible.

Secondly, we have the Health Centre—which is not just concerned with curing sick people, but is also a base for preventive medicine. It uses the people's desire for curative medicine as a means to interest them in the much more important preventive work. I say more important quite deliberately, for the health problems of this country will never be solved unless people learn how to protect themselves from diseases like bilharzia, malaria, worms, tuberculosis, diseases caused by malnutrition, and so on. This means, of course, that the work of the Health Centre is not, and cannot be, confined to the Kibaha site. At present, trainee doctors, nurses and health visitors, all come here for part of their training; and the organization is such that they spread the benefits of their knowledge, and themselves gain knowledge, by working in the villages within a ten-mile radius of this place. . . .

Part of preventive medicine is, of course, good feeding, and the Farmers' Institute at this Centre plays an important part in helping farmers and their wives to learn about methods of agricultural production. Many different courses are run at this Farmers' Institute, and it deals with practical problems as they are experienced by farmers in this Region. I understand, also, that Kibaha has already become the place where modern poultry-keepers get their young chicks, and that the tree nursery is becoming increasingly important to the Regional plans for an expansion of fruit growing and urban beautification.

These three basic services have been formed into a single co-operative unit by the existence of common services. Thus, we have what is, in effect, a community centre serving all the people in all the different institutes. We have good housing, co-operative shops, a bank, a post office and, I am pleased to say, a public library. This latter can form an important base for the further expansion of adult education in this area.

I think I have already given enough reasons to explain my interest, and that of Government, in Kibaha. The Swedish Ambassador just now read out a number of criticisms which have been made of Kibaha, and I must confess that I find this display of modesty refreshing, but also somewhat amusing. Of course, it is true that we have learned from the experience of Kibaha. It was built by man and perfection would have been strange, to put it mildly. But I would like to make it quite clear that the Tanzania Government would like more Kibahas, and as many as possible! The criticisms do not worry us. Some of them touch a little bit of truth here and there, and can be used in any new project which we are able to undertake, either alone or in co-operation with others. But the important thing is that Kibaha is here, and it is working, and it is doing a good job. Let those who do not create continue to criticize; their contribution to our development is comparable to the contribution to literature of those whose sole activity consists of criticizing other writers!

Responsibility for the future of this great project now rests firmly and squarely in the hands of Tanzania. From now on we pay for its upkeep, although I am very pleased to say that the four Nordic countries have agreed to continue to provide staff for the posts which we are not yet able to fill with qualified Tanzanians. We are grateful for this promise of continued assistance. Until now, however, if anything had gone wrong at this Centre, we would have had the comfort of being able to shift the blame on to others—even if the fault was basically ours. That comfort is now withdrawn from us. The responsibility is clearly ours. But I am confident that, with the help we have received, and with the help we will continue to receive from the Nordic countries, we shall succeed in maintaining what has been created, and in building upon it. I believe that we shall take full advantage of the opportunity which has been provided for us.

Let me, therefore, take this opportunity to express on behalf of all of us in Tanzania, our very great appreciation to all those who have worked on, or in connection with, this project until now.

It would be invidious to mention any parti ular name, for it has been a co-operative effort, and no one from outside can properly assess who has done what, and how they have done it. We only know that between them all they have created this fine Centre and made it work. We only know that, because of their activities, Kibaha is being handed over to us as a going concern.

Your Majesty, and Your Excellencies, the representatives of Sweden, Norway and Finland, I would ask you to convey to your Governments and your peoples our very warm appreciation of the help which has been given to us by the creation of this Centre and its transfer to us. Tanzania accepts your gift of work and money in the spirit of brotherhood and human unity in which it was given. We assure you that we shall do our best to take full advantage of the opportunity which has been created here by our combined efforts. We shall do our utmost to maintain this place as a worthy and living reminder of international co-operation and international brotherhood.

22

Yugoslavia's Experimentation

On 26 January 1970, President Tito and Madame Broz, then on a state visit to Tanzania, were entertained at a dinner given by President Nyerere in the State House, Dar es Salaam.

President Nyerere first outlined for his Tanzanian listeners his guests' life of struggle and sacrifice, leading up to the Yugoslav Partisan struggle from 1941 to 1945 against the German invaders. He went on to pay tribute to President Tito and the Yugoslav people for their willingness to defend their national independence and to experiment in working out the most appropriate socialist organization for their circumstances.

President Nyerere concluded his speech with an appreciation of Yugoslav technical assistance to Tanzania.

. . . At this point let me voice a suspicion that this Yugoslav experience of a guerilla struggle for freedom has been important to Africa. For I believe that it has influenced the kind of sympathetic understanding and practical assistance which the people of Yugoslavia have given to the freedom fighters of Southern Africa. Their socialism and their own desire for freedom would have led to support for this cause in any case. But President Tito and his colleagues know what is involved in such a struggle; they know its difficulties, its sufferings and its political and military possibilities. Therefore, they do not indulge in loose and easy criticism of what has been, or has not been, achieved. Instead, they help the movements when they can, and in whatever way they can. We in Tanzania, whose brothers are directly involved, and whose own security is indirectly involved in this struggle, greatly appreciate the Yugoslav attitude of helpfulness in these matters. We hope that our brothers, and we ourselves, will be able to learn from the Yugoslav experience until our struggle is as successful as theirs was.

But, of course, independence was only a beginning for Yugoslavia, as it is for the African countries. It was a divided country almost brought to its knees by four years of continual struggle, of which President Tito became leader in 1945. We in this continent sometimes talk as if the problems of national unity, and of development, exist only in Africa. Yugoslavia is a demonstration that these problems are not unique, and can be overcome. . . .

Nor is it only in political organization that the Yugoslav people, under the leadership of President Tito and the Yugoslav Communist Party, have shown a willingness to think for themselves about their own problems. They have consistently searched for the most appropriate methods of achieving their socialist goals of equality, of an end to exploitation, and of economic and social well-being for all the people. The Yugoslav schemes of industrial self-management; their willingness to use different methods of organization in different areas and different circumstances; and their refusal to accept any strait jacket for thought; all these and many other developments are a contribution to world socialist experience, as well as an attempt to deal with local problems.

Indeed, Yugoslavia is a country which every nation trying to build socialism should be watching with sympathy and interest. Of course I am not saying that all the experiments have worked out as hoped, or that Utopia will soon be achieved. From reading his speeches to Parliament and Party Congresses, I know that President Tito makes no such claim. But what I am saying is that the people of Yugoslavia are thinking for themselves about their own problems; they are trying new methods in dealing with the problems of building socialism, and they have not been afraid to abandon an experiment when it has proved a failure, and to try again. The people of Yugoslavia are therefore making progress in creating a single socialist nation out of a country with a long history of division, exploitation and poverty. For that alone, we would salute them.

But in fact all this has been done in the midst of the international cold war, and while frequent attempts were being made to persuade Yugoslavia, or to force it, into becoming a puppet of stronger nations. And the people have resisted all persuasions and all

attempts at intimidation. They have withstood economic pressures
and military threats. The result is that Yugoslavia is now universally
accepted as a truly independent, non-aligned nation. Yet it has not
taken refuge in isolationism. While maintaining their right and ability
to determine their own internal and international policies, the people
of Yugoslavia have continued to look out to the world as a whole
and to play their full part in its development.

This brief summary will be quite sufficient to explain why Tanzania
has such a high regard for the Yugoslavia people and their leader.
For we too are trying to build socialism in a manner appropriate
to our circumstances and, at the same time, to retain our independence of thought and action in a world of giants. Tanzania also,
has renounced isolationism; like Yugoslavia, we are determined
to play our part in the world as a non-aligned nation which is
involved in international co-operation on a basis of national equality
and sovereignty. . . .

23

A Survey of Socialist Progress

On the third anniversary of the Arusha Declaration President Nyerere broadcast to the nation a survey of progress towards socialism. He began by quoting those parts of the Declaration which defined socialism and which laid down the qualifications for leadership in Tanzania. He then went on:

. . . Our first job was to see that socialism was understood and accepted, especially by the leaders. Has it now been accepted? For my part, I reply without hesitation that, on the whole, our leaders did accept the Arusha Declaration and its conditions for leadership.

We can divide our leaders into four groups. First, there are those who were unable to accept, who resigned from their positions of leadership, and a few of whom left Tanzania for different places. This was not a big group. The second group was those who understood the Declaration and fully accepted it in their hearts from the beginning. This was not a very big group either. The third group was those who understood the Arusha Declaration and accepted it obediently because TANU had made the decision. This was a very big group. But the fourth group was those who pretended to accept the Declaration so that they did not lose their jobs. I think even this group was quite large, although not as large as some people assumed. All that was at the beginning.

But now I think the group which thoroughly believes in the policies of socialism has greatly increased. Most of this increase came from among those who accepted the Declaration just because TANU had made the decision; yet I believe—indeed I know—that even from among those who at the beginning just pretended, there are some who have been convinced. I do not want to say more on this matter because what I know you also know and sometimes you know better.

But I think all of us agree that socialism is much more accepted now than when we first adopted it as our policy. And it is not just we ourselves who recognize that. The feudalists and capitalists know that their hopes of defeating our socialist policies by using TANU and Government leaders have been very much reduced. You will notice that I said reduced, not ended; the appetite of a hyena does not end as long as he sees a bone.

Although we cannot say that we do not have any TANU or Government leader who just pretends to accept socialism, we can honestly claim that socialism has been accepted by Tanzania, the number of leaders who are convinced believers is increasing, and the number of hypocrites continues to decline. And this commitment is a very important thing; a commitment to socialism is half the battle in building socialism. For my part, I sincerely congratulate our leaders for their acceptance of socialism. They have discouraged the hyenas!

Our second job was to see that those sectors of the economy which we had made the property of the people were being well run for the benefit of the people. And here I want to congratulate all the workers in these industries, together with their leaders. For the capitalists hoped very much that we would be unable to run these things properly.

Let us try to see how well we have managed in these matters. Do our people, or our nation as a whole, get better service now than before nationalization? Is it the same, or worse? To answer those questions fully I would have to talk for a very long time indeed. So I will just give some examples. Take first the banks—which were the first things we nationalized.

The National Bank of Commerce is giving more and better service to the people of Tanzania than the private banks ever did. In three years it has opened 39 more Agencies—thus increasing the service available to people in the rural areas and smaller towns. It has increased the amount of lending to parastatal organizations by 300 per cent—which means that we, as a community, are able to spend that much more on development. Shs.312 million more money is deposited with our Bank than was deposited in the private banks when we took them over. Yet, despite all this extra work, the fees and loan rates of our Bank have not increased at all, and in the last financial year it made an operating surplus of Shs. 31 million—all of which can now be used for development work in Tanzania, whereas previously any surplus was sent abroad to the private owners as profit.

That is a great achievement in a short time, especially when it is remembered that almost all the experienced managers were withdrawn by their employers, and that all the reorganization had to take place without any interruption of normal service. I think all the workers in the Bank, in the Central Bank, and in the Treasury, deserve our congratulations. They must not relax, for the banking system is the corner-stone of modern development; they must do even better. But their efforts have certainly given us a good foundation.

The National Insurance Corporation is also doing quite well now after a very difficult period. When we took over the insurance business, we found that almost no one in Tanzania knew the work. The foreign companies had used our country as a market, concentrating all the business of drawing up policies and meeting claims at their head offices in other countries. Although we were able to recruit some foreign experts to help us, the understandable result of this situation was some delays in dealing with applications for insurance and in settling claims; during 1967 and 1968 these delays were very serious. Now, after some experience and training, things are a little more speedy—although we are far from good enough yet. But the workers recognize this problem, and they are studying and working hard.

In the meantime, we have, as a nation, already benefited from having our own Insurance Corporation. Even while they were expanding the business and learning the job, the workers in the Corporation have enabled it to earn a gross surplus of over Shs. 2 million during the year ended September 1968—and all that money remains in Tanzania. Previously all surpluses on insurance were exported in the form of dividends. Further, all the insurance premiums received, and all the money put into reserves ready to meet any claims, is now available for use in development work in Tanzania until it is required by the owners, who are also Tanzanians. Therefore, while we urge the workers in this business to improve their speed and efficiency, we should also congratulate them on what they—together with our management—have achieved despite the very great difficulties of starting up a modern insurance business and expanding it so rapidly.

Then there is the Tanzania Sisal Corporation. As everyone knows, the world price of sisal dropped very low in 1964, and has remained low ever since. The response to this low price made by many of the private owners had been to allow their estates to run down, to cease new planting, allow machines to deteriorate, and dismiss the workers. All this meant that even the amount of foreign exchange which we can earn at the low price was in jeopardy; cleared land was just being abandoned to the bush, and workers' interests were ignored.

By nationalization, and efficient management afterwards, we have made one large, efficient and viable economic unit out of a lot of private farms. We have resumed planting where necessary, bought new machinery, introduced new crops in places where they would be more economic, retained all the workers who had been employed on the estates we took over, and reduced the average production costs of sisal in every estate we took over! As a result, sisal still accounts for 10 per cent of our foreign exchange earnings, future production is assured, and we have been able to convert heavy losses in the cordage mill into small profits. Workers on these estates have been able to earn more, and although some of them have had to move from one area to another, none has been declared redundant. Thus nationalization has already justified itself in this industry too.

It is impossible for me to go into as much detail about all the other industries. The National Development Corporation existed before February 1967, and was already important to our economy. At that time we greatly expanded its responsibilities, making it responsible for all the publicly owned manufacturing, agricultural, and mining activities. Later we split it, setting up separate Corporations to deal with agricultural, tourist, and trade companies. But throughout the organizational changes, the NDC has continued to expand its services to the public sector and to prepare new investments which will provide economic growth.

One field of public enterprise where much improvement is still necessary is in the distribution of goods. It is important that the business of importing and exporting, and of wholesaling, should be in public hands as soon as possible, and indeed that is what we decided to do when we adopted the Arusha Declaration. In this country most of the merchants are Asians. Therefore, as well as the usual problem of a small group of people monopolizing the trade of the whole country, we have the additional problem that this group consists of foreigners or people of a different colour. This colour question inevitably makes our problem more difficult. Yet really the problem is the same one—that of preventing a small group from controlling a large sector of the economy on which all the people depend. And therefore the solution is exactly the same regardless of this colour question: it is to put this sector of the economy into the hands of the people's institutions. That is what we intend to do this year. To carry out these plans we shall use the NDC and the STC. First we shall expect the NDC and its companies to undertake the wholesale distribution of the goods they produce. This will reduce the pressure on the State Trading Corporation.

Second, we shall expect the State Trading Corporation to hold discussions with the merchants, in order that those who wish to do so can work under this Corporation and thus conform with the Arusha Declaration. I know that the merchants will not like this. But I also know that many will agree because this is the desire of the nation, and that others will agree because they are afraid of losing their means of livelihood. That is natural. The affairs of a nation are not dealt with by holy people or saints; they are run by ordinary people, each person for his own reasons. And for the country what matters is that its affairs are run in the manner its peoples decide; the individual motives are less important. I want all citizens, together with our brothers the Asians, to understand this problem and to help us to straighten it out.

We shall not concern ourselves with retail trade, although we shall be ready to assist NUTA and the co-operative societies to enter into it. But in fulfilling all these objectives, it is important that we should ensure that the work of distribution does not fall into chaos as a result of this revolution. I am confident that in this matter too we shall succeed.

Now I want to explain a little about our progress in the rural areas. How much have we done in relation to our decision to put increased emphasis on development in the rural areas? And how are ujamaa villages progressing? Here too it is important that we understand what we set out to do before we can measure whether we have succeeded or not.

Our peasants are very much behind in modern development. Our policies demand that we speed up the development plans for the rural areas; but this development could be exploitative or socialist. Because of our general socialist policies we have agreed that we must have socialist rural development and we said that we shall start ujamaa villages. Therefore our first job was to explain what an ujamaa village is, and why we want to start them. We said that an ujamaa village is a place where people live together and work together for the benefit of all of its participants. We explained that this was the only way to bring socialist development, that is development which does not involve exploitation.

Peasants have a reputation for refusing change. It is said that they want to live and work in the same way as their forefathers did. If their forefathers lived on separate shambas, then they will wish to live apart from their fellows; if their forefathers worked individually, then they will like to work on an individual basis. This custom, and the belief that the peasants would insist upon continuing it, was the hope of the capitalists and feudalists. They hoped that the peasants would oppose ujamaa villages; and if they did so, the only way of bringing development without exploitation would have been closed. Yet because people would not stop wanting development, by their opposition to socialist development they would have had to agree to development through exploitation.

I must agree that it is not easy to change the ideas of peasants. But factories bring progress; a factory is a place where many people work together, whether it is for their own benefit, or for that of the capitalists, or for the benefit of the nation as a whole. The working together is unavoidable. You cannot tell the workers in a shoe factory, or a textile factory, that they will be better off if each one of them has a back-yard factory in which he makes shoes or clothes. A factory like that would not be a factory at all; it is just stupidity, and no foundation for progress. A factory which is able to bring modern development is that which employs hundreds or thousands of workers together.

This is a thing which every wage earner recognizes. But unfortunately it is true that many peasants still think that the way to progress is for every individual to have his own little shamba. But such shambas cannot bring progress. If we want progress we have to start big farms. These can be capitalist, like the old private sisal estates, or state farms like the sisal estates now, or they can be co-operative farms. The farm of an ujamaa village is a co-operative farm.

So I repeat: our first job was to explain to the people the idea and the customs of ujamaa villages. Those who lived together but did not work together had to understand the benefits of working together. Those who neither lived together nor worked together had to be given the explanation about the benefits of living together or, even if they did not live together, of at least working together.

What has been the result? We have started well. Thousands of people who used not to live together in villages now do so. Mtwara Region has had the greatest expansion; we now have more than 400 villages in that area. More than half the people of Rufiji District now live in new villages. Tabora and Tanga Regions also have many villages now. These are the most advanced Regions. But there is not a single Region which does not now have some villages. Also, in some places where people used to live together but not work together, they have started to work co-operatively. Sumbawanga is a good example of this. In Sukumaland people who live separately have begun to cultivate a shamba in one place. They call this a 'block farm'. Now some of these people have seen for themselves the benefit of working together, and they are agreeing to move so that they live together in an ujamaa village near their shamba.

Thus in the rural areas socialist practices have been accepted. We never said that within three years all the Tanzanians in the rural areas would live together and work together for their common benefit. But the steps we have so far taken, and especially the spread of understanding about the benefit of socialist villages, is a very big step indeed.

Our problem now is not a lack of understanding or a refusal to accept socialism. Our problem is development programmes. It is not enough for a thousand people to gather and announce that their intention is to produce clothes or shoes together. There has to be a plan, machines, skilled people, and leadership which is able to start the factory for shoes or clothes. Similarly, it is not enough for the peasants of a village to gather together with the good aim of cultivating together; they too must have a plan, the tools, the knowledge, and the leadership which will enable them to start a good modern shamba.

Plans to take water, schools, or dispensaries to the villages have begun in many places, and this will continue until they exist everywhere. But it is also essential that we have good plans to increase the output of the villagers.

This work of drawing up development plans has been agreed upon. We have begun to choose teams of experts of different kinds under the leadership of TANU, which will go into the villages and help the villagers to draw up their economic development plans. The job of these experts will be to help the village in the same way as the Government gets help from experts in drawing up the development plans for the whole nation. The village will be able to use these experts to draw up its own development plan.

It is obvious that we do not have enough experts to be able to send them to every village or even to every Region. But we must start. Therefore we have begun in those areas where progress in starting villages has been greatest—i.e. Mtwara, Rufiji, Tanga and Tabora. We have also decided that we should encourage further growth in West Lake and Sumbawanga. We shall try to assemble more teams, and in any case when one of the existing teams has finished the plans of one village it will move on to another; and if it finishes the plans of one District or Region, it will go on to the villages of another District or Region. For now we have entered the stage of planning. The stage of explaining and persuading (although that will continue for those who still need it) is really ending everywhere. This in itself is big progress.

There are very many other things we have been doing towards implementing the Arusha Declaration which I have not talked about today. We have made progress in education—in making it more relevant to our objectives and our circumstances. We have strengthened the administration at Regional level. The new Five-Year Plan provides for the emphasis on development to shift to more labour-intensive and rural projects, and so on.

In fact we have made good progress over the last three years. We have done this because our public servants, and the workers in parastatal organizations, have responded magnificently to the challenge of building socialism through self-reliance in Tanzania. We have made this progress also because all the peasants and workers of this country have given their clear support to the Arusha Declaration, even when this has meant personal sacrifices to them in the short run. We have a right to be proud of our beginning.

But as we begin the fourth year since the Declaration, there are certain dangers we must guard against. First, we must not get complacent. The achievements so far are good only because it is the beginning; we have to go faster in the future. But we must still go carefully. We cannot afford to reduce our economic output while we socialize our organization; even if the improvements are slow, people must be able to see them year by year. And we must avoid arrogance. We must not think that because we are trying to build socialism we know everything that should be done throughout Africa and the rest of the world—or even that we know all the answers to our own development problems! We must be willing to learn from others; and especially important is that our leaders must be willing to learn from our peasants and workers. But our nation must also be willing to learn from the mistakes and achievements of other countries.

Most important of all, we must not be afraid of initiative. Unless we try, we cannot succeed. If we had not dared to demand our independence, we would not be independent today; and if we had not dared to announce, and to begin to implement, our socialist beliefs, today I would not have been able to discuss our successes in socialism. Every Tanzanian must have the courage to *try*. He must take the initiative to suggest new ideas, and he must be courageous enough to accept new ideas from others. And especially, if the ideas are good, he must try to implement them.

24

Developing Tasks of Non-Alignment

The 1970 Conference of Non-Aligned Nations was held in Lusaka during September, but the Preparatory Conference took place in Dar es Salaam, and was opened by President Nyerere on 13 April 1970. The President then argued that in changing world circumstances the only way of achieving the objectives of the Non-Aligned Conference is through economic co-operation among the poor.

First, let me welcome all our guests to Tanzania. We are very happy to have you with us for this important Preparatory Meeting of the Non-Aligned Conference, and I speak on behalf of everybody in Tanzania when I express our good wishes for the success of your work.

You have a great deal of work to do at this Conference. Obviously, the first responsibility of the Preparatory Conference is to fix the place and date of the Summit Conference, and to make other procedural arrangements for such a meeting. Yet I do not believe that any government would have sent such a high-powered delegation to this gathering if that was all it had to do. Indeed, a meeting would not have been necessary just to fix a date and a place; these things could have been arranged through diplomatic channels—with a considerable saving of time and expense!

For the fact is that the Summit Conference will be the more successful the greater the amount of ground which has been cleared before hand. If this Preparatory Conference can spell out areas of unanimous agreement, the later meeting will not have to spend time on such matters. And on other issues discussion can illuminate the problems involved, so that our different governments can give further consideration to these questions before the Heads of Government meeting. Then we are likely to make real progress at the Summit Meeting.

This preparation is important because the next Non-Aligned Conference has a more difficult task than either of those which have preceded it. Our first Conference in 1961 was held when the world was still divided into two fairly clear and opposing power blocs. Therefore, just by the fact of meeting and asserting their independence of either bloc, the member states of that Conference were taking an important political action. They were announcing that a refusal to become an ally of either side was not a temporary aberration of a few states; it was an important new international development which the big powers could not ignore. The Conference was saying, in fact, that a third force existed in the world— a group of sovereign states which insisted upon making their own judgement on world issues, in accordance with their own aspirations, needs, and circumstances. The Conference members did not claim to have great armed forces, and their meeting did not mark a change in the military 'balance of power'. But the Conference declared the existence of boundaries to the exercise of that military power. Its members made clear that they were not going to be willing participants in the cold war struggle. The dangerous game of threat and counter-threat, which was being played between the big powers and their 'allies' or 'satellites', no longer involved every nation of the world.

That was the first Conference. The 1964 Conference was a reassertion of that same fact, made necessary by a growth in the number of independent states, and some changes within the two blocs. It enabled a discussion of the changing problems as the non-aligned states were experiencing them; and it provided a forum through which we could reiterate our own quite independent view of world affairs.

Since that time considerable further changes have taken place within, and between, the two major power blocs. They are no longer so monolithic; both the USA and the USSR have had the—for them—unpleasant experience of some of their 'reliable allies' becoming less reliable! And both have, at different times, reacted with force, or by intrigue and subversion, against other members of their own group. Thus, inside the power blocs there is obviously a restless movement of peoples struggling to express their own desire for peace and freedom—and indeed for a little bit of non-alignment!

Further, the two great powers have come together for joint action on certain issues, and developments inside the People's Republic of China have made it impossible to continue to deny that country its status as an independent world power in its own right. The cold war has thus become less simple; the so-called 'Iron Curtain' has become less solid, and whether a 'Bamboo Curtain' exists or does not exist, the People's Republic of China does exist. The 'Power Game' has become three-sided, and those wishing to stand outside it have further complications to contend with.

These developments have not made non-alignment an outdated concept. For it is not, and never has been, a matter of neutrality—of treading a delicate tightrope between contending forces. Non-alignment is, or certainly ought to be, a policy of involvement in world affairs. It is not that we have no views, or that we wish to be available as mediators and arbitrators if the opportunity occurs. Such a role can be an honourable one; but it is not the major role of non-aligned states. Our role arises from the fact that we have very definite international policies of our own, but ones which are separate from, and independent of, those of either of the power blocs

By non-alignment we are saying to the big powers that we also belong to this planet. We are asserting the right of small, and militarily weaker, nations to determine their own policies in their own interests, and to have an influence on world affairs which accords with the right of all peoples to live on this earth as human beings, equal with other human beings. And we are asserting the right of all peoples to freedom and self-determination; and therefore expressing an outright opposition to colonialism and international domination of one people by another.

This non-aligned role has still to be defended. Our right to it is accepted in theory now, but its practice remains difficult and dangerous for us individually—though the dangers are not now necessarily those of a military invasion. For even while the power blocs have become a little less monolithic, the big states remain big states. And they clearly retain the urge to determine the policies of others in their own interests. In recent years we have seen plenty of evidence of this urge to dominate. Indeed, barely a month goes by without further evidence of externally organized or supported *coups d'état*, or sectarian rebellions, or of economic blackmail.

But it is no longer enough for non-aligned states to meet and complain to each other and to the world about international bullying. Everyone now knows that this international bullying goes on. And we have already declared our intention of standing up to such behaviour, and of refusing to become permanent allies of any big and bullying power. Also, we have declared our opposition to colonialism until it has become a series of hackneyed clichés.

Our non-alignment exists. It has already had, and it still has, a tremendous importance in the world. It has been a factor in the restlessness of peoples in satellite states; it has been a factor in smudging the edges of the cold war; it has been a factor in reducing the imminence of violent confrontation between the great powers. And it has prevented the division of the whole world into two—or even three—powerful and bitterly hostile groups.

All that we have already achieved. Simply to meet and to repeat our goals and intentions is therefore meaningless. Worse, it would imply that we have doubts about ourselves, and our ability to continue along the path that we have chosen for ourselves. For a big man does not keep shouting that he is big; a clever man does not keep shouting that he is clever. It is the small and stupid who constantly reiterate their claims to size and intelligence, hoping to convince themselves if no one else—and, of course, earning derision in the process.

The next Non-Aligned Conference, therefore, will achieve less than nothing simply by its assembly. This time the Conference has to lead to a development of non-alignment; it has to lead to action which will help non-aligned states to protect their non-alignment. And it has to do this in the context of the world as it exists in the 1970s.

Yet how can our Conference achieve this objective? The member countries have adopted different ideologies, and pursue different internal policies. We even differ in our foreign policies—and sometimes quarrel among ourselves! Only on opposition to colonialism and racialism do we all agree, yet even on that issue we differ on the tactics which should be pursued. In other words, we are not ourselves a 'bloc'. And if we tried to become one we would split, and split, and split again.

For non-alignment says nothing about socialism, or capitalism, or communism, or any other economic and social philosophy. It is simply a statement by a particular country that it will determine its policies for itself according to its own judgement about its needs and the merits of a case. It is thus a refusal to be party to any permanent diplomatic or military identification with the great powers; it is a refusal to take part in any alliances, or to allow any military bases by the great powers of the world.

And the fact is that the non-aligned nations differ in almost every conceivable way as regards the circumstances they have to deal with. Some of us have to live with a powerful neighbour; some of us have to live next door to a nation dominated by a great power; some of us live in places where none of the big nations have yet shown any interest—either in pushing us around, or in our economic development! Some of us border colonial states where freedom fighters are operating; some of us have mineral resources which depend on one or other of the big nations for their development and their marketing; and so on. Indeed, all that the non-aligned nations have in common is their non-alignment; that is, their existence as weak nations, trying to maintain their independence, and use it for their own benefit in a world dominated politically, economically, and militarily, by a few big powers.

Let us be honest with ourselves. We can do virtually nothing about these facts of geography and history in military terms. We cannot fight the giants on any basis of equality.

And to talk of alliances between us for mutual defence in modern terms, is also to talk of dreams. That is a brutal fact, and it is as well to accept it. Even together we do not have the capacity to mount the kind of defence system which could make an attack on one of us comparable in its nature to an attack by one developed country against another. And in any case, we are scattered over different continents and separated from each other by states which have chosen a different path from non-alignment. Nor do we have that degree of mutual knowledge, understanding and political agreement which are essential to realistic combined defence arrangements.

It is a fact of our life that if any of the big powers attacks us with military force, our only hope is to wage prolonged guerilla warfare; and as yet very few of us would be very proficient in waging such a war. A neighbouring non-aligned state is unlikely to be able to

give us effective help without endangering its own existence—
although, again, it may be able to support our guerilla activities.
If, on the other hand, we asked an opposing big power to come to
our aid, we are taking another risk. For occasionally they may help
and then go away again, but very often such a request would really
mean that we were simply choosing our masters; our real independence would have been surrendered in exchange for the assistance
against other aggressors. And even the United Nations would be
unable to help us if any of the big powers is involved and uses
its veto.

This is the military position which has always existed for non-
aligned states. We knew it when we chose this policy of non-
alignment. For it is a function of our size and our power, and has
nothing to do with non-alignment as such. Indeed, it is a position
which applies just as much to small powers which have allied themselves to large powers. Our liability to military invasion is not
increased by non-alignment; if anything, the experience of the 1960s
would suggest that some small aligned nations have developed a
healthy envy for the non-aligned nations! I would add, incidentally,
that there is need among the non-aligned nations for sympathy
and understanding towards the small, aligned states.

This does not mean that none of us faces, or may face, a threat
of military attack from a big power. It simply means that we have
to deal with such a possibility in the context of our real situation.
And the basic reality of that situation—the thing which is itself
the cause of our military circumstances—is our economic weakness.
Further, the truth is that this economic weakness very often enables
the big powers to impose their will without using their military
strength at all. With much less difficulty to themselves—and less
danger of getting themselves bogged down in endless anti-guerilla
activities—they can use their economic strength for the same
purposes of reducing our independence of action.

The real and urgent threat to the independence of almost all the
non-aligned states thus comes not from the military but from the
economic power of the big states. It is poverty which constitutes
our greatest danger, and to a greater or lesser extent we are all poor.
We are certainly all trying to develop. We are all short of capital,
and many of us are short of the expertise which is just as vital
to development. It is in these facts that lies the real threat to our

independence. For in seeking to overcome our poverty we each inevitably run the risk of being sucked into the orbit of one or other of the big powers.

Each of our states needs to look outside for some capital investment. We try to lay down conditions so that it will not bankrupt us, nor jeopardize our future independence. But we also have to accept conditions—that is natural and inevitable. Sometimes they are conditions about the rates of interest, sometimes about marketing, sometimes about exclusive purchase from, or sale to, the 'donor' country; or sometimes they involve receiving goods which we can sell in order to raise development money. These are all conditions which we have to consider; we accept them or reject them according to their nature and our general circumstances. If we accept them we do so knowing that we reduce our field of economic choice—our economic independence of action. That is a price we have agreed to pay; it is a deliberate and an economic decision.

But then we sometimes find that the aid, or the loan, or the personnel, is dependent on other factors which we had not specifically agreed to. We are told it will be taken away if we make a particular political decision which the donor does not like. Alternatively, it happens that when we are seeking support for economic projects, we find ourselves being encouraged to act in a certain manner because aid will be forthcoming if we do so. At every point, in other words, we find our real freedom to make economic, social and political choices is being jeopardized by our need for economic development.

It is pointless to answer that we can refuse to sell our freedom in this manner. We all say that our nations and our policies are not for sale. And we do stand up against the most open and blatant attempts to intimidate us with economic weapons. Many of the nations at this Conference can give examples of aid being withdrawn as a result of their political decisions. But the fact is that every one of us agrees to little compromises here and there when we are conducting supposedly economic negotiations.

We have no alternative. The world supply of disinterested altruists and unconditional aid is very small indeed. And however self-reliant we try to be in our economies and our development, we are up against the fact that progress out of poverty has everywhere, throughout history, required some outside injection of capital or expertise. Even the largest states of the world have used outside resources; small ones have to use more. It becomes a question of how far we will go, and what kind of compromise we will make. We cannot refuse to make any. For our own people will refuse to accept poverty without hope of change. We must have economic development or we have no political stability; and without political stability we have no political independence either, but become playthings of any other nation which desires to intervene in our internal affairs.

The fact is that our political independence depends upon the degree of our economic independence, as well as the nature of our economic development depending upon our political independence. These things are inter-linked in the modern world. And because of that interdependence, our economic relationships with one another, and individually with the great powers of the world, are matters with which the Non-Aligned Conference must be concerned.

For it is through these questions of trade, and of aid, that our action in world affairs can be influenced, if not controlled. A nation which sells 90 per cent of its exports to one foreign power—to take an extreme example—has to think many times before taking action which might provoke that purchaser to declare an economic boycott of its goods. A nation which gets even 50 per cent of its economic assistance from one allied group of powers, has to consider very carefully the effects on its growth of a decision which that alliance will consider unfriendly.

Yet, I repeat; we cannot respond to these facts by denouncing all aid, all foreign investment, and all technical assistance. In so far as these are essential to our development, and cannot be replaced by a re-allocation of our internal resources, we each have to seek for them, and accept them, on the best terms we can get. All that any of us can do, individually, is to try to avoid becoming dependent on any single big power for our total economic advance—and even this is not always possible. It is in these facts that lies the real threat to freedom, and to non-alignment.

But in economic matters we non-aligned states, as a group, can help ourselves and can reduce the danger to any one of us. Economics in my opinion, is not the same as defence. We can help to bolster our freedom from economic domination by working together, by co-operating for our mutual benefit.

There are many ways in which this can be done, and I do not believe we have yet given to these possibilities a fraction of the attention which they deserve. We even find ourselves being pushed into joint undertakings by outside forces—by those to whom we go for capital. Very often the most economical use of money and skilled manpower—the very things we are desperately short of—requires joint projects by two, three, or four underdeveloped states—whether these are non-aligned or otherwise. Often the economies of scale make it absurd to build separate manufacturing units for a single domestic market in each of neighbouring states; together they could build one factory which would serve them all at much lower cost. Yet instead of seeing these things for ourselves, and taking the initiative of working out joint schemes which will meet all our needs, we wait for some big capitalist to come along and take the initiative. Consequently we lose at least part of the advantages of our joint action. Instead of going together, as a united group, to negotiate for the capital or the expertise, we allow others to come and deal with us separately. We even allow them to act as 'go-between' when sorting out the many problems involved in our international economic co-operation.

Really, is it not absurd that small, weak, and non-aligned nations should allow representatives of the big powers to make our joint action a condition of their help? If they make the proposals, and seek the support of each of us, the joint project may still be viable and beneficial to us all. But it is likely, to say the least, that if we have taken the initiative ourselves, and worked out the proposals ourselves, we shall be able to obtain outside financial or manpower support on a rather better basis. Our real freedom will be greater at the end because we have worked together voluntarily. For together we are an attractive proposition for financialists and can get better economic terms. And together we can less easily be intimidated by political conditions, or blackmailed at a later stage.

There are very many things in which the non-aligned powers can work together for their mutual strengthening. Indeed, there is usually no reason why non-aligned countries could not also co-operate with other undeveloped nations which have chosen a different policy, because their weakness is the same as our weakness. Neighbours can join together for the development and extension of electric power. Nations selling a particular primary commodity—

or ones which are to a degree interchangeable—can organize joint sales operations on a co-operative basis instead of competing in the world market. Air lines, shipping lines, international road transport undertakings, can be jointly owned and run. Research into agricultural, industrial, and even health problems in tropical countries, could be organized jointly. And in all these matters the initiative can be taken by us; then, as a united group we can seek outside support if this is still required.

Some of the nations represented here have begun to organize this kind of international co-operation among themselves. But we are not yet taking it seriously enough. It must be extended. And it need not be confined to co-operation between neighbours, although for certain projects geographical propinquity is obviously essential. Indeed, the past six years have seen a considerable expansion of this kind of joint negotiation, with the weaker nations acting together on one side and the developed nations on the other. The most obvious example of this is seen in UNCTAD, but there are many others.

We must go further. We assume too easily that we have nothing to sell each other, and nothing to teach each other. When one of our nations needs to import something—whether it is consumer goods or capital goods—do we always examine first what other undeveloped or small nations have to offer? Or do we go automatically to the traditional suppliers or to other old industrial nations? If the lack of credit availability is a problem, do we ever investigate the possibility of a barter arrangement between ourselves? And when we are trying to expand a new sector of our economy, do we always have to go to the developed nations for training and expertise? Is it not a fact that each of our nations has gained experience in some field or other which the rest of us could learn from?

I believe it is essential that our next Non-Aligned Conference should consider the question of how we can help to strengthen non-alignment by economic co-operation. This is the field in which we can really effect changes in our vulnerability to outside pressure. It is one which we can do something about if we act together.

Of course, economic co-operation is not easy. All of us have now had sufficient experience to realize its difficulties. We must face up to them: they will not disappear as a result of grand words in conference resolutions—or opening speeches!

In particular we have to acknowledge that within the under-developed world there are the poor, the not so poor, and the very poor nations. There are nations which have begun to make a little progress, and those which still flounder in the morass for want of a stick to hold on to. And each of our nation states has to deal with its own problems—each government has to cope with the urgent needs of its own people, even when it is aware that a particular action might have adverse effects on its often poorer neighbour. Do these facts of nationalism, and of degrees of poverty, mean that we really cannot work together at all?

Does the clever, or the lucky, worker do better as a member of a trade union, or does he benefit personally by trying to ingratiate himself with his employer? What security has he individually, and what happens to his human dignity when he stands alone? Do the unskilled and the semi-skilled workers benefit more by fighting each other for the division of the wages the employer is offering, or by combining in opposition to that employer? For these are the real analogies of our position.

Some of us are lucky—for geographical or historical reasons; we have minerals or some other asset which the developed nations are prepared to pay for at the present time. Some of us have already developed the simplest industries—such as textiles—and fight to prevent others getting these things for themselves. Yet our luck, or our development, is only comparative to those even worse off than ourselves. And it can disappear for reasons quite outside our own control—new technological developments in the rich nations, or new mineral discoveries elsewhere.

When we really consider the modern world, and its division between the haves and the have-nots, not one member of this Conference is anything but a pauper. And like paupers, we shall really win a decent and secure livelihood, and maintain our dignity and independence, only if we act together.

The fundamental question we have to answer, therefore, is whether we recognize and accept that the progress of each member of the Non-Aligned Conference depends on the progress of all. For this is the truth which we reject at our peril.

On many occasions we have reminded the wealthy nations that their prosperity is bound up with our becoming effective markets for their goods. We have pointed to the lesson of history—that the bankruptcy of the poor nations leads inevitably to economic disaster for the rich. Recent world economic statistics support our case by showing that trade increases fastest among the wealthy; that both sides benefit when economic relations are conducted on the basis of real equality. The developed nations always acknowledge these truths; they bow their heads reverently when they cannot simply shrug and pass on. But they do not make any fundamental change in their economic attitudes towards the rest of us. Are we, within our own group, to act in a similar fashion? Or will we recognize our economic and political need for each other? If we are to do this, the less poor among us have to act in a manner which eases the development of the more poor, and thus allows us all to maintain a solid and united front. And the more poor have to acknowledge that these others cannot stand still in their development, but that we have to co-operate for mutual benefit, with give and take on both sides.

It is therefore not going to be easy for us all to work together and stay together. Working together will mean that each one of us may sometimes have to accept something slightly less to our advantage than we might have got—on that single occasion—by ourselves. This is the price, and the difficulty, of unity. Then, too, the big powers will try to prevent us from forging a real united front, and if we succeed they will constantly endeavour to break it up. They will approach us individually, offering this little concession, that little advantage. Yet if we succumb to these temptations they will continue their domination over us; they will even strengthen their control over our political freedom because they will have again demonstrated their effective power. Yet in economic unity we do have a defence for our freedom, if we have the courage to pursue it. A real determination to help each other, and to stand together on economic matters in relation to the developed and wealthy nations of the world, can lead to a new situation.

But is this possible? I said earlier that a military defence alliance between us is a dream; is talk of real and continuing economic unity any more realistic? Is this kind of 'trade union loyalty' possible between poor nation states, or does our nationhood force each government to pursue only the short-term interests of its own citizens? Will any of us be able to withstand the political bribery of some immediate short-term advantage for our own people and our own economies?

The answers to those questions depend on ourselves, and our ability and willingness to defend our own national independence. For independent nationhood in any real sense will become increasingly impossible for any of us unless we combine and co-operate together. Economic co-operation among ourselves is an essential part of the struggle to maintain our political freedom. Without it we shall each become ever more involved in the economies —and thus in the power—of the big states.

It is certainly true that our separate nationhood creates difficulties, as it means that each of our governments is responsible only to the people of its own state. But I believe that we can make our peoples understand that their freedom depends upon co-operation with other poor states. And we can make them understand, also, that economic strength is a greater safeguard for their freedom than such military power as would be within our capacity. For our people know from direct and personal experience that a hungry man, or a man trying to improve his standard of living, is at the mercy of those who control the food and the means of production. It is for this reason that wage-earners combine into trade unions in order to improve their effective power; it is for this reason that our peasants have begun to form marketing co-operatives so as to receive more for their produce. What they know, and what we know, to be true for the workers and peasants of our nations, is also true for those undeveloped nations who are struggling to be free in a world dominated by a few powerful countries. We must work together, as a united group; or, one by one, we shall be forced to follow the policies determined by other nations.

Ladies and gentlemen: all the member nations of the Non-Aligned Conference have recognized that it is impossible to be independent as diplomatic or military tails to a large kite. That knowledge caused us to choose non-alignment. We must now apply that same truth to economic matters. We shall never be really free while our economic weakness, and our economic aspirations, force us to our knees as supplicants or as scavengers of the world's wealth. Separately, that is, and will remain, our position. We shall beg or wheedle our way towards a little development here, a little investment there—all on terms determined by others.

But together, or even in groups, we are much less weak. We have the capability to help each other in many ways, each gaining in the

process. And as a combined group we can meet the wealthy nations
on very different terms; for though they may not need any one of us
for their own economic health, they cannot cut themselves off from
all of us.

Such a change is within our power. It does not demand
an economic strength which we do not have. It requires only a
political consciousness and a political will. And these depend upon
our courage and the intensity of our desire for real independence.

It is this question of economic self-reliance and economic co-
operation which I believe must be given special consideration at
the next Non-Aligned Conference. We shall undoubtedly reiterate
the truths which we have already spoken—about the need for real
action against colonialism and racialism, about the need for nuclear
disarmament, about the importance of supporting the United
Nations, and so on. But this time our meeting must do more. It must
recognize that freedom and economic backwardness are incompatible
in the modern world. And it must work out a combined strategy
for overcoming the poverty which now endangers the real independence of every member of our group.

Your Excellencies, ladies and gentlemen: on behalf of everyone
in Tanzania, I wish this Preparatory Conference great success in
its deliberations.

25

Arusha Declaration Parliament

The President addressed the last meeting of the 1965-1970 Parliament on 6 July 1970. He surveyed the work which it had done, and discussed the importance of elections in a socialist society as well as the requirements of the Tanzania system.

Mr. Speaker, Honourable Members:

In June 1965, I came to this House to announce the dissolution of the Independence Parliament, and in September of that year we had our first election under the One-Party State Constitution. Since then we have made many changes in Tanzania; it is appropriate that, at this last regular meeting of what may be called the Arusha Declaration Parliament, I should remind Members of our purposes and our achievements, as well as mention some of the things which remain to be done.

OUR CONSTITUTION

The elections of 1965—like those which will be held later this year—were conducted under a constitution drawn up by us, and designed by us to meet our own needs and circumstances. It marked a great change. For Tanganyika began independence in December 1961 with a constitution drawn up at a time when TANU was concerned almost exclusively with one thing—independence. For that reason we concentrated our attention on the powers of the Governor-General; the control of the Government over the civil service, the police and the army; and on the relationship between the judiciary, the people and the Government. In addition, British agreement to our constitution was necessary. For all these reasons the Independence Constitution of Tanganyika was neither particularly suited to the needs of our development nor was it entirely ours. Yet it achieved our purposes; for it secured our complete political independence and it enabled us to draw up our own Republican Constitution without interference from anyone. That constitution came into force in December 1962.

By the beginning of 1963, therefore, Tanganyika was operating under a constitution devised by the Government of this country and accepted by the Parliament and people. Yet gradually we became dissatisfied with it. We became increasingly aware that real democracy in Tanganyika was not finding expression through the machinery we had set up. Therefore we appointed a Presidential Commission, which travelled the country obtaining the people's views of the constitution and listening to their ideas, before drawing up proposals for a democratic one-party state. This report was considered by, and amended by, the National Executive of TANU; it was also accepted by the Afro-Shirazi Party in so far as its proposals affected Zanzibar. In July 1965, Parliament then passed the constitution based on that report. Ever since then the United Republic of Tanzania has been operating on a constitution which was drawn up and devised by Tanzanians, and which was based on a realistic appreciation of our own history and our own needs.

This constitution, which has been amended as we found it necessary, is called an 'interim constitution'. But we must not be unduly perturbed by that title, for it does not reflect any doubts about our electoral system and Party structure. Like all other provisions of the constitution, these could of course be changed if not less than two thirds of the Members of this House so decided. But I am bound to say that nothing so far has indicated the necessity for basic amendments to the one-party election system, apart from the changes which were necessary to implement the leadership qualifications and which have already been made.

In fact, the only reason why our constitution is called 'interim' is because, at the time of the Union between Tanganyika and Zanzibar in 1964, we acted quickly knowing that only by immediate action would we ever achieve our ambition for unity. Recognizing the problems of such a procedure, we decided that we would regard our arrangements as being interim while we gained experience of the necessities and the problems involved. Then, if it became necessary, either or both of the Parties could ask for the arrangements to be reconsidered. I would add that in practice we have been discussing advances and problems as they have arisen, and a number of consequential constitutional amendments have already been passed by this House.

The timing and circumstances of the Union also account for the fact that elections to the National Assembly are held on the mainland but not in Zanzibar. For our action was taken within a few months of a violent and bloody revolution in Zanzibar, which had been the necessary and inevitable result of the island's history. Zanzibar had become independent in December 1963 under a constitution carefully and cleverly devised by the colonial Government and the Sultan's Government in order to frustrate the freedom and the development of the mass of the people. There had been two elections before independence, but both were a sham, in that they did not result in a Government which reflected the people's expressed wishes. Not surprisingly, the people of Zanzibar refused to accept this, and at the first opportunity they overthrew the Sultan's Government. They did this at great cost in lives and under circumstances which inevitably left a heritage of bitterness, as well as a realistic recognition that attempts might be made to subvert the new régime and return the masses to the control of the minority. It was for this reason that the electoral system which was appropriate to, and desired by, the people of the mainland could not be adopted by Zanzibar. Not only were the people understandably suspicious of elections because of their experience; they also knew that elections at that time could be used by anyone who wished to confuse the people and nullify the then fragile institutions of the people's government.

However, I will return later to a discussion of the Union between our two sovereign nations. My purpose for the moment is simply to point out that the word 'interim' in the title of our constitution does not imply any instability or lack of control by the people over their own destiny. Neither does the word imply any time deadline after which the Union is in jeopardy. It is simply a public acknowledgement that when both sides are ready we shall look again at the present arrangements of union and see whether any alteration is required. So far we have not felt this to be urgent, but it may be that during the next Parliament discussions on this subject between TANU and the Afro-Shirazi Party will be begun.

Our present constitution thus governs the way we govern ourselves. It defines the powers and the duties of all our different political institutions, and is the basic law of this country, which must be followed by everyone. The constitution defines the role of the Party, the Parliament, the courts and the President. It says what the President may do at his own discretion, and what he may do in co-operation with Parliament; and it lays down the supremacy of the people, specifying the manner in which they may legally exercise and effect their rights through TANU, the courts of this country, the Permanent Commission of Enquiry, and through their elected representatives. Our constitution is, in other words, the basis of Tanzania's orderly development. Following it ensures that the unity of our people, and their rights, cannot be lightly tampered with, and that effective government and development activity is still assured.

OUR ACHIEVEMENTS

What then have we achieved over the last five years under this constitution? The answer is, a very great deal. Let us look first at the Union.

(a) *The Union*

Without any question, the manner and the implications of the Union between Tanganyika and Zanzibar is the most misunderstood aspect of Tanzania's political development. It may not matter very much when foreigners get confused, but unfortunately there are many times when Tanzanians themselves appear to misunderstand it!

Under the constitution there are two governments in this United Republic: the Union Government and the Zanzibar Government. The constitution lays down the powers of each; but at the time of Union it was clearly specified that Union Government powers, in so far as they required the assumption of duties previously carried out by the Zanzibar Government, would come into effect gradually. In practice, this integration of Union matters has been effected by agreement between the two Governments, and not simply by the President exercising his legal authority. This procedure has been adopted because our Union is a voluntary coming together of two equal nations; it is not the result of one state conquering another. Yet in fact, almost all the affairs included in the schedule of the Act of Union have now been integrated. Not only this, there have also been constitutional amendments to provide for certain matters to be transferred to the Union from the Zanzibar Government. Thus it has been possible for the whole United Republic to comply with and benefit from the Treaty for East African Co-operation; and questions relating to mineral resources have been transferred to the Union.

For all these reasons not even our enemies now talk of a 'Union in name only'. We have already reached a position where the Union seems natural and inevitable to our people, so that when difficulties occur we automatically think of a solution in the context of the Union. We take its existence for granted. Perhaps I should add that this has its own dangers! When it is young, every living thing must be cared for and guarded very carefully.

In 1960 I said that if the countries of East Africa want to federate it will be easier to do this before independence rather than after, because independence brings its own problems. We have now seen the truth of that statement, and there is no need for me to enlarge upon the problems of securing unity in Africa. But the Union between Tanganyika and Zanzibar is a demonstration that unity can be achieved if the will exists, in spite of the difficulties. The fact that our Union has become stronger over the past five years is thus a great achievement which is an encouragement to all those who desire the unity of the whole of Africa.

(b) *East African Community*

There is, however, another area in which our country has moved towards our ambition for greater unity in Africa since 1965. In December 1967, the Treaty for East African Co-operation came into effect, with provision for a real common market between Kenya, Uganda and Tanzania, and arrangements for jointly controlled common East African services. I do not need to go into details about this Treaty; you are all familiar with it. I will only remind the House that it was carefully worked out by the sovereign governments of our three nations to maximize for each country the benefits of co-operation. There are already signs that it will achieve this objective.

Of course, this move to unity in East Africa has not been without its problems for any of the countries involved, and some difficulties of implementation will continue to be experienced. But that is the nature of international co-operation, and experience suggests that nothing which is worth doing is easy to do. In any case our Treaty for East African Co-operation has already achieved sufficient success to be widely hailed as an example of what can be done to increase co-operation in our continent; indeed, it has set something of a fashion for similar efforts elsewhere. I believe, therefore, that co-operation in this part of Africa will gradually expand both geographically and functionally in the years to come. Certainly that is my hope and that is what our Government has been working for.

(c) *Political Development within Tanzania*

The past five years have been, if anything, even more eventful internally, and once again we have many achievements to our credit.

First I must mention the successful completion of our first Five-Year Development Plan. It is true that not all the projects included in that Plan were fully implemented; we cannot claim that. But we did achieve a degree of success which was quite remarkable in the light of our large ambitions and the resources of men and money which were, in the ultimate, available to us. In particular we discovered at the end of that Plan that we had been pursuing a policy of self-reliance long before we officially adopted it! For, as you know, the extent to which we had financed the First Plan from within our own resources was out of all proportion to our expectations when we drew up the Plan. Over 70 per cent of the development expenditure under the Plan had been found from within Tanzania, as against something like 22 per cent which we had expected to provide. We can take some satisfaction in that achievement.

But in some ways the most important achievement of the past five years (and the only ones which I intend to enlarge upon today) have been the changes leading up to, and consequent upon, the

Arusha Declaration—changes in which the members of this House have played a full and important part.

The Arusha Declaration was, and is, a statement about both politics and economics. These two aspects are equally important and cannot be separated from each other. For the Declaration is about the way in which we shall make a reality of human equality in this country, and how our citizens will achieve full control over their own affairs.

Since the Arusha Declaration three years ago, our practical emphasis has been on the necessity for public ownership and control over the economy. It was this aspect which required immediate action because it involved considerable changes in the institutions which existed before 1967. But the nationalization of the banks, of insurance, of food manufacturing plants, and of the wholesale, export and import trade, only makes a country socialist if the nation is governed by the people themselves through their freely-elected representatives. This is specifically emphasized in the Arusha Declaration. Socialism is not possible without democracy, any more than it is possible without a full acceptance of human equality, regardless of race, tribe, religion or sex.

State ownership and control of the key points of the economy can, in fact, lead to a greater tyranny if the state is not itself controlled by the people, who exercise this control for their own benefit and on their own behalf. For socialism is not an alternative to political democracy; it is an extension of it. It is a system by which political democracy is made an effective reality in the lives of the people, because of their control over the instruments with which they earn their livelihood. Socialism, in other words, means the extension of political democracy to include economic democracy; it does not exist while either of these aspects is missing. The people cannot say that they control the economic institutions of their country if they do not at that same time control the political institutions through their ability to choose their own leaders. Political control and economic control by the people cannot be separated.

I think it is important to stress these two components of socialism so that the House understands the significance of its own position and its own actions. For the National Assembly has been one of the people's institutions which has accepted the Arusha Declaration, and helped to implement it. Since February 1967, an important part of the work of this Parliament has been to pass the necessary legislation and to supervise developments so as to ensure that our policies result in the quickest and greatest possible benefit to the people.

No one can say that this House, or the Government either, has made no mistakes in these matters; that would be an exaggeration. And anyone who suggested that we have achieved our objectives would show that he does not understand our goals. We are trying to build socialism; we are not yet a socialist country. But we have many things to be proud of.

First of these is the fact that our leaders, including the Members of Parliament, accepted the leadership qualifications of the Arusha Declaration. There was a certain amount of grumbling at the beginning and some M.P.s even suggested that the qualifications were hard on people who were just beginning to enjoy the fruits of capitalism. But M.P.s were not the only leaders to have such a reaction—as anyone will know who attended the special TANU Conference in February 1967! And in any case, a little reluctance to do the kind of duty which demands self-sacrifice or unpleasant effort seems to be human nature; what matters is that the duty is recognized to be right, and that it is done. In this respect the National Assembly has a fine record. Only one M.P. actually left Parliament on the issue, and one slipped out of the country partly for this reason—although on other pretexts. Incidentally, I hope it will not have escaped notice, or been forgotten, that the one man who refused to comply with the socialist leadership qualifications was the M.P. who talked more about socialism and quoted more socialist textbooks than any other Member of this House! Perhaps this fact will help us to recognize that shouting about socialism, and being a socialist building socialism can be two very different things!

Apart from this, however, the House has co-operated with the Government and Party in passing a great deal of very important legislation. Bills considered here have dealt with questions relating to public control of the economy, changes in the educational system, the wages and incomes policy, the National Library Service, the reorganization of Government machinery to make it more effective for our new purposes, compulsory selective National Service and all the necessary financial provisions for giving emphasis to the rural areas as far as possible.

It may interest the House to realize that, apart from the many Bills relating to the national Budgets, an average of 42 Acts have been passed each year since 1965. Of course, it does not follow that speedy passing of legislation is necessarily an indication of good work by this Assembly! Speed is sometimes essential, but at other times it could indicate a lack of interest in the job, or a lack of care and preparation in the consideration of proposals put to Parliament by Government. In general, however, I think that has not been true of this National Assembly, although some proposals and Bills, especially those of a technical nature, have found the House at a loss. There have, however, been many occasions when the debates of the House have enabled Government to improve Bills under discussion, or to improve proposals submitted for debate.

I am not saying that I believe Parliament has always been right when it forced Government to give further consideration to Bills submitted; understandably perhaps, I feel that Government's proposals were sometimes unpopular with the House for wrong or insufficient reasons! Yet if Members were not persuaded, then they were right to force Government to reconsider the proposal concerned. For this meant that the Government had failed properly to explain its purposes or the reasons why it believed that its proposals would fulfil those purposes. And if M.P.s were not convinced, then they could not explain these things to the people. Parliament was thus carrying out one of the functions I outlined in my Address to this House on 12 October 1965. I said then that provided both Government and the National Assembly members are 'honest and able to advance arguments for their views, the people will be better served by reconsideration of the proposals than by automatic affirmative vote'. So even on those few occasions when Government and the National Assembly have had differences of opinion, I believe that this House—and our constitution—has served our people, and given us cause for pride.

Political development, however, involves much more than Acts of Parliament, or National Assembly discussion of White Papers, or Private Members' Motions. As far as our people are concerned what matters is the impact our policies and administration make on their daily lives. They care about the actions they experience, not our intentions or the Acts in which those intentions are inscribed. The people are not God; they do not judge us on our wishes or intentions, but on the results of our actions. In this respect serious deficiencies unfortunately still exist.

The Annual Reports of the Permanent Commission of Enquiry have shown something of the extent to which some officers of our Party, our Government, and our courts have abused their powers, to the detriment of the peasants and workers of Tanzania. It is true that the last Report shows that the number of complaints has begun to lessen, and if this is the result of our improvement it is very good indeed. But we must not forget that the Permanent Commission receives complaints only from the most literate, aware, or energetic and courageous of our citizens; its Reports understate, rather than overstate the problem. This means that while we can be proud of the existence and the workings of the Permanent Commission of Enquiry—which was itself set up by this Parliament —we must not be complacent. We must work until all our people are able to rely on enjoying the respect and freedom within the law which is due to them as citizens of our country. This will be achieved only when every officer of Government, Local Government, and Party, and every judge and magistrate, acts consistently as an intelligent and humane servant of the community. In this matter we all have a heavy responsibility. For it is the job of the officers of Government and Party and of M.P.s to explain policies to the people, to listen to them, to answer their questions freely and openly, and then to see that the policies are implemented properly, fairly, and with decent humanity even against those who transgress against our laws.

Yet I do not want to give a false impression. We have made mistakes and we have failed in many respects to do the things we set out to do. But we have worked hard and we have made many changes of great benefit to the peasants and workers of this country. While, therefore, it is appropriate that all of us should meet the citizens we seek to serve with a decent degree of humility and a consciousness of work still to be done, we do not have to meet them dressed in sackcloth and ashes! For we have much to be proud of. Over the past five years there have been many developments which have made the lives of our people much better. Water supplies, roads, bridges, schools, dispensaries, hospitals, improved technical services for the peasants, better working conditions for the wage-earners—in all these things our record is as good as any in Africa, and better than that of most underdeveloped countries.

We have made a good start. Further, much work has begun which will bring great benefit in the future. For example, the real importance of securing public ownership of the banks, insurance, all the major industries and so on, cannot yet be apparent to the villagers of Tanzania because it takes years to build up these institutions in the manner we require. The importance of our action in this respect can, perhaps, be usefully compared to the experience of an ujamaa village which starts a new farm. The people plant some crops like maize, beans, and groundnuts, which will provide their food almost immediately; but if they are wise they also plant things like tea which will begin to bring profit only after three years, and fruit trees which produce only after five or six years. If they are very far-seeing they will also have planted a small softwood plantation which will bring profit to the village only after 15-20 years, and even a hardwood plantation which will provide a steady income only after 40 or 50 years. The work of planting all these crops—both long-term and short-term—will have to be done by the founder members of the village. And although the results will not become apparent for years, the planters will have prepared a good heritage for their children and grandchildren through their long-term planning and investment.

Yet if the members of the village have not understood that some of their work will not bring immediate results, or if they have not wholeheartedly agreed to prepare this heritage for their descendants, then they will get disgruntled when the return on their labour is very small for the first two or three years. A side effect of this will be that they will change their leaders at the next opportunity! For the members of an ujamaa village have—and must have—the right to change their leadership, and they will make their choice on the basis of their understanding, not because some visiting expert economist knows that their work has been of great long-term importance. Thus the members may change their leaders because the present ones have not brought quick progress. They will be making a mistake, yet even so it is vital that they have this opportunity regularly to choose the leaders they want. For if the members do not have confidence in their leaders they will not work hard and they will not co-operate in villages' plans; so no progress will be achieved—either long-term or short-term.

THE NEXT ELECTION

In just the same way the adults of Tanzania have, and must have, the right to elect their representatives in Parliament every five years. And they too, will make their choice on the basis of their present experience and their understanding of what has been done and why. We shall have our next Presidential and (on the mainland) Parliamentary Election in the next few months.

Elections are expensive to run, and introduce an element of personal uncertainty in the life of every leader. But they are essential to this nation, and indeed to every leader who accepts his role as servant of the people.

Firstly, the periodic right to choose or to reject a particular representative is the only way in which the people can be sure that their M.P.s and President will be truly and exclusively responsive to their interests, their needs and their desires. Secondly, only by periodic elections can the Members of Parliament know that they continue to enjoy the confidence of the people. And only with such knowledge can we be certain of the people's co-operation and backing in the plans we make for our nation.

These are two very practical reasons for having elections at least every five years, but there is another even more fundamental reason.

The Government of this country—of which the President and the National Assembly are both parts—is intended to be the mechanism through which the people govern themselves. Our jobs exist only because it is impossible for the work of government to be done by the people directly. We are therefore elected to speak and act on their behalf. We can do this, and the people are therefore able to govern through us, only while both we leaders, and the people themselves, know that they will have a chance to decide that there is another person better able to speak for them. For it is the people's confidence, and the people's wishes about policies, which elections are intended to reflect. Further, it is the work they want done in the future which is important to them, not the things we have already done on their behalf; they neither will, nor should, choose their representative out of gratitude.

I know that there are, even in Tanzania, some beliefs that periodic elections are dangerous. It is said that they give to the enemies of our people and of our political system an opportunity to sow confusion; it is said that they could be used to destroy our unity; that they could be used to get rid of good leaders and replace them with bad leaders; or that elections could be an opportunity for rogues who oppose our policies of socialism and self-reliance; and so on. I know that some of the people who have these doubts about elections are very well motivated; they are anxious only to prevent disaster coming to our country. Indeed, I can assure you that I myself am aware that periodic elections do bring these dangers. Yet I am quite unable to see what we can put in their place.

We have rejected the system whereby our leaders are chosen by their mothers—that is, where a person becomes a leader just because he was born to a certain wife; this is a hereditary system—a sultanate. We could say that when our national leaders have once been chosen by the people we should leave them in position for life—meaning that we leave the question of their removal from office solely to God. This system has been proposed many times in Tanzania, although just for a few of our leaders, not all of them. But until now we have rejected this idea. It may be that in religious matters such a system is very appropriate; I do not know. But for matters of this world this system does not differ very much from the hereditary system which we are opposed to.

Let me explain. The wife of a sultan may give birth to a child who grows up to be a very good leader of the nation. That is good fortune. But she may also give birth to a very tyrannical leader. Under the hereditary system you will then have to wait until God removes this tyrant and his wife gives birth to a better leader. But how sad for the people if the next leader is also a tyrant—like his father! It is the same with elected leaders. You may choose a very good leader; that is good fortune. But you may make a mistake and choose a tyrant. What will you do then? There is nothing at all that you can do! You have to endure him until he dies as a result of an accident or disease. And I say that deliberately. Because you cannot logically and legally get rid of a man you have elected for life either by votes or by the use of weapons. Under a system of electing a leader for life you have surrendered the right to remove a man once you have selected him. You have retained only the right to choose in the first place. It is obvious that such a system is no good for us.

Nor can we lead a country as if it were a Church, with the priests and bishops of politics choosing and rejecting each other as leaders, without the believers having any chance to choose or to throw out their leaders. The Church can explain why they have this system. But it is very difficult to get an explanation which would justify a government concerned with this world being run on the same basis. Secular leaders of the people must have trust in the people; that is the only way they can be trusted by the people. A system where leaders choose themselves from among themselves rests on a foundation of mutual trust among the leaders; but it shows that the leaders have no trust in the people.

To sum up, only while there is this kind of recurring opportunity for choice, can the people rest confident that they govern themselves, and no one else governs them; only while this opportunity remains are we, their representatives, forced to overcome our indolence or our selfishness and serve them to the best of our ability. Without free elections the people of an independent country do not govern themselves; they are governed by masters. They may have good masters or bad; their masters may be local or foreign; but they are still masters. And if your masters are good, thank God; if they are bad, God help you!

OUR TYPE OF ELECTIONS

It is, however, one thing to recognize the need for some kind of elections; it would be quite a different thing to assume that the electoral system has to be the traditional Western multi-party system. For to fulfil its purpose an electoral system must do two things. It must allow the people to elect a competent government which reflects their feelings and ideas; and it must enable them to do this without damaging the society in which they live, or the long-term objectives they have set themselves.

Our system of one-party democracy was designed by us in the belief that it would enable us to do both these things. For we recognized that the people of mainland Tanzania were united behind TANU and further, that this unity is our greatest strength in the struggle against poverty, as well as against any outside enemies. Our electoral system, therefore, provides the people with an opportunity to choose between two TANU candidates, each of whom is standing after a democratic process of party selection. By this procedure our Party is able to ensure that all candidates in the General Election are people of good character, loyal Party members, and qualified under the Arusha Declaration rules. At the same time, the fact that the Member of Parliament or Local Council is elected by all Tanzanian citizens reduces the danger of the Party getting out of touch with the people. Nor can a Parliamentary seat be used as a reward for past loyalty, regardless of present competence. For TANU is unable to assign a seat to any individual; that choice remains with the people of each constituency. Our system has no 'safe seats'!

I would add that one result of our system is that individuals who have served the nation well are sometimes not elected, even when the United Republic could still benefit from their services in Parliament or Government. But the possibility of defeat for a national leader is unavoidable; in every constituency the people must have the right to select their own representatives. In the exceptional case of an over-riding national need for the services of a person who is not elected, the President has the necessary powers. This provision in our constitution has, however, to be used sparingly; it has not been, and must not be, regarded as a reward for past services, only an indication of future national requirements.

The importance of national unity to Tanzania is also reflected in our prescribed manner of campaigning for election. There are two important aspects to this. First is the fact that the campaign is organized by and paid for by TANU, with the candidates travelling together and speaking on the same platforms. No candidate in our elections is expected to run a private campaign on his own behalf; indeed, we must take care that such 'private enterprise' does not enter into our system. For private campaigning would give rise to the possibility of bribery and corruption, thus introducing an advantage to candidates of greater wealth or lesser morality. It would also lead to divisions within our society, as groups form around individuals and urge their cause, perhaps on communal grounds.

This brings me to the second important provision in the laid-down procedure of campaigning. It is of fundamental importance that nothing shall be said or done by anyone involved which encourages division between our citizens on grounds of race, tribe, religion, or sex. In our society every citizen is of equal worth and must be judged on the basis of what he does, not what he looks like, or what he believes about God. If we allow candidates to campaign, however indirectly, on the basis of their birth, or their parents' birth, their tribe, or their religious affiliation, then the whole basis of TANU policy is undermined. Who is a Tanzanian citizen is laid down by law, and only citizens will be standing for election. On that point, therefore, nothing more needs to be said. All that matters is whether an individual is a good person, a capable and an honest man or woman, and hopefully, a good socialist! It does not even matter whether his parents or his relations were or are any of these things; we cannot control what others do, only how we ourselves live and act.

CONCLUSION

Mr. Speaker: I have been talking for a long time, but I want to conclude by pointing out that in the next five years we shall be building upon the work we have already done. And, as according to the English proverb, 'nothing succeeds like success', I think we can look forward with confidence.

For we set out to establish a democratic one-party state. In spite of the doubts freely expressed by many people, we have succeeded in this aim so far. We set out to consolidate the union between our countries, Tanganyika and Zanzibar. In spite of many anticipated difficulties, and despite the gloomy prophecies of many people, we have had great success. We set out to establish the proposition that even a small and poor nation should resist the bullying of large nations and should remain the master of its own destiny. Our United Republic has acted in that manner; we are not a client or satellite of any nation, but we have survived.

And finally, we have decided to act boldly in the implementation of our ambition to build a self-reliant socialist state. I suspect that our success so far has given encouragement to others.

Our work is not finished. But as I do not anticipate the necessity, or the opportunity, to address this House again, I wish to express, on behalf of the Government, the Party, and all Tanzanian citizens, our appreciation of the work which Members have done over the past five years.

Some present Members of the House will seek a renewal of the people's confidence. Some of these may be elected and others may be defeated. But I wish to say now, that whatever the people's decision about their representatives for the coming five years, this House has served the nation well. Every Member will be able to take pride in saying to his children, and his children's children: 'I was a member of the Arusha Declaration Parliament'.

Mr. Speaker: to you and every Member of this House I wish the happiness of continued service to the people of Tanzania, and to our socialist beliefs, in whatever field our people may decide is most appropriate to their interests.

26

Learning from Hungary

On 23 August 1970, President Nyerere welcomed President Losonczy of Hungary at a state dinner in Dar es Salaam. After paying tribute to his guest, and speaking of his own visit to Hungary in 1969, the President went on to refer to that country's experience of co-operative farming.

. . . The progress of your co-operative agriculture was particularly interesting to us; what we saw during our brief visit caused us to ask that Tanzanians should have an opportunity to stay with you, and see developed co-operative farms in operation. I am glad that the Hungarian Government was able to respond to our request, and that 29 of our young Agricultural Officers are now studying the practical aspects of co-operative agriculture in Hungary. On their return they will take part in the development of co-operative and socialist villages in Tanzania.

We appreciate this help very much, for although the co-operative farms of Hungary are mechanized to an extent which is at present inappropriate here, the involvement of the members in decision making is far from inappropriate. Indeed, it must be the basis of our rural socialist expansion. For—as you, Mr. President, pointed out to me when I was your guest—experience has shown that it is impossible to build socialist agriculture by using force or intimidation. The peasants must be persuaded and convinced about the new methods of organization; they must participate voluntarily, and they must make their own decisions about their farm. I would add that the Hungarian success has shown that this can be done, and that the reputed conservatism of rural peoples is an exaggeration. They have learned to be cautious, and to judge by results not by words; but that is very different from rejecting change. Let me add that in my experience our two peoples are the same in this matter. We are at an early stage in the development of socialist agriculture, but our peasants are moving in ever increasing numbers from individual production to co-operative production and co-operative living. . . .

27

Relevance and Dar es Salaam University

In the presence of a very large crowd of workers and Peasants, as well as staff and students, the University was inaugurated on 29 August 1970, at a colourful open air ceremony on the University campus about eight miles from the centre of Dar es Salaam. The President, speaking as Chancellor of the University, used the opportunity to discuss the function of a university and the meaning of the 'relevance' which was frequently demanded of it.

It is with great pleasure that I have come to this campus today to preside over the formal inauguration of the University of Dar es Salaam. On the good foundation built by the University College of Dar es Salaam, which was a constituent part of the University of East Africa, we are now embarking upon our independent existence as a University. This is therefore an occasion for rejoicing. It is also an occasion which calls for re-dedication and renewed endeavour by all those involved. For it is now our responsibility to shape this institution so that it gives the maximum service to the people of Tanzania and their socialist objectives.

To do this effectively, however, it is first necessary that we should be clear in our own minds about the function of a university in the modern world, and about the particular tasks of the first University in Tanzania. Only when we have done this can we avoid the twin dangers, on the one hand, of considering our University in the light of some mythical 'international standard', or, on the other hand of forcing our University to look inwards and isolate itself from the world in which we live.

Mr. Chairman, a university is an institution of higher learning; a place where people's minds are trained for clear thinking, for independent thinking, for analysis, and for problem solving at the highest level. This is the meaning of 'a university' anywhere in the world. Whatever it may be called, an institution is a university only if that definition can be truly applied to it.

Given this definition, a university has, in my opinion, three major and important social functions. From one generation to the next it transmits advanced knowledge, so that this can serve either as a basis of action, or as a spring-board for further research. Second, a university provides a centre for the attempt to advance the frontiers of knowledge: it does this by concentrating in one place some of the most intellectually able people who are not preoccupied by day-to-day administrative or professional responsibilities, and through its possession of good library and laboratory facilities. And third, a university provides, through its teaching, for the high-level manpower needs of the society.

The comparative importance of these three functions at a particular university will vary from time to time, according to the resources which the community is able to allocate to it, the pressures which society exerts on it, and the accident of personalities and abilities among its members. But the three functions are interlinked. A university which attempted to prohibit any one of them would die—it would cease to be a university.

Thus, if it tried to cut itself off from the rest of the society, and evade its role as an institution of high-level training, the university's isolation would soon lead to intellectual anaemia. For, as its members lost touch with the purpose of their activity—which is man in society—it would cease to have any attraction for intellectually able people. If, on the other hand, a university became so much of a training institution that none of its members had the opportunity to expand their own knowledge and to search into the unknown, then it would cease to be relevant as a high-level training institution. For it would become unable to make any contribution to a society which was changing all the time—it would be locked in the past.

It is in the context of this definition, and these functions, that young and backward nations seek to establish their own universities— Tanzania being no exception. For although a university is, by its nature, inevitably expensive to establish and to maintain, the full value of university activity can only be obtained when the university and the society it serves are organically linked together. A nation without a university can be served by graduates from foreign universities; specific research needs can often be met by scholars based at a good foreign institution. Tanzania knows this by experience. But these are short-term expedients; they help a society while it is establishing or strengthening its own institutions, but they cannot replace them.

For learning of all kinds has a purpose: that purpose is to increase man's power over himself and his environment. In other words, the function of learning is the development of men, and of mankind. And development must start from where you are. You cannot teach calculus to an illiterate peasant—he first has to learn to read and write and to understand numbers. Similarly, a university is wasting time and effort if it ignores the society in which its student grew and learned his preliminary lessons.

Learning is part of living; it cannot be divorced from the community. A child learns from his family before he ever goes to school—and while at school he continues to learn from his experiences outside the school compound. Successful school teaching then builds upon the student's total experience; it introduces new knowledge through using that already acquired. Thus a child is taught to write its name; it is taught to read the written symbols of things it already knows—the *kuku, mama, ng'ombe, nyumba*, and so on. New facts and strange concepts are discovered in such a way that the process of discovery is part and parcel of the process of growing up. Only if this method is used will the new knowledge make sense to the student, and be of use to the society which he knows, in which he lives, and where he will work. And if the society is itself changing—as ours is—then the school education must keep pace, and help the student to be part of those changes. But this can only be achieved by gradually extending the horizons of knowledge with which the students entered the institution, and by showing that the new material can be related to their experiences outside the classroom.

This is why so many young men and women have difficulty when they are forced to go to an entirely different society in order to obtain higher education. The new learning is offered in a form which does not easily fit into their previously acquired knowledge. And even when they triumph over these problems and absorb the academic knowledge they travelled for, they then have to make other adjustments when they return home. It is very much easier, and more profitable for the community, if a graduate's life and learning are an integrated whole, each relevant to the other and part of the other. Then the problems a graduate meets when applying his knowledge to the service of the society will be related to his studies, and the social attitudes of the community in which he is working will be compatible with those he absorbed as part of his academic knowledge.

Quite apart from the learning process itself, however, there is another way in which university education is linked to the community. It is provided at the expense of the community as a whole. I know that we who have received education do not like being reminded of this fact; but it is better to remind ourselves than to be reminded by others. The peasants and workers of a nation feed, clothe, and house both the students and their teachers; they also provide all the educational facilities used—the books, test-tubes, machines, and so on. The community provides these things because it expects to benefit—it is making an investment in people. It believes that after their educational opportunity the students will be able to make a much greater contribution to the society; they will be able to help in the implementation of the plans and policies of the people.

The community's investment will, however, have been a bad one if the student is ill-equipped to do any of the jobs required when he is called upon to make this contribution. In such a case the university will have failed in its task. The same is true if the graduate is unwilling to fulfil his responsibilities without demanding further privileges from the community. For, I repeat, the purpose of learning is the advancement of man. Knowledge which remains isolated from the people, or which is used by a few to exploit others, is therefore a betrayal. It is a particularly vicious kind of theft by false pretences. Students eat the bread and butter of the peasants because they have promised a service in the future. If they are unable or unwilling to provide that service when the time comes, then the students have stolen from the peasants as surely as if they had carried off their sacks of wheat in the night.

Thus, new nations establish their own universities because they need a type of higher education appropriate to their problems and their aspirations. This is not to deny that much knowledge is international. The laws of chemistry apply everywhere: an economic analysis is valid or invalid wherever it is made. But the kind of problems which are examined at a university—the means through which advanced and theoretical knowledge is taught—do and should vary according to the background, and the anticipated requirements, of the students. Is more time spent studying the chemistry of ice formation, or of volcanic eruptions? Are the tools of economic analysis acquired by considering mostly developed or developing, capitalist or co-operative societies? In a tropical new nation which aims to build socialism, the emphasis at the University will be very different from that applied in highly industrialized and capitalist nations with temperate climates.

The kind of intellectual skills taught and practised is, however, only one of the reasons for having a national university. Another is that an educational process inevitably encourages the development of certain social attitudes and beliefs. It is certainly true that university education must encourage the students to think for themselves. But the ethos of the university and the surrounding society does have an automatic and unavoidable influence on the students.

Are students encouraged to debate, or simply to listen? Is it obviously assumed that in the absence of an imposed discipline they would completely disregard the interests of their fellow members of the university, or does the university structure support an expectation that students will work in co-operation with each other and with the wider community? Are the students led to believe that they are the future masters or the future servants in the society? These and similar things affect the students' growth as surely as the quality of the food they eat and the formal lessons they receive. Of course, some people will absorb the ethos of the university and the society more easily than others; some may even react against it. But its importance in the educational process can be seen everywhere. It follows that a country which is trying to build socialism on its cultural foundation cannot ignore the social atmosphere in which its students are being educated. For they are being given special educational opportunities simply because the society needs special services from them if its goals are to be achieved. The skills and the attitudes they acquire are therefore of equal importance.

This is the background to Tanzania's decision to establish its own University. Our nation has decided to divert development resources from other potential uses because we expect to benefit by doing so. We believe that through having our own higher educational institution in this country, we shall obtain the kind of high-level manpower we need to build a socialist society, and we shall get the emphasis we need on investigating the particular problems which face us. In other words, we expect that our University will be of such a nature that all who pass through it will be prepared both in knowledge and in attitude for giving maximum service to the community.

In its teaching activities, and in its search for new knowledge, therefore, the aim of the University of Dar es Salaam must be service to the needs of a *developing socialist Tanzania*. This purpose must determine the subjects taught, the content of the courses, the method of teaching, and the manner in which the University is organized, as well as its relations with the community at large.

Thus our University, like all others worthy of the name, must provide the facilities and the opportunities for the highest intellectual enquiry. It must encourage and challenge its students to develop their powers of constructive thinking. It must encourage its academic staff to do original research and to play a full part in promoting intelligent discussion of issues of human concern. It must do all these things because they are part of being a university; they are part of its reason for existence.

And because this is a Tanzanian University, it must do these things in such a manner that the thinking is done in the framework of, and for the purpose of serving, the needs of Tanzania's development towards socialism. The University of Dar es Salaam must be a University; and it must be *our* University—relevant to the present and future society of Tanzania.

In this connection I must add that we have a past error to correct, and a present danger to avoid. For we have always recognized that Harvard University must try to understand American society, and be understood by it, in order to serve America. And we have always known that London University and Moscow University must each try to understand, and be understood by, their respective societies in order to serve their nation's people. Yet it is only recently that we have realized a similar necessity in Africa. Our universities have aimed at understanding Western society, and being understood by Western society, apparently assuming that by this means they were preparing their students to be—and themselves being—of service to African society.

This fault has been recognized, and the attitude it involved has been in the course of correction in East Africa—and particularly in Dar es Salaam—for some time. But there is now the danger of an understandable—but nevertheless a foolish—reaction to it. This is that the universities of Africa which aim at being 'progressive' will react by trying to understand, and be understood by, Russian, East European, or Chinese society. Once again they will be fooling themselves into believing that they are thus preparing themselves to serve African society. Yet surely it is clear that to do this is simply to replay the old farce with different characters. The truth is that it is Tanzanian society, and African society, which this University must understand. It is Tanzania, and the Tanzanian people, who must be able to comprehend this University. Only when these facts are firmly grasped will the University of Dar es Salaam be able to give full and proper service to this society. The University of Dar es Salaam has not been founded to turn out intellectual apes whether of the Right or of the Left. We are training for a socialist, self-respecting and self-reliant Tanzania.

WHAT IS RELEVANCE IN THE UNIVERSITY?

It is, however, not enough just to say that. Our University prepares people to work in the *future* Tanzania; it seeks to teach that which will be useful in years and decades to come. Yet we cannot accurately foresee the future; we can only try to predict the probable outcome of man's present goals, present knowledge, and present investigations. And of course, Tanzania does not exist on a planet by itself. It is part of Africa, and part of the world; it is increasingly affected by what happens outside its own borders. In any case, we are human beings who are entitled to the accumulated wisdom of mankind—and who have a corresponding duty to contribute to man's pool of knowledge. We should therefore be extremely foolish if we tried to cut ourselves off intellectually from the rest of the world on any grounds, whether these be geographical or ideological. For even if we succeeded in doing that, we should certainly not be able to deflect the effects on us of others' ideas, knowledge, and actions—indeed, we should be less capable of doing so because of our ignorance!

Thus we would be inviting our own destruction if we gave too narrow a definition to the word 'relevant' when using it in relation to our University studies. Knowledge is international and interrelated. We need to know and to understand as much as we possibly can; we need to learn from the past and present of all parts of the globe. All knowledge is relevant to us, even if we consider ourselves only as Tanzanian citizens and ignore our existence as human beings.

It is only by starting from that basis that we can avoid blundering into national disaster through deliberate blindness.

But having said that, and having accepted that, we still have to select; we still have to determine our priorities. For it is impossible for us to learn everything. Still less can we teach everything at a University inevitably restricted in size and scope by the limitation of our resources. To plan is to choose. On what basis, then, shall we determine the kind of disciplines, the kind of knowledge taught at our University? On what basis should the University syllabuses be determined?

The answers to these questions can be deduced from an understanding of our present national circumstances and national goals. Tanzania is a backward and poor country, most of whose people live in the rural areas. Our economy depends upon agriculture, but we need to diversify it. We aim to revolutionize the conditions in which our people live, so that everyone is assured of the basic necessities of life and is able to live in decency and dignity. But we are not only trying to develop; we are determined to do this on the socialist basis of human equality. We want to establish a free society where all citizens are equally assured of justice. And while doing all this, we need to safeguard our national independence against all external or subversive attacks.

It follows that at our University the implications of these conditions and these ambitions must be studied and taught. Students must learn to anticipate the kind of problems which might arise from any combinations of these circumstances and desires. And they must have their minds orientated towards solving such problems; analysis has to be followed by action, and a university education must lead to a positive and constructive approach to the difficulties which might face our nation in future. Further, while the students acquire this understanding and this problem-solving approach, they must also be learning the skills necessary for the implementation of policies. For it is not enough to work out that the solution to a problem of underdevelopment in one area is to build a particular bridge. We must also have the ability—the skill—necessary to construct that bridge.

Thus, University 'relevance' is not a question of drawing up syllabuses which talk about 'Tanzania' all the time. It is a question of intelligent and knowledgeable tutors relating their discipline to the student's, and the society's, past, present, and anticipated future experience. It is a question of the teaching being oriented towards solving the problems of Tanzania—as they are, and as they can reasonably be expected to be in the future.

When determining whether a particular subject should be offered, the University should therefore be asking itself 'what contribution can a study of this subject make to Tanzania's future?' Similarly, when a tutor is preparing his syllabus, his lecture or seminar, he should first ask himself 'What needed understanding, or what new information, am I trying to convey to the students?'; he should then go on to ask 'What knowledge of, or from, our own society is relevant to this matter?'. And finally, 'What has mankind's heritage of knowledge to teach us in this connection?'. If the University authorities, and the professors and lecturers, always bear in mind the reason for the existence of the University, the principles on which our society is based, and the purposes of our policies, then their courses will be relevant, and the institution itself will be relevant.

For ultimately this question of the relevance of a particular subject, course, or lecture, can only be determined by those who are familiar with the subject as well as knowledgeable about our social goals. Certainly the academics must be able to explain to laymen the importance of a particular study and its relationship to the society. But we must avoid the trap of allowing unqualified people to decide on its inclusion in the University teaching just by looking at the name of a course, or at a syllabus outline, and then stating firmly 'this is relevant, that is not'. The traveller knows where he wants to go; but the man who knows a forest intimately is the one who can guide him to his objective by the shortest and easiest route—for the first few yards of a path are not always a good indication of the terrain it will cross or the point to which it will ultimately lead.

This does not mean that all the planning of teaching and research at the University can be left to the sole discretion of the academic staff. The community has too much at stake to allow any one group such complete control. Ideas about what is needed, and can be done, should come both from University staff and from the community at large. The decisions must then be made on the basis of whether a particular course is likely to contribute to our development; whether it is one which is appropriate to a University institution rather than some other (and possibly less expensive) educational body; and whether this use of our resources is justified in the light of possible alternative uses in other sectors of the economy. Such decisions must necessarily be made by the representatives of the whole society. But they must be reached in the light of advice given by those qualified to tell what can be gained from a particular study. And once a course has been decided upon, the academic staff must be allowed to decide how to conduct it. If they cannot do that properly, and for our service, then they should not be employed at the University.

And ultimately, the community has to judge the University by results. When a fruit tree is growing, the farmer can tell whether it is being attacked by pests, whether it is in danger of dying from lack of water or nutrients, or whether its shoots look healthy. He can tell from the leaves whether it is the kind of fruit he wanted, or whether he planted the wrong seed by mistake. But he can only tell whether it is a good tree when, year after year, it has produced a great deal of large and sweet fruit. If he tries to examine its roots while it is still growing, or to transplant it every year, he is more likely to destroy than to improve it.

The same thing is true of our University. Having made clear why we are establishing it, and what we expect from it, and having done our best to select administrators and teachers capable of fulfilling our intentions, we have then to trust those we employ and those we select to attend it. We can watch and warn. We can demand that they should explain what they are doing and why—and we can tell them to change if that is necessary! We can instruct the staff to examine themselves and their work every year—to conduct 'postmortems' with the students at the end of every course and to use the experience as they gain it. But we should be stupid to try to bind the University staff hand and foot, and move them like puppets.

The University must be allowed to experiment, to try new courses and new methods. The staff must be encouraged to challenge the students and the society with arguments, and to put forward new suggestions about how to deal with the problems of building a socialist Tanzania based on human equality and dignity. Further, they must be allowed, and indeed expected, to challenge orthodox thinking on scientific and other aspects of knowledge—it is worth remembering that Galileo was very unpopular when he first argued that the world went round the sun! The staff we employ must lead in free debate based on a concept of service, on facts, and on ideas. Only by allowing this kind of freedom to our University staff will we have a University worth its name in Tanzania. For the University of Dar es Salaam will be able to serve our socialist purposes only if we accept that those whom we are paying to teach students to think, must themselves be allowed to think and speak their thoughts freely.

CONCLUSION

Mr. Chairman: I have tried, today, to outline the basic purposes of our new University, and to explain some of the things we expect from those who work and study here. There are many important aspects of the University's life and work which I have not referred to; for the job to be done cannot be discussed in one brief speech—we will work its implications out together as we develop.

In conclusion, therefore, I simply want to say that every single individual working or living on this campus, as well as very many people outside it, has a part to play in the work ahead. For this will be a socialist University in a socialist country only if all members of the community recognize their common involvement and their mutual responsibility to each other and to the society at large. And it must be remembered that the community extends from the men who look after the grounds, or wash the dishes, or type the letters, to the Vice-Chancellor and his staff, as well as the students.

Of course, we shall not have a socialist University after today's ceremony, any more than we have a socialist society because of the Arusha Declaration; indeed it is impossible for the University to be fully socialist unless the society in which it operates is fully socialist. But I believe that the University of Dar es Salaam can help our people to attain their goals, both by its work and by its example. Let us commit ourselves to the attitudes, the organization, and the work, which this requires.

28

At the United Nations General Assembly

Like many other Heads of Government, President Nyerere addressed the 25th Anniversary Session of the United Nations in New York, giving his speech on 15 October 1970. After calling for China's admission to its seat during that Session (the vote was finally won a year later, on 25 October 1971), he went on to discuss the question of Southern Africa, and the responsibilities of member states in relation to it.

It is, I know, customary to congratulate an organization which has successfully survived for 25 years. Yet I feel that it would be a little odd for me, as the representative of the United Republic of Tanzania, to offer congratulations to the United Nations on its 25th Anniversary. For the United Nations is not an abstract thing; nor is it governed and run by creatures from outer space. The United Nations is us—its members. It does not exist apart from us; it can do only what we, its members, are prepared to do, acting together. This means that to congratulate the United Nations is to congratulate ourselves—which is rather dangerous! For self-congratulation is all too liable to lead to complacency and self-satisfaction—neither of which is, I believe, warranted at the present time in relation to ourselves as the United Nations.

In saying this, Mr. President, I do not intend to belittle that which we have achieved, nor to under-estimate the importance of the fact that, after 25 difficult years, the United Nations still exists. And I must mak clear that I am not wishing to minimize the value of the work which has been done by successive Secretaries-General of the United Nations, and their staffs. The task of servants of this organization has been—and still is—extremely important to world peace; it is also difficult beyond assessment for men and women who are concerned to live up to the high ideals of the United Nations' Charter.

Therefore I would like, through you, Mr. President, to express gratitude and congratulations to the Secretary-General and his staff, for both their achievements—which are many—and for their efforts in the cause of peace and justice. In this expression of appreciation, I would like to include all the members of the peace forces still at work under the auspices of the United Nations. Their thankless task has saved many lives, and has provided more time for us—the masters of the United Nations—to deal with the problems which threaten world peace.

Whether we use the time thus made available to us is, of course, not within the control of United Nations' employees. They remind us of what has to be done; they prepare Papers for us to consider. But the consideration and the decision-making is a matter for the nation states which are members of the United Nations. The failures—where there are failures—are ours. And it is about one of these areas—where the Secretary-General has constantly reminded us of a danger and where we have virtually failed to act—that I intend to speak this morning.

Before I do so, however, there is one other matter I must mention, and that is the question of membership of the United Nations.

Mr. President, it is not always easy, at a given point in time, to determine which is the real government of a country that is going through a period of revolutionary upheaval. For that reason, the United Nations—I believe wisely—usually gives the incumbent government the benefit of doubt until the position clarifies itself. But there comes a time when we only make ourselves ridiculous by refusing to face the facts of change—whether we like that change or not. And that point has been reached and passed in relation to China.

The territory and people of Mainland China—that is, about $3\frac{3}{4}$ million square miles, and now about 700 million persons—have been under the effective control of the Government of the People's Republic of China in Peking since 1949—for 21 years. Yet they are still represented in our councils by a so-called Government of

China, which in fact controls only Formosa—an island of approximately 13,900 square miles in area, and a population of about 15 million people. And even this control continues only because of the intervention of an external power.

How much longer does the General Assembly propose to allow this absurd state of affairs to continue? For it cannot go on indefinitely. I would like to suggest that an appropriate way of celebrating the 25th Anniversary of the Organization would be the admission of the People's Republic of China to its seat here. Only by such an action shall we end the situation whereby we pretend to decide questions of peace or war in the absence of the most populous nation on earth.

Having made that point, Mr. President, I want to come back to my major theme today—which is the question of peace or war in Southern Africa.

Nothing could be more relevant, or more important, to this Assembly. For the purpose of the United Nations is the preservation of peace. But no one has ever suggested that this meant the preservation of evil. On the contrary, the Charter of the United Nations makes it quite clear that peace can only be maintained—and should only be maintained—on the basis of 'promoting and encouraging respect for human rights and for fundamental freedoms for all, without distinction as to race, sex, language or religion'.

The task of the United Nations is thus much more than the prevention of violence between men and nations. It has to promote justice and human equality. And it has to fight against the forces of injustice, and inequality.

In particular, the United Nations has to act against the forces of racialism and colonialism. For these represent the kind of tyranny and oppression which deny all hope to men, and which therefore force them to express their humanity through violence. A man can change his religion if he wishes; he can accept a different political belief—or in both cases give the appearance of doing so—if this would relieve him of intolerable circumstances. But no man can change his colour or his race. And if he suffers because of it, he must either become less than a man, or he must fight. And for good or evil, mankind has been so created that many will refuse to acquiesce in their own degradation; they will destroy peace rather than suffer under it.

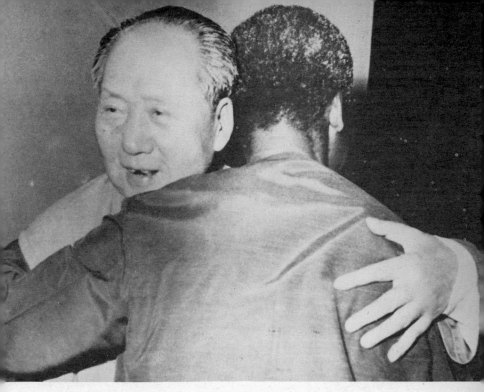

1 Chairman Mao and the President meet again in Peking in 1968 (T.I.S.).

2 In Moscow, during October 1969, the President had long official talks with his hosts. But there were also social meetings—as in this photograph taken at a lunch party in the House of Receptions. The President is with Prime Minister Kosygin, President Podgorny, and Mr. Mazurov, Deputy Prime Minister (Copyright: A.S.P., London).

3 During his State Visit to Hungary in October 1969 the President visited the publicly owned 'Ikarus' Bus Factory at Budapest—and was given a bus fitted out as a mobile dispensary. Hungarian President Pal Losonczi is fourth from the left (front row) in this photograph (Copyright: Interfoto Mti).

4 King Frederick IX of Denmark and the President in interested conversation at State House, Dar es Salaam, during the State Visit of the Danish King and Queen, January 1970 (T.I.S.).

5 President Tito and Madame Broz of Yugoslavia pictured with the President at State House, Dar es Salaam in January 1970 (T.I.S.).

6 President Obote of Uganda, and President Nyerere, leave Dar es Salaam for the Non-Aligned Conference in Lusaka, September 1970 (Adarsh Nayar).

7 The President delivered his speech 'Church and Society' to the Maryknoll Sisters' Conference on 16 October 1970 at their Headquarters outside New York, USA (T.I.S.).

8 The President and his party with Pope Paul when the President was returning from the United Nations in October 1970 (T.I.S.).

9 The old search for water is still much too common—this photograph comes from Shiny District (T.I.S.).

10 In the same District, the villagers of Mwamalasa Ujamaa Village have clean tap wa provided by a combination of self-help work and Government finance (T.I.S.).

12 In October 1970 work on the Tanzania/Zambia railway was formally started at a ceremony attended by President Kaunda and President Nyerere as well as a visiting Chinese Minister This photograph shows the two Presidents examining a map of the railroad (T.I.S.).

11 The President discussing design work for *vitenge* with a worker at the Friendship Textile Mill, Dar es Salaam (Daily News).

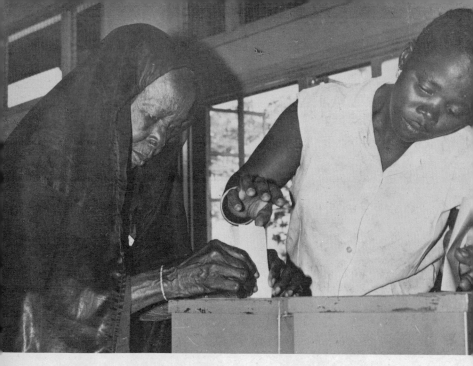

13 The Presidential, Parliamentary, and Local Elections were all held simultaneously in October 1970. This photograph was taken at a Polling Station in Mtoni, near Dar es Salaam (T.I.S.).

14 In January 1971 the President paid a State Visit to India. He is seen here with (r. to l.) Prime Minister Mrs. Gandhi, President V. Giri, and the Indian Vice-President Mr. G. S. Pathak (T.I.S.).

15 The Mass Literacy Campaign now covers the whole of Tanzania—this class is in Monduli District (T.I.S.).

16 The President's interest in adult education is reflected as he visits this class in Ruvu during 1971 (T.I.S.).

17 The President enjoys a joke made by the retiring Chief Justice Georges when replying to the President's speech at a Dinner given in his honour in March 1971 (T.I.S.).

18 The President spent some weeks in Dodoma District in 1971, helping the people in their move into ujamaa villages. Here he is mixing mud for brick-making (T.I.S.).

19 The Prime Minister of Sweden, Mr. Olof Palme, was a guest at the TANU National Conference in September 1971 (Adarsh Nayar).

20 On his return from a visit to President Kenyatta at Nakuru, President Nyerere was greeted by the First Vice-President of the United Republic, Sheikh Aboud Jumbe, and the Second Vice-President and Prime Minister, Mr. Rashidi Kawawa (T.I.S.).

21 A large Buffet Dinner was given on 9 December 1971 in honour of the 10th Anniversary of Tanganyika's independence. Traditional Tanzanian dishes were cooked for the occasion by members of Umoja wa Wanawake (the national women's organization). With the President in this photograph are (l. to r.), Lady Seretse Khama, President Barre of Somalia, President Micombero of Burundi, and President Seretse Khama (T.I.S.).

That is the position in Southern Africa now. The apartheid policy of South Africa—now being imposed also in Namibia—and the colonial oppression of Portugal in Mozambique, Angola, and Guinea Bissau, have goaded the people to desperation.

No one can say that the peoples of these territories did not try to secure change—even some movement towards justice—by peaceful means. They tried political organization, trade union organization, and tribal welfare organization. They tried petitioning to their rulers, and to international organizations; they tried peaceful public rallies; they tried the publicizing of their wrongs through the press of the world. Indeed, perhaps they tried too long, and thus enabled the forces of oppression to strengthen themselves too much, before they finally recognized the situation for what it was. For all their efforts were met with increased oppression and an increase in the sufferings imposed upon them.

But the position is now obvious. Efforts to achieve peaceful change towards justice from within the states of Southern Africa have failed—miserably failed.

As far as the peoples of Southern Africa are concerned, therefore, the choice is now clear. They can acquiesce in their own humiliation and accept their position as third-class subjects of an alien ruling power, or they can fight for their manhood. They are now making that choice. And they are doing it for themselves. They are choosing future life at the cost of physical death and suffering for many.

What free nation, or what free people, dares to tell the masses of South Africa, of Rhodesia, of Namibia, and of the Portuguese colonies, that they are wrong? Who is it that can tell these people that they should acquiesce in the daily humiliation of themselves and their children? Certainly the United Nations cannot do so. For this would be to deny the basic premiss of human equality, and thus to deny the basis on which we meet here.

No one who genuinely believes in human equality has the right to demand that the peoples of Southern Africa should refrain from making war on racialism. But, if we used our strength in support of humanity, we could make their fighting unnecessary. For the United Nations—the nation states acting together—has the power to put such pressure on the states of Southern Africa that change would have to come. It is a question of our will; it is a question of whether the preservation of peace by the removal of injustice is sufficiently important to us. If it is, we shall exert all pressures short of war. If it is not, then war will grow.

Until now, we have not acted in support of our verbal condemnations of apartheid and colonialism. We have given the peoples of Southern Africa no hope of change. So they have begun to take up arms in their own defence—in defence of their manhood and their right to a life which is more than brutal existence. Yet so far the fighting is more a warning to the world than a real threat to the power of their oppressors—although it has certainly frightened them.

One thing, however, the beginning of the fighting has already done. It has forced the rest of the world—all of us—to face up to the situation. We can no longer pretend that we have no concern with affairs in Southern Africa. Now we have to make up our minds: whether we support the freedom struggle; whether we support the South African and Portuguese racialist and colonialist Governments; or whether we propose a new version of the non-intervention which helped the fascist regimes of Europe into power in the late 1930s.

For Africa there is no choice. We have to support the freedom fighters. Theirs is merely a continuation of the freedom struggle which has already resulted in 41 African nations being represented in this General Assembly. For the national freedom and human equality for which these peoples are fighting are not only the same rights which the rest of Africa claimed and won; they are also the only basis on which the free states of Africa exist. For no one would claim that Tanzania, for example, has a right to be independent because of its military power, its economic strength, or the high level of education of its people. Tanzania is independent because the United Nations, and Administering Authority, acknowledged the right of its people to demand national freedom, and because they acceded to that demand when it was firmly and clearly made.

Yet if this right to self-determination existed for Tanzania, then it does exist for Southern Africa—and if it does not exist for those peoples, then it does not exist for us either. This is recognized both by South Africa, and by Tanzania. It is the root cause of the conflict between the free states of Africa and the apartheid régime of South Africa. For apartheid is the modern form of slavery—and Africa can no more survive half-slave, half-free, than could the United States of America. Our efforts to build non-racial societies are made more difficult because of apartheid. Conversely, the example of our freedom, and our efforts in support of human dignity, are a continual irritant to the slave-masters of South Africa and Portugal.

This is why, Mr. President, talk of a non-aggression treaty between South Africa and Tanzania is such nonsense. Our conflict is not that of two states quarrelling about a border or something of that nature. The conflict is about apartheid versus humanity, and about our right to freedom. For racialism is itself an aggression against the human spirit, as colonialism is the result of a past aggression against a people and a territory. We in Tanzania, and the other peoples of Africa, have been—and still are—the victims of these aggressions. It is impossible for us to sign a non-aggression treaty with aggression itself. No country which considers itself a friend of Africa should try to persuade any African state to sign such a treaty with the murderers of our humanity. For an African Munich would no more bring peace than did that of Europe in 1938. It would be a betrayal, and as such it would weaken the struggle for justice everywhere. But ultimately it would not succeed in preventing the people from fighting for their freedom.

Yet although Africa has no choice but to side with the freedom struggle of Southern Africa, it has at the present time very little power to affect the outcome. We are all poor nations. We have no effective economic power to use. Further, we do not even manu-facture arms which could be made available to the freedom fighters. All that we can do is to allow those peoples of Southern Africa to receive help through our territories and to use our land for their offices, their hospitals, and so on, until they have effectively re-occupied their homeland. This little we do. And we do it because we have already, without effect, implemented all the non-violent pressures within our power.

And what of other—non-African—nations? They all claim opposition to apartheid, and to colonialism. Yet the sad truth is that—far from using their power for justice—many nations rep-resented in this Assembly give continuing and expanding practical support to South Africa, and to the Portuguese colonial war effort.

Does anyone imagine that one of the poorest states of Europe could, unaided, fight colonial wars in three territories, which are together twenty times its own size? On the contrary; its NATO membership allows it to almost disregard its domestic defence needs, and devote its armies to Africa. Its membership of EFTA strengthens the Portuguese economy, and thus helps that country to meet an otherwise intolerable burden. And things like the planned foreign investment in the Cabora Bassa project enable Portugal to increase its exploitation of our continent.

The same pattern can be seen in relation to South Africa. Despite all the expressed opposition to apartheid, South Africa's foreign exchange deficit is now financed by new investment from abroad. And powerful nations still put more time, effort, and money, into expanding their trade with South Africa than with the whole of Africa north of the Zambesi. But this is not all. In absolute contravention of the United Nations arms embargo, France—and to a lesser extent some other European nations—continue to provide arms for South Africa. Indeed, it is noticeable that to France the obligations of friendship and peace go only one way. For many French-speaking countries in Africa are very sensitive to criticism against France; they value their friendship with that European power and do not like to embarrass that country. But France does not seem to be equally concerned to avoid embarrassment to her African friends, or to consider their attitudes on matters affecting the African freedom and unity to which they are publicly committed. And now another great European power is considering the resumption of arms sales to South Africa—and using the French practice as one of its justifications.

Mr. President, national leaders do not like it when their sincerity is called into question. Let me just say, therefore, that Africa and the freedom movements have to judge who are their friends, and who are the allies of their enemies, by actions not by words.

Yet we are sometimes given an explanation. We are told that the arming of this racialist state is an aspect of the defence of the 'free world', and does not imply any support for apartheid. Really, Mr. President, do words change their meaning? What have freedom and the present régime in South Africa to do with one another? Can you avoid aiding a murderer if you give him a weapon?

There is another aspect of this, which is of very great importance to the future of the world. For, if the Eastern bloc nations make arms available to freedom fighters, and the Western bloc nations sell arms to South Africa and to Portugal, what is the likely result? Africa will become a hot front to the cold war. The freedom struggle of Southern Africa will become confused by a power conflict which is irrelevant to it; and Western countries will then find that their exclusive concern with what they see as the danger from communism, has led them to take the side of South Africa in a conflict with the rest of Africa. And the rest of Africa will find that it is fighting against the nations with whom it has long ties, and in alliance and alignment with others from whom it has desired only normal friendly relations.

Yet although Africa recognizes this danger to the peace of the world, we cannot draw back. We cannot ask the peoples of Southern Africa to acquiesce in their humiliation and their misery. We cannot fail to support them. For the deliberate attempt to deny the humanity of non-white peoples, which is what apartheid means, is an affront to every person in Africa. And because humanity is in fact one and indivisible, and because freedom is indivisible, it is also an affront to every free man, regardless of colour.

The war has already started in Southern Africa. Yet even now it would be possible for us to restore peace, if we only acted for justice. For if the world would really recognize this evil for what it is, and isolate the nations concerned, then change would be inevitable. It might not be quick, but it would be certain; and that certainty would provide new hope for the peoples of Southern Africa. The régimes of South Africa, and Portugal, need the world; they cannot survive without it. This they know—it is why they work so hard to obtain 'certificates of respectability' in the form of contact of any kind.

We in Tanzania recognize that nations find it difficult to make sudden changes in their trade and economic policies; we know that inherited patterns of investment and trade cannot be suddenly disregarded. We are neither fools nor impractical idealists. But it is one thing to recognize the facts of an inheritance while you work to change that pattern. It is another thing altogether to intensify that pattern of friendly and trade relationships with a country like South Africa. Up to now that is what has been happening—despite all our words. We in Tanzania are asking that the world—and particularly the powerful nations of Europe and America—should change direction, and should move towards actions which will increasingly isolate South Africa. Only by such policies can we hope to secure change without the horrors of war.

Mr. President: the issues of Southern Africa have been discussed so often that some members of the United Nations express boredom, and ask why the matter is raised yet again. But the peoples of Southern Africa are not bored by their oppression; they are suffering it. They are not tired of repeating that they are oppressed, because their repetition is a cry for help.

The issue in Southern Africa is one of principle. It does not allow for compromise, because compromise on a matter of human rights is a denial of those rights. We are none of us perfect. Certainly I do not claim that Tanzania is faultless, or that offences against human rights never take place in my country. But it is one thing to try and to fail, and to try again. It is an entirely different matter to base the whole structure of your society on a denial of human rights. With a society of that kind, we compromise at our peril. For ultimately, humanity will not be denied.

Mr. President: the prime function of the United Nations is to establish and to maintain peace. We know that there can be no peace without justice. The greater the movement for justice, the greater the chances of peace. I ask that all members of the United Nations should work for peace in Southern Africa by acting for justice now.

29

The Church and Society

On 16 October 1970, President Nyerere visited the Headquarters of the Maryknoll Mission outside New York City. Many members of this religious order continue to work in Tanzania, and at their request the President (himself a practising Catholic) addressed a Congress of Maryknoll Sisters which was in session at that time. This address has been widely circularized, in the original and in many translations.

Poverty is not the real problem of the modern world. For we have the knowledge and resources which could enable us to overcome poverty. The real problem—the thing which creates misery, wars and hatred among men—is the division of mankind into rich and poor.

We can see this division at two levels. Within nation states there are a few individuals who have great wealth and whose wealth gives them great power; but the vast majority of the people suffer from varying degrees of poverty and deprivation. Even in a country like the United States, this division can be seen. In countries like India, Portugal or Brazil, the contrast between the wealth of a few privileged individuals and the dire poverty of the masses is a crying scandal.

And looking at the world as a collection of nation states, we see the same pattern repeated. There are a few wealthy nations which dominate the whole world economically, and therefore politically; and a mass of smaller and poor nations whose destiny, it appears, is to be dominated.

The significance about this division between the rich and the poor is not simply that one man has more food than he can eat, more clothes than he can wear and more houses than he can live in, while others are hungry, unclad and homeless. The significant thing about the division between rich and poor nations 'is not simply that one has the resources to provide comfort for all its citizens, and the other cannot provide basic services. The reality and depth of the problem arises because the man who is rich has power over the lives of those who are poor, and the rich nation has power over the policies of those which are not rich. And, even more important, is that our social and economic system, nationally and internationally, supports these divisions and constantly increases them, so that the rich get ever richer and more powerful, while the poor get relatively poorer and less able to control their own future.

This continues despite all the talk of human equality, the fight against poverty, and of development. Still the rich individuals within nations, and the rich nations within the world, go on getting richer very much faster than the poor overcome their poverty. Sometimes this happens through the deliberate decision of the rich, who use their wealth and their power to that end. But often—perhaps more often—it happens 'naturally' as a result of the normal workings of the social and economic systems men have constructed for themselves. Just as water from the driest regions of the earth ultimately flows into the oceans where water is already plentiful, so wealth flows from the poorest nations and the poorest individuals into the hands of those nations and those individuals who are already wealthy. A man who can afford to buy only one loaf of bread a day contributes to the profit accruing to the owner of the bakery, despite the fact that the owner already has more money than he knows how to use. And the poor nation which sells its primary commodities on the world market in order to buy machines for development finds that the prices it obtains, and the prices it has to pay, are both determined by the 'forces of the free market' in which it is a pigmy competing with giants.

'For he that hath, to him shall be given; and he that hath not, that also which he hath shall be taken away from him.'

Both nationally and internationally this division of mankind into the tiny minority of rich, and the great majority of poor, is rapidly becoming intolerable to the majority—as it should be. The poor nations and the poor peoples of the world are already in rebellion against it; if they do not succeed in securing change which leads towards greater justice, then that rebellion will become an explosion. Injustice and peace are in the long run incompatible; stability in a changing world must mean ordered change towards justice, not mechanical respect for the *status quo*.

It is in this context that development has been called another name for peace. It is this context which gives urgency to your deliberations on participation in the development of peoples.

MAN IS THE PURPOSE

The purpose of development is man. It is the creation of conditions, both material and spiritual, which enables man the individual, and man the species, to become his best. That is easy for Christians to understand because Christianity demands that every man should aspire towards union with God through Christ. But although the Church—as a consequence of its concentration upon man—avoids the error of identifying development with new factories, increased output, or greater national income statistics, experience shows that it all too often makes the opposite error. For the representatives of the Church, and the Church's organizations, frequently act as if man's development is a personal and 'internal' matter, which can be divorced from the society and the economy in which he lives and earns his daily bread. They preach resignation; very often they appear to accept as immutable the social, economic, and political framework of the present-day world. They seek to ameliorate intolerable conditions through acts of love and of kindness where the beneficiary of this love and kindness remains an 'object'. But when the victims of poverty and oppression begin to behave like men and try to change those conditions, the representatives of the Church stand aside.

My purpose today is to suggest to you that the Church should accept that the development of peoples means rebellion. At a given and decisive point in history men decide to act against those conditions which restrict their freedom as men. I am suggesting that, unless we participate actively in the rebellion against those social structures and economic organizations which condemn men to poverty, humiliation and degradation, then the Church will become irrelevant to man and the Christian religion will degenerate into a set of superstitions accepted by the fearful. Unless the Church, its members and its organizations, express God's love for man by involvement and leadership in constructive protest against the present conditions of man, then it will become identified with injustice and persecution. If this happens, it will die—and, humanly speaking, deserve to die—because it will then serve no purpose comprehensible to modern man.

For man lives in society. He becomes meaningful to himself and his fellows only as a member of that society. Therefore, to talk of the development of man, and to work for the development of man, must mean the development also of that kind of society which serves man, which enhances his well-being, and preserves his dignity. Thus, the development of peoples involves economic development, social development, and political development. And at this time in man's history, it must imply a divine discontent and a determination for change. For the present condition of men must be unacceptable to all who think of an individual person as a unique creation of a living God. We say man was created in the image of God. I refuse to imagine a God who is poor, ignorant, superstitious, fearful, oppressed, wretched—which is the lot of the majority of those He created in his own image. Men are creators of themselves and their conditions, but under present conditions we are creatures, not of God, but of our fellow men.

Surely there can be no dispute among Christians about that. For mankind has never been so united or so disunited; has never had such power for good nor suffered under such evident injustices. Man's capacity has never been so clear, nor so obviously and deliberately denied.

The world is one in technological terms. Men have looked down on the Earth from the Moon and seen its unity. In jet planes I can travel from Tanzania to New York in a matter of hours. Radio waves enable us to talk to each other—either in love or abuse—without more than a few seconds elapsing between our speech and the hearing of it. Goods are made which include materials and skills from all over the world—and are then put up for sale thousands of miles from their place of manufacture.

Yet at the same time as the interdependence of man is increased through the advance of technology, the divisions between men also expand at an ever-increasing rate. The national income per head in the United States is said to be more than $3,200 a year; in Tanzania it is approximately $80—that is, it would take a Tanzanian 40 years to earn what an American earns in one year, and we are not the poorest nation on earth. Further, it has been estimated that, while the rich countries are adding approximately 60 dollars a year to the *per capita* income of their citizens, the average increase of *per capita* income in the poor countries is less than 2 dollars per year. It has been estimated that up to 500 million people on the earth today are suffering from hunger—from never having enough to eat. Further, one out of every two of the world's peoples is suffering from malnutrition—from deficiencies of protein or other essential health-giving foods. And finally, let me remind you that even within the wealthiest countries of the world, the misery and oppression of poverty is experienced by thousands, or even millions, of individuals, families and groups.

So the world is not one. Its peoples are more divided now, and also more conscious of their divisions, than they have ever been. They are divided between those who are satiated and those who are hungry. They are divided between those with power and those without power. They are divided between those who dominate and those who are dominated; between those who exploit and those who are exploited. And it is the minority which is well fed, and the minority which has secured control over the world's wealth and over their fellow men. Further, in general, that minority is distinguished by the colour of their skins and by their race. And the nations in which most of that minority of the world's people live have a further distinguishing characteristic—their adoption of the Christian religion.

These things cannot continue, and Christians, above all others, must refuse to accept them. For the development of men, and the development of peoples, demands that the world shall *become* one and that social justice shall *replace* the present oppressions and inequalities.

MAN IS A MEMBER OF SOCIETY

In order to achieve this, there must be economic development and equitable distribution of wealth. The poor nations, the poor areas and the poor peoples must be enabled to increase their output; through fair distribution they must be enabled to expand their consumption of the goods which are necessary for decency and for freedom.

For what is required is not simply an increase in the national income figures of the poor countries, nor a listing of huge increases in the production of this crop or that industry. New factories, roads, farms, and so on, are essential; but they are not enough in themselves. The economic growth must be of such a kind, and so organized, that it benefits the nations and the peoples who are now suffering from poverty. This means that social and political development must go alongside economic development—or even precede it. For unless society is so organized that the people control their own economies and their own economic activity, then economic growth will result in increased injustice because it will lead to increased inequality, both nationally and internationally. Those who control a man's livelihood control a man; his freedom is illusory and his equal humanity is denied when he depends upon others for the right to work and to eat. Equally, a nation is not independent if its economic resources are controlled by another nation; political independence is meaningless if a nation does not control the means by which its citizens can earn their living.

In other words, the development of peoples follows from economic development only if this latter is achieved on the basis of the equality and human dignity of all those involved. And human dignity cannot be given to a man by the kindness of others. Indeed it can be destroyed by kindness which emanates from an action of charity. For human dignity involves equality and freedom, and relations of mutual respect among men. Further, it depends on responsibility, and on a conscious participation in the life of the society in which a man moves and works.

The whole structure of national societies and of international society is therefore relevant to the development of peoples. And there are few societies which can now be said to serve this purpose; for there are few—if any—which both accept, and are organized to serve, social justice in what has been called the Revolution of Rising Expectations.

Certainly it is difficult to argue that the societies in which the Catholic Church operates, and has most influence, are organized for social justice; it is impossible to demonstrate that these societies serve social justice. Under capitalism the greatest advances in technology and economic growth have been achieved. But the decisions as to what goods shall be produced, and how they shall be produced, are made by a small number of people who have obtained control over land and capital. And the determining factor in all their decision-making is whether the activity will yield a monetary profit, or power, or prestige, to them as owners of the land or capital. The needs of mankind are secondary, if they are considered at all. There is 'no profit' in producing cheap houses, so they are not produced; there is 'no money' for schools and hospitals. But luxury apartments can be built, and six-lane highways; for these things money can be found. And the result is a few men living in great luxury, using the wealth produced by man for their own grandeur and to ensure their own power. At the same time masses of men, women and children are reduced to beggary, squalor, and to the humiliation of that disease and soul-destroying insecurity which arises out of their enforced poverty.

Let us be quite clear about this. If the Church is interested in man as an individual, it must express this by its interest in the society of which those individuals are members. For men are shaped by the circumstances in which they live. If they are treated like animals, they will act like animals. If they are denied dignity, they will act without dignity. If they are treated solely as a dispensable means of production, they will become soulless 'hands', to whom life is a matter of doing as little work as possible and then escaping into the illusion of happiness and pride through vice.

Therefore, in order to fulfil its own purpose of bringing men to God, the Church must seek to ensure that men can have dignity in their lives and in their work. It must itself become a force of social justice and it must work with other forces of social justice wherever they are, and whatever they are called. Further, the Church must recognize that men can only progress and can only grow in dignity by working for themselves, and working together for their common good. The Church cannot uplift a man; it can only help to provide the conditions and the opportunity for him to co-operate with his fellows to uplift himself.

THE MEANING OF SERVICE TODAY

What does this mean for those who give their lives to the service of the Church?

First, it means that kindness is not enough; piety is not enough; and charity is not enough. The men who are now suffering from poverty, whether they are in the Third World or in the developed world, need to be helped to stretch themselves; they need to be given confidence in their own ability to take control of their own lives. And they need to be helped to take this control, and to use it themselves for their own purposes. They need their uhuru, and meaningful uhuru. This is important to the Church, as well as to mankind. For until men are in a position to make effective choices, few of them will become Christians in anything but name. Their membership of the Church will be simply another method by which they seek to escape from a consciousness of their misery; if you like, religion becomes a kind of opium of the people.

Everything which prevents a man from living in dignity and decency must therefore be under attack from the Church and its workers. For there is, in fact, nothing saintly in imposed poverty, and, although saints may be found in slums, we cannot preserve slums in order to make them breeding grounds for saints. A man who has been demoralized by the conditions under which he is forced to live is no use to himself, to his family, or to his nation. Whether he can be of much use to God is not for me to judge.

The Church has to help men to rebel against their slums; it has to help them do this in the most effective way it can be done. But most of all the Church must be obviously and openly fighting all those institutions, and power groups, which contribute to the existence and maintenance of the physical and spiritual slums— regardless of the consequences to itself or its members. And, wherever and however circumstances make it possible, the Church must work with the people in the positive tasks of building a future based on social justice. It must participate actively in initiating, securing, and creating, the changes which are necessary and which will inevitably take place.

Only by doing these things can the Church hope to reduce hatred and promote its doctrine of love to all men. Its love must be expressed in action against evil, and for good. For if the Church acquiesces in established evils, it is identifying itself and the Christian religion with injustice by its continuing presence.

Secondly, the members of the Church must work with the people. It may sound odd to be saying this to the Maryknoll Sisters, but it is important that we should stress the working with, not the working for. For it is not the task of religious leaders to try to tell people what they should do. What is necessary is sharing on the basis of equality and common humanity. Only by sharing work, hardships, knowledge, persecution, and progress, can the Church contribute to our growth. And this means sharing in every sense as 'members one of another'. For if the Church is not part of our poverty, and part of our struggle against poverty and injustice, then it is not part of us.

I think another changing function of religious members is in relation to the social services. In many areas of the world—and particularly in Africa—the Catholic Church has built its own schools and its own hospitals. These have been invaluable; they have provided education and medical care when there would otherwise have been none. But I believe that such provision should be an interim measure, and that, wherever possible, the Church members should be working with, and through, the organizations owned and controlled by the people themselves. Nuns and brothers should be working in state schools and nursing in state hospitals; they should be District Nurses in a national, regional or city structure. By adopting this kind of policy wherever it is possible the Church will be showing that its purpose is service to the people, and not control over them. By separating the provision of service from its evangelical activities, the Church will make clear that it desires men's conversion to Christianity to come from conviction, not from gratitude or from the compulsion of indebtedness.

Finally, I believe that members of religious organizations must encourage and help the people to co-operate together in whatever action is necessary for their development. What this will mean in practice will vary from one country to another, and from one part of a country to another part. Sometimes it will mean helping the people to form and to run their own co-operative villages. Sometimes it will mean helping the people to form their own trade unions—and not Catholic trade unions, but trade unions of workers regardless of religion. Sometimes it will mean the Church leaders involving themselves in nationalist freedom movements and being part of those movements. Sometimes it will mean co-operating with local governments or other authorities; sometimes it will mean working in opposition to established authorities and powers. Always it means the Church being on the side of social justice and helping men to live together and work together for their common good.

Let us admit that, up to now, the record of the Church in these matters has not been a good one. The countries which we immediately think of as Catholic countries are not those in which the people enjoy human dignity, and in which social justice prevails' Nor are they countries in which there has been great economic progress. The Church is not without influence in Latin America; I am told that one-third of all the Catholics of the world live in that sub-continent. Yet we do not associate that part of the world with progress and social justice. On the contrary, the conditions of poverty, of exploitation, and misery, in Latin American countries are too well known to require comment from me. Spain, where the Church is powerful, is not a paragon of freedom and justice. It may not be completely irrelevant to mention also that Italy and France have the largest Communist Parties in the Western World. All these things are a reflection of failure on the part of the Catholic Church, its leaders, and its workers.

There are priests (and sometimes bishops) in many countries of Latin America, Jesuit brothers and lay priests in Spain, priests and bishops in Rhodesia and South Africa, and some in other countries of the world, who work with the people and speak for them. Some of these priests have been assassinated, some have been imprisoned, some have been tortured; some, unfortunately, have been dismissed or re-located by the Church hierarchy. But all of them are redeeming the reputation of Catholicism and organized Christianity, and are showing what can be done and what must be done, even if it is at the cost of great sacrifice. Their work is invaluable; but we have to admit that they are too few and have much leeway to make up.

For until quite recently the Church was silent on the great issues of man in society, or even sided with those whose exclusive concern was their own power and the accumulation of riches. Even now, despite the teachings of Pope John and Pope Paul, and the deliberations of the Second Vatican Council, the most usual practice of the Church is the upholding of the established order—regardless of its implications. It is this practice which we have now to change. For these individual Churchmen and women who are working for social justice need the comfort and support of the whole Church in their suffering for the teachings of Christ. They are acting according to the dictates of their conscience and, in doing so, they are showing us the way forward. But all too often they find that they have to work in isolation from their Catholic brethren. They find that the whole Church has not yet committed itself to justice here on earth.

In the Portuguese colonies in Africa we see the same thing. For centuries the Church has, without protest, accepted forced labour, torture, exploitation and alien domination Even now the Church refuses to speak up against the colonialism and oppression in Mozambique, Angola and Guinea Bissau. It is true that in recent months His Holiness has received in audience three of the nationalist leaders; but this is only a beginning. Unless it is followed up by open speech and by action, the identification of the Catholic Church with Portuguese tyranny will continue.

I am not asking that the Church should surrender its functions or allow itself to be identified with particular political parties or political doctrines. On the contrary, what I am saying amounts to a demand that it should stop allowing itself to be identified with unjust political and economic power groups. For the Church should want to be identified with the pursuit of social justice. And that is what I am asking you to promote. The poor and the oppressed should come to you not for alms, but for support against injustice.

CO-OPERATION WITH NON-CATHOLICS

It is necessary to recognize, however, that others—non-Catholics and non-Christians—will also be working to promote social justice; we have no monopoly of virtue! We must not be afraid of this. On the contrary, we should welcome other workers for justice. It is not necessary to agree with everything a man believes, or says, in order to work with him on particular projects or in particular areas of activity. The Church must stand up for what it believes to be right; that is its justification and purpose. But it should welcome all who stand on the same side, and continue regardless of which individuals or groups it is then opposing.

A good does not become evil if a communist says it is a good; an evil does not become good if a fascist supports it. Exploiting the poor does not become a right thing to do because communists call it a wrong thing; production for profit rather than meeting human needs does not become more just because communists say it leads to injustice. Organizing the society in such a manner that people live together and work together for their common good does not become an evil because it is called socialism. A system based on greed and selfishness does not become good because it is labelled free enterprise. Let the Church choose for itself what is right and what is wrong in accordance with Christian principles, and let it not be affected by what other groups or individuals do or say. But let it welcome co-operation from all those who agree with its judgements.

> 'Then shall the king say to them that shall be on his right hand:
> Come, ye blessed of my Father, possess you the kingdom
> prepared for you from the foundation of the world.
> 'For I was hungry, and you gave me to eat; I was thirsty, and
> you gave me to drink; I was a stranger, and you took me in;
> Naked, and you covered me; sick, and you visited me; I was
> in prison, and you came to me.
> 'Then shall the just answer him, saying: Lord, when did we see
> thee hungry and fed thee; thirsty and gave thee drink? And
> when did we see thee a stranger and took thee in? And naked
> and covered thee? Or when did we see thee sick or in prison
> and came to thee?
> 'And the king answering shall say to them: Amen, I say to
> you, as long as you did it to one of these my least brethren,
> you did it to me.'

We know that we are fallible men and that our task is to serve, not to judge. Yet we accept into the Church (provided only that they come to mass every Sunday and pay their dues or contribute to missionary activities) those who create and maintain the present political and economic system. But it is this system which has led to millions being hungry, thirsty and naked; it is this system which makes men strangers in their own countries because they are poor, powerless and oppressed; it is this system which condemns millions to preventable sickness, and which makes prisoners of men who have the courage to protest. What right, then, have we to reject those who serve mankind, simply because they refuse to accept the leadership of the Church, or refuse to acknowledge the divinity of Jesus or the existence of God? What right have we to presume that God Almighty takes no notice of those who give dedicated service to those millions of His children who hunger and thirst after justice, just because they do not do it in His name? If God were to ask the wretched of the earth who are their friends, are we so sure that we know their answer? And is that answer irrelevant to those who seek to serve God?

> 'Not every one that saith to me, Lord, Lord, shall enter into the kingdom of heaven; but he that doth the will of my Father who is in heaven, he shall enter into the kingdom of heaven.
> 'Many will say to me in that day: Lord, Lord, have not we prophesied in thy name and cast out devils in thy name and done many miracles in thy name?
> 'And then will I profess unto them; I never knew you; depart from me, you that work iniquity.'

Yet this is not all. Just as we must not be afraid of working with men of different religious convictions or of none, nor must we allow ourselves to be frightened by new ideas, new plans, or new projects. The world needs new ideas, new organizations, as much as it needs to apply the truths of Christianity; indeed, we need new ways of applying these truths in the technological world of the twentieth century. It is the job of the Church to find these new paths forward, and to recognize them when they are pointed out by others. Fear of the future, and of the needs of the future, is no part of Christianity Ours is a Living Faith: if you like, a Revolutionary Faith, for faith without action is sterile, and action without faith is meaningless.

> 'I am come that they may have life and may have it more abundantly.'

THE ROLE OF THE CHURCH

What all this amounts to is a call to the Church to recognize the need for social revolution, and to play a leading role in it. For it is a fact of history that almost all the successful social revolutions which have taken place in the world have been led by people who were themselves beneficiaries under the system they sought to replace. Time and again members of the privileged classes have joined, and often led, the poor or oppressed in their revolts against injustice. The same thing must happen now.

Within the rich countries of the world the beneficiaries of educational opportunity, of good health, and of security, must be prepared to stand up and demand justice for those who have up to now been denied these things. Where the poor have already begun to demand a just society, at least some members of the privileged classes must help them and encourage them. Where they have not begun to do so, it is the responsibility of those who have had greater opportunities for development to arouse the poor out of their poverty-induced apathy. And I am saying that Christians should be prominent among those who do this, and that the Church should seek to increase the numbers and the power of those who refuse to acquiesce in established injustices.

The same is true as regards the international scene. The poor and backward countries are beginning to speak up, and to protest against their condition. But they gain strength and effectiveness because of countries like the Scandinavian nations and Canada, which are beginning to recognize the insecurity and the injustice of their wealth in a world of poverty, and which are beginning to take a leading part in urging change.

I am saying that the Church should join with these nations and, if possible, help to increase their number. I am saying that it should be one of the group of nations and institutions which reject domination by the rich for the benefit of the rich. And it should be the function of Church members in wealthy countries to enlarge the group opposed to international exploitation of the poor and oppression of the weak.

Only by its activities in these fields can the Church justify its relevance in the modern world. For the purpose of the Church is man—his human dignity, and his right to develop himself in freedom. To the service of man's development, any or all of the institutions of any particular society must be sacrificed if this should be necessary. For all human institutions, including the Church, are established in order to serve man. And it is the institution of the Church, through its members, which should be leading the attack on any organization, or any economic, social, or political structure which oppresses men, and which denies to them the right and power to live as the sons of a loving God.

In the poor countries the Church has this same role to play. It has to be consistently and actively on the side of the poor and unprivileged. It has to lead men towards godliness by joining with them in the attack against the injustices and deprivation from which they suffer. It must co-operate with all those who are involved in this work; it must reject alliances with those who represent mammon, and co-operate with all those who are working for man. Its members must go out as servants of the world, as men and women who wish to share their knowledge and their abilities with those whom they recognize as their brothers and their sisters in Christ.

Friends: there was a time when the Christian Church was persecuted and its members held in contempt and derision. Are the societies in which the Catholic Church now operates so just, or so organized for the service of God and man, that it is unnecessary to risk a similar rejection in the pursuit of social justice? I do not believe so. I believe with Teilhard de Chardin that: 'A Christian can joyfully suffer persecution in order that the world may grow greater. He can no longer accept death on the charge that he is blocking mankind's road.'

Reverend Chairman: it is appropriate that I should conclude with two quotations from the Encyclical Letter of His Holiness Pope Paul VI on the Development of Peoples:

'If someone who has the riches of this earth sees his brother in need and closes his heart to him, how does the love of God abide in him?
... To quote St. Ambrose: "You are not making a gift of your possessions to the poor person, you are handing over to him what is his. For what has been given in common for the use of all you have arrogated to yourself...."
'That is private property does not constitute for anyone an absolute and unconditioned right. No one is justified in keeping for his exclusive use what he does not need, when others lack necessities....'

Later the same Letter says:

'To wage war on misery and to struggle against injustice is to promote, along with improved conditions, the human and spiritual progress of all men, and therefore the common good of humanity. Peace cannot be limited to a mere absence of war, the result of an ever-precarious balance of forces. No, peace is something that is built up day after day, in the pursuit of an order intended by God, which implies a more perfect form of justice among men.'

30

Choosing a Representative

In October 1970, Presidential elections were held throughout Tanzania, and Parliamentary and Council elections were held on the mainland. In a broadcast, on 24 October, President Nyerere spoke of the importance of the election and the meaning of it in Tanzania's one-party system.

... The choice before the voter is a very real one and a very important one. For TANU's policies are broad, and cover many aspects of politics and economics. It is inevitable, therefore, that each individual candidate, as well as each voter, will be more interested in one aspect of TANU policy than in another aspect. There is nothing wrong with this; on the contrary, it is a good thing. We need people with different interests and different kinds of knowledge in our Parliament and in our Councils. For deciding that we want to build socialism on the basis of self-reliance in Tanzania is only the beginning; it only settles the direction in which we shall move. Afterwards our Councils and our Parliament have continually to make new decisions about *how* we shall move to socialism. ...

... Thinking about their particular interest in different aspects of policy will help you to decide which of the candidates, in Parliamentary or in Local Government elections, you think best expresses your own interests and your own desires. But I hope that both candidates in each election will be intelligent enough to recognize that not everything can be done at once, and that nothing in this world is free. For the fact is that, if a person is urging more communal services or better communal services, he or she is probably also urging that you, as the voters, should be willing to pay more local rates or more taxes. For if they are promising lots of new activities if they are elected, and if they are promising that all these will be done without any cost to you, or effort on your part, they are either deliberately misleading you—thinking you are fools—or they themselves are fools. We can develop ourselves but we cannot do it without work and sacrifice, and we cannot achieve development overnight.

There is another thing which is worth remembering when considering how to vote. A good TANU supporter or a good candidate must be loyal to the Party, and accept the decisions made according to the TANU Constitution. But it is not necessary that he or she should agree with everything which is proposed by an established TANU leader, or even by the National Executive. Nor does he have to applaud everything which we have done—for we have inevitably made some mistakes. TANU members must act in accordance with TANU's decisions, but they can still argue that these decisions should be changed. For TANU's policies will remain alive and responsive to the people's needs only if TANU members and TANU candidates can criticize the execution of TANU policies, and also the priorities which we have up to now given to different aspects of those policies. We need a Parliament, and District Councils, which are made up of honest and loyal people; but we also want their members to have ideas of their own and to be capable of arguing about how best we can fulfil our socialist objectives. A Council or a Parliament full of people who can only say 'yes', 'yes', to other people's ideas would not help our progress or our democracy. . . .

Under our one-party system, only two people can stand for each position, so the TANU District Councils and the National Executive Committee had to decide which two of the people nominated were, in their opinion, the most able or the most suitable. Even so, when you hear the candidates addressing meetings, or from your own private knowledge, you may feel that one of the candidates is a more genuine person, and more selfless than the other. Or you may come to believe that one will be better able to express his views, or better able to work through the national machinery of administration in the service of his ward or his constituency, and of our nation. It is so that you may be able to come to such decisions that the election campaign is organized.

All these things a voter should think about when he is deciding whom to vote for. But the vote is secret. You do not need to tell anyone how you intend to vote or how you have voted. Of course, if anyone offers you money for your vote, he should be immediately reported; similarly, if he offers any goods or advantage to you, on condition that you give him your support. Again, if any candidate tries to get an advantage by organizing a private campaign, voters would be well advised to think whether such a person is sufficiently honest and trustworthy to be entitled to the responsibility of Council or Parliamentary office. Under our system, candidates for election are supposed to work only in, and through, the official campaign which is organized by TANU. It is only through this means— through the public meetings and through the written material which is circulated by TANU—that he should be seeking your vote.

None of this means that you cannot discuss the different candidates with your friends, if you wish to do so. And if you, as an individual who has listened to the two candidates, wish to explain to others who were not at a meeting why you think one is better than the other, this is your right as a citizen. But it is also your right to refuse to discuss the candidates, or to refuse to say how you will vote. The vote is secret. . . .

You are not being asked to give a vote of thanks for past service when you cast your vote in the polling booth on 30 October. You are being asked to give a vote of confidence in the ability of the candidate to serve you in the future. A very good person may, in your opinion, now be too old, or too sick, to do as good a job for the next five years as he did in the past. The past is one indication of a person's ability to serve, but it is not everything. . . .

But leadership should not be treated like the wearing of clothes. . . .

An election is not like an opportunity to buy from a new selection of khanga. With your votes you are choosing people to lead our country for the coming five years. If you do not now have confidence in the previous leader, you can try another leader if you believe that he will be better. If your previous representative did his work well in the past period, and you have no reason to doubt that he will continue to work well in the future, and if it is not obvious that his opponent would be better, do not change your representative just for the sake of change. . . .

31

The Tanzania/Zambia Railway

The building of the railway between Dar es Salaam in Tanzania, and Kapiri Mposhi in Zambia, was inaugurated at twin ceremonies in October 1970. President Kaunda of Zambia spoke at Dar es Salaam before the two Presidents and their Chinese guests flew to Kapiri Mposhi, where President Nyerere spoke on 28 October.

. . . It has been left to the independent states of Zambia and Tanzania to bring to fruition a project which has been talked about for many years. For it was in 1947 that the idea of a railway linking what was then Northern Rhodesia and what was then Tanganyika was first considered. As early as 1952, preliminary economic and engineering reports were completed: one of these was prepared by the East African Railways and Harbours and showed this link to be both possible and worthwhile. Yet nothing happened. Only under pressure from the nationalist movements of our two countries, and after Tanganyika had become independent, was there any progress at all. Then, when it became clear that a UNIP Government would soon be able to act on this matter, the colonial government of Northern Rhodesia asked for a World Bank Report on the question. The World Bank Commission, however, was given terms of reference which virtually prejudged the issue; the result was the only adverse report there has ever been on the economic feasibility of this project.

Fortunately neither Tanzania nor Zambia has ever faltered in the conviction that a railway link between our two countries is of the utmost importance. Our two governments were determined that it should be constructed. We knew that, in the long run, the unity of Africa requires that our continent should be linked by railway lines from north to south. We knew also that linking Zambia with the north is vital for the security of free Africa—and especially vital for our two frontier states.

Developments in Southern Africa, and particularly the unilateral declaration of independence by the Smith régime in Rhodesia, did, however, make this project very urgent. For a railway link with the port of Dar es Salaam is vital for the full implementation of Zambia's policy of linking herself to the free African states to the north. In colonial times Zambia had communications only with the countries of Southern Africa. Despite the fact that Tanganyika was also administered by the British Government, no links at all had been created between our two countries; even the road was designed only for light traffic during dry weather. Consequently, when the Smith rebellion of November 1965 was met by a policy of economic sanctions, the most immediate result was grave problems for newly independent Zambia.

But despite all the difficulties of its economic and communications inheritance, Zambia responded whole-heartedly to the African decision to boycott Rhodesia. Of course, Zambia could not make her boycott immediately and 100 per cent effective. Of course, the immediate effect of reducing imports from Rhodesia to the very minimum had to be a temporary increase in the importation of goods from South Africa. But the people of this country, under the leadership of President Kaunda and UNIP, did more than anyone would have believed possible, and made sacrifices which few outsiders understand even now. Indeed, I am disgusted by those who were mainly responsible for Zambia's predicament, and who now, from thousands of miles away, dare to criticize the Government and people of this country for their actions at that time, and since. No one could have done more without causing chaos and collapse; only a fierce determination for freedom enabled this country to do as much as it did.

President Kaunda: those who dare to criticize what has been done by the people of your country towards the isolation of Rhodesia, and of South Africa, are beneath contempt. And when they not only ignore, but also oppose, all the efforts which Zambia is making to overcome the effects of its inheritance, and use Zambia's residual trade with Southern Africa as an excuse for actions which will strengthen the enemies of this country and of freedom, then words cannot express our feelings.

Of course, it is not only Zambia which will benefit when this railway line is completed. Tanzania will receive immediate and direct benefit too. It will gain—as Zambia will—by the increased trade which will be possible. It will gain through Zambia's use of Dar es Salaam harbour, rather than Portuguese-controlled Beira. It will also gain because this railway will reinforce the alliance for freedom which exists between our two countries, and which helps us both to withstand the pressures exerted upon us by the enemies of African dignity and African freedom.

Nor is this all. The whole of Africa will benefit from this railway. We shall benefit because it will strengthen Zambia and therefore strengthen the forces of freedom. We shall benefit because trade between different African countries will become easier, and thus the development of us all will increase. And in particular, the countries of Eastern Africa will benefit by the closer contact the railway will make possible. I would add that I believe this railway will make Zambia's membership of the East African Community even more natural—and mutually beneficial—than it already is.

Yet despite all these advantages, I have noticed one very odd thing about the international reactions to this railway project. It is that some of those nations which have had the effrontery to criticize Zambia for her residual trade with nations to the south, also criticize us for building this railway! They make it clear that they admit our right to build the railway. They sometimes even admit the obvious fact that only when the railway exists will Zambia be in a position to choose for herself with whom she trades, and through which country her goods pass. Thus—under pressure—they admit that a railway to the north will increase the reality of Zambia's freedom. Yet some of them also suggest that, by building this railway now, Tanzania and Zambia are coming under Chinese influence!

I can only respond to this suggestion by some amazement. First, is the fact that from 1918 to 1961 a Western country controlled both Tanzania and Zambia—surely that was long enough for them to have at least begun the railway they were talking about from 1942 onwards? Indeed, Western countries could have acceded to our requests for help with this project right up until 1965. They failed to do so. But more interesting—and in a way more frightening—is the self-revelation which this Western criticism implies. For this criticism implies that in their view aid is always an instrument of domination. And this criticism comes from those who dominated Africa and, in varying degrees, are still dominating Africa. The Chinese have no colonies in Africa or anywhere else in the world; and their present leadership, at least, is genuinely and fervently anti-imperialist; and so are we.

Therefore, let me make it absolutely clear—and in this I know I speak for the Governments and peoples of all our countries—we are extremely grateful to the Chinese People's Republic for their help in the railway project; we are grateful for the spirit in which the offer of assistance was made, and for the manner in which this assistance is being given. A railway is a railway; that is what we want, and that is what we are being helped to build. But there is something more; this railway will be our railway. It will not be a Chinese railway, because the Chinese are not building a Chinese railway! What is happening is that the People's Republic of China is giving us an interest-free loan of Shs. 2,865 million—that is, 286,500,000 kwacha—for the construction of the railway and the provision of rolling stock. Tanzania and Zambia will jointly repay this loan when it becomes due—but that will not be for some time after the railway has begun to contribute to the development of our economies. For, under the Agreement, we only begin repayment in 1983; we then continue to pay gradually until repayment is completed in the year 2012! These terms are more than generous; an interest-free loan, with a grace period of 15 years from 1968, and then payment over 30 years—this is real 'aid'. Thus, to say the very least, the Chinese people are not planning to make a profit from this railway. Indeed, they are making a gift to us, for it would be very expensive to borrow this amount of money at commercial rates of interest. Let me state quite clearly that we appreciate this loan, and we appreciate the fact that it is interest-free. We greatly appreciate all this help with the building of our railway. And—I repeat—the Chinese people have not asked us to become communists in order to qualify for this loan! They know that we would not sell our independence, even for the railway; and they have never at any point suggested that we should change any of our policies—internal or external—because of their help with this railway. They have simply offered us generous terms in money, and in men.

For there will be about 7,000 Chinese technicians working in either Tanzania or Zambia by December of this year. More than 4,000 are already here. I would like to express our welcome to these men and women—who have already shown us an example of hard work and dedication in the fulfilment of the jobs they have undertaken. Because of this number of technicians, the 1,900 kilometres of line will be built within six years, despite all the physical difficulties of the route.

I said that we welcome these technicians, and I want to emphasize that. For we are not afraid of the Chinese people who will be working here. Despite all the indoctrination we have had over a long period, we believe that the Chinese people are human beings, not ogres.

Of course we shall learn from the Chinese technicians who will be working in Tanzania and Zambia. We hope to learn their technical skills—and experience in Tanzania has shown us that they are willing to teach these technical skills. Further, we hope to learn something of the history and the ideas of the Chinese people. For the world needs unity in its diversity; and it needs international understanding between peoples of different backgrounds, different political beliefs, different religions and different histories. Indeed, we believe that the peoples of Zambia and Tanzania, and the Chinese people who are working here, will all learn from each other. And we believe that friendship between a great nation and two small nations will be increased because of this contact. Certainly I hope that this will happen, for we need friendship between Africa and the people of China, just as we do between Africa and the peoples of other continents.

To suggest that this means Tanzania and Zambia are going to be hostile to Western countries is absurd. The railway has, and will have, nothing whatever to do with our attitude to the countries of Europe and America. Our attitude towards each country in the world is determined only by its actions towards Africa and towards world peace. It is not determined by our need for aid, nor by the help that we get. As we in Tanzania and Zambia have said many times, we want to be friendly with all nations and we allow no one to choose our enemies for us.

Yet we in Africa do have an enemy—our enemy is the racialism and colonialism which now exist in Southern Africa. Our hostility to the apartheid régime of South Africa, and that of Rhodesia, and our hostility towards Portuguese colonialism, is neither increased nor decreased by the building of this railway. Of course, the fact that Southern Africa is not free does make one important difference to this railway project. For if the peoples of Southern Africa were governing themselves, they would be represented at this meeting today, and they would be joining in our happiness at this development. As it is, we know that the régimes to the south bitterly oppose the building of this railway, because of the strength its completion will give to Zambia, to Tanzania, and Africa as a whole. For they do not want us to become strong; they want us to be their puppets.

For this reason it is important that we understand one thing. It is quite likely that the agents of the Southern Africa régimes will intensify their efforts to sabotage our freedom and our work. It is therefore essential that, throughout the construction period, and when the railway is completed, all the peoples of Tanzania, and of Zambia, should accept a responsibility for guarding this railway. We must guard it against sabotage, and we must also guard it against the effects of hostile propaganda. For the governments of the south could achieve their objectives by political subversion and by spreading disunity, just as well as by placing high explosives on the line. It is up to us to ensure that neither of these things happens. And in particular, it is up to us to ensure that the unity within Zambia, and the unity within Tanzania, remains firm. We have to make certain that no one succeeds in driving a wedge between Tanzania and Zambia on the one hand, and the people of China on the other.

I do not believe that attempts to divide our peoples will succeed. For many years agents of Southern Africa have tried hard to cause chaos in Zambia, and they have failed. They have tried to spread dissension between Zambia and Tanzania, and they have failed. In both cases I believe they will continue to fail. The same kinds of people have also tried to undermine the negotiations between our two countries and China. In this, too, they have so far failed. I say 'so far', because they continue in many ways—some crude, some subtle—to try to cause dissension between our two countries and China. They must continue to fail.

For it was September 1967, when the first Agreement was

signed between the three Governments, under which the People's Republic of China undertook to carry out detailed surveys for the design and construction of this railway. This Agreement was implemented so quickly that work had begun by December of that same year, although the official start was not until April 1968. These surveys were completed during the first half of 1970: since then preparations have been going ahead for the construction work.

Indeed, although we are celebrating the official beginning of the construction today, and although the Agreement for the interest-free loan was not finalized until July 1970; preliminary work has been going on since April 1970. Both the Chinese people and ourselves practised the slogan: 'Work first, words later', once the basic principle had been agreed. . . .

I have already said that Tanzania and Zambia have jointly received an interest-free loan of Shs. 2,865 million from the People's Republic of China. But I have also pointed out that this money has to be repaid. It is important that we should not be under any illusions about this. China is helping Zambia and Tanzania. But the responsibility remains ours. Ultimately it is the money of the peasants and workers of our two countries which will pay for this railway. How much they have to pay, and how effectively they are served, depends upon the workers on this project. It is important, therefore, that all of our citizens work as hard and as well as they are able to do, that they learn as much and as quickly as they can, and that they guard all the equipment against theft or misuse. This railway is a vital part of our economic development. Anyone who damages the work which we are undertaking today is damaging all the people of Tanzania, and of Zambia. . . .

We have done well up to now. . . .

But, of course, however hard we, in our two countries, had worked, this ceremony would not be taking place except for the warm and energetic co-operation of the Government and people of the Chinese People's Republic, under the leadership of Chairman Mao Tse Tung. China is not a rich country. It is a developing country. There is no question but that the equipment and skills which are being made available to us could have been used within China, and for the progress of the people of China. This we know; the help we are getting represents a real sacrifice of urgent needs. Our knowledge makes us even more appreciative of the generous help which is being given to us, so generously and so completely without political conditions.

Mr. Minister, I hope you will convey our very warm gratitude to Chairman Mao Tse Tung, to your Government, and to all the citizens of the People's Republic of China. We accept their help in the spirit in which it is given—as a gesture of international solidarity between the poor and the less poor of the world, and between China and Africa. I hope you will make it clear that words do not adequately convey our appreciation. Instead, we shall try to express it through our endeavours to speed the work which you are doing with us, and through our determination to use this railway for the exclusive benefit of the peasants and workers of Africa.

Friends, let us go forward together. Let us build the future now.

32

East African Co-operation is Alive

When laying the foundation stone of the Soroti Pilot Training School in Uganda on 27 November 1970, President Nyerere spoke of the need to acclaim the successes of East African Co-operation.

... In fact, most of the work of the East African Community does not show very quickly, and least of all can it be judged by buildings. For the Community is not a matter of buildings. It is a matter of working together, of planning together, of harmonizing our national development, and of running joint services. And all these things are going on all the time.

It is true we hear a lot about the problems of the East African Community. And indeed they do exist! It would be quite possible for some academic to write a book about them! But to what end? The thing about problems of international co-operation is that they get solved if the will to co-operate is there. In East Africa I think we can claim that this will for united action does exist, and that therefore our problems will gradually be overcome—and be replaced by new ones! For the partial surrender of national sovereignty to an East African body inevitably means difficulties; it means negotiation, argument—and compromise. All these things are a part of co-operation, and East Africans have always known it.

The trouble is that newspapers talk about difficulties much more than they talk about successes. Hard, steady work for unity is not exciting—it provides no headlines. Writing long letters, having long meetings, discussing terms, negotiating which of three countries shall have a particular headquarters within its territory, or a particular institution within its jurisdiction—all these things are hard, detailed work. And when a meeting takes place and reaches agreement, there is no news—or at most a few lines to be tucked into the bottom of a news column. But if the arguments get heated, and the meeting breaks up without coming to a decision at that time, then the dispute is news. That fact is a real problem if you like!

Do not let us be misled by this. The East African Community is succeeding. It is succeeding in practical everyday terms. Sometimes signs of its success become visible. The building of this School; the opening of the East African Telecommunications link; the scatter inter-communications link; new office buildings in different cities of East Africa; the new Headquarters at Arusha; and the decentralized administration of our common services: all these things are signs of that success. So, too—at a different level—is the increase in East African trade which took place in 1969—and which, I believe, is taking place again this year. For this expansion of trade is of fundamental importance, and is a direct consequence of the Treaty for East African Co-operation. So, too, is the fact that this inter-East African trade is becoming more balanced, and therefore of obvious benefit to all the participants.

Mr. President, all such things as this are successes. Why do we not talk about them more? Success breeds success—but not if it is unrecognized in the first place!

Let us remember, also, the East African Common Services. They are ours. Sometimes people talk as if the East African Airways, and the East African Railways, and the East African Posts and Telecommunications services belong to no one—they are just there! This is absurd. It is also dangerous. For the planes of East African Airways are our planes; it is our name which they carry to a large number of the international airports throughout the world. The East African Railways—with the 70 new diesel engines which have just been ordered—are our Railways; the line is ours, the engines are ours, the carriages are ours. The research stations, which exist throughout East Africa, are all of them ours. The Development Bank, which is already helping the establishment of industries in all three territories, is our Bank. All these things belong to us. We are responsible for their existence and we benefit from their work. It is important that we recognize this.

For all the things I have mentioned—and many more—mean that East Africans have a great deal to be proud of. So let us be proud! Why do we under-estimate our achievements? The fact that problems exist is in itself an achievement, for it is a sign of life. There is nothing which is worth doing which does not cause problems in the doing of it; there is nothing achieved which does not give rise to new problems as it creates a new situation. East African co-operation is alive; its problems are those of action, achievement, and advance.

33

South Africa
and the Commonwealth

On arrival at Singapore for the Commonwealth Conference in January 1971, President Nyerere circulated a document to all Heads of Government arguing the special responsibility of Commonwealth countries to refrain from selling arms to South Africa. The Conference spent a great deal of time on this subject and almost all countries expressed strong opposition to the proposed British arms sale. Although the Prime Minister gave no ground at the Conference, the British Government's later announcement referred only to 'legal obligations under the Simonstown Agreement'—which they said required the selling of a few helicopters. These had not in fact been sold up to April 1973.

At a press conference in the United States in December 1970, and as reported by the BBC, Prime Minister Heath said: 'The Commonwealth has always existed and worked on the basis that members respect each other's interests'. Tanzania certainly has no quarrel with that description of one aspect of the Commonweath. It implies a mutual responsibility between Commonwealth members, as well as the complete national sovereignty of every individual member to pursue his own country's interests. In other words, it is a recognition that, while every Commonwealth member has complete freedom to make its own decisions, each nation has also, by its membership, accepted an obligation to try to the best of its ability to pursue its own interests and needs in such a manner that its actions will not adversely affect the basic interests of other members.

This combination of complete freedom and inter-responsibility is an important and fundamental part of Commonwealth membership. There is one other. By the composition of the Commonwealth, one basic principle is implicitly accepted by every member. If we are not opposed to racialism, we have no business sitting down together in an association which consists of representatives of all the racial groups in the world.

The Commonwealth is based on the equality of all its members, despite our great inequality in wealth, in power, and in experience. Yet it remains true that, for historical reasons, the United Kingdom has, up to this time, a very special position in the Commonwealth. Its Queen is the Head of the Commonwealth. Economically and politically it is the most powerful member—the only one with permanent membership of the Security Council. And all other Commonwealth members were at one time governed by the United Kingdom; many of us have yet to celebrate a decade of independent existence. We are all equal members, all bound to consider the interests of others when making our own decisions; but we have reason to expect that the most powerful among us, whose actions are most likely to affect other members, will not make the least effort to harmonize her interests with those of her Commonwealth partners.

It is in this context that the British proposal to sell arms to South Africa has to be considered.

SOUTH AFRICA AND AFRICAN COMMONWEALTH COUNTRIES

The South African Government is a minority government elected by, and supported by, that group of its citizens who are defined, by South Africa, as white. The other four-fifths of its citizens are excluded from political and economic power. They suffer daily degradation, humiliation and discrimination in every sphere of life. They suffer these things not because of what they have done, or even what they believe, but simply for what they are. They suffer for being Africans, Indians or Coloureds, as defined by South Africa.

There is nothing accidental about the sufferings and the degradation of the non-white peoples of South Africa. They suffer because the South African Government, and the white people who elected that Government, are committed to racialism. White supremacy is to them a doctrine of faith—an ideology. The mass removals of non-white peoples from one part of the country to another; job reservation, which excludes non-whites from any skilled or semi-skilled jobs; 'influx control', which breaks up families of non-whites; the Group Areas Act; the Pass system; the allocation to the 70 per cent of the population who are Africans of 13.7 per cent of the land (with no land at all allocated to the 2 million Coloureds or the 600,000 Indians): all these things add up to a tyranny unequalled elsewhere in the world. And it is a tyranny based entirely on race, which is maintained by deliberate racial legislation combined with ruthless administration, and enforced by a Secret Service and a Police Force of a viciousness which has not been equalled since the days of Nazi Germany.

All this means that the South African régime is at war with the majority of its own people—with something like 83 per cent of them. And this 83 per cent have no choice in the matter at all. They cannot join the ruling group even if they are themselves racialists; they are for ever Africans, Coloureds or Indians, and therefore, according to the South African régime, they are for ever inferior and subject to the decisions of their white masters.

It is for this reason that the nations of Africa, in particular, are committed to absolute hostility to the South African régime. Even though we are living in free states ourselves, we cannot acquiesce in a system which denies our humanity, because it denies the humanity of our brothers on grounds of characteristics which we share. We are determined that Prime Minister Vorster and his supporters should be put in the dock of world opinion, and that they shall be condemned.

We make no apology for the fact that we want to see the present régime of South Africa overthrown. We want to see South Africa governed on the principles of humanity, with the equality of every citizen recognized regardless of his race or colour. In other words, we want to see the apartheid policy of South Africa replaced by a system which accepts the principle of human equality and which is working for the implementation of that principle. If anyone fails to understand the depths of Africa's feelings on this matter, then he does not understand apartheid, or he does not understand the reaction of people who have suffered from racial discrimination. It is, in fact, impossible for Africa to understand how anyone who really opposes racialism can fail to share Africa's hostility to the South African régime, even if they are not prepared to do anything against that régime.

For in reality South Africa is only a peculiarly African problem in the sense that it exists in the continent of Africa. It is true that the majority of the victims of apartheid are Africans; but there are also 600,000 South Africans of Indian descent, a few hundred South Africans of Chinese descent, and approximately 2 million people of mixed African, Indian and European descent. And on the other side, those imposing apartheid are Europeans who claim that their actions are in defence of a 'European Christian civilization' and the whiteness they share with the white people of Europe and America. Thus, all members of the Commonwealth could be expected to feel equally concerned about the evils of South African apartheid, because the humanity of all Commonwealth citizens is being questioned by the policy.

But it is not really enough to say that. For different members of the Commonwealth have different strengths, both in relation to each other and in relation to South Africa. African Commonwealth members—even taken together—are very weak compared with South African economic and military strength, and therefore compared with her international influence. Similarly, the economic, military and political strength of the African Commonwealth countries is miniscule in comparison with that of the old and white members of the Commonwealth, each of which is separately on a par with, or stronger than, South Africa. If, therefore, the problem of racial tyranny and the propagation of racialism by South Africa is of concern to us all, then it is not unreasonable to expect more action from the white Commonwealth members in helping to defeat this evil, than the non-white members are capable of mounting.

Britain, in particular, would seem to have a special responsibility in this matter. For although it would be absurd to blame the present-day British leaders for the actions of British Governments at the beginning of the twentieth century, it would be equally absurd for us not to recognize the lessons and the implications of the history of those years. In the first decade of this century, following wars between Britain and the Boers of South Africa, British Governments put all their energies into establishing good relations between the Boers on the one hand, and Britain together with South Africans of British descent on the other. In their exclusive concentration on that aspect of the problem, the interests of the African peoples were left to the protection of entrenched constitutional clauses, and the anticipated influence of the more 'liberal' Cape Province. The result we all know; it is this result we are dealing with now. This is not the fault of anyone at our Conference—it is doubtful whether any of us was even born at that time! But it does mean that we all, and Britain especially, have a responsibility to see that similar mistakes are not made again. This has been the background, and the lesson, which has caused Africa's continued pleading with Britain not to acquiesce in independence for Rhodesia except on the basis of majority rule. It is a further reason why one would expect Britain to avoid any action which could strengthen still more the South African régime which has developed out of that error. In fact, one would expect Britain to be helping to end the harm which was, perhaps inadvertently, done then—not because of any personal guilt about that past (which would be stupid) but simply in the spirit of putting right things which had gone badly wrong.

We in Tanzania do, of course, understand that Britain and some other members of the Commonwealth may not have the same order of foreign policy priorities as we do. Every government thinks first of the security of its own citizens and its own homeland. But we do expect that they will have South Africa's racialism on their list of priorities even if it is not at the top. For Tanzania, however, which borders a white-dominated state, opposition to racialism is, and must be, the very top priority of our foreign policy—and South Africa is the leading racialist state. Therefore, both because Commonwealth membership implies an endeavour to respect other members' interests, and because we believe that all Commonwealth nations are involved in this problem, we do feel that we have a right to ask that other Commonwealth countries should at least not make the African people's position relative to the South African régime worse than it already is. Only if their own very existence is under immediate and obvious threat would it be possible for us to understand how another member could think that an action which strengthens South Africa is compatible with their continued Commonwealth membership.

This attitude applies, of course, to arms supplies. For the selling of arms is something which a country does only when it wants to support and strengthen the régime or the group to whom the sale is made. Whatever restrictions or limits are placed on that sale, the sale of any arms is a declaration of support—an implied alliance of a kind. You can trade with people you dislike; you can have diplomatic relations with governments you disapprove of; you can sit in conference with those nations whose policies you abhor. But you do not sell arms without saying, in effect: 'In the light of the receiving country's known policies, friends, and enemies, we anticipate that, in the last resort, we will be on their side in the case of any conflict. We shall want them to defeat their enemies.'

BRITAIN'S NEED FOR THE SIMONSTOWN BASE

The British Government has said that it is considering the sale of arms because it needs the Simonstown Base for the defence of the Cape route. It says, further, that South Africa has the same interest in the Cape sea route and that, if Britain does not agree to sell arms, the South Africans may renounce the Agreement under which Britain can use the Simonstown Base.

Britain's need for Simonstown is a matter which only Britain can determine, because only Britain knows her own defence secrets. The fact that it is reported that no British ships are stationed in Simonstown now, and that her contribution to the defence of the Cape route at present consists of three naval officers and six ratings, is perhaps irrelevant to the fact that, under the Agreement, the Simonstown Base would be available to Britain in time of war. It does, however, suggest to the uninitiated that Britain's need at this time is not extreme. It is also difficult for the non-military mind to imagine that, if Britain was involved in a war with the Soviet Union, South Africa would side with the Soviet Union, or even fail to give Britain and her allies any facilities she needed to fight the Soviet Union effectively.

There are, however, other aspects to the Simonstown Agreements. First, they were negotiated in 1955—that is, before any African Commonwealth country was an independent state. Among the African members of the Commonwealth, Ghana obtained independence in 1957, Nigeria in 1960, Tanzania in 1961, and the others still later. In 1955, none of these developments was expected to happen so quickly. The Simonstown Agreement therefore refers to British and South African co-operation in the defence of Africa; it was also thought to have some relationship to Britain's Far Eastern colonies. But Britain is no longer responsible for the defence of Africa. And South Africa is the enemy of the rest of Africa, and of humanity in general.

Even leaving aside these considerations, the fact is that, under the Agreement, Britain's obligation to supply, and South Africa's obligation to purchase from Britain, certain naval equipment, expired in 1963. From 1964 up to 1970, South Africa has acquiesced in the continuation of the Simonstown Agreement despite the fact that Britain joined in the arms embargo called for by the United Nations in 1963.

CONTINUITY OF POLICY

The British Government has further argued that the supply of arms to South Africa now would not mark a major change in policy, but is merely a logical extension of practices about which African states have made no previous complaint. It is said that, although Britain undertook, in 1964, to ban the sale of arms to South Africa, she has in fact continued to sell spare parts, and has had military man-oeuvres with South Africa, in accordance with the Simonstown Agreements, throughout the period since 1955. It is said that if Africa did not, and does not, object to this, it is illogical to object to the sale of more naval weapons, and weapons intended by Britain to be used in defence of the sea routes.

The truth is, of course, that Africa has not liked these practices, and does not like them now. But we are very well aware of the problems of inheritance. African states themselves inherited many Agreements which they have since regretted but not felt able to renounce. Indeed, many African governments have themselves entered into Agreements which change of circumstances, or greater knowledge, has caused them to regret. It would therefore be un-realistic for us to complain, in 1970 or 1971, about Britain fulfilling the minimum of engagements with South Africa which she undertook in 1955. What we do expect, however, is that a government inheriting obligations which are contrary to its interests in changed circumstances, will do the minimum it is obliged to do, and will endeavour always to lift these obligations from its back.

And circumstances have changed. Africa is a different place now from what it was in 1955. South Africa has left the Commonwealth, and twelve free African states have joined it. During the same period the South African Government has intensified its attacks on the interests of the majority of its citizens, and has improved its capability for effective oppression of its non-white citizens.

There is also the developing situation as regards Namibia. In 1966 the United Nations General Assembly Resolution ended South Africa's right to administer that country, and established instead an eleven-nation council which has the task of transferring the administration to an independent Namibian government. Until now no concrete action has been taken to implement that Resolution, but this is not to say that it never will be taken. The Resolution certainly creates a different situation in this United Nations Trusteeship Territory from that which existed in 1955. Further, in July last year the Security Council (with Britain abstaining) passed a Resolution calling again upon all members to desist from the sale of arms or spare parts to South Africa. Canada has, since this Resolution, stopped the supply of spare parts, having previously stopped the sale of new arms.

On top of all this is the Rhodesian situation. Rhodesia is in rebellion against Britain; its administration is being carried on by an illegal régime. Britain has asked for, and received, United Nations' support for economic sanctions against Rhodesia. But the Rhodesian régime has been able to withstand the effect of those sanctions, and maintain its rebellion, because of the support which it receives from its two white-dominated neighbours—Portugal and South Africa. Further, the South African Government has its armed forces operating in Rhodesia, despite both formal and public protests by the British Government. Is it not ironic that, after this deliberate South African action against Britain and British interests, the British Government should now be considering selling arms to South Africa? One would have expected that the new Rhodesian situation by itself would have been sufficient for the British Government to view South Africa with the kind of suspicion which is incompatible with anything except the most formal of diplomatic relations.

In other words, the point about this current British proposal is that Britain is proposing to make a new commitment in new circumstances. It is ignoring all the changes which have taken place since 1955. It is ignoring the fact that its supply commitments of 1955 have been fulfilled; it is even ignoring the fact that, against its declared wishes, South African armed forces are now operating in a British colony.

Thus, Britain is saying that it still supports South Africa despite everything which has happened in South Africa and in Rhodesia since 1955. It is supporting it despite the failure of South Africa to make any response whatsoever to any of the representations which have been made by the British Government in opposition to apartheid and inhumanity, and it is still supporting it despite the fact that a large number of its Commonwealth partners have, as their first priority in international affairs, a commitment to the opposition against South Africa's racial doctrine.

The British Government has argued that, because it is only proposing to sell naval weapons, and weapons designed to be used in relation to naval warfare, the interests of the Africans and of Africa will not be affected by this sale. There are three points to be made in this connection. First, it is impossible to ensure that any particular weapon will not be used for a purpose different from that for which it was designed. Even submarines can be used to control the movement of freedom fighters along a coast, or to land spies or saboteurs in territory occupied by those you are fighting against. It is absolutely impossible for Britain to ensure that any weapons she supplies will not be used in South Africa's struggle against the freedom fighters, who are now operating in Rhodesia, Mozambique, Angola and Namibia, and who will one day operate in South Africa itself.

Secondly, ships can be used to intercept other ships. South African naval vessels could easily be used to intercept shipping destined for East African ports on the plea that these ships were, or may be, carrying supplies for the freedom fighters of Southern Africa. If this happens, is it still possible to say that Britain's arms supply is irrelevant to the conflict between Africa and the South African régime?

And thirdly, South Africa is the most heavily armed nation in the African continent. As we have seen, it could obtain arms from other countries. It is anxious to obtain British arms because it wants to commit Britain publicly to its support. It is for this same reason that African Commonwealth members are so concerned that Britain should not supply arms to South Africa. Even though we have so far failed to prevent South Africa getting supplies from other countries, like France, we do not expect that a country officially committed to non-racialism, as Britain is both by its membership of the Commonwealth and by the declarations of successive Prime Ministers, will give this kind of moral support to racialism incarnate.

DEFENCE NEEDS

Britain has, however, explained that she is considering this proposal because she is worried about her defence interests in the Indian Ocean. She has pointed to the existence of increasing numbers of Soviet naval ships, and clearly feels worried by the effect of this Soviet presence. The worry has been expressed in both military and political terms; that is to say, it has been suggested that the Soviet Union may interfere with British shipping and, alternatively, that the presence of Soviet ships in the Indian Ocean will incline those nations which border the Indian Ocean to be more receptive to political pressure from the Soviet Union just because of the presence of these ships.

The first question which African states are forced to ask is how worried is Britain by this threat? Is it worried enough to make any defence efforts of its own? Or just worried enough to disregard the interests of her African Commonwealth partners? The second—and most important—question is what alternatives has Britain considered as a way of dealing with this anticipated threat? Has she considered alternative dispositions of her own naval forces? Has she discussed this problem with her allies outside the context of South African sales? Has she asked the Commonwealth to discuss the problem which she sees, in any other way than in the context of the sale of arms to South Africa?

Tanzania, for example, is a non-aligned state. But we recognize that Britain and many other Commonwealth partners are members of different alliances. We accept as a fact that many of our Commonwealth partners feel threatened by the Soviet Union, or even by

China. Our failure to share these feelings in relation to ourselves does not mean that we are incapable of understanding them or the policies which other Commonwealth members have adopted. All that we are asking is that, in planning to counter moves by nations they fear, Commonwealth members should avoid strengthening a nation which is hostile to free Africa. For we in Tanzania are the enemies of the present régime in South Africa; and we fear South Africa because of our opposition to the régime in power there.

The threat we feel cannot be removed by assurances to us, whether given directly by South Africa, or by Britain about arms she is supplying to South Africa. For the basic quarrel which South Africa is involved in is a quarrel with her own people and with humanity; free African states are involved because of the Africanness we share with South African citizens. A non-aggression pact between South Africa and the free African states is therefore nonsense, or it is a betrayal. We independent states could be sure that South Africa would not attack us without a non-agression pact. All that we have to do is acquiesce in her racialism and in the subordinate position that Government has allocated to black and brown people. For us to sign a non-aggresion pact would, in fact, be tantamount to doing just these things.

LET US COMBINE OUR INTERESTS

Britain's reason for considering a proposal which would strengthen South Africa is said to be because of her desire to prevent the Soviet Union from extending its influence in the Indian Ocean area. But two African states border the Indian Ocean, and four border the Eastern Atlantic—another part of the Cape route. Some at least of these determine their foreign policy more by their opposition to South Africa than by any other single factor; to all, this is a very important element. If, then, those we have regarded as friends move from a position of comparative neutrality on this issue to a positive act in support of South Africa, we shall be forced to look again at all our international relations. For, compromise on the South African issue we cannot do. Nor can we do nothing in response to actions which further strengthen South Africa in its opposition to us.

Surely the British Government would be best serving its own interests if it tries to combine British interests with those of free Africa, and of those members of the Commonwealth who share our bitter hostility to racialism and colonialism? We do not believe it would be so difficult as all that. Commonwealth members normally start from a position of basic sympathy with each other and a desire to understand each other's problems, even if we cannot come to the same conclusion about the action which is necessary. Because of our past history, and because of our present circumstances, the African states want a secure and confident Britain, and a Britain which realizes, as we do, the role which she can play in the modern world. All that we ask is that she should not pursue her legitimate interests at the expense of ours.

In brief, the problem amounts to this. Britain believes that she has defence problems in the Indian Ocean. Africa lives in bitter opposition and hostility to South Africa. Britain and Africa are both members of the Commonwealth of Nations, which is based, as Mr. Heath said, on the principles of respect for each other's interests. The problem before us, therefore, is that of reconciling two interests which overlap. We in Africa believe that they can be reconciled, that Africa can accept Britain's defence needs if Britain accepts Africa's unalterable hostility to South Africa.

But if Britain is not willing to reconcile these two interests, and if supplying arms to South Africa means more to her than the interests of her Commonwealth partners, then responsibility for damage to the Commonwealth and for African hostility towards Britain will be clear. It will belong to the British Government. We all of us live in the world. We react to the actions of others as they react to ours. As Mr. Heath said in a different context, one action by one country can 'easily trigger off a chain reaction'. And in this case there can be no question of acting in ignorance of the importance with which other members of the Commonwealth regard this proposal.

But I do not believe that there has to be any allocation of responsibility for a chain of events which would damage many, if not all, of us. We can reconcile our interests if both sides wish to do so. And we in Tanzania do wish to do so. I am pleading for friendship with Britain because we in Tanzania value it. I am pleading for the Commonwealth because we believe in it and we need it. But we cannot, and we will not, abate our opposition to racialism for any purpose in the world. We have learned this from Britain too—that, even if you are alone, you do not give up your opposition to tyranny or your fight against it. And I do not want to believe that Britain is saying that tyranny is not tyranny when the victims are black or brown.

Africa and other active non-racialists have achieved some success in getting the world to understand the evil of apartheid and the need for international pressure against the South African régime. The United Nations support for an arms embargo is part of that success, and the incompleteness of that embargo in practice is a measure of the work which still has to be done. A reversal of British policy on the arms embargo would, however, mean more than a set-back, for Britain is a major power whose actions have international repercussions. Other developed nations would undoubtedly find that they, too, had a national interest in breaking the embargo. Then, instead of Africa and non-racialists elsewhere just having France to deal with, we should find that the arms embargo is completely non-existent. We should have to start all over again. But the time scale will not allow that; the cold war divisions of the world would get an irreversible hold on the African continent long before such an international agreement could be obtained for the second time. The British Government may not intend that what it calls its 'limited arms supply' should have the effect of smashing the embargo, and of introducing a new front to the cold war she is engaged in, but that will be the inevitable result of their action.

But, let me repeat something which has been said many times. There is no question about Britain's right to decide to sell arms to South Africa. No one questions her *right*. The decision is hers. No one does, or ever has, doubted that. The purpose of this paper, and of all Tanzania's previous communications on this subject, is to ask her to look for other means of solving the problem she feels faced with. We are not asking the British Government to ignore Britain's interests. We are asking that she should try to solve her problems in the context of her opposition to racialism. And we are saying that we believe this can be done; that we are anxious to do what we can to help within the context of our own basic principles.

Let the Commonwealth members sit together and work out our different problems without considering the needs or desires of this non-member—South Africa—whose basic doctrine of faith, and every action, is a denial of everything the Commonwealth stands for. We can do it if we want.

34

The Indian Ocean as a Link

In January 1971, President Nyerere travelled straight from the Common-
wealth Conference at Singapore to begin a state visit to India.
President Giri honoured his guest at a state banquet in the Rashtrapati
Bhavan on 23 January 1971, where President Nyerere replied to the
toast by paying tribute to India's stand on principle at the Common-
wealth meeting. He also spoke of the need to expand trade and other
relations between the two countries.

This state visit had to be cut short owing to the coup d'état *in Uganda.*

. . . History suggests that there was contact between Indians and
the peoples of East Africa before either of our areas was colonized.
Yet it was during East Africa's colonial period that contacts between
our two countries became institutionalized. Both of us were 'used'
for the benefit of the colonial power; joint activity and co-operation
was imposed on our peoples.

But although peoples from this sub-continent were brought to
East Africa for the purposes of Europe, I think it is fair to say—and
now possible to say!—that both of us received some incidental
advantage. Certainly we in Tanzania did so. For although the main
Tanzanian railway lines were built while my country was occupied
by the Germans, Indian people still found themselves involved in
its construction. And peoples from what is now this Republic were
active in commerce and trade while mainland Tanzania was still
being subdued by its first colonizer.

Since the independence, first of India, and later of Tanzania, the
ties between us have been changing in form. As you, Mr. President,
have just indicated, they are now developing according to our
deliberate choice, and for our mutual benefit. . . .

Further possibilities of co-operation, over a wide range of activities, became clear in our very good and useful official talks this morning. I was extremely pleased to find that these confirmed my long standing belief that Tanzania could use India's experience, to its own great benefit—and that India is very willing to help us do so.

On trade too, we must look more into the possibilities of working together. Many of the things which Tanzania is accustomed to buying in Europe may be obtained from those developing countries —like India—which are some steps ahead of us in economic development. . . .

. . . It is no use the underdeveloped nations just complaining about the domination of the rich countries in the world economy. We have to work among ourselves to see how the Third World can be made a little more self-reliant. This does not imply any desire that we should isolate ourselves from the rest of the world, any more than Tanzania's domestic policies of socialism and self-reliance mean an isolation from all other countries. It simply means recognizing that the poor are the ones who are concerned with their poverty, and who have the responsibility of advancing themselves.

I believe this is particularly relevant to economic relations between Tanzania and India. For trade between us has no canal to pass through, and it does not have to pass near any hostile power or naval base. We must treat the Indian Ocean as the link it can be, not the barrier others would like it to be! . .

35

Socialism and Law

On 31 March 1971, President Nyerere proposed a toast at the farewell dinner given by the Government to Chief Justice Georges, a Trinidadian who was returning home after six years of work for Tanzania. The President spoke of the relationship between socialism and law.

My purpose is a very simple one. The Government, the Party, and the people of Tanzania, want to say thank you to Chief Justice Georges for the great contribution he has made to our development over the past six years.

In saying this I am not suggesting that the Chief Justice has been a great builder of buildings, or a great farmer, or a great politician! I am using the word 'development' in its proper sense, as meaning the growth of a people in freedom, and the growth of a society which upholds and protects that freedom. In Tanzania, at least, we know that economic development is only one aspect of real growth; the parallel development of justice among the people is of at least equal importance.

Thus it is true to say that the judiciary has a very important role to play in the development of Tanzania—and the Chief Justice is their leader. For the job of the judges, and the magistrates, is to see that the Rule of Law operates in this country. In other words, they have to try to see that people's actions are judged according to the law, and that every individual can claim the rights he or she is entitled to under the law—as well as being forced to carry out the duties imposed by law! Unless these functions are carried out properly, then we shall never develop into a socialist society; for socialism cannot exist without law, because freedom cannot exist without law, and socialism and freedom are—ultimately—indivisible.

But the Rule of Law is not enough for freedom; still less is it enough for socialism! As we know only too well—and as we can see in Southern Africa today—laws can be used to suppress freedom, and to impose the most dreadful tyranny. For whether, in fact, the Rule of Law supports freedom and justice, or socialism, depends upon whether the laws passed by Parliament are directed to those ends. And I hasten to add that the judges, and the Chief Justice in particular, bear no responsibility for the laws which are passed—at least in this country!

In Tanzania, however, we are trying to build a body of laws which does serve these purposes of human freedom and equality—that is, which does serve the cause of socialism. And if these are to become meaningful and useful to our people, then the Judicial System has to uphold them in every way. In particular, the judges in our courts have to interpret these laws, and enforce them, in a manner which is understandable to our people and acceptable to them. Judges cannot change the law—though they can draw attention to laws which need changing if justice is to be upheld. But they can, in their judgements, reflect the society of which those laws are a part, or they can pronounce according to some other, self-chosen, social ethic.

In Tanzania we expect that our judges shall do the former! This means that our judges and magistrates must understand our society, and the aspirations of the people. Further, they must be seen to have this understanding and sympathy; for—as has been said many times before—justice must not only be done, but must also be seen to be done. People must trust their judges, and their magistrates, because they know them to be men like themselves—though with an unimpeachable degree of integrity.

It is in this matter of obvious identification with the people that Chief Justice Georges has conducted a little revolution of his own—and changed our expectation of Chief Justices! He has joined with the people in their political, economic, and social activities—both large and small. He has visited ujamaa villages—and other rural areas. He has joined in the people's *ngoma*; he has talked with people on a man-to-man basis; he has worked with them on nation-building projects. He has taught, and he has learnt. And he has listened to a great number of speeches at mass rallies and in Party commitee meetings—so much so that it is a pity to inflict another speech on him this evening!

The Chief Justice has, in fact, shown by all his actions that the independence of the judiciary does not mean the isolation of the judiciary from the life of the nation. He has shown a recognition of its true meaning; that in the consideration of cases, and in the giving of judgements, a judge or magistrate takes orders from no one, but uses his own brains, his training in law, and his independent judgement about the issues in dispute and the facts involved. And he does this regardless of other factors, because he knows that this is the service the people have demanded of him. . . .

36

Ten Years After Independence

President Nyerere submitted to the TANU National Conference in September 1971 a long report on the first ten years of independence. This surveyed the achievements of those years and also discussed some of the failures and outstanding problems.

INTRODUCTION

In Bagamoyo in December 1961, I made what many people regarded as a rash statement. I said that in the coming ten years we, the people of Tanganyika, would do more to develop our country than the colonialists had done in the previous forty years. Those ten years will be up on 9 December this year. Have we justified my prophesy? More important, how does life feel to the people of Tanzania? What progress have we made in dealing with the 'poverty, ignorance and disease' which I referred to on that day? And, following from that question, what new problems of development have we reached in 1971?

This report is intended to give a general answer to those questions. It will reveal much that we can be proud of but also some things which give very little cause for satisfaction and really show only how far we have yet to go, and how much we have to do. For over the past ten years we have made many mistakes and some of these we have hardly begun to correct. It is necessary that we face up to these matters now and realize the kind of effort which is called for. Yet in doing this we must not allow ourselves to be discouraged; for the truth is that we have done a great deal in the past ten years. We have made many changes, we have done a lot of building and we have now created a base from which our nation can advance more quickly and more freely in future.

We certainly did not have a very good base in December 1961. The independence we celebrated that month was politidal independence only. It was a vital and very fundamental event, for it gave to this nation the legal right to make its own decisions on all matters. Without that we could make no progress, and we were therefore right to celebrate on 9 December 1961. But we were also right to recognize that what we had won was the right io begin work—and nothing more.

The fact is that political independence always exists within a framework of a nation's actual strength and its relative position in the world as regards economic, diplomatic and military power. In other words, an independent nation's legal power to make any decision it wishes is in practice restricted by that nation's real capacity. Its legal independence and its real independence may thus be quite different things. And in December 1961, Tanganyika did not attain economic power—and certainly not economic independence. We gained the political power to decide what to do; we lacked the economic and administrative power which would have given us freedom in those decisions. For it is no use deciding to import more goods than you have foreign currency to pay for, or deciding to provide free books for all children if you have neither the teachers, the buildings nor the money to make a reality of that decision. A nation's real freedom depends on its capacity to do things, not on the legal rights conferred by its internationally recognized sovereignty.

AT INDEPENDENCE

Tanganyika achieved independence by a peaceful process, and the new Government was therefore able to take over an existing administrative structure of Central and Local Government. But its Constitution was modelled on that of the United Kingdom and took very little account of the historical, geographical and cultural realities of this country. The structure of its civil service was also modelled on that of the United Kingdom, and was designed for the administration of a nation, not for its development. Further, it was not a local civil service: as late as April 1960, only 346 of the posts classified as 'senior' were filled by Africans. By independence the position had improved somewhat; 1,170 out of 3,282 senior posts were held by citizens of this country.

The economy of the newly independent Tanganyika was also typically colonial. It depended on the production of subsistence foodstuffs and primary commodities for export; almost all the monetary sector had grown in accordance with the needs of foreign countries. Thus, the largest single export was unprocessed sisal, with raw cotton and coffee following behind. (Together the value of these three crops accounted for some 54 per cent of the total domestic product.) The sisal was grown on foreign-owned plantations, although four-fifths of the coffee and virtually all the cotton were the result of peasant production. Some other commercial crops, like cashew nuts and various types of oil seeds, were also grown by peasant farmers as a sideline, and had begun to contribute to the export revenue; while tea, pyrethrum, and tobacco had been introduced to the country but were being produced almost entirely on foreign-owned estates.

The vast majority of the farmers of Tanganyika were, in fact, still just subsistence producers, or were selling the very minimum of their low output in order to pay taxes. Further, the subsistence agriculture was still mostly based on a shifting cultivation pattern, with the units being small and output depending entirely on the vagaries of the weather and the good health of the individual peasant at critical moments during the production process. The net result was a life of poverty and insecurity for the masses of the people, while a small number of foreign companies or private farmers from Europe were obtaining a comfortable life—often at the expense of their exploited workers.

The industrial sector of the Tanganyika economy in December 1961, was so small as to be hardly worth noticing. In so far as small factories—such as breweries and cigarette manufacturing plants—did exist, they were alien owned and controlled, just as all the commercial and financial institutions were alien owned and controlled. The only exception to this was the marketing done by the co-operative unions, such as the KNCU, the BNCU and VFCU. All other exporting and all importing was done by private businessmen, with hardly a Tanganyikan African among them.

Thus, overall, the wealth produced in Tanganyika at independence provided for its people very little more than subsistence at a low level.

Any surplus produced above this was mostly exported to the home territories of the foreign companies or the agricultural estate owner.

For that reason it is not surprising that the social services were at a very low level. The bulk of the health and education services were in fact still being provided through voluntary agencies—religious missions or charities which received subventions from the tax revenues of Tanganyika. This meant that not only was the total provision ludicrously inadequate, but it was also concentrated in areas of Christian mission activity, and the services were often thought to require at least a willingness to be 'converted'. In some cases this was not true, though the non-Government secondary schools did, as a rule, restrict attendance to members of their own faith.

The same inadequacy was evident in the public services. Indeed, even the infra-structure for economic development did not exist. For example, the trunk road system looked outwards, doing more to connect the periphery of the country with our neighbours than it did to pull the nation into an integrated unit—and the roads were not very good anyway. In 1961 there was a bitumenized road between Dar es Salaam and Morogoro, one between Arusha and Moshi, and another between Korogwe and Tanga. Apart from that, there was very little tarmac outside the towns. Many of the other 'major' roads became virtually impassable during the rainy season, and only in the few areas where the important cash crops were grown was there anything even pretending to be a feeder road system.

Hidden within this picture of a small and hardly growing economy there was also a major social problem, for the entire political, economic and social structure of the country was based on racial divisions. Not only were most of the major economic activities foreign-owned; their managers, technicians and professionally qualified workers were almost all non-Africans, and the rates of pay in both private and public employment were based on race. Even when he could get such an opportunity, the African worker in the private companies, and in the public service, got less pay for doing the same job than an Asian worker, who himself got less than a European. The racial disparity was, however, seen mostly in the large differentials which existed between the non-skilled labourer, earning perhaps Shs. 50/- a month, and the top officials in Government, earning about Shs. 5,000/- a month—with top rewards in private industry being even higher.

The public service provided in the urban areas reflected the same racial bias; the areas where Europeans lived had electricity, water in the houses, and paved roads. In the African areas, such services were—to put it mildly—very much fewer, despite the greater number of people involved. In education, too, there were European schools, Asian schools and African schools, although some of the voluntary agency Asian schools had begun to accept African children. In Dar es Salaam, and in other major towns, there was a European hospital and an African hospital.

This pattern continued in every aspect of life. Thus, although there was not in Tanganyika the formal and all-pervading colour bar which some neighbouring countries suffered from, the whole society during the colonial period was organized so as to separate people of different races, give privilege to those of European origin, and make the African people feel that they were inferior. By the time of independence TANU had, it is true, asserted the political equality of Africans, with inevitable effect upon social discrimination, but racial consciousness and an underlying sense of inferiority remained to plague the new country. Indeed, traces of this can still be seen today, ten years later.

The Inevitability of Change

A change in all these conditions was clearly necessary, and had been a major purpose of the independence struggle. Change was also inevitable. For not even the accession to political power gave to the people of Tanganyika the possibility of preventing change in their society. This country could not have cut itself off from its neighbours, or from the world at large. Even an attempt at national isolation would have involved change; because the country was already involved, through geography and trade and language, with other parts of the world.

The question before the new nation, therefore, was not whether to change, but what kind of change it would have. The nation had to decide whether this change was to be deliberately chosen and implemented, or was to be merely a side effect of development elsewhere. In other words, one of the first issues which the newly independent people, through their Government, had to settle, was whether to use their acquired decision-making power to initiate, lead and control changes in the society. The alternative was to remain fairly passive while the society absorbed changes initiated from outside, like a sponge absorbing water.

There were other vital questions to be answered, too. For it is not enough to say that a 'nation' will decide something. A nation is its people, and they are scattered, in our case, over more than 350,000 square miles of land. Who is it, then, who will use the decision-making power acquired with independence? In whose interests will they use that power, and what will be their objectives and their method?

Looking back over the past ten years, we have to ask ourselves what use the people of Tanzania have made of their independence, how the country has been governed and by whom, and what use has been made of the circumstances which existed in the country in December 1961. For circumstances can be used as an excuse for inaction, or they can be seized and made to work for the objectives which have been decided upon.

Tanganyika's Advantages

And despite its poverty, Tanganyika did have many advantages which other newly independent countries have envied. Our overall poverty did not hide great inequalities between citizens—hardly any Africans would have been recognized as rich in any other country except Tanganyika. And, although a handful of members of the Asian community were wealthy, the majority of this community too were either themselves poor or were what in Europe would be called lower middle-class.

Further, the very fact that our country had experienced almost no economic development meant that there were no islands of wealth surrounded by vast areas of misery. The Districts we had come to think of as rich were those like Kilimanjaro, where the people had lifted themselves above misery, and had begun to provide primary school education for their children and had often built themselves reasonable houses to live in. In fact, taken as a whole, the economic differences between citizens of Tanganyika were minor, because so few had been absorbed into the colonial economy or colonial administration. There were a few people who were conscious of the fruits which could be gained from such absorption, but even they had hopes or expectations rather than existing wealth. We did not have a 'class' structure in a classical sense; we had a racial economic structure, and a division between expatriate and local people. Our other economic differences between Africans were of marginal importance.

Tanganyika had other advantages, too. Its ten million people consisted of many different tribes—123 African and a few Asian. But almost everywhere Swahili was understood, and the vast majority, at least of the men, could speak it. This common language was of inestimable value, both for the independence struggle and for the unity of the new nation.

Another advantage which the new nation enjoyed was that its nationalist party was fiercely secular and its members came from all regions as well as from town and country alike. Moreover TANU was an organized mass movement which reached down to almost all the villages and hamlets in the country, and every street in the African areas of the towns. In some places it was strong and in others comparatively weak, but everywhere it existed.

All this meant that Tanganyika had very important strengths in 1961. Its strength lay in its weakness and in the unity of its people. There were comparatively few citizen vested interests which had to be taken into account in determining policies, and its people were not filled with mutual hostilities or suspicions, but had experienced years of working together for a common purpose. At independence, therefore, these strengths were waiting to be exploited and used for future development, or to be dissipated through quarrels about how to get and use those other kinds of strength which the new nation lacked.

AFTER INDEPENDENCE

There were undoubtedly some people in Tanganyika who continued to believe that with independence all their problems would disappear. But this was not the feeling of the majority. For many years TANU had campaigned on the slogan *Uhuru na Kazi* (Freedom and Work). And, as the independence date approached, TANU leaders had been stressing that 'what we have .won is the right to work for ourselves, the right to design and build our own future'. The real commitment with independence was thus to 'build the nation', and to establish 'dignity for all'. This involved a commitment to work for economic and social growth; it involved also a commitment to real independence for the nation.

The most immediate task after independence, however, was the assertion of the dignity of all Tanganyika citizens. It was for this reason that within weeks of independence there was a shock deportation of five Europeans who publicly insulted Africans after 6 December. Those deportations were intended to have and did have, a psychological effect on the whole society. They showed that, whatever else we had not achieved when the Tanganyikan flag was raised on the flagstaff, we achieved the right to be treated as human beings.

But that was only the beginning. Much more fundamental was ending racial discrimination in the health and education services, in social life, and in wage rates. This was done quickly. By the end of 1962, this work had almost been completed. There was by then a single educational system, hospitals were reorganized to deal with medical problems and not races, private clubs were in the process of being forced to bring their racial exclusiveness to an end, and wages based on race were being rapidly phased out.

Africanization

At the same time a deliberate policy of 'Africanization' of the public services was being pursued in the full recognition that this was itself discriminatory. For before all citizens could be treated equally, it was necessary to rectify the position in which the nation's civil service was dominated by non-Africans, and to make it reflect in some measure the composition of the society. Therefore, until January 1964, Africans were appointed and promoted in preference to anyone else, and many of their promotions were very rapid and involved the suspension of normal qualification requirements about experience and education.

This policy inevitably meant that some people were appointed or promoted to posts for which they were unqualified, and some had to be replaced as they proved unequal to the increasing demands made upon them. It is important to realize that even those who were later replaced contributed a great deal in the early days of independence; many of them were the victims of our needs, which refused them the time and opportunities to grow into the jobs they were given. And in fact many of the people who were promoted so rapidly did succeed in their new tasks—some are still doing them today.

The urgency of this Africanization policy arose out of the need to build up the self-confidence of the people of Tanganyika. Once we had demonstrated—to ourselves and others—that being an African did not have to mean being a junior official, the nation was able to accept that in some fields we can, without shame, hire the skilled people who are needed. This had been done by January 1964, and we were therefore able to revert to a policy of priority to citizens regardless of their racial origin. This is the policy today. Every citizen has the right to be considered on his or her merits, regardless of race, religion or sex.

In fact, in regard to our aim of ending discrimination against Africans in Tanganyika, we have been so successful that we have forgotten what we have achieved. Today the humanity and equality of Africans is no longer challenged inside Tanzania by non-Africans. The Africans are, as they always were, a majority in Tanzania. But now they control Tanzania. Therefore, if there are racial problems in this country, it is an African responsibility—just as, in countries like America or the United Kingdom, the so-called colour problem is really a white problem. It is now basically our responsibility to correct the vestiges of our racialist inheritance. Thus for example, it is our fault that some of the forms in our hospitals still ask the 'race' of the patient, and it is our responsibility to end this.

Early Constitutional Changes

The second priority task for the new nation was to re-design its political institutions so that they reflected the history, geography and culture of our people, rather than those of our ex-colonial masters. Only when the people really felt involved in the decisions made on their behalf could they feel that the Government making them was theirs in every sense. But it was not only our past which mattered in this connection; our political institutions had to be made appropriate to the development tasks which they would have to fulfil.

There were two vital aspects to the constitutional change which these conditions required. The first was that all Tanganyika citizens must have the right to vote; TANU had been demanding that for years, yet even the independence Parliament had been elected on a restricted franchise. Only after this change had been effected could TANU's commitment to human equality be made a reality in political terms.

The second important and urgent change needed was the ending of the system whereby a foreign Queen was the Head of State, even though her representative in this country was nominated by the Tanganyikan Government. It was not only her 'foreignness' which was the problem: the conception of a Head of State who had virtually no power, and a Prime Minister who did have power, was alien to our traditions and confusing to our people.

It was for these reasons that immediately after independence the new government began to work out a Constitution providing for an Executive Presidency and a really representative Parliament, which had to work together to make laws, and both of which were directly responsible to the people. The first Presidential Elections, on a one-man one-vote basis, therefore took place in November 1962, and the Republic of Tanganyika came into existence exactly one year after independence. From that time onwards it was clear to everyone that this country was being governed under a Constitution worked out by us and in accordance with our needs and aspirations.

It was during 1962, also, that the TANU Constitution was amended. For until that time the first objective of TANU, according to its Constitution was 'to prepare the people of Tanganyika for self-government'. That was obviously outdated! After this revision, TANU for the first time became specifically committed to a socialist philosophy, although what this meant was not defined. Indeed, the change was generally regarded as showing in a vague way our commitment to the principle of human equality and our intention of building a Tanganyika concerned for the welfare of all its citizens.

Economic Developments

Before independence—that is, during the period of responsible self-government—a Three-Year Economic Development Plan had been prepared by the Government, and steps were being taken towards its implementation. This Plan, which was based on a survey of the economy prepared by the World Bank, was really little more than a series of public expenditure projects. It did, however, outline the main priorities as they were seen at that time. These were the development of agriculture and the livestock industry, the improvement and development of communications, and the development of secondary and technical education. Of the total planned expenditure amounting to Shs. 480 million, Shs. 380 million were expected to be obtained from external sources.

In fact, although implementation of the Plan went ahead during the succeeding years, it was rapidly outdated. There was a general expansion of education, greater expenditure on agricultural advice services, and improvements in road and other communications. Yet, as the new nation got into its stride, dissatisfaction grew up about the proposed rate of growth, and there was a new consciousness of the need for wider participation in development. In 1962, therefore, a political call was made for 'self-help schemes', and all over the country people began to build village schools, dispensaries, roads, and so on, on their own initiative. Unfortunately, the work was unplanned and unco-ordinated, and it was soon found that more classrooms were being built than there were teachers to work in them, more dispensaries than there were drugs to use in them, and that many roads led only to a river or stream for which no bridge could be provided. Nonetheless, this experience did show that the people were anxious to help themselves, and required only leadership and technical assistance. And despite all the problems and disappointments which were experienced, new services—estimated to be worth some Shs. 60 million—were provided by the people's own efforts during those first one or two years after independence.

Other developments took place during this period which were, in fact, socialist developments, although once again they suffered from an enthusiasm which was not tempered by planning and co-ordination. Thus, there was a very rapid expansion of the co-operative movement in the country, but at the same time a slackening of the standards of organization required before a co-operative society was registered. As a result, groups which were too small to be economically viable were recognized as co-operative societies, and even given local monopolies in marketing—at the expense of the peasants. Also, the lack of supervision meant that dishonest persons found it only too easy to steal from the new societies.

Dissatisfaction with this state of affairs mounted to such an extent that the whole co-operative movement was in danger of being discredited, and in January 1966, a Presidential Commission was set up to examine the situation and to make recommendations for its rapid rectification. The Report was published the same year, and Government accepted its major recommendations. After the consequent reorganization, the co-operative movement has been able to develop while giving increasing and ever-improving services to its members and to the nation as a whole.

Also beginning in 1962 was the gradual redirection of Government expenditure in favour of the poorer areas and the poorer people. And this was combined with a shift in taxation so that it bore more heavily on those who could afford to pay. Thus, it was in these early post-independence years that the hated Poll Tax was abolished and replaced by the Personal Tax system, under which people with less than a certain income paid nothing.

Land nationalization was also effected in 1962, although it passed almost unnoticed! It meant that freehold ownership of land was abolished and development clauses imposed on all leasehold ownership rights. By this Act of Parliament, and without any fanfare, Tanganyika achieved a basic socialist objective which more aggressive socialist parties elsewhere in the world had almost given up advocating because of its difficulty! This was one of many respects in which Tanganyika's lack of development enabled us to jump straight from a basically traditional economic organization to a socialist economic organization, without going through long agonies resulting from private ownership of a basic resource.

Another foundation for socialist growth which was laid in these early years was the establishment of the Tanganyika Development Corporation in July 1962. This was given the task of building up an industrial base for the nation. But $2\frac{1}{2}$ years later it, together with the Tanganyika Agricultural Corporation, was absorbed into the

National Development Corporation, and given the more definitely socialist task of building up public enterprise. The new NDC was, however, allowed to go into minority partnership with private concerns, as and when this seemed appropriate for the purpose of maximizing total investment. And, in practice, emphasis was given to the latter aspect of its responsibilities until 1967.

TANU also moved into the development field during these early years, setting up the Mwananchi Development Corporation and initiating a wide variety of economic activities. Two things however were gradually realized: that TANU was not equipped for this kind of work; and that in any case it was undesirable for TANU as such to engage in this kind of development activity. Most of the activities and projects of the Mwananchi Development Corporation were therefore eventually taken over by the National Development Corporation.

Reform of the trade union movement, to make it appropriate for the conditions of Tanzania, was also begun soon after independence, as the Tanganyika Federation of Labour was strengthened in relation to the separate unions. Later, a further reorganization resulted in the TFL being replaced by the National Union of Tanganyika Workers, in which the separate unions became merely sections. Thus, the industrial side of the labour movement was gradually prepared for its role in a socialist economy even before much other progress had been made in that direction.

There was one field in which very little change took place during the first two years of independence—and the country paid a heavy price. For although the Police Force did succeed in becoming much more the servant than the master of the citizens, and although considerable progress was made towards the Africanization of the Police Officer Corps, similar developments did not take place in the Army. Some changes in the Army were, of course, inevitable—it could no longer be the King's African Rifles after Tanganyika became a Republic! Some officer training was also begun. But in general the Tanganyika Army was as cut off from the society, and the developments of the new society, in January 1964, as it had been in December 1961. The mutiny which then took place, and which endangered the whole country, made radical action necessary. The old Army was therefore disbanded and a new one created from members of the National Service. These lessons of the past were thoroughly learnt, and from its beginnings, the new Army was organized so as to instil among all its members a commitment to the nation and the national policies of development.

The One-Party Democracy

While all this activity was going on, TANU was falling into the background. Its nation-wide organization was hardly being used, because both the Party and the nation as a whole were unsure of the role TANU could play while the state constitution provided for competing political organizations. For the fact that there was no other political organization consisting of more than a handful of people did not alter the constitutional theory that the State and the Party had to be kept separate.

By following this theory, however, the nation was wasting one of the few resources it had—a mass organization which the people trusted, and through which they could both express their views and co-operate with the projects being executed through the state machinery. In 1963, therefore, TANU called for the establishment of a democratic one-party state. The implementation of this was postponed while the hope of an early East African Federation was being pursued, but finally a Presidential Commission was set up at the beginning of 1964. The Commission was directed to investigate the people's wishes and to make recommendations on how a democratic one-party state could best be achieved. The Members appointed travelled in groups all over the country, consulting with the people about the different alternatives which international experience had suggested, and gaining ideas of what the new constitution was expected to be like. The Presidential Commission reported early in 1965 and its recommendations were, in large measure, accepted by both the Party and the Government.

In September 1965, therefore, Tanzania's first Parliamentary election on the basis of adult suffrage was held under the new One-Party Constitution. This allowed the people to choose between two TANU-approved candidates; it meant that opportunists or incompetent people could no longer hide behind the Party banner because of past services, and it meant, too, that the people could choose which of two TANU candidates they thought would best express their wishes and their ideas in the coming five years. Many individuals who had served the nation and the Party well in the past were electorally defeated in this process; for the people were for the first time able to express their views about an individual's future capacity for service without fear of weakening the national progress.

The Union

Perhaps the most important long-term development in these early years, however, was the Union between Tanganyika and Zanzibar, which took place in April 1964. This followed the premature negotiations for an East African Federation, which lasted from June 1963 to early 1964, and the revolution which took place in Zanzibar in January 1964.

TANU and the Afro-Shirazi Party had long had close and cordial relations. The overthrow of the Sultan and a Government which achieved power through gerrymandered elections, enabled this Party co-operation to be transformed into what it was hoped would be the first steps towards greater East African unity.

From the beginning, the Union has been the subject of much international misunderstanding, and it has attracted a considerable amount of criticism from outside. And there have been many problems. A union between two free nations can never be without difficulties. The policies of two sovereign states with a very different recent history had to be merged into one. The international trade arrangements, and very different tariff structures, had to be unified, and so on. A system also had to be worked out which would give fair expression in a single system to two countries of very different size and population. Despite all this, the Union was created and it has survived seven years which were difficult for Tanzania and for the whole of Africa. For the first time in African history, two nations submerged their sovereignty into one, and progress towards unity in Africa was shown to be a matter of political will on the part of the people and their leaders.

SOCIALIST DEVELOPMENT

During 1966 there was a gradual realization that, although some economic progress was being made, and although we were still talking in terms of a socialist objective, the nation was in fact drifting without any sense of direction. A lack of co-ordination between our different objectives and policies was resulting in confusion; some of our people were getting disheartened; and there was a widespread tendency to look to others for our salvation instead of concentrating on our own efforts and resources.

The effect was already visible. In particular, there was an increase in the amount of economic inequality between citizens, and this was leading towards attitudes of social inequality. The growth in economic differences was inevitable as the Africanization policy was pursued in the public services and urged upon private enterprise. But the problem was not simply that a small number of educated individuals were getting great responsibilities and being paid comparatively highly for them. The real problem was that these same people were able to get access to credit facilities and technical advice, and that some of them were therefore venturing into other income-earning activities.

This kind of thing did not go unnoticed by the mass of the people, and they resented it. For they could not get loans from the banks to build houses for renting, or to start a bus service, or to employ labourers on a large farm. A small number of people were thus pre-empting the capital and technical resources of the nation, and were using them for their own profit. The country was beginning to develop an economic and social *élite* whose prime concern was profit for themselves and their families, and not the needs of the majority for better basic living standards. We were beginning to see the development of a true class system.

At the same time, the urban areas were growing rapidly and most of the emphasis of Government activity was on their obvious need for better public services. There was even a tendency towards prestige building, especially in Dar es Salaam. And even the Party was becoming less effective in its leadership of the masses, because individuals were seeking office in it in the hope of thereby bettering their own economic position. The general interest in greater welfare was being used as a catch-phrase rather than being pursued as a policy.

The Arusha Declaration

In October 1966, prompted by the shock of University students, resistance to a period of compulsory National Service, all Ministers, and senior and middle-grade civil servants, accepted a wage cut amounting, in some cases, to 15 per cent. But this action did not deal with the basic problem, which was that we had determined our national objective in such general terms that it was not guiding us to where we wanted to go. Therefore, although we had made good progress in some respects, on balance we were drifting away from our basic socialist goals of human equality, human dignity, and government by the whole people.

In January 1967, at a conference in Arusha, the National Executive of TANU faced up to this problem, and its conclusions were published as 'The Arusha Declaration' on 5 February. The Declaration defined what socialism means in the context of Tanzania, it set out qualifications which had to be fulfilled by all in leadership positions in politics and public service, and it demanded a much more serious commitment to self-reliance in our development.

This policy was accepted by a special TANU National Conference as were, in due course, the more detailed policy pronouncements, 'Education for Self-Reliance', 'Socialism and Rural Development', and 'Freedom and Development'. With these four papers, the Party gave a clear statement of its commitment to socialism, and what it means for Tanzania; and it indicated some policy implications of this commitment. The policies were accepted with acclaim by the nation as a whole.

The importance of the Arusha Declaration is difficult to over-estimate. It provided a guideline to the people, the Government and the Party, to which all future policy decisions could be compared. After it there has been no excuse for decisions which, although good in certain respects, would divert our development from its purpose of serving the whole people.

Of course, the Arusha Declaration would have been meaningless if it had not been followed by actions. It was. In the week following the publication of the Declaration, key sectors of the economy were taken into public hands, with compensation paid to previous owners. Banks, insurance, and food processing factories were the first to be taken over. Eight of the larger import/export and wholesale businesses were also nationalized, and formed the nucleus of the State Trading Corporation; this was later to become the nation's main organization for external and wholesale trade. In addition to this, the Government took a controlling share in such major manufacturing industries as existed—which was a very short list—and announced that it would shortly secure a controlling share of the sisal industry.

By these actions the Government fulfilled its obligations under the Arusha Declaration, Part 2 (B). For almost all the other industries existing in Tanzania were already publicly owned or controlled before the Arusha Declaration. Thus, no action was required as regards land, forests, mineral resources, electricity, telecommunications and railways because all were already in Government hands or under Government control.

This sudden expansion of public ownership was achieved and followed through with remarkably little dislocation of the economy. Even in relation to the banks, where the previous owners withdrew all the expatriate senior staff, the difficulties of reorganization were over in a matter of weeks and international exchange (the only aspect of their business which had suffered from any delays) was being conducted normally. Most other take-overs were effected without major problems to the consumers.

The total effect of this series of measures cannot, of course, be seen for many years. But already the nation has saved large amounts of foreign exchange and, much more important, been able to implement its own decisions in relation to the economy in a manner which would have been impossible otherwise. For by the nationalizations Tanzanians became able to decide positively, as well as negatively, what would happen as regards the economy of their country.

There are, of course, other implications of this. Internally, we can no longer blame the actions, or lack of actions, of others for our economic failures. Of course, we cannot remain unaffected by what happens in the world markets, but in 1967 it became our responsibility to take actions which maximize the advantage to us, or minimize the disadvantage to us, of the world economic situation as it changes from week to week or day to day. We have thus, through the nationalization measures, gradually extended our economic independence, even though we remain subject in many respects to events over which we have no control. The sense of service, the initiative, and the business acumen of Tanzanians is now the crucial factor in our development,

An equally important result of the Arusha Declaration, however, has been a new consciousness that the development of a nation means the development of its people, rather than the erection of imposing buildings or impressive roads. Of course, in a country like Tanzania, dispersing your effort to benefit the masses of the people, who live throughout our 360,000 square miles, means that the results of much of the work are not very visible. It is still easier to point to the industrial and business developments which have taken place since the Arusha Declaration than it is to display developments in the rural areas. Indeed, more money has in fact been spent on such urban developments than has been put into the rural areas in this post-Arusha period. Despite much change we have not yet succeeded in making our practice keep up with the change in consciousness.

Even as regards the ujamaa village policy, progress is difficult to quantify in any meaningful sense. We can say that something approaching 8 per cent of our population are now living in what they call ujamaa villages. But in many of these villages, only the first steps towards 'living together and working together for the good of all' have in fact been taken. And few of them as yet give any sign of the kind of life which this form of organization will in time make possible. Only by knowing a particular area before an ujamaa village was established, and revisiting it later, can the progress really be seen. But in fact it is there. The members are a little better off; there are more water supplies, schools, and so on. And, most important of all, the peasants are beginning to control their own lives, and are less at the mercy of weather, wild animals, ignorance, stock thieves—and unscrupulous leaders.

The TANU Guidelines

But although great advances have been made since 1967 in many respects, there is one field in which experience has shown that more emphasis is required. We have gradually realized that public ownership of enterprises is not enough. These enterprises may be—and in most cases in Tanzania have been—managed well, and with the intention of serving the interests of the Tanzania people. But they are still being managed for the people, and only by them in the sense that the decisions are taken by Tanzanians appointed by, and responsible to, an elected Government. Consequently, the people who are not in management positions in the public corporations, still do not feel that these corporations are theirs. Even the workers in the organizations frequently feel that they are working for 'them', and not for themselves.

This means that there is a need to develop new methods of public participation in the planning operations and management of the public corporations. Much more effective public supervision of the implementation of parastatal policies is also needed. We have, in fact, to change the attitude that only 'experts' can make decisions in economic matters, and that 'experts' can be identified by their formal educational qualifications. We have, instead, to help the people make the decisions for themselves. Those with technical knowledge of any kind have to develop the ability, and be willing, to explain the facts and the problems to the people, so that the latter may make decisions which are not only theirs, but which are also practicable and forward-looking. In other words, we have to get to a position where the public can make suggestions to management, as well as receive suggestions from management, and where in both cases the people are equipped to make judgements which are in their own long-term interest.

It was with these things in mind that the TANU Guidelines were drawn up in February 1971. In fact, just as there had been some tentative moves in the right direction before the Arusha Declaration was adopted, moves towards greater workers' control had already begun before TANU published its Guidelines. But the Guidelines call for much more than that. They also remind us that our Party is still a Party committed to the fight for freedom—freedom for Tanzania and for the whole of Africa. Therefore the Guidelines put a great deal of emphasis on the building of our country and the defending of it. The Guidelines call for a leadership which is of the people in economic as well as political matters. They call for new attitudes and practices in order to facilitate public participation in all decision-making.

Not very much progress has been made in these matters up to now. We are still not organized for *leadership*, only for persuading people to accept what experts and political leaders believe 'is good for them'. But we should not be discouraged by slow progress. In many ways the TANU Guidelines call for a more difficult change than the Arusha Declaration did. In fulfilment of the Arusha Declaration, concrete steps could be taken—a change of ownership or the relinquishing of private profit-making activities. The TANU Guidelines call for an understanding, both by management and by the people at large, of the real meaning of socialist and democratic activities. It will take time for the all-pervading implications of this to be realized.

There is, however, one danger in our present position. It is that decision-making will be slowed down as people in positions of authority realize that the old practices are being rejected but fail to understand how else to proceed. This we must not allow to happen. The TANU Guidelines call for public decision-making, following public discussion of the issues involved. They do not call for a stop to decision-making, and must not be allowed to be used as an excuse for refusal to accept responsibility. Just as Standard Bank branches continued to operate on the old basis after nationalization while the reorganization was being worked out, so the old practices of decision-making must continue while new methods of public involvement are being prepared and implemented. Our country cannot afford to stop its activities in order to prepare for the next stage of its progress.

WHAT WE HAVE ACHIEVED: GENERAL PROGRESS

What is it then that we have achieved during the last ten years? A full report is impossible. What follows is intended to be a general survey of the things we have succeeded in doing as a nation since Tanganyikan independence.

Definition of the Goal

The first thing we have achieved is a definition of what we understand by socialism, and an acceptance of a national commitment to build a socialist society. Because of this, our progress is now towards a definite and understood goal. We know where we are going, and the general route which has to be taken.

A general understanding of the Arusha Declaration is the key to our success; and this is beginning to be achieved. The document is being increasingly read, studied and understood; it is now an important element in the education of both children and adults. This is a vital advance, for it is with the Arusha Declaration that all our proposals must be compared. If they are consistent with it, then they will help us to progress along the right lines; if they are inconsistent with it, then whatever their other advantages they are not right for Tanzania. The more this kind of comparison can be made at grass-roots level, the greater will be our progress. This is what is beginning to happen; the people are questioning proposals in the light of the Arusha Declaration.

And in fact the spirit underlying the Arusha Declaration already permeates a good deal of our national life. Our people receive good service at rates of pay which are very low in comparison with those prevailing in many other developing societies. Further, although the battle against corruption is not won—for continued vigilance is always necessary—we have in large measure avoided this disgrace. And on top of this is the increasing rate of ujamaa village development in the rural areas and its first signs in the urban areas.

Thus, on the spread of understanding about our goals and the way to reach them, and on the widespread commitment of our people to socialist progress, the people of Tanzania can congratulate themselves. But this must not lead us to complacency, for there are very many problems remaining—some of which we have hardly begun to think about.

For example, we have not universally accepted the need for the self-discipline which is necessary if we are to get rid of the discipline of fear or of possible starvation. In our factories we have begun to talk about workers' participation and control, but have we even begun to educate the workers in their responsibilities to the rest of the nation? Sometimes it would appear not, for in recent months there have been too many cases of workers putting down their tools because of complaints about individual managers, or because they want a larger share of the returns from a profitable industry regardless of the fact that it is owned by the nation and its profits go to general good. And while demanding that they themselves should not be dismissed without proper investigation and without warnings, some of our workers do not seem always to be willing to concede similar rights to the people they accuse; instead they make the whole nation suffer over their disputes.

Again, what sanctions are appropriate for those who destroy, or waste, or misuse, public property? Under capitalism, the sanction for such actions against the employer is the sack, and fear of the boss was a motivating force for everyone in industry, from the foreman, to the general manager. But we are fighting against this kind of fear of the 'boss'. So how can we, and should we, ensure that public property is carefully looked after and efficiently used? For the fact is that if one kind of discipline is not replaced by another kind, we shall not achieve socialism—only mob rule and a speedy end to all our ambitions for national progress and greater well-being for all our people.

These, and many similar problems have still to be worked out. But they are urgent, for we cannot build socialism simply by rejecting the ideas and practices of capitalism. Nor do people become angels the moment the nation has decided to turn towards socialism. On the contrary, the fact that we were all brought up under colonialism and capitalism means that we have many attitudes and habits of personal acquisitiveness which we are carrying into the new society. And we cannot just wait for socialist education to rectify such practices. For people learn by what is happening in the society around them, not just from books or speeches! Thus we have to find some method of ensuring that people act like socialists towards their work responsibilities, and towards public property, even if they—and the society—have not yet become socialist!

The Organization

The appropriate organization for socialist advance is also a metter which we have to keep under constant review, always watching to see that in each field it helps us to move in the direction we want to go. It may be that such a review is again necessary, especially with the aim of greater decentralization. Yet this does not mean that there has been any lack of progress since independence; it can mean that we have outgrown the changes we first made.

Thus, after its initial hesitation, TANU has been re-activized and democratized. It has become more effective with the development of the ten-cell system. The nation has developed a system of administration which is, on the whole, appropriate to our needs, and which gives the people a real opportunity to express their wishes. In particular, our one-party system has enabled a strong and unified Central Government to remain responsive to the will of the people, at the same time as allowing it to give the lead which is necessary if Tanzania is to make progress towards its goals and is to be respected in the world at large. We have begun to tread the long and difficult road towards worker's democracy in public industry, and have begun the process of building local self-government at ujamaa village level.

The economy of the country has also been reorganized to meet our purposes. All the major industrial and commercial institutions of the country are now under public ownership or control, so that it is no longer possible for external forces to determine the size or shape of our economic growth. This is true not only at national level; District Development Corporations are now being established and some have already begun new productive enterprises of local importance. At the other end of the spectrum, the Railways, Harbours, Posts and Telecommunications, and the Airline, are jointly owned by the three East African Governments; they are thus able to serve the peoples of all three territories on a more economic and rational basis than would be possible without this international co-operation.

Further, co-operative marketing of our crops, and some of the goods manufactured in small units, has been very greatly expanded; and the co-operative movement is now paying increasing attention to co-operative production, as well as to co-operative savings and credit societies. The new (and as yet few) 'multi-purpose co-operatives' are in fact the sign of the future. They will be based on the ujamaa villages, so that the members will receive the benefits of co-operation in all their productive and commercial activities.

Finally, through the publicly owned financial institutions, including the new Industrial Development and Rural Development Banks, we have organized ourselves for the financing of an expanded productive capacity.

Administratively, too, the Government is much more appropriately organized for development now than it was in 1961. The early development of the system of Regional and Area Commissioners has helped to ensure that national decisions are implemented throughout the country, and also that the special needs of particular areas can be brought to the attention of the Government and TANU without difficulty. The establishment of the Regional Development Funds and the Regional Development Committees has also assisted us towards our ambition of enabling the people of a particular area to determine their own local priorities and implement their own decisions.

At a national level, the Ministry of Economic Affairs and Development Planning, and Ministry of Regional Administration and Rural Development between them, ensure ever-increasing co-ordination of our development efforts, and their proper direction towards the development of people rather than of things. The other Ministries have also been allocated responsibilities in a manner which is intended to enable us to think developmentally, and to execute our national policies.

The War Against Poverty

What progress, then, have we made in the war against poverty? In one sense the answer can only be found in the lives of the people; in their health, their education, their clothing, and their housing. But there is much more to this question than that: a useful answer also requires that we look at all the manifold things which have been done to build up the economy of the country and provide for future growth. For a farmer who has cleared, ploughed and planted a large acreage may, before the harvest, appear as poor as a man who has not done so—indeed, he may seem poorer because he has spent money on the equipment and the seeds he has used. Yet the real position of the two men is very different. Not only will the former be very much richer after the harvest; he will also have laid the groundwork for future growth. The farmer who has done nothing more than subsistence planting, on the other hand, will be as badly off in the second year as he is in the first.

Thus, there are two aspects to this question which cannot be separated. After ten years we have to ask ourselves how much, if at all, the life of the people has improved, and we also have to consider what groundwork we have laid which will lead to a continuing improvement in the future.

Another difficulty in answering this questionas regards a nation is that we can only report figures, and these must be totals or averages for the whole country. They can therefore only give an *overall* indication of our position and our preparations for the future; they can rarely reflect the reality in a particular area.

Finally, it must be borne in mind that, when an individual in Tanzania is considering his wealth now as compared with ten years ago, he is usually thinking of the money in his pocket at the end of the month, and what it will buy. But that is not a true comparison of his relative well-being when there has been a big increase in the proportion of the nation's wealth which is spent on community activities like health, education, roads, water supplies, and so on. For in reality every man has two pockets: one holds the money which he is free to spend on his private needs at his own will; the other holds his share of the public services. Thus, even if there has been no change over ten years in the amount a man has to spend on food, clothes, shelter and recreation each month, his standard of living may have improved. This will have happened if at the end of the period, but not at the beginning, he can go to a hospital or dispensary, or his children can go to school, or he himself to adult classes, or he can travel to work or get goods brought to him more safely, comfortably and cheaply, and so on. All these things are an improvement in his condition of life— and are more vital to it than extra consumer goods like watches, carpets, or cars.

All this means that, although figures hide a great deal about a nation's development, they also reveal things which are often ignored when an individual is considering his comparative position at two periods. It is in this context that we have to consider Tanzania's progress since 1961.

That there has been a great improvement in the general health and welfare of the people is without question. A very large number of our people look healthier and feel healthier; their dress is better; a very much larger proportion wear shoes now than ever did before. This is, as yet, especially true in the towns, but there are also a very large number of people in the rural areas who have good clothes now even if they are too sensible to wear them for work, who have shoes, who can go to a clinic or dispensary for their illnesses, and who have a little money in their pockets. Not nearly as many of our children sit quietly in the apathy of malnutrition as was the case ten years ago—mostly they are active, and stand a much better chance of living to adulthood than they used to do.

Figures to illustrate these matters are difficult to give because of the inadequacy of our statistics. Yet it would appear from an analysis of the census figures of 1957 and 1967 that the average life expectancy at birth has gone up from something like 37 or 38 years to something like 41 years. It would also appear from the same source that infant mortality was between 200 and 250 per thousand live births in 1957, and is now between 160 and 165 per thousand live births. Maternal mortality figures have also greatly decreased. Considering only the mothers who give birth in hospitals and maternity clinics (because other figures are less reliable), 47 mothers died in 1961 out of every 10,000 who gave birth, whereas now the figure is 27 per 10,000.

Although these figures must be treated with caution, they show so great a change that we can be sure of the big improvement which has taken place. For infant and maternal mortality rates are universally accepted as a good general indication of the health of the adult women in a population, and therefore by inference of the children and men. Life expectancy figures have a similar function of revealing a general level of health. In our case, of course, they do not only show a little improvement on the past; they also show how far we have to go. For in Europe a baby born alive will, on average, live to about 70 years of age; not 41!

Public Revenue and Expenditure

These improvements in health are among the many things which have become possible because of an increase in the total wealth produced by the nation, the better distribution of that wealth among the inhabitants, and the greater concentration on community expenditures rather than individual expenditures.

Our total wealth has certainly gone up, although really comparable figures are rather difficult to give. Thus, it was estimated—though without much precision—that at the time of independence the national income per head (that is, the total wealth produced in the country divided by the total population) was something like Shs. 380/- per year. Since that time, a new and more reliable basis for such calculations has been worked out and, on that basis, plus the fact that the population in 1961 was larger than we thought, a better figure for 1961 is probably between Shs. 460/- and Shs. 490/-. Certainly that is the figure we must think of when comparing with the present position, where the national income per head is calculated to be approximately Shs. 670/- a year. This 40 per cent increase, however, is after allowance has been made for a much larger Tanzanian population—which appears to be increasing at something like 2.8 per cent every year! In other words, the total production of wealth has increased by very much more than 40 per cent; indeed even in constant prices it has increased by something like 60 per cent, but our output now has to be divided between 13 million people instead of between 10.2 million.

That looks quite good; but we should not forget that we aimed at a higher performance than this. In fact, since 1967 the average annual growth for the production of goods and services has been between 4 and $4\frac{1}{2}$ per cent in constant prices; this is about one-third lower than the growth targets of both the First and the Second Five-Year Plans.

This does not merely mean a disappointment in our hopes about the individual standard of living for Tanzanians; such a failure has important implications for our whole progress. For expenditure on new development is often committed in the expectation that revenue from a higher national income will enable the nation to raise the money required; or schools are built in the belief that tax revenues will increase by a certain amount and thus enable the recurrent costs to be met. When we achieve a one-third lower increase in the national income than we were anticipating, this means that work on certain projects could have to stop half way, or something else may have to be forgone in order to use the school we have built, and so on. Failing to meet a target is thus a very serious matter, as it causes a lack of balance in our economy, means that we may get involved in commitments that we cannot meet, and also disappoints people as they fail to receive services or improvements in their living standard which they had been led to expect.

But how have we distributed and used the wealth we have produced? In fact we have made efforts to distribute our wealth more fairly between citizens, and we have nothing to be ashamed of in the amount we have taken from our private consumption pockets in order to use it for community needs.

Thus, between 1 July 1961 and 30 June 1971, we have spent something like Shs. 3,400 million on what is classified as 'Development Expenditure', and Shs. 2,300 million of this came from our internal resources—either by taxes or by internal borrowing. This figure includes a transfer over the period from Government revenues to the parastatal sector of Shs. 590 million, which has been spent on the expansion of our productive investments.

Thus, only 33 per cent of our total Government development expenditure in the past ten years has come from outside in the form of loans or grants. This shows the degree to which we are relying first on our own resources and only looking outside when it is absolutely necessary, and when we are sure that we shall be able to repay on the due date. In fact, our 'self-reliance' in this respect has increased since the Arusha Declaration. In the last four financial years, an average of nearly 74 per cent of our total development expenditure has come from internal resources, as against an average of 56 per cent over the previous six years.

At present, our total Government indebtedness is Shs. 2,441 million, of which 42 per cent is owed to people and institutions within Tanzania. It is possible, however, that in the future we may be able to allow ourselves to borrow from abroad a higher proportion of the money we spend on development. This is, of course, assuming that we can raise loans on acceptable terms and without political strings attached to them—conditions which we will always insist upon in the future, as in the past. But if we are able to do this, our development programme will be able to proceed faster than otherwise, for finance is now a limiting factor for us.

Yet, in truth, development expenditure and recurrent expenditure cannot really be separated. For example, running a school is included in the latter category; but its major purpose is the development of our future citizens and their greater capacity for skilled work—in other words, education is part of development as well as being valuable for itself. The two things are very intimately linked in another way, too; it is a waste to spend development capital on building a hospital if you are not prepared to set aside recurrent revenue every year to provide a medical attendant and the drugs which are prescribed. Thus, the rise in our recurrent expenditure from Shs. 494 million in 1961/62 to something like Shs. 1,634 million in 1970/71, is a reflection of many things. It reflects the greater public services which are available to our people now as a result of past development efforts; it reflects continuing development expenditure of a certain kind; and it also reflects a continuing commitment to emphasizing the provision of basic public needs rather than more and more individual consumer goods. Looking around the world, the experience of other countries (including the richest) suggests that in this we are on the right path for the future health, happiness and well-being of our people and their society.

There is one other aspect of our revenue-raising activities which is important to the kind of society we are creating. Our taxation policy has become much more progressive—that is, a much greater proportion of the public revenue comes from those with larger incomes than those with smaller incomes, both because of the direct taxation rates and because the indirect taxes are much heavier on luxury goods than on essentials. Thus, for example, income tax and personal tax currently account together for Shs. 415 million, and sales tax for another Shs. 217 million, as against a total of Shs. 120 million in 1961, and all these taxes fall on the wealthier sections of the community.

It may be easier to understand what this means when we consider that a Minister in the Tanzania Government receives an annual income of Shs. 48,000/- plus a free house. If he is married with three children he will pay Shs. 9,304/80 in personal tax and income taxes. A Principal Secretary earning Shs. 48,600/- (with no free house) who is also married with three children will pay personal tax and income taxes of Shs. 9,352/-. A man earning the Government minimum wage in Dar es Salaam, that is Shs. 2,160/- a year, will pay a total of Shs. 30/- a year in direct taxes. But that is only the beginning; all the 'durable consumer goods', such as a car, a refrigerator, etc., which the man on the high income is likely to want to buy, are also very heavily taxed. Thus, for example, the cheapest car on sale in Dar es Salaam, which has a list price of Shs. 9,000/- carries a 'Registration Tax' of Shs. 3,150/-, while a popular larger car which has a list price of Shs. 26,500/- carries 'Registration Tax' of Shs. 10,600/-.

The take-over by Government of many of the services which were previously the responsibility of the local authorities also has the effect of spreading the burden of public consumption from the poorer to the richer people and areas. And the fact that revenue from Excise Duty is now becoming increasingly important in relation to Customs Duty is an indication of a different kind: it shows how our economy is changing in structure towards greater self-reliance

But we have only just started along this road, and it is important that we continue a lot further along it. For we are still laying the foundation for our future growth as much as we are producing for our present enjoyment.

This is not to say that our conditions have failed to improve already. They have done so—a great deal.

Health

One of the problems in evaluating progress in the health of a nation (apart from the figures already given) is that statistics normally refer to sickness and the provision of services for sickness! Indeed, the truth is that the best way to measure the improvement—or lack of it—in the health of the people of Tanzania over the last ten years, is to walk around and look at them! But there is one thing at least which is certain; the consumption of protein foodstuffs such as milk, fish, eggs, and even meat, has increased more than the population has increased. This is bound to have a good effect on national health in the course of time.

It is also true that the incidence of some of the major communicable diseases has been reduced. Whereas there were 3,027 cases of smallpox notified in 1961, and about the same number every year until 1967, a rapid decrease followed until there were only 32 cases reported in 1970, and none at all between January and August this year. This change began with the commencement of the smallpox vaccination campaign which got under way in 1968 with the help of WHO, and which has now led to an estimated 60 per cent of the population being protected against this disease. Polio cases also appear to be greatly reduced in number, and although similar progress cannot be recorded in the other major diseases, it does appear that at the very least we have held our ground in respect to them. This is itself an achievement when one considers the experience of some other African countries. Also, the strengthened basic health services mean that the suffering caused by many illnesses, and the severity of them, has been much reduced.

Thus, for example, anti-malaria drugs and simple medical care for this disease are now within easy reach of almost everyone; death is less common from it, and the length of time during which a sufferer is incapacitated has, in general, been reduced.

For there has been an increase in the medical services available, and the position will improve still further in the future because of the continuing expansion of staff training. The Dar es Salaam Medical School, which was started in 1963, and became part of the University in 1968, now has an intake of between 30 and 40 students a year. This will be increased to 100 in the next few years, and the School will become a comprehensive faculty of the health sciences. Training still takes place elsewhere as well and, whereas in December 1961, there were 403 registered doctors and 22 licensed doctors working in Tanganyika, in December 1970, there were 489 registered doctors and 100 licensed doctors. In addition, there are 83 Chinese doctors working in the rural areas. It is also interesting to note that, whereas in 1961 only 12 of the registered doctors were Tanganyikans, in 1970 the comparable figure was 123.

The expansion in the numbers of Medical Assistants and Rural Medical Aids being trained is also notable. In 1961 there were 4 schools training these two groups of health workers, with a total output of 74 a year, whereas in 1971 there are 9 such schools with a total output of 270. And whereas there were 14 schools for nurses in 1961, with an annual output of 235, there are now 22 schools with a combined output of 422—with some of these being trained to a higher standard than ever before.

In addition to this, the organization of the health service has been rationalized, expanded, and directed more to serving the needs of the rural areas. One example of this is the integration of Government and non-Government medical services, so that available facilities are used to the maximum advantage. Thus, 11 voluntary agency hospitals have been provided with Government funds to function as District hospitals—and some of these have been completely handed over to Government. Also, suitable voluntary agency dispensaries now receive Government finance to act as rural health centres, and Government has taken increased financial and other responsibility for the running of local authority health services where this was necessary to ensure reliable, good service to the people of the area.

In figures, there will be 122 hospitals in mainland Tanzania by the end of 1971, as against 98 ten years ago; 90 rural health centres as against 22; and 1,400 rural dispensaries as against 975 at independence. Further, training in simple first-aid is now being given to selected members of ujamaa villages so that they can man 'health posts' which are being established on an experimental basis in some villages. It is as yet too early to assess the results of this important new development.

Quite spectacular progress has been made in the field of mother and child care. It is estimated that more than 60 per cent of the pregnant women now get ante-natal care, as against some 30 per cent in 1961, and about 30 per cent of children are now born in various health institutions as against 11 per cent at independence. The importance of this arises from the fact that a confinement in a clinic is less likely to result in the baby's death than if it takes place outside.

Much remains to be done for the health of our people, and it is essential that the money we allocate to this service should be spent to the maximum advantage. For although it is true that the Health Budget has increased from less than Shs. 5/-, to about Shs. 10/- per person per year, this is still a very small amount. Yet an increase could only be made by reducing some other expenditure, or by increasing taxes—neither of which we can easily do.

There are, however, two methods by which we can increase the effectiveness of the money we allocate for health. The first of these is to put greater emphasis on preventive medicine. Given our general state of health, we often have to cure before we prevent. Nevertheless it is cheaper, as well as better, to prevent illnesses than to cure them; and this can often be done by greater health education, by better hygiene, and by sensible prophylactic medicine for people at special risk. Tentative steps in this direction have been taken, with more emphasis being given to preventive medicine in the training programmes. But it is necessary that we should act more positively and with a greater sense of urgency in this matter.

All members of the medical profession should see it as an important part of their task to teach their patients, and the people in their locality, how to remain or become healthy. And every TANU leader should make it his or her business to learn how he can help. For cleanliness in our streets, and in our yards, does not need special training courses; a declaration of war upon flies should not need a debate at a TANU Conference. Nor is it good enough to grumble about bad municipal refuse collection; to a large extent each area could become 'self-reliant' in this matter. Yet through such means as this we could make great headway towards better health, without more money.

The second step is equally important. We have to 'think Tanzanian' in relation to health as in other things. It is no use our laying down such high standards of building, sanitation, and equipment for our rural health centres, etc., that we can only afford to build one or two a year instead of the hundreds which are needed. What is important to our people is that they should have services available; they don't need palaces. It doesn't matter if these services are available in a mud hut, provided that this hut is kept scrupulously clean, that light and air can get through it, that it has clean water available, and some means of sterilizing thermometers and other instruments. And an improved local-type building, whitewashed inside every few months, and thoroughly scrubbed every day, with a simple water tank and filter, and a gas or paraffin heater, etc., can be provided quite cheaply. Indeed, in many cases the members of an ujamaa village could do such building and maintenance themselves if they had a minimum of guidance. The same principles apply to all other rural medical services; all the time we must be concerned to see how cheaply we can provide the basic facilities and not how beautiful they look to visiting Presidents or tourists.

Even in towns the same attitude must be adopted. We now have some wonderful hospitals, with elaborate equipment. But do we realize how much these buildings and this equipment costs to maintain? In future we must think ten times before we undertake such recurring expenditures; for in health as in other things we must concentrate first on the basic necessities. We cannot afford to provide facilities for a few people to get advanced treatment for special heart diseases while the masses of our people are not able to get treatment for the common diseases which make their lives a misery. That is a hard doctrine, but it is a question of priorities. To plan is to choose!

Education

In a socialist country universal primary education would be provided free for all children, and post-primary education would be readily available to all who could benefit from it, however old they may be. Such conditions do not exist in Tanzania; we are only working towards socialism and are far from having achieved that objective.

The poverty of Tanzania does not allow for the kind of expenditure which would be necessary for such universal services, however much we would like them. Priorities have had to be worked out and strictly adhered to. Certainly these priorities have changed as our circumstances changed and as we became more aware of our national requirements. But one thing has remained fairly constant: that is the decision that the limited resources at our command must be used first to prepare citizens of this country for the competent execution of the jobs which the community wants done. Post-primary education in particular is thus provided in accordance with the manpower plan forecasts; although we are working towards universal primary education, we cannot make available at public expense 'education for education's sake' beyond that level.

Yet for our country education is a necessity. Hence, something like 20 per cent of Government recurrent expenditure is devoted to this service, and has been for years. Whereas in 1960/61 we allocated Shs. 50 million to recurrent costs and a further Shs. 8 million to development, the respective figures for the current year are Shs. 310 million and Shs. 60 million.

The problem is that, even with this great emphasis on education, we cannot do a fraction of what we would like to do. We have decided that an early objective must be universal literacy; we want to provide for all our citizens the basic tool with which they can become more efficient in their daily work, and which they can use to improve their own education.

At independence, however, we inherited a society which was basically illiterate, and where the number of people with even secondary school education was very small indeed. Thus, for example, in 1961 there was a total of only 11,832 children in the secondary schools in Tanganyika, and only 176 of these were in the Sixth Form! This meant that, in order to provide for efficient Africanization of our administration and our economy as quickly as possible, the new Government was forced to give first priority to the expansion of post-primary education. We did this to such good effect that in 1971 we had 31,662 children in secondary schools, of whom 1,488 are in Form VI.

The University College of Dar es Salaam was opened with 14 law students a few months before independence—it began that year as a result of decisions made in the period of 'responsible self-government'. But in 1961, altogether, there were only 194 Tanganyika students at the University Colleges of East Africa and 1,312 studying overseas, either at university level or below. The figures were very different by 1971—with 2,028 students at the Universities of East Africa and 1,347 studying overseas, some of these in post-graduate studies. It must also be remembered that these figures reflect a steady growth over the whole period; our country is now receiving the services of many young men and women who have received their Fifth and Sixth Form, and their University education, all since independence. The establishment of the University of Dar es Salaam has also meant that the subjects available to our students, and the content of their courses, are becoming ever more relevant to the needs of this country.

The same thing is true of primary schools. There has been a big expansion in numbers—from 3,100 to 4,705 primary schools, and from 486,000 primary school pupils in 1961 to 848,000 in 1971. Further, a much larger proportion of the children now do the full primary school course, for in 1961 most pupils left school after four years. Thus, in 1961, 11,700 children completed the primary school course, whereas this year 70,000 are expected to do so.

Yet these achievements must not blind us to the terrible fact that almost the same proportion of our children now as in 1961 fail to find a place in primary school. We have provided primary school places for only about 52 per cent of the children of primary school age—that is how far we are from our objective of universal primary school education! And it is absurd to think that passing resolutions at TANU Conferences, or asking questions in Parliament can solve this problem. There is no short and simple answer to it. Yet it would be criminal if we allowed our failure to be enveloped in a cloud of self-congratulation about what we have achieved in education. Those children without school places must remain as a real challenge to us for the future.

It is not, however, only numbers which matter in education. The type of education given in our schools is equally important. This was recognized when we adopted the policy of 'Education for Self-Reliance' in 1967, and since then we have been trying to change the content of the education provided by our education system. We are trying to ensure that lower levels do not direct their attention solely to preparing their pupils for secondary school or university, but that at each level attention is concentrated on the needs of the majority. For we have recognized that, for the foreseeable future the majority of our primary school pupils will not go to secondary school, and the majority of our secondary school pupils will not go to university. In Tanzania they will leave full time learning and become workers (not necessarily wage earners) in our villages and towns.

We have made quite good progress in this endeavour so far, but our task is far from complete. Not all the syllabuses have yet been changed in accordance with the new policy; not every teacher has yet received the necessary re-training and re-orientation. We must try to do more on this, because wrong education could cause difficulties for the nation as well as for the individual in the future. But it is no use being impatient; replacing most of the books used is an expensive business, and in any case, they have first to be planned, written, and printed. It is no use replacing one set of bad books by another.

The policy of Education for Self-Reliance has, however, further implications, as it says that all schools 'must be economic communities as well as social and educational communities'. And it asks, 'Is it impossible for secondary schools at least to become reasonably self-sufficient communities, where the teaching and supervisory skills are imported from outside but where other tasks are either done by the community or paid for by its productive efforts?'

Virtually every school now has a farm or a workshop attached to it, and visitors see the children putting various degrees of effort into the work when a teacher is not nearby. It is also true that some schools have produced quite good crops, and have developed a pride in their production. But it is a much rarer school where the pupils are involved in the planning of the farm, the keeping of records, and the allocation of its returns to different purposes—in other words, where it is theirs and they are able to go forward on a co-operative basis. And still more rare is the school where the productive unit is regarded as an integral part of the life of the school.

The fact is that we have a very long way to go before our educational policy is properly understood and properly applied. Schools are places of learning—we do not want to change this. A school should not become either a factory or a shamba. But working in a school factory or shamba should become a normal part of the process of learning and living. This is what we have not yet grasped; we do not accept in practice that school pupils have to live, and work as they live, as well as learn, and that learning and living are parts of a single process. We are still trying to graft 'working' on to 'learning', as if the former is an 'extra' being added to education just for the good of our souls. Living, learning, and working cannot be separated.

Our failure to implement fully this policy of education for the young is, however, nothing as compared with the extent of our failure in the field of education for adults. As early as 1962 we recognized in words that national progress could not wait until school children had been educated and had grown up to take their places as active citizens. And we said then that this meant that education for adults was essential.

Yet despite the words, very little practical emphasis was given to adult education by Government until recently. It was talked about by politicians, but it was really done only by voluntary agencies and as a sideline by some Government field workers! This position has begun to change. During the last 18 months an organized and concerted adult education campaign has been under way, with the active and irreplaceable support of school teachers throughout the country. Further, the Ministry of Education has appointed Adult Education Officers in each District, and is providing free to each student, literacy text-books which were specially prepared to interest, and educate, adults about the nation's objectives while they are acquiring the literacy tool.

It is as yet too early to say whether the six Districts which were challenged to eradicate illiteracy before the end of 1971 will in fact succeed in reaching this objective. But efforts are going on in those areas and elsewhere, so that in the first half of 1971 something like 560,000 people in the country were attending literacy classes, and another 280,000 were attending other, more advanced, classes. One further lesson learnt from the experience of the past is also being applied now; it is no use teaching someone to read and write and then leaving him without anything to read! Post-literacy books and magazines are being prepared and distributed by the Ministry of Education, and this work will be expanded.

In addition to this 'mass education', a great deal of other education activity is now going on in Tanzania. For all the public enterprises are engaged in various worker training schemes; and seminars are constantly being held for Government employees, for TANU workers, for voluntary social workers, or for other different kinds of groups. Some of these seminars have as their major purpose the improvement of job skills; but a very large number of them are directed also towards spreading an understanding of our socialist objectives and what the particular group can do to further them.

Yet although this effort is now being made, we have not, as a nation, grasped that just as working is a part of education, so learning is a necessary part of working. A factory or a shamba is a place of work; we neither want to change this, nor could we do so. But learning must become an integral part of working; and people must learn as and where they work. At present education at the work places is regarded as an 'extra', whether it be thought of as an imposition or as a special treat! We still do not think of working and education as being necessarily connected together.

But they are connected unless a worker is to become simply an appendage to a machine—endlessly tightening nuts or endlessly copy typing. And for a Tanzanian to be regarded in this way simply as a 'unit of production' would be quite contrary to everything we are trying to do. It would be to treat people as an instrument of development instead of as the masters of development.

It is therefore essential that work places become places of education as well as of work. Classes must be organized there, for literacy, skills, politics and anything else in which a group of workers are interested. Of course this education cannot replace work; but it can and must supplement it, and be part of the working day.

These classes must become an integral part of the factory life—so normal a thing that it is their absence which is noticed, not their presence! An occasional 'course' is not enough: Workers' Councils, Workers' Committees, the management, or the TANU or NUTA Branch could take the initiative in this matter, then discussing with the management and the workers as a whole, how, when and what class should be organized. It does not matter who gets them going; the important thing is that they should start and be kept in being. At the moment we have, as a new thing, many literacy classes in different factories in Dar es Salaam. But this is not enough. We must go very much further than that.

If we are to make real progress in 'adult education' it is essential that we should stop trying to divide up life into sections, one of which is for education and another, longer one of which is for work—with occasional time off for 'courses'. In a country dedicated to change we must accept that education and working are both parts of living and should continue from birth until we die. Then we may begin to deserve the praise that was given to Tanzania by the man who said that our policy is 'revolution by education'. At the moment, and despite our undoubted achievements, such praise refers more to what we say than to what we do.

WHAT WE HAVE ACHIEVED: THE ECONOMIC SECTORS

Agriculture

All that we have done in the social and public service sectors, and indeed all other economic expansion, has depended on agriculture. That was, and remains, the basis of our economy. Unless we had expanded output in this field, virtually no other progress would have been possible. Similarly, if we had done nothing about socialization in the rural areas, then the effect and the longevity of our other socialist measures would have been very greatly reduced. Fortunately, agricultural production has expanded, and we have begun to move towards socialism in the rural areas.

The output of all our major, and many of our minor, crops (except sisal) has increased very greatly. Once again, it is only possible to compare the position in 1961 as against 1970, because it is dangerous to count on expectations about output when the weather can have such a devastating effect on the final result. That factor must also be remembered when comparing these two years: 1961 was quite a bad year from a weather point of view, while 1970 was not.

Bearing that in mind, it is still very much worth looking at the increases in output in certain crops. Using metric tons as the unit of measurement (equivalent to 2,205 lb.), our cotton production went up from approximately 30,000 to approximately 79,000 tons, coffee from 20,000 to 55,000; and pyrethrum flowers from 1,300 to 3,800. It is worth noting, also, that the processing of this latter crop is now done in Tanzania, whereas previously all the flowers had to be sent to Kenya for extraction to be done. Sugar production went up from 29,000 tons to almost 90,000; cashew from 28,000 to 118,000; and sunflower seeds from 6,000 to 13,000. It is because of these increases that the other expansion of our economy was able to take place. Yet it would be idle to pretend that we have done anything like enough, or that we have really made much progress in modernizing our agriculture.

For the truth is that these increases have been achieved more by increased acreage than by any other single factor. It is believed that in 1964 something like 29 million acres were being cultivated and that the figure in 1970 was nearer 39 million but, because there has been no agricultural census, these are only the roughest of estimates.

It would be wrong to say that there has been no improvement in the methods of husbandry practised in Tanzania or that there has not been any introduction of modern ranching methods for livestock. Yet unfortunately it would be more true to say that than to imply that a revolution in method has taken place in our rural areas. No such revolution has been effected. Our cotton is grown very much as it was grown ten years ago. Better seeds are used because of the work done at the Ukiriguru Research Station, and this has helped a lot. But only about 5 per cent of our cotton farmers are using fertilizers; even the number of oxen-ploughs used in the cotton areas is very small indeed. A visitor to a cotton farm in Sukumaland or elsewhere, returning after an absence of ten years, will probably see nothing new in method or in tools. He will still hear the same message being broadcast—plant early, uproot and burn the plants after harvest, etc.—and he will see that these messages are still necessary because otherwise the work does not get done!

The same thing is true of all our old crops; the methods are those of the past. Indeed the situation is even worse as regards foodstuffs, because our colonial governors used to concentrate all their attention on cash crops and we have followed their example by not bothering about the methods used for the production of food.

Only in regard to the new cash crops have we farmed at all well, for in relation to these the peasants are taught and supervised from the beginning. Tobacco and tea are the most important examples of this, and as a result our tea is now recognized as being of high quality in a competitive market, and our tobacco production has increased from 2,700 metric tons in 1961 to 21,400 metric tons in 1970. And it is in these crops—especially the latter—that the use of fertilizers has really expanded. It is therefore even more disgraceful when one considers that whereas Tanzania used 7,000 tons of fertilizers in 1961 we used only 23,000 tons in 1970. If we had really been carrying through an agricultural revolution in Tanzania during that period, the expansion in the amount of fertilizer used would have been nearer 30 times than 3 times!

The use of better tools has also extended very slowly indeed. At one time we imported a lot of tractors and put them under the control of co-operative societies which used them to plough for their members. But this soon proved to be uneconomical, because the use of the tractors was not properly organized and they spent more time moving on the roads or waiting for repairs than they did actually at work in the fields. Now tractors are used mostly on state farms with just a few being owned by the more advanced ujamaa villages.

The small expansion of tractor use is, however, of much less importance to us than the slow progress we have made in spreading the use of animal-drawn implements. It ought by now to be a common sight in our countryside to see ujamaa village members, or even individual peasants, doing their ploughing and harrowing, etc., with such tools. But in most areas all that we see are people with backs bent under the hot sun, breaking the land with heavy hoes just as their ancestors have done for centuries. We must move faster in this matter. It is true that in the last few years 21 ox-training centres have been established; but when one considers the size of our country and the number of our people it is obvious that this number is ludicrously small. Even last year only about 12,000 ox-ploughs were sold in Tanzania—2,300 of which wcre locally made.

We have, it is true, extended the training of agricultural field officers both for arable farming and for the veterinary sector. Whereas in 1961 there were three Ministry of Agriculture Training Institutes, by 1971 there had been added to these, four Centres for the training of Field Assistants, 17 Farmers' Training Centres (which take members of ujamaa villages for special courses), an Agricultural Faculty of the University, and several centres for specialized training in such things as farm management, agro-mechanics, land planning, and so on.

Once again however, the content of such courses is as important as the fact that they are taking place, and changes have recently been introduced which should make these more useful. For greater emphasis is now being given, especially at the more advanced levels, to the economics of farming, in the hope that the people trained will be able to help our ujamaa village members to organize their crops and their time to better effect. But the technical knowledge about different types of crops, and about what will grow where and how, remains as important as ever. And we must do much more, for although the expansion of training courses is good, we have not reached the stage where a peasant can easily get new information—or pass on the information he gains through experience. The growth in ujamaa villages will, however, make it easier for us to apply the lessons learned at these training courses, because agricultural field workers can reach a larger number of people at one time—and be reached by them.

There is one other thing we must also learn. For we still appear to think that the only person who can teach anyone anything about agriculture is a man who has certain certificates or certain formal educational qualifications. This is just not true. Such things can help provided the course leading to the certificate is practical and directed towards the needs of our countryside. But learning is not a matter of getting certificates; and in agriculture especially, we must accept that fact quickly, and make arrangements to learn from anyone who is a good farmer.

What all this means is that the considerable increases in agricultural production which our nation has recorded are due mostly to the sweat of the peasants. Yet, although we must be dissatisfied with the amount we have done to help them improve their methods, it would be wrong to say the extended activities of the Ministry of Agriculture have had no effect. They have helped. The expansion of services has just not been great enough or dynamic enough. It is worth mentioning at this point, however, that most of the extra activities of the Ministry—for example, the wages of the Field Officers and Assistants, the running of the Farmers' Training Centres, and so on—are classified in the national accounts as 'Recurrent Expenditure' not 'Development Expenditure'. Yet this kind of work is basic to development. It is not much use the nation spending money on making ox-ploughs available if the farmers do not know how to use them; it is no use urging the farmers to apply fertilizer if they have no way of learning how and when to do so. Agricultural expenditure is, and ought to be 'Development Expenditure', however it appears in the national accounts.

Although it does not yet show very much in the production figures, the organization of production in our rural areas is also beginning to change. With the establishment of a few publicly-owned, and usually mechanized, large farms, and the rapid growth of ujamaa villages, our rural areas are beginning to move towards a socialist pattern. Unfortunately, it is not at present possible to give figures of the proportions of the total output which come from the different types of farms—though certainly up to now peasant agriculture is still responsible for the bulk of most crops.

This must change. If we are to become a socialist society the greatest part of our agricultural production must result from co-operative or publicly-owned farms. So far we have established the machinery for state farms and ranches, but we cannot claim to be giving them the attention and care that they need if they are to succeed. In at least one case, indeed, state farms are at present getting a lower yield per acre than the nearby peasants, despite the amount of machinery, etc., which they have! Yet if capitalist farmers can make profits out of large units, it is obvious that properly conducted state farms should be able to make a great contribution to our national output, and also to help their neighbours with services and advice.

At present, the Production Division of the Ministry of Agriculture runs some farms, a few of which are doing reasonably well, but not all. The National Agricultural and Food Corporation is also active in this field, with ranches and some arable farms in the process of formation or—in a few cases—expansion after they were taken over from NDC when NAFCO was established in 1969. So far, rice, wheat, sugar, tea, limes and maize are among the crops being grown on these publicly-owned farms, and dairy farming is being introduced. Yet although it would be absurd to forget that there is always a time period between establishing a new farm and getting maximum production from it, we should not be satisfied with our progress. We must keep the public-farm sector under constant review.

But the real socialization of the rural areas depends upon the spread and the success of ujamaa villages. For these are, or will be, the co-operative farms which are under the direct control of the producers, who will themselves decide what to grow, how much, and so on. Further, these are not just economic units; an ujamaa village is, or will become, an economic, a social and a political unit. Its people will not only produce their crops together, so that they talk of 'our shamba' and 'our output'; they will also run their own affairs, supervise their own schools, organize the improvement in their own living conditions, and become a community for all purposes.

It is much too early to discuss the success or failure of this rural socialist policy. For although a few such units did exist previously, it was only in September 1967, that the development of ujamaa villages became official TANU and Government policy, and therefore only after that date that there was official help and encouragement given to them. Further, all such villages must be established voluntarily, and the members must themselves decide at any one time how much they are willing to do co-operatively, and how much they want to continue on an individual basis. For an ujamaa village can only come into being in its full sense when it has the whole-hearted support and commitment of the people involved; it will inevitably, therefore, come into being by stages.

Thus, although there were in June 1971, thought to be something like 2,700 'ujamaa villages' in existence, with a total population in the region of 840,000 people, most show more of a commitment to a future of ujamaa than to the practice of it. In some cases, the people have only just come together to live in a village; in such circumstances they usually continue with their individual farming practices for a year or so. Co-operative farming is usually started, and expanded, quite slowly. In other cases (particularly in Iringa Region), the people have begun to work together on a co-operative farm before moving into a village.

In fact, among these 2,700 ujamaa villages there can be found almost every stage of development, from one or two of the older ones where all farming is done co-operatively, through those where cash crops are farmed co-operatively, to those where only a few acres are farmed together, with the proceeds being used for village needs. Sometimes people describe themselves as living in an ujamaa village, when in fact they are doing nothing at all together. This is usually because it is their first year of living as a community and all the members are concentrating on ensuring that they have some sort of shelter and food for the coming season.

There is nothing wrong with this method of development; on the contrary, it is probably the best way for our nation to proceed; for we have no blueprint which tells us all the answers to questions about how such villages should be run and should operate. Indeed, different types of land, different climates, different peoples and different crops mean that there should not be a single model; for an ujamaa village will only succeed when it takes all these things into account in its organization and practice. By our present method we shall learn as we go along, and learn from each other. Indeed this is already happening as members of newer villages visit those which are older or more advanced, and study what is being done and how.

Yet already a number of interesting things can be seen. For example, whereas at one time it was the general practice for an ujamaa village to be started on completely new land, with members leaving their old homes, an increasing number of villages are now being created by the transformation of existing communities—Mwanza Region is a good example of this trend. It is also clear that the rate at which ujamaa villages are being established is increasing. Between early 1970 and July 1970, the number increased from about 800 to about 1,200; in the next six months an extra 500 were started, and in the following six months an extra 700. And, of course, none of these figures include the recent mass movement of people in Dodoma Region into ujamaa villages—a movement which represents the biggest challenge and the biggest opportunity for the ujamaa village policy, because of the particularly difficult nature of the land and climate in this Region.

There is, in other words, good reason to believe that we are making progress in the execution of our policy for socialism in the rural areas. Certainly Government has done, and will continue to do, everything possible to help and encourage this development. Priority is given to ujamaa villages in the allocation of new schools or class-rooms, dispensaries, clinics, water supplies, advisory services, etc. Everything now depends upon the leadership which is given to the people—a leadership which must mean doing, not just saying—and our determination to learn as we go along from our own experience and from each other.

Industry

If our nation is to develop, however, we cannot continue to have an exclusively agricultural economy. It is encouraging, therefore, that the expansion of manufacturing and processing since independence has been very great. A large proportion of our simple consumer goods, which used to be imported in 1961, are now made within Tanzania, and the number and variety is increasing every month. Thus, for example we now produce almost all our own textiles; we make our own matches, blankets, cycle and motor car tyres, household and plastic products, furniture, shoes, steel wire, bags, foodstuffs of all kinds, and so on. We produce our own cement, refine our own oil, assemble lorries, and make simple agricultural implements. In by no means all of these things are we the only supplier of our market, but none of them did we do in 1961. Then, we had just begun to make our own cigarettes and beer, manufacture plastic shoes, and mill our own flour—and very little else besides.

The importance of this change is difficult to over-emphasize. For it is not just a question of national pride; this industrial development has an effect on the whole economy. It creates employment for Tanzanians and is a source of training for them as they work; the money which is spent on these goods circulates within the country—the worker buys food, clothes and other things from his wages thus providing still more employment and stimulating further activity. At the same time we are saving foreign exchange.

In 1961 we had to sell overseas the products of our farmers, even to buy clothes made out of the cotton we had grown; to buy such simple things as matches, we had first to find a foreign purchaser for our cash crops. Now we can save the foreign exchange which our farmers earn, and spend it on complicated goods needed for development.

Inevitably we have had some difficulty with certain of our new Tanzania-made products as regards quality and price. These are not small matters, for it is a waste of effort and money to make matches which do not light, or textiles which do not wear well. Nor is it very helpful to a poor peasant if he is forced to pay much more for a Tanzania-made product than he would have had to pay for a comparable imported one. It is vital that great attention should be paid to these questions by the workers in our new industries; their job is to produce good, hard-wearing and functional products even though they may be simple at this stage.

Yet it would be absurd to pretend that this can always be done immediately. The community must accept that either in price or design—or both—Tanzanian products may not be quite as good as the imported things when they first come on to the market. A householder who is learning to make his own chairs from wood off his own farm is unlikely to produce a very nice chair at his first attempt. But if his wife refuses to use it because of its imperfections, she will either have to go without a chair altogether, or she will have to give up buying a new cooker because some of the money for it has been spent on buying more beautiful chairs. Tanzania, as a nation, has the same kind of choice.

And this situation will change. The householder is likely to make a better chair at his second attempt, because of greater confidence in the use of his tools, because he will have studied the faults in his first effort, and examined those made by more skilled persons. Similarly, our Tanzania factories will improve as they learn from experience. Indeed, that has already happened with some products. Our matches now work; the cloth from our textile mills is of better quality and more to the taste of our people than when it was first produced; and so on.

In price, too, there may be a differential, with Tanzania prices being higher than those for comparable goods from developed countries. Sometimes, and in relation to certain products, this can also be corrected in time; but that will not always be so. For sometimes this difference will arise because the developed countries are able to produce in much larger quantities and can therefore use methods of mass production which our market does not justify, or which demand elaborate machines for which we do not have the foreign exchange. But the basic question is the same: if we insist on purchasing such goods from abroad, rather than paying a few extra cents for small items, or extra shillings for large items, then we shall be unable to spend our foreign exchange on things which we are quite unable to produce for ourselves. We should remember, however, that some local products have been cheaper from the beginning. We have got so used to paying 15 cents for a box of matches that we forget the price of 20 or 25 cents we used to pay for imported ones!

But there is another important thing about our industrial production now. By far the greater part of it is produced in factories and workshops which we, as a nation, own completely, or in which we own the majority of the shares. This is not true of all goods: we have not excluded all private manufacturing activity in Tanzania. But it is true of the most important goods. And our instrument for this public ownership in manufacturing industries and mining is the National Development Corporation.

National Development Corporation

After its formation in January 1965, the National Development Corporation was reorganized in 1969 when the whole parastatal sector of the economy was rationalized. Several of its subsidiaries were then transferred to other parastatal corporations. Yet even so, the NDC's total investments in mid-1971 were valued at Shs. 330 million, as against Shs. 24 million at its inception.

The NDC, which is responsible for public investment, initiation, and management in the manufacturing, processing and mining industries (and which is involved in procurement and distribution within these fields), is thus the largest single parastatal organization. It has 22 operational subsidiary companies in which it has total or majority control, five companies in which it owns 50 per cent of the shares, and six others in which it owns a quarter or more of the shares. In addition, the NDC owns or controls a number of other companies and projects which are still being developed. Its interests therefore cover a very wide field; they include such things as the Williamsons Diamond Mine, a steel rolling mill, factories producing textiles, shoes, school supplies, meerschaum pipes, blankets and books. And its units vary in size from the Friendship Textile Mill, which employs more than 3,000 people, to the National Small Industries Corporation, which directly employs only 21 people, but which organizes and provides facilities for a large number of small craftsmen working on a cottage industry basis.

This variation reflects the many different purposes of NDC investment. For its task is not only to organize the production of high-quality goods at reasonable prices, and to save imports, or earn foreign exchange by exports. It also has the task of increasing wage employment and of diversifying economic activity in the rural areas. Thus, the NDC companies are occasionally very capital intensive, like the steel rolling mill or the fertilizer factory which has an investment of Shs. 162 million but employs only 800 workers. And sometimes they are labour intensive, like the National Cashew Company which deals with the hand decorticating of nuts in some ujamaa villages of Coast and Mtwara Regions. This will eventually employ about 3,500 workers, but the total capital investment will be only Shs. 3.5 million.

Thus, the NDC cannot look only at profitability when considering whether to initiate or maintain an enterprise. It has to consider the development of Tanzania as a whole.

However, the NDC as a Corporation, and in the course of time its individual companies, has to earn a surplus which can be invested in future development. So far, and after balancing out losses in new companies or those with special marketing difficulties, this has happened every year, although the total surplus has never been anything like enough to meet the new investment projects of the Corporation. It is essential that we should make extra efforts in this connection, for we cannot rest at our present position, and past investments must make a real contribution to the financing of new investments. Only thus will we build our industrial sector on the basis of self-reliance.

Yet their surplus is not the only contribution which NDC Companies make to national funds. They pay taxes like any other company, and these now total something like Shs. 175 million every year. This is an important contribution to our public revenues.

The Distributive Sector

As regards the distributive and foreign-trade sectors of the economy —as in so many others—the new nation inherited a structure which was mostly foreign owned, and which was very fragmented. Even by 1968 there were still some 400 private importers, 400 private wholesalers, and about 3,600 private sub-wholesalers, operating on the mainland of Tanzania—and this was after the nationalization of the major import/export firms. Yet Government has not only intended to control importing through a system of licences, and thus safeguard our foreign exchange position. It decided also to take importing and wholesaling into public hands so as to ensure that they operate solely for the benefit of the consumers, and with the minimum of fuss. We are making progress towards this.

Although some of the different parastatal corporations and companies have been given responsibility for the sale and distribution of their own manufactures, the bulk of this task has been given to the State Trading Corporation—and a difficult task it is. Tens of thousands of different items have to be kept available after having been procured, locally if possible or otherwise from the cheapest and most reliable foreign sources. At the same time the internal distribution structure has had to be reorganized to avoid waste and exploitation while ensuring that an adequate service to the customer is maintained. In addition, the STC is the Government institution most responsible for the rationalization of brand purchasing and the maximum use of such overseas credits as are available to us on good terms.

In these circumstances, and after less than five years of existence, it is hardly surprising that the STC has experienced more problems than any of the other public enterprises. For it has been expanding its activities throughout; at no time have we given the STC time to consolidate its existing operations before instructing it to undertake new tasks. A leisurely progress towards socialization has been impossible, because the necessity to rationalize the whole distribution system, and the need to reduce the period of business uncertainty have all required quick action. Positive public control of all foreign trade and wholesale distribution agencies had to be secured before full advantage could be taken of our other economic advances.

Yet despite its difficulties, the STC has not been running at a loss: on the contrary, after making provision for something like Shs. 20 million income tax over the period, it has earned a net surplus in the region of Shs. 27 million—all of which has been, or is being, re-invested in training or other improved facilities.

And the socialization has proceeded. In this year, 1971, we have reached a position where by far the greater part of our wholesale distribution is in public hands, and parastatal organizations have a monopoly in all the most important commodities. Thus, STC alone handles over 40,000 group products, and its turnover has increased from Shs. 353 million in its first full year of operation (1967/68) to something more than Shs. 630 million in 1970/71—an almost 80 per cent increase in four years.

Before becoming too proud of this, however, we must remember that this increase is the result of our deliberate policy, not because of any virtues of STC! In particular, we have to recognize that this Corporation is not yet geared for 'service' in the sense of making things easy for the consumer or retailer. We hear many complaints that the STC office closes at set times, regardless of the fact that customers' buses arrive later; in both town and country goods 'run out' although they are in plentiful supply; and everywhere there is a lack of helpfulness. Thus, for example, certain customary brands of goods may no longer be available, yet customers are only occasionally offered the alternative local or other product with some encouragement to try it; usually they are just told that what they want is not available—so they go off dissatisfied and still not knowing that their needs could be met. Then we grumble about people's conservatism!

There are other problems also, such as those of ensuring regularity of supply to shops, and of co-ordinating imports and local production, which the STC has not yet overcome. But in urging all the workers of this Corporation to make further efforts, we must remember that the STC is a young organization. While being aware of its deficiencies we must help it forward with constructive criticism, and not fall into the trap of doing our enemies' task for them by destructive attacks.

Looking now at foreign trade, we can see a similar advance

towards socialist organization. In 1961 virtually all imports were handled by private firms. In 1970 the STC was dealing with something like 42 per cent of the total imports (though about one-fifth of these were still being imported by private firms under licence); Government, the smaller parastatals and the East African Community, together, were importing more than 50 per cent of the total, the NDC was responsible for another 5 per cent; and only 3 or 4 per cent was still being handled by private firms.

Public ownership and control also dominates our exporting system now. Most of the collection, grading, packing and storage of agricultural commodities is done by the co-operative movement, with overseas buyers coming in at auction or other central sales points. And even here, the STC, on behalf of the nation, is now becoming active, while organizations like the Sisal Marketing Board, and the various NDC firms, also sell direct in many cases. Altogether something like 60 per cent of our exporting is now done entirely by public enterprises, and most of the remaining 40 per cent is bought by foreign agents from the Marketing Boards or other public institutions.

Thus, it is fair to say that the nation is basically succeeding in obtaining control and ownership of the wholesale, import and export trade in accordance with the Arusha Declaration. What remains is to increase our efficiency of operation, and our drive and initiative in finding good export markets.

Foreign Trade

From all that has already been said, it will be obvious that our economy is changing in type. It is no longer entirely geared to the export market; increasingly it is being organized to produce the goods which Tanzanians require.

This is not only true as regards manufactured goods, but also in agriculture. Sugar consumption has increased, and the sugar is now produced here; we produce wheat which our people eat to an increasing extent; and so on. And different areas are beginning to concentrate on the crops which they can best produce, so that an internal market is developing. Thus, for example, maize is transported from the Iringa area to Arusha or Sukumaland, while Iringa Region gets wheat from Mbeya or Arusha, and so on.

Of course, this development is only possible because of the improved communications and transportation system. When one Region of our country has a drought now, we can usually supply it from another Region which is in surplus, or from stocks; it is no longer necessary automatically to look to other countries for help and to use the transport system from our ports to the afflicted area. All this means that our real independence has been increased by a growth of an internal market; we can mostly help ourselves in times of difficulty, and we can use our own resources to increase our well-being when conditions are good.

But none of this reduces the importance of exports to our national development. There are many manufactured goods which we do not produce for ourselves, some of which we are not likely to produce for a long time. And only by exporting shall we be able to get the foreign currency to pay for these necessary imports. Indeed, the more we export, the more we will be able to spend on development goods and other essentials.

Exports have, in fact, increased considerably—by 73 per cent in money terms between 1961 and 1970, going up from about Shs. 973 million in 1961 to Shs. 1,689 million in 1970. It must be remembered, too, that this increase in value hides a great fall in the world price of some of our most important export crops (for example, sisal), while the prices we obtain for others have not gone up anything like as much as the prices of the kind of goods we import. The 'terms of trade' have moved against us since independence.

These figures hide a considerable change in the direction of trade. Thus, for example, in 1970 we sold goods to the value of Shs. 115 million to China and the East European countries, whereas in 1961 the total value of our exports to those areas was Shs. 9,000!

The totals also conceal the first signs of a change in the type of our exports. To countries other than our East African Community partner states, we sold processed and manufactured goods to the value of approximately Shs. 181 million in 1970, in addition to the oil which had been imported and refined here before being sold to Zambia, Burundi and Congo Kinshasa, and which had a total export value of about Shs. 111 million. In 1961 comparable goods to the value of only Shs. 68 million were sold. A similar development has taken place in our exports to Tanzania's partners in the East African Community. Not only has the total increased; we sold them manufactured and processed goods to the value of Shs. 64 million in 1970, whereas in 1961 the figure had been about Shs. 15 million.

Despite these changes, our most important exports are still primary products, with coffee, cotton and sisal—now in that order—being the most important in 1970. But even among primary commodities there were changes. Cashew nuts had become very important by the end of the period—increasing in exported value from Shs. 36 million in 1961 to Shs. 115 million in 1970 (which represented an increase in quantity from nearly 40,000 tons to well over 77,000 tons). Tea had also risen in importance, as had tobacco, although oil seeds and nuts, and meat exports, had declined—the latter at least partly because of greater consumption at home without a comparable increase in sales on the market.

This diversification in the market for our exports, and some change in their type, is matched by similar changes as regards our imports. Thus, for example, whereas in 1961 consumer goods accounted for something like 45 per cent of our imports, they only accounted for 9 per cent in 1970. That is a tremendously important change and reflects the new kind of economy we are building up. But although the value of imported consumer goods had gone down from approximately Shs. 455 million to Shs. 160 million, this does not mean that our total imports have gone down. On the contrary, they have increased from a total value of Shs. 794 million in 1961 to Shs. 1,939 million in 1970. What that change does mean, however, is that our importation of capital goods—the kind we use for development projects—has gone up from Shs. 308 million to Shs. 996 million—that is, from being 31 per cent of our imports to being 53 per cent of their total value. The importation of intermediate goods has also increased by about 300 per cent; these are the kind of goods on which further work will be done in this country—such as crude oil, industrial chemicals, and vehicle parts which will be assembled by Mtava in Dar es Salaam.

Our imports also now come from many countries with which we had very little or no trade in 1961. Thus, for example, our total imports from China in 1970 were valued at Shs. 265 million, as against nothing in 1961; most of this increase is, of course, accounted for by the TanZam railway or the consumer credit connected with it. But our imports from countries like the United States of America, and from the European Economic Community members, have also gone up by a very large amount. Even the imports from our traditional suppliers—the United Kingdom and other Commonwealth countries—have increased, although not so fast as those from other parts of the world.

Generally, it can be said that Tanzania's participation in international trade is now organized for Tanzania's benefit. This does not mean that we are satisfied with the prices we get for our exports, or have to pay for our imports! But we can, and do, search out the best markets in which to sell or buy; and we can, and do, engage in hard negotiating on our own behalf.

Banking

Both internal and external markets, however, require currency and credit. And at independence Tanganyika had no currency of its own. It used the East African shilling, which was issued by the East African Currency Board. Neither did the country have a Central or Government Bank; both central and local government used one of the private commercial banks for all their transactions.

Such a situation was obviously unsatisfactory for an independent nation, but action was delayed in the hope that an East African Federation could be established. But when it became obvious that this was not going to happen quickly, the Bank of Tanzania was established as the Government Bank. This Bank also became a 'bank of issue', and Tanzanian currency began circulating in 1966. By this means Tanzania was able, for the first time, to accumulate and manage its own foreign currency reserves. Then when the commercial banks were nationalized in 1967, the nation was able to secure complete control of its own currency and credit, and marshall all its financial resources for its developmental and social objectives.

Nationalization of the private banks was not, of course, without difficulty. Seven banks had been operating in this country, and all had been using different systems of management and accounting. (The Co-operative Bank was brought in at a much later stage.) The first task of the National Bank of Commerce was therefore to set up a single Head Office, and to ensure that a single system of operations was effective and practicable throughout all the

branches and the sub-branches. The second step was the rationalization of banking services, so that duplication in those towns
where the different private banks had been competing was reduced
to a single effective branch. New branches or sub-branches could
then be opened in areas which had previously been denied such
a service. Both of these steps were taken quickly and with great
success.

Since these first tasks were completed, the Bank has begun to
pay special attention to the rural areas, including some of the less
urbanized towns, such as Maswa, Geita, Mto-wa-Mbu, Masasi,
Mafia, Sumbawanga and Makambaku. In some places new branches
or sub-branches have been opened; in other areas mobile services
are now being provided, and these will be used as a gauge for the
future expansion of the branch system.

One of the big problems which the National Bank of Commerce
had at the outset was the small number of people with the training
and experience which equipped them for management positions,
and also the very restricted training schemes for bank employees—
indeed, these existed only in the very largest of the private banks.
This problem has, of course, been intensified by the expansion of
the NBC's activities. What it means in this vital sector of the
economy can be gauged by the fact that the Bank's work force at
the end of December 1967, consisted of 1,211 senior and middle
level people, plus junior service personnel—and 344 of the former
were non-citizens. At the end of June 1971, the comparable figure
was 2,151—which includes 247 non-citizens. Thus, there has been,
nearly 80 per cent expansion in the number of senior employees
but a reduction in the proportion of non-citizen staff from 28.6
per cent to 11 per cent.

All this, and the continuing improvement in the standard of
service, has been achieved by a thorough-going and extensive system
of training. Indeed, 117 different in-service courses had been given
by 30 June 1971, involving over 1,600 participants. In addition, 60
staff have been sent abroad for specialized training for periods
ranging from 3 months to 2 years. Tanzania's own Institute of
Banking and Insurance will open early in 1972.

It is worthy of note that since nationalization the Bank has earned
a surplus of Shs. 139 million—which has more than paid the
compensation due to the previous owners, and all the rest of which

is now invested within Tanzania, whereas previously most. of it would have been sent abroad.

Insurance

Insurance is another field in which public ownership has brought immediate and great benefits to the economy of Tanzania, as well as benefiting large numbers of its people through the greater availability of services.

Originally set up in competition with private insurance companies (all of which were foreign owned), the National Insurance Corporation took a monopoly of life insurance business in February 1967, and that of all other insurance in January 1968. Since then, great efforts have been made to expand insurance facilities to those sections of the population which were previously denied them.

In th's connection, individual life insurance has been greatly expanded, and the Corporation has also initiated group insurance plans, under which many groups of workers have already achieved a degree of personal monetary security. The NIC is now considering plans to extend group insurance benefits to members of ujamaa villages, co-operative societies and marketing boards, thus taking the benefits of insurance to people who live deep in the rural areas. At the same time as doing this, the Corporation has been expanding its general, commercial and industrial risk insurance to keep pace with the expanding economy.

While providing these services, often at a cheaper rate than before nationalization, the National Insurance Corporation has managed to accumulate a surplus of some Shs. 82 million during its first three years of operation. This is quite apart from its reserve funds! It is worth reminding ourselves that, if this business had not been taken into public ownership, all these funds would have accrued to foreign insurance firms and would have been invested abroad. Instead, the funds have been invested in Government Stocks, in real property, and in the share capital of the other parastatal organizations.

This work has been done despite very great staff problems. Immediately after nationalization, the Corporation had about 60 employees; these formed the nucleus with which all insurance business had to be taken over and expanded. There are now 580 employees of the Insurance Corporation, of whom only eight are expatriates. The work of training has thus been, and remains, a matter of very high priority for the Insurance Corporation. As it proceeds, faster, better and wider service will be possible. The groundwork has been laid.

Water

There are three other basic economic and public services to which some reference must be made in any report about Tanzania. These are water, electricity, and road, railway and harbour development. The first of these is water, because one of the major problems of rural development in most parts of Tanzania is the dearth or irregularity of water supplies. Although a water point does not have a spectacular appearance, it can often be more important for the progress of the people in the area than an imposing building, or a factory, put somewhere else; progress in this matter is thus an indication of the seriousness of Tanzania's development efforts.

On that basis Tanzania has nothing to be ashamed of—although nothing to be complacent about either. In 1961, Shs. 2.4 million was spent on rural water supply works by the Central Government, with local authorities contributing perhaps another Shs. 600,000/-. In 1971, by which time Government had taken over full financial responsibility for both development and maintenance, something like Shs. 22 million will be spent. In practical terms this means about 100 new major Government rural water supply projects in 1971, as against 20 in 1961, and the rate of expansion is at present being greatly increased in accordance with the 20-year rural water supply programme which has been worked out.

In fact, it has been estimated that, whereas 300,000 people in the rural areas were served with water supplies in 1961, the comparable figure for 1971 is 1,400,000. Although this still leaves the vast majority of the people in the rural areas without such a service, it is an indication of our progress, as well as the distance we still have to go. It must be realized, too, that these figures do not include simple well-digging, which has also been greatly expanded, and in which many voluntary organizations are helping. Thus, the Community Development Trust Fund alone has provided the materials for 1,050 wells, with the people of the villages concerned doing all the labour without pay. (Self-help is an important part of most small rural water developments.) It is also relevant that, whereas before independence the consumer had to pay up to 5 cents a *debe* for the water he collected from a standpoint, that charge has now been lifted. Both in towns and villages, water is provided free unless it is laid on into a house.

In the urban areas there has also been a great expansion of water supply, particularly in Dar es Salaam. The supply capacity in the capital was 3 million gallons per day in 1961; it is 9 million gallons now, and is expected to be 11 million gallons a day by the end of 1971 or early in 1972. This three-fold expansion has been made necessary by the growth in the population and by the industrial development in the city, and it is for the same reason that preparations are being made for still further expansion in the coming years.

Electricity

In 1961 TANESCO was operating in 14 towns; by the end of 1971 it will be operating in 22. Eight extra towns with electricity is not great progress in ten years. But that figure does not give any idea of the real expansion of electricity supplies; this can be better gauged when it is considered that, whereas about 144 million kilowatt hours were sold in 1961, something like 380 million kilowatt hours will be sold in 1971. This great increase is mostly a reflection of the nation's industrial development although increased public and private consumer demand has taken place.

Of course, a lot of this extra demand has come from the growth of Dar es Salaam, but it is no longer possible to isolate that as the only factor. For the central and north coastal area, including Morogoro and Tanga, is now linked by transmission lines. This system is served by a hydro-electric station at Hale, as well as a diesel station at Ubungo—where further expansion work has already started. Arusha and Moshi will also be linked up to this system; at the moment they are served from the generation at the Nyumba ya Mungu Dam, which was also built after independence and which it is expected will be integrated into the enlarged system. But other areas such as Mwanza have also experienced a great expansion in electricity consumption—in this case the sales have increased from 4 million kilowatt hours to 25 million kilowatt hours over the last ten years.

Roads and Railways

As in all figures, comparisons of the road situation at different periods depend upon classification! Certainly it is sometimes difficult to decide what in Tanzania should be called a 'road'—a reasonable answer depends upon the vehicle which is being considered and the time of year! An example of this difficulty can be illustrated by the fact that an official British publication at the time of independence gave the road mileage of Tanganyika as '20,464 excluding village roads'. But that was certainly not a figure for what are called 'classified roads', i.e. all-weather roads of some reasonable standard. Using a definition of that kind, there were in December 1961, 660 miles of 'bitumenized major roads', 310 miles of 'engineered gravel major roads', and 8,026 miles of 'other main earth roads'—a total of 8,996 miles! Comparable figures for mid-1971 are 1,550 miles, 595 miles, and 8,405 miles—a total of 10,550 miles, to which should be added the 5,880 miles of 'regional roads' which have been taken over from District Councils in order to effect improvements in standard and maintenance.

In fact, of course, anyone who has driven in our country in 1961 and 1971 does not need figures to tell him of the improvements. Almost any journey ten years ago was an 'expedition', where you arrived on time if you were lucky. This is no longer true. All our major towns are now connected with reasonable roads—the East African Safari has to find different routes than it used previously in order to maintain its reputation for being over very difficult surfaces!

There is a first-class bitumenized road from Dar es Salaam to the Kenya border; the road from Dar es Salaam to Zambia can no longer be called a 'hell run' by any stretch of the imagination, despite the large amount of traffic on it since 1965, and it will be completely bitumenized in the near future. The road to Rwanda is also now of a good standard—although unfortunately the bridge across the Kagera River, which is being built by Rwanda, is not yet completed. And, perhaps even more important, Tanzania is now united by its road system, even though we have taken these energetic steps to improve our road links with our neighbours in order to promote inter-African trade.

On railway development there is no need for very much to be said. The Ruvu-Mnyusi link was completed after independence, but had been decided upon before. Its importance is that it links all the railways in Tanzania with the rest of the East African system in Kenya and Uganda. It is true that the short railway from Mtwara has had to be dismantled—indeed, some of its equipment was used in this Mnyusi link. But it had been running at a heavy loss for many years because it was built by the British to support the Groundnut Scheme in the south. When that scheme collapsed, there was too little traffic to make this railway worthwhile.

The really big development, however, is the railway which is now being built to link Tanzania and East Africa to the Zambian rail system. This enormous undertaking is now well under way. By the end of 1971, if all goes well, the first 502 kilometres (out of a total of 1,900) will be completed and will become operational—thus providing a much easier means of transporting the equipment needed for the more difficult terrain further along the line.

And that is not all the work which has been done so far; the communications system of the railway is expected to be completed on the Tanzania side by the end of September, and four or five stations on the first section will be in operation at the same time. Work has also started on the very many bridges and tunnels which are needed on the next stretch of the line. Our brothers in Zambia and ourselves have good reason to be pleased with the progress made, thanks to the incredibly hard work of our Chinese friends and of the Tanzanian and Zambian workers on this project.

This immense project has added to the pressure on the harbour and port of Dar es Salaam, which is in any case now handling a great deal of Zambian traffic, as well as most of the increased Tanzanian overseas trade. In fact, the port has been working for years at a rate in excess of its theoretical capacity, despite an increase in the number of its deep-water berths from three to six. The completion of two more deep-water berths within the next six months will help the great efforts which have been made to avoid delays in ship turn-round. And plans are in hand for further expansion before the TanZam railway is completed.

Mtwara port has also been used for some of the Zambian traffic, and Tanga port—which at present has excess capacity—is expected to become increasingly busy as the fertilizer plant, the steel rolling mill, and other factories in the north, reach full output.

FOREIGN AFFAIRS AND SECURITY

It is, of course, difficult to talk in terms of 'progress' in relation to foreign affairs. It is quite easy to say that we now have a Permanent Mission to the United Nations and 17 Heads of Mission stationed abroad—some of whom cover several countries. But the purpose of foreign affairs is not simply to place ambassadors and high commissioners in other countries! All that this number of missions does is to indicate our involvement in the world at large, and the extent to which Tanzania is now able to have direct relations with foreign governments.

On that score there is no doubt about the great change which has taken place since independence, when our contact with other countries, and indeed our knowledge of them, was confined almost entirely to Britain, America, and one or two of the other larger Western countries. Now our relationship cuts right across all the cold war barriers and is particularly strong with some of the other non-aligned nations.

In fact it is fair to say that Tanzania has been playing a very full part in the spread and the development of the concept of non-alignment, and that we have also participated actively in many international conferences designed to secure united action by the poor nations of the world in the defence of their own interests. We have often given a lead in such conferences, as well as taking a clear stand on all issues relating to human equality, colonialism, and Third World progress, at the United Nations. In the process, we have earned hostility from some countries. What is much more important, however, is that we have earned the respect of all. No one thinks that Tanzania is his puppet, and the occasional allegation that we are the puppet of a third nation is the product of the accuser's chagrin that we have refused to be his nation's stooge.

In fact we are now almost universally accepted as being a non-aligned nation, anxious to be friendly with all who respect our integrity, and who accept the principles of human equality. Thus we have, during these past ten years, moved from our colonial position as a member of the Western bloc, to the position where we are really independent in international affairs. Our job now is to maintain this position despite all the pressures which will continue to be exerted upon us from different directions.

There is one thing, however, on which we have never pretended to be non-aligned. That is, on matters relating to the liberation of Africa. In this we have been active and we shall continue to be active. Yet we cannot pretend that the last ten years has done more than see the battle joined.

In the Portuguese territories of Africa, the people have now taken up their weapons and are fighting for their freedom. Tanzania is proud to give support to these freedom fighters—diplomatically, morally, and by allowing them to receive their supplies through our territory when necessary. We look forward to the day when we can celebrate their independence with them. That may yet be a long time ahead, for the forces against them, and against us, are very powerful. But we know they will never give up the fight, and they may rest assured that this country will never draw back either.

In Rhodesia the situation is now, in many respects, worse than it was ten years ago. The minority régime has declared itself independent and has pursued the nationalist movement with great ruthlessness and with considerable success. For despite great heroism by individuals and groups, the liberation forces of Zimbabwe are unfortunately split, and spend a lot of time and energy quarrelling among themselves. Yet it is also clear that the rebel Rhodesian régime feels very insecure. It is for this reason that it depends so heavily on support from the apartheid government of South Africa, and it is for this reason that it continues to search for what is called a 'settlement' with the United Kingdom. One thing is certain: neither Tanzania, nor the OAU, nor the people of Zimbabwe will recognize any 'settlement' until the majority of the people of that country have secured control of their own destiny.

In South Africa the nationalist forces continue to exist despite the most ruthless and cruel oppression which can be imagined. Time and again one is forced towards the belief that organized opposition to apartheid has been completely smashed. But then one sees a new sign that this is not true; that, on the contrary, there are some heroic people still living and working in that country for the day when the principles of human equality will be the policy of a democratic South African government. We salute these heroes, and all those who suffer in the torture chambers and prisons of South Africa.

The other major objective which we announced at independence was progress towards African unity. Some progress there has been —though very much less than we hoped for. Yet it may be that our ambitions at that time were unrealistic in the sense that they expected progress too quickly. Africa is very far from united; even in the struggle against colonialism and racialism, it now appears that different states are adopting different policies.

Yet all is not lost. The Organization of African Unity, formed in 1963, does still exist, and most African governments at the very least take note of its decisions and feel the necessity to twist and turn in the pretence that they are observing OAU resolutions, even when most blatantly ignoring them. The name of the OAU is taken in vain by its members as often as it is respected. But the fact that no African nation is willing to leave the Organization, or to ignore it, is a sign that, however weak it is, the OAU has a worthwhile function. We shall continue to work for its greater effectiveness.

In more regional matters, there has been greater progress. It is not necessary to refer again to the Union between Tanganyika and Zanzibar. But the establishment of the East African Community, despite all i's current difficultie., is still an example to the rest of Africa of what must be done. Tanzania was disappointed in the failure of the negotiations for an East African Federation, but this ambition remains; all that has changed is that a different route towards it has had to be adopted.

Finally, Tanzania has been an active member in what is called the Good Neighbours Conference of East and Central African States. In fact, our relations with our neighbours have not always been good; we have continuing problems with Malawi because of its Government's friendship towards South Africa, Rhodesia, and the Portuguese; and, since January this year, the *coup d'état* in Uganda has brought bilateral co-operation to a standstill. But these are temporary set-backs. In general, Tanzania takes an active part in all efforts to further co-operation and unity on this continent. We shall continue to do so.

None of this means that we have broken, or that we wish to

break, old associations and friendships. It is true that our relations with Britain have been through many periods of difficulty as we have reacted to what we consider to be Britain's unfriendly actions in relation to African affairs, or as Britain has reacted to our opposition to colonialism. Tanzania has paid a heavy price in terms of economic aid for her stand on some of these matters; but neither in relation to Britain or any other country have we ever wavered in our pursuit of the policies we believe to be right because of our desire to develop our country at maximum speed. This is beginning to be understood in the world—and increases the respect with which our country is regarded.

Despite these difficulties with Britain, however, Tanzania has been able to maintain its membership of the Commonwealth and, through that institution, to rally much support for the principles we espouse, as well as to make new contacts and new friendships. Of particular importance in this connection has been the friendship which has grown up between Tanzania and Canada—a friendship which is based on mutual respect and a mutual understanding of the importance of working for racial equality in the modern world.

Our natural ties with India have also been enhanced by our common membership of the Commonwealth. Links with Guyana and with other West Indian nations, as well as united action on many matters, have been facilitated by our Commonwealth membership, and it has also given us new contacts with the small Pacific island nations, like Fiji and Western Samoa. In general, therefore, the Commonwealth has proved valuable to Tanzania, and our country has been able to play a full part in it. We hope that future circumstances will permit us to continue as members.

In addition, Tanzania's friendship with other small nations of the world has been built up. Of particular importance has been the great mutual understanding which has developed between the Scandinavian countries and ourselves. In recent years friendship with the small nations of Eastern Europe has also developed. Indeed, the list of our friends would be much too long to write down. They vary from Malta, with a population of approximately 320,000, to the People's Republic of China, with a population of something like 700 million people. With this latter country, indeed, our relations have become particularly important, because of China's size and its willingness to help our peaceful revolution on the one hand and

on the other, our ability and willingness to help China break out
from the isolation in which other nations were endeavouring to
confine her.

National Security

At independence Tanganyika inherited a very small Army of about
2,000 men, still equipped with 1914 War rifles. While it is no part of
Tanzania's ambition—nor within her capacity—to become a military
power, the threats to Tanzania's security from the colonialist and
racialist countries of the South have made reorganization and
expansion essential. Since independence, therefore, the numbers in
the Armed Forces have been increased, their weaponry has been
modernized, and an Air Wing and a Naval Wing have been created
or are being created.

More important, the Armed Forces of Tanzania are now an
integral part of the society, and their loyalty has been proved time
and time again since the reorganization in 1964.

Even so, it is not possible for Tanzania to maintain a standing
army large or powerful enough to defend the wide borders of this
country without the full and active co-operation of the population.
Work is just beginning, therefore, on the formation of a Militia
Force—a force of workers and peasants who will be trained to take
up their rifles if occasion demands. In full co-operation with, and
under the leadership of the Party and the TPDF, we intend that the
militia shall make the occupation of our land so expensive to an
enemy that he will finally give up any such attempt.

Many of the militia men will in fact have had some military
training during their membership of the National Service. This was
first established in 1963 and now has camps all over the country
where young men and women receive training in practical skills
as well as in the use of rifles, machine guns, etc.

The National Service is, in fact, basically not a military force at
all; its job is to make a contribution to the development of our
economy, at the same time as it provides education in politics and
skills for its members, and inculcates a sense of discipline which they
will carry into their post-Service life. It therefore runs farms, builds
roads, and does many other productive activities in the country as
these are needed. In particular, the National Service has proved its

worth in emergency situations. Examples of this have been their work in connection with the resettlement of refugees from the Rufiji flooding, their help in gathering bumper harvests in different parts of the country, and currently their participation in the Dodoma Region ujamaa village preparations.

The National Service was at first an entirely voluntary organization, but since 1966 all young men and women who receive senior secondary school or post-secondary school education spend two years in the National Service. A large part of the service of these members is, however, spent in doing the jobs for which they have been trained.

The Police Service has also been expanded and modernized since independence, though it is still a very small Service in relation to the population of Tanzania. More important in this case than expanding numbers, however, is the change in the attitudes of the Police, and to the Police, which has taken place since it became the people's own Service and not a creature of the colonial government.

Finally, in this connection, mention must be made of the Prison Service. We still have prisons in Tanzania because, unfortunately, we still have crime. But, despite the pressure on it, the Prison Service has won an international reputation for its enlightened methods and for the training which it gives to those who have been convicted. The Service rightly sees its major task to be preparing the convicted persons for an honest life as full and responsible citizens of our country.

CONCLUSION

Without any question at all, the people of this country have justified the statement I made in Bagamoyo in December 1961. We have achieved much more for the development of our country in the last ten years than was done in the previous forty years.

We have achieved more in material terms. Our country looks very different now, and is very different now, from what it was in 1961. In physical terms this shows up most in our capital city. At that time driving in from the new Airport you saw all the factories which existed; now the airport road has many more factories and workshops, yet the real industrial area has spread behind those buildings and along the Morogoro Road. We even surprise ourselves when the things we produce in this country are displayed every year at the Saba Saba Fair. Nor is this kind of development restricted to Dar es Salaam. Arusha and Moshi and Mwanza and Morogoro have all, to a less extent, shared in this progress, with most other towns also looking different now from what they did ten years ago.

But it is not only as regard business and commercial buildings that our towns have changed. In Dar es Salaam there are large estates of modern low- and medium-cost housing; smaller estates exist in other towns. There are many more schools, hospitals, better roads, better lighting, and better water supplies.

In the vast rural areas the changes are less evident because they are inevitably smaller and more scattered. Yet they exist. There are new stores, new water supplies, new clinics, new roads—and whole new farms and villages.

More important even than this is the progress we have made in nation-building—that is, in developing the people of this country. Hundreds of thousands of adults are literate now who were not literate in 1961. Hundreds of thousands of people now take an active part in their own village government, their District government, and indirectly in their National Government. The people are more self-confident; not only is the future theirs to determine, but they know it is theirs to determine.

We have achieved a very great deal in ten years.

Change Brings Problems

We have tackled many problems, and we have solved some. But we cannot be satisfied. In particular it is now obvious that despite our efforts in recent years, we have not in practice yet got our priorities right. We talk about rural development and about concentrating on the essentials of life, but we have not really succeeded in re-orienting our actions for that purpose. We should look again at this, remembering that our object is to make sure that every Tanzanian has available, first water, then a school for his children, and then a dispensary for simple medical treatment. Only after that should we spend money on unrelated things, except defence and security which, unfortunately, must always be maintained. Every other expenditure should be questioned in that context. How does it help us to reach those objectives?

Yet in the process of tackling past problems and solving some of them, we have created many new ones which also have to be dealt with. For change always brings problems, both for the individual and for the society. Indeed, the kind of problems a nation is faced with is an indication of the level of development it has reached.

Some of the problems of change can be avoided by careful planning, and where this is possible, efforts have been made—not always with success—to do so. But some problems reflect an almost inevitable lack of balance in development.

Thus, for example, a young man or woman with a full primary school education in 1961 regarded himself, and was regarded by others, as being educated. He expected wage employment—probably in an office. But now, with 70,000 students graduating from Standard VII this year, and an increasing number every year in the future, none of this is true. Not only is there insufficient wage employment to absorb all these people; they are needed in the ujamaa villages and on the farms of our country. Nor do they have much formal education in comparison with the thousands who now graduate from secondary school every year. Yet the expectation of these young people, and of their parents, has not changed to keep up with this development. Many still feel disappointed at what they regard as a failure to get wage employment. The attitudes have not kept pace with the real changes.

Many other examples could be given. Thus, despite the great care which has been taken over foreign exchange ever since the nation introduced its own currency in 1966, we are now running into the foreign exchange problems which come with development. Yet this is only to say that our capacity to develop has now caught up with our resources; for many years the limiting factor on our progress was men, not money. And because of our conscious efforts in relation to foreign exchange, we have been able to avoid foreign indebtedness of such a nature as to endanger our independence of action. We are able to implement and enforce the priorities which we have democratically decided upon.

In our case, too, there are the special problems of socialist growth as distinct from economic growth without a social purpose. One of these problems is that the process of socialization costs money and time—both of which are thus taken from physical development activities. For not only do you have to pay compensation for the enterprises which are taken into public control; the reorganization, and training of people in new attitudes, and in new skills, all take money as well as time. And the very fact that the socialist institution is different, and usually much larger than the private undertaking it replaces, means that the people who are given responsibility to run it on behalf of the nation have to gain experience—and inevitably they make mistakes in the process.

These costs must be recognized, for they are inevitable. But they are also very much worthwhile. Without paying them, we shall never succeed in our purposes; we shall never build the kind of nation we want. Again we can illustrate this point by an analogy; a man who has inherited a tumbledown cottage has to live in even worse conditions while he is rebuilding it and making a decent house for himself. In the same way, Tanzania has to accept the existence of problems which are created by the very fact of trying to convert the colonialist and semi-capitalist economy we inherited into a nationalist and socialist economy.

We have to encourage initiative in business, commerce and agriculture, without the vision of great individual wealth for the person or group concerned. We have not yet solved this problem.

Further, while ensuring public control of our economy and public direction of our development, we have to overcome tendencies towards bureaucracy. In other words, we now have the problem of how to liberate the citizen, not only from private exploitation, but also from the frustrations which arise from organized officialdom and inefficiency. And all the solutions to these problems have to be found while we are deliberately reshaping the Tanzanian society towards the pattern we have worked out, and in a world which is at least half hostile to the whole process.

Our problems now are those of combining organization for the common benefit with freedom to develop democratically at all levels. There is no simple solution to any of them, and certainly not one solution which can be quickly applied to them all. There is no short cut. We have to work out these problems as we deal with them.

In a sense our position is similar to that of a nation at war—for indeed we are at war, only with poverty. A commander-in-chief has to keep overall control of the war in face of conflicting demands for the resources which are available. But he will never lead his forces to victory if no one on any front does anything without consulting him, or if he rejects all their suggestions, or lets their ideas get bogged down in 'proper channels'.

And military planning is easier than national planning, for all members of the armed forces are subject to rigid discipline; within their own ranks all that is important is that they should understand what is being done and why, so that their morale remains high. This is not true of a nation at war with poverty. For the participants in this—that is, all the citizens—must have freedom and increased well-being even while they are participating in the struggle. Indeed, as far as we are concerned, the people's freedom to determine their own priorities, to organize themselves, and their own advance in welfare, is an important part of our objective. It cannot be postponed to some future time. The people's active and continued voluntary participation in the struggle is an important part of our objective because only through this participation will the people develop. And to us, the development of the nation means the development of people.

Let Us Celebrate

As I said on the 7th of July this year, our Party has passed through two stages of work. The first was that in which we demanded uhuru after becoming conscious of the indignity of being ruled by others. This stage took seven years.

The second stage is that which we have just completed; it was that of questioning ourselves, defining, and agreeing on the kind of nation we want to build. Now we have agreed that we want to build a nation with true independence, not one which has only 'flag independence'. We have agreed that we shall decide our own affairs in accordance with our own wishes and for our own benefit. We shall never agree to be puppets, tools or stooges of other people or of any other nation. This has been decided and understood by us and the world understands what we have said.

But we have also agreed that this freedom from external interference is not enough by itself. We shall refuse to allow Tanzania to be a tool or stooge of any nation; but we have also decided that no Tanzanian should be used for the benefit of another Tanzanian. We have agreed that we shall build a nation on the basis of equality, and have rejected the idea of having within our nation a class of masters and a class of servants. Further, we have understood that the masters we have rejected are not only the colonial masters, and the slavery we have rejected is not just that of being used by people of other nations. Rather we have rejected the very idea of masters and slaves, even if the one who wants to become the master and have others as his slaves is a fellow Tanzanian of ours. When we said we have been oppressed long enough, exploited long enough and disregarded long enough, we were not talking only about other nations but also about any Tanzanian who was accustomed to, or hoped to, oppress, exploit, or humiliate his fellow Tanzanians. In other words, we decided that we would build a nation based on equality and brotherhood—a socialist nation.

Thus, during the second stage, we decided that we wanted to build a nation which was truly independent and truly socialist. Now our Party is entering into its third stage; and this is the stage of actually building and defending that kind of country. It is a stage of building with determination, and defending with determination, a free and socialist nation.

We shall celebrate on 9 December 1971. And our nation has, and will have, something worth celebrating. But just as the celebration on the 9 December 1961 was only a beginning, so will be the celebration this year. It is the beginning of our third phase. We have achieved our uhuru; we have defined and accepted the kind of Tanzania we want to build and live in; now we must seriously build and protect such a Tanzania. And there is no true freedom and socialism without freedom and work. *Uhuru na kazi.*

37

Welcome to Olof Palme

President Nyerere gave a state banquet on 25 September 1971, during the official visit of the Swedish Prime Minister, Mr. Olof Palme. After expressing appreciation for the kind and the amount of Swedish aid to Tanzania, the President went on:

... Mr. Prime Minister: we do appreciate all this assistance. But it is not the real reason for our warm feelings towards Sweden, or for our pleasure in your presence. This, I believe, stems more from the fact that Sweden's neutrality is not a neutrality towards the great moral issues of our day. For Sweden's support for the struggle of the oppressed people of the Third World is well known here. We have noticed the assistance given to the people of North Vietnam, and the peoples of Guinea Bissau, Mozambique, Angola, Namibia, Rhodesia and South Africa. We know that this support does not take the form of arms supplies for the liberation struggles, because the Swedish nation does not, as a matter of fundamental policy, get involved in military commitments anywhere in the world. But what is important is that the people of Sweden have found other ways of expressing their solidarity with the peoples concerned. Thus, Sweden makes available health equipment and supplies, educational materials, food relief, and other essentials of any liberation movement which involves the simultaneous development of the human beings involved in the struggle.

Nor is that all. At the United Nations and at other international conferences, the voice of Sweden—and of other Scandinavian countries—is heard in support of humanity and justice. Your people, Mr. Prime Minister, help Africa to demonstrate—and help to remind us—that this struggle is one for humanity and is not just a matter of colour. The importance of this can hardly be over-estimated; for if the world is really to make progress towards peace and justice, we have to forget colour, and we have to overcome the great economic disparities which now divide the developed and the underdeveloped countries. The internationalism of the majority of the people of Sweden, and especially of its Government, is one of the most hopeful signs that mankind can achieve this goal.

For we must remember that our guest tonight is the leader of a rich party, which is governing a rich country. Therefore, when the Swedish people support human equality and oppose imperialism, it means that they are making a deliberate choice of principle, not acting in the hope of personal or national betterment. And when a young Swedish politician and Minister, like Mr. Palme in 1968, attacks the American actions in Vietnam, he is doing so because he is willing to risk his political career, and accept political difficulties for his country because he believes in certain principles. Mr. Palme: we know that sometimes you have had what I might call 'a little trouble' because of your stand on issues like Vietnam and human equality; I hope that, without being accused of interfering in Swedish affairs, I can say how pleased we are that you have overcome these 'troubles' and how much we hope that you will continue to do so. . . .

38

A Long-Term Optimist

After his return from a month in his home village of Butiama, the President gave his annual reception for diplomats on 13 January 1972. In his customary manner he spoke only briefly in referring to the past twelve months and expressing his good wishes for 1972.
  He concluded by expressing his long-term optimism.

. . . Externally, it is our hope that the world will continue to change in the direction of human equality and justice. For despite the fact that the world is still very much dominated by big power politics, I believe that much of the present ferment is the birth-pangs of a new kind of world—one in which all human beings have a reasonable chance for a decent life in dignity and freedom. I certainly do not expect this kind of world to be born in the next 12 months—or even in the next 12 years! But I am a long-term optimist. I believe that mankind does struggle upwards, in however halting a manner, and however many set-backs we experience as we progress. . . .

39

East African Industrial Co-operation

The East African Legislative Assembly meets alternately in Kenya, Uganda and Tanzania. President Nyerere opened its session on 8 February 1972 in Dar es Salaam.

This speech was made after the Community had survived great difficulties following the January 1971 coup d'état in Uganda and Tanzania's refusal to recognize General Amin's régime. Bilateral difficulties between the two partner states continued, and the E.A. Authority did not meet throughout 1971 and 1972; however, the various Ministerial Councils carried on with their periodic meetings, and the day-to-day work of the E.A. Community continued. It was at this time that President Nyerere re-emphasized the importance of regional co-operation and even called for its extension.

. . . At this Session, and indeed on all other occasions, the members of this Assembly should think East African. They have to try to understand the motivation and the problems of other partners in the Community, as well as recognizing and speaking for the interests of their own nation. For, in spite of its inevitable frictions. co-operation between our three nations is of vital importance to the economic development of all the partner states; indeed, we would all benefit by an extension of it into the industrial sphere.

For in fact, although we have a Common Market in East Africa, we are ignoring its greatest potentialities—at great cost to each of our nations. We say that we want to establish a real industrial base in East Africa; we want to produce our own steel, our own tyres, our own lorries, our own fertilizer, and so on. Yet whenever any of our nations considers such a project, we come up against the fact that our national market is too small to make such production a viable economic proposition in the near future. To produce any of these things as cheaply as we can import them, we have to use modern mass-production techniques—which involves massive capital investment, and consequent heavy losses if we produce for only Kenya, or only Uganda, or only Tanzania. In many instances, however, such investment would be justified and sensible if the output served the whole of East Africa; and our Common Market theoretically allows this to happen.

In practice, however, this is not happening. Each of the partner states goes ahead on its own, trying to interest foreign firms or foreign governments in such a project. And the foreign firms do sometimes agree. After all, their main concern is to sell their machinery to us, either for purposes of extending their competition to East Africa, or simply as a means of making immediate profit for themselves. In either case, the costs of the necessary subsidy will have to be borne by us. So we have the absurd position where both Kenya and Tanzania, in partnership with competing foreign firms, set up a tyre factory—each of which requires the whole East African market to be really economic.

If we allow this state of affairs to continue, we in East Africa will be throwing away one of the major potential advantages of our international co-operation. That is what we are doing now; we are ignoring the fact that the East African market, taken as a whole, justifies investments which would beggar each of us separately. And the answer, at least theoretically, is simple. It is the allocation among our states of those industries which need the whole East African market.

We did try to work out such a system of allocation once before. But although the Kampala Agreement of 1965 was right in accepting the principle of allocating industries, it had a major flaw. For we tried to use the allocation of industries as a means of rectifying the imbalance in the economic development of our three nations. This was wrong; it meant that if Kenya accepted the allocation of industries, she was agreeing to hold up her own development.

Fortunately, the problem of economic imbalance has now been dealt with by the system of transfer taxes, and by the rules governing the East African Development Bank. We can, therefore, look again at this question of industrial allocation, without the complication of trying to make it serve purposes other than the national use of our Common Market.

What is needed is for the organs concerned to sit together and to consider what are the industries which need an East African market if they are to be a viable proposition. Having made such a list, we can then find industries of equal value and allocate one to each partner state—doing this as often as it becomes possible to consider local production of this kind of manufacturing. Each industry would be owned within the state concerned, and under national control and in accordance with each nation's economic philosophy; but its products would be marketed freely throughout the three territories. Thus, although one industry would be in Kenya, one in Uganda, and another in Tanzania, all three would be East African industries. And the result would be a benefit to the whole area, as well as economic advancement for each of our countries.

In the machinery of the East African Community now, we have the ability to take this initiative, to conduct the necessary negotiations between the partner states, and to reach agreements of mutual benefit. We should use this machinery and use it *now*. . . .

. . . Mr. Chairman: the institutions, and the fact, of co-operation in East Africa have been under great strain since the *coup* in Uganda in January 1971. They survived, and it is very good that they did so. For the break-up of the East African Community would not only mean an economic loss; it would also be a terrible set-back to the Community's fundamental long-term objectives. These are, I believe, much more than the economic benefits which our present regional co-operation brings with it, or allows in the future. Our economic co-operation is, and to be meaningful must be, just a stage in Africa's growth towards unity; a unity through which we can obtain and defend the freedom of all Africa— freedom from colonialism, from racialism, and from exploitation of any kind.

But these long-term objectives mean that simple survival at our present stage is not enough. We must move forward to strengthen unity for our ultimate purposes, or we shall slip back to the exclusive consideration of narrow national interests defined only in money terms. That would lead to strains within the Community of a different kind—strains which would not deserve the kind of dedicated service which contributed so much to the Community's survival last year. This we must prevent. Therefore, because the possibilities of advance on the political front have receded for the time being, we must work for what is currently possible—that is, for an expansion of functional co-operation.

In saying this I am not implying that economic co-operation has priority over political co-operation. On the contrary, I believe that economic co-operation alone would mean reducing to a mercenary level all the struggles of our people for human dignity. Our real objective is a political one—greater freedom for us all. But under our present Community arrangements, co-operation in East Africa is organized by governments and headed by those in control of governments. In consequence, it is always insecure while the Governments of East Africa remain subject to violent overthrow. To counter that insecurity, and to safeguard the Community, it is therefore necessary that we should seek to involve more and more people in the implementation of regional co-operation—thus making it more and more difficult for the Community to be jeopardized by a flagrant disregard of its rules. This wider involvement can be achieved by a further advance on the economic front. But, while we accept the inevitability of limiting our advance to this front at the present time, we have to recognize that even this will become easier to negotiate if there is in each partner state a clear determination to pursue Africa's political objective of complete independence.

One final point, which is relevant to the current political problems between East African States.

There is a distinction between the responsibilities each partner state has as a member of the Community and the political relations of the partners one to another. If we all hold fast to that distinction and, regardless of our bilateral disputes, work to strengthen the Community where we can, then East Africa will come through this crisis stronger and better equipped to deal with the real problems of the development of its peoples.

40

Rumanian Independence

On 27 March 1972, President Nyerere gave a dinner at State House, Dar es Salaam, for President and Madame Ceausescu who were on a state visit to Tanzania.

... Mr. President; Rumania has a long history of struggle for independence and for its people's right to determine their own destiny. You achieved legal independence more than a century ago, but your people early discovered that legal independence does not necessarily mean real independence. Indeed, although neo-colonialism is a new word, I have the impression that it could have been invented by Rumania at almost any time after 1859, and that it certainly can be applied retrospectively to most of the first century of Rumanian independence! But the Rumanian people have also shown that it is not necessary to acquiesce in alien economic domination, and that neo-colonialism is not an inevitable price for economic development. Instead, the Rumanian people have expressed, through your Government, and that of your recent predecessors, Mr. President, their determination to build a socialist economy, and to do this in freedom. We in this United Republic have the same determination. We intend to be Tanzanians and also to build socialism.

But neither for Rumania nor for Tanzania does this mean a dream of isolationism. The people of Rumania know that they are Europeans as well as Rumanians. The people of Tanzania know they are Africans as well as Tanzanians. The people of Rumania know that they are East Europeans, and the people of Tanzania know that they are East Africans. And both of our peoples know that they are human beings, inhabitants of one world—and that, a world inescapably united by modern technology. Therefore, both of our peoples and our Governments rejoice in every opportunity for international co-operation on the basis of equality. . . .

41

Decentralization

During 1971 and the first half of 1972, Government worked out a new system of decentralized planning and administration. The Government changes of February 1972 were designed to assist in making these effective through the appointment of senior politicians as Regional Commissioners and by the appointment of a Prime Minister. President Nyerere broadcast on this subject in January, and in May put out a Paper explaining the proposals and their purpose. The following extracts from this Paper explain the philosophy and purpose of the changes.

The purpose of both the Arusha Declaration and of Mwongozo was to give the people power over their own lives and their own development. We have made great progress in seizing power from the hands of capitalists and traditionalists, but we must face the fact that, to the mass of the people, power is still something wielded by others—even if on their behalf.

Thus it has gradually become obvious that, in order to make a reality of our policies of socialism and self-reliance, the planning and control of development in this country must be exercised at local level to a much greater extent than at present. Our nation is too large for the people at the centre in Dar es Salaam always to understand local problems or to sense their urgency. When all the power remains at the centre, therefore, local problems can remain, and fester, while local people who are aware of them are prevented from using their initiative in finding solutions. Similarly, it is sometimes difficult for local people to respond with enthusiasm to a call for development work which may be to their benefit but which has been decided upon and planned by an authority hundreds of miles away.

These difficulties do not only frustrate the ordinary people in the villages. They also cause frustration for the District and Regional officials of Central Government, and for Local Government officials, who ardently desire to work for the development of their Region, but who find all their ideas—and their enthusiasm—buried in the mass of papers flowing backwards and forwards to Dar es Salaam. For at present, these officials have, in reality, very little local power. They have to consult the Ministries in Dar es Salaam for almost everything they wish to do, and certainly about every cent they wish to spend.

The problem is made worse by the fact that, at present, each functional officer is responsible only to his own Ministry in Dar es Salaam, so that it is extremely difficult to work out a Regional, or District development or problem-solving scheme which calls for co-ordinated action. Thus, for example, if all the different functional officers based in a District get together to work out the solution to a particular village problem, each one of them has then to apply to his own Ministry for any little money which may be necessary, or even sometimes for permission to devote his or her own energies to that project. Then if one Ministry refuses permission, the whole scheme can fall to the ground.

In that example I have assumed that permission was refused by one of the Ministries in Dar es Salaam for what appeared to that Ministry to be very good reasons. But the most frequent complaint in the Districts and Regions is that they cannot get answers to their letters at all. They write and write, sometimes five times, and hear nothing, yet it is impossible for them to visit Dar es Salaam from a place like Sumbawanga, or even Morogoro, without permission— which they cannot get!

Nor is this complaint heard only on one side. The Ministries also complain of the difficulty of getting answers to their questions. Further, they argue—quite understandably—that, because the Principal Secretary to the Minister is legally responsible for finance (and has to account for all expenditure to the Public Accounts Committee of Parliament), the Ministry Head Office must supervise and agree to the spending of every cent of Government money. Yet, in practice, the unfortunate fact is that this endeavour to safeguard the nation's money can result in great waste, as equipment or skilled people are left idle waiting for approval to begin work.

Or workers spend hours, and many shillings worth of stamps, finding out what happened to a few shillings which was spent on moving maize to where it was urgently needed, instead of the stamps it was voted for.

On top of all these frustrations, there is the fact that great confusion often exists between the responsibilities of the District Councils and those of the Central Government officials at the local level. All too often local people get sent from one office to another and back again, because the subject they are interested in has really fallen between everyone and is not being dealt with at all.

For all these and many other reasons, it is necessary that we should reorganize the administration of Government so as to make it more appropriate to our goal of socialist development. We have to work out a system which gives more local freedom for both decision and action on matters which are primarily of local impact, within a framework which ensures that the national policies of socialism and self-reliance are followed everywhere. The system must enable the Central Government to give guidance and assistance to local people, as well as to check on their work, while it reduces the amount of red tape and bureaucracy which is at present in danger of strangling our people's enthusiasm. Also, it must be possible for help to be given to areas with special difficulties or special needs, and the system must ensure the maximum use of scarce resources. Finally, projects which are of national importance must remain under national control, even though they may be situated in one particular area—a decision which does not preclude greater delegation of authority to the responsible officers on the spot.

The Government's proposals have been worked out with these objectives in mind. . . .

In addition, if these proposals are worked through properly, the mass of the people will find that it is easier for them to practise self-reliance in their own development, and to take part in decision-making which directly affects them. Further, they will find it less difficult to call to account those public servants who are responsible for local activities of Government. For if a villager has a problem now, he is liable to be pushed from the District Council to the Area Commissioner's Office, from there to the Region, and from there to Dar es Salaam, where he—or his letter—will wander between one office and another. But if this new system works properly, the villager should be able to go straight to the District Office and find the person responsible for the subject he is interested in.

There is, however, one danger which must be guarded against. The transfer of power to the Regions and Districts must not also mean a transfer of a rigid and bureaucratic system from Dar es Salaam to lower levels. Nor is it the intention of these proposals to create new local tyrants in the persons of the Regional and District Development Directors.

These officers will have overall responsibility, but the Decentralization exercise is based on the principle that more and more people must be trusted with responsibility—that is its whole purpose. We are trying to eradicate the thicket of red tape and the tyranny of 'the proper channels', not to plant them out all over the country. It is essential that this should be understood by everyone, for those who cause the new system to become enmeshed in bureaucratic procedures will, as they are discovered, be treated as what they will be—saboteurs.

What this really means is that the spirit of Mwongozo must permeate the entire implementation and operation of Decentralization. Personal responsibility for duties assigned will, of course, exist. But it must be recognized as responsibility to lead, to guide, and to help; officers are intended to be servants entrusted by the people with certain duties, not gods whose orders must be obeyed for fear of damnation. And in so far as procedures are necessary for the efficient carrying out of the people's business, they must be simple procedures, understood by the people, and operated with sympathy and understanding.

It will, of course, take some time before the new arrangements are fully operational. Provided that Parliament passes such legislation as is necessary, it is intended that, in principle, the new system should come into operation at the beginning of the 1972/73 Financial Year or as soon thereafter as practicable. In any case, however, the 1972/73 Development Budget is obviously being prepared under the existing system; it will therefore be 12 months later before the full effects on planning and financial control are felt throughout the country. But, after that, our people should begin to become conscious of their own control—and the nation should be able to see what effort it is really making in the rural areas. . . .

TANU

All these proposals refer to Government reorganization. But their success will depend upon TANU accepting enlarged responsibility for initiating ujamaa villages and other co-operative activities. Further, because the District Development Councils will refer their draft development proposals to the District Executive Committee of TANU for approval, the Party at this level will also have new responsibilities. For in these matters they will act in the same manner as the National Executive Committee does to Government development proposals. That is to say, the Party District Executive Committee will consider the *policies* being implemented by the proposed Plan, not the detailed projects. For example, the Party could say to the District Development Committee that their proposals give too much emphasis to schools and not enough to water, but they would not argue about whether a water project should go to one village rather than to another. Or, again, they could say that the proposals give too much emphasis to big buildings or to elaborate schemes rather than to many small productive activities. The job of the TANU District Executive Committee in other words, is that of guarding policy.

From this it is obvious that the Decentralization proposals will provide a new opportunity for local TANU leadership, as well as local Government leadership. For in addition to their new formal responsibilities, the TANU branches throughout the rural areas could, and should, make themselves into the active arm of the people, so as to ensure that every advantage is taken of this increased local responsibility. The necessary strengthening of the relevant departments of TANU is now under consideration by the NEC.

There is a further point which is relevant to the democratic nature of our society. Up to now, Parliament has been able to call any Minister to account for all the activities of his Ministry—or lack of them—in the country. When this new system is in operation, some departmental Ministers will be unable to answer certain detailed questions about local development. For example, the Minister for Health would be able to answer any point relating to technical or other medical assistance to a new health centre or dispensary, or a question about the training of workers for such rural services. But there will be other questions—about its size, architecture, location, etc.—about which he will know nothing. Such questions will have to be directed either to the Prime Minister, to whom Parliament votes the money for the Regions, or—usually more appropriately—to the relevant Regional Commissioner. But in practice it should not be necessary for M.P.s to ask questions in Parliament about specific local developments, for they will be members of the DDCs and RDCs, and can raise all such problems there.

This does not affect the *right* of M.P.s to ask questions in Parliament. It simply means that, as power has been decentralized, so the real place to get certain problems solved has been decentralized, and an intelligent M.P. will act accordingly.

But there will be other types of questions which he may still need to ask in Parliament—questions about overall policy, about technical assistance to Regions, and, of course, questions about 'national' matters. For—to take an example—the Minister for Health will still be responsible for health matters throughout the country. But he will, in future, exercise this responsibility (a) by running the national institutions like Muhimbili Hospital, (b) by giving policy guidance to the Districts and Regions, and helping them as necessary, and (c) through the provision of training for technical personnel, etc.

And in fact, this decentralized system should increase the reality of democracy in our society because it brings power closer to the people—they will be in real contact with those persons in Government and TANU who have responsibility for development in their area. Indeed, it will be one of the functions of TANU, and of the members of the Development Committees, to hold frequent meetings to consult with the people, to answer their questions, and to explain. For this purpose they will be able to call upon the Development Directors and the Functional Officers at District level to explain problems and opportunities. (Indeed, the officials should themselves ask for such meetings.) Thus, local democracy will become more real, even as the institutions of development will become more efficient.

CONCLUSION

The organization which is still being worked out will be important in the new development. But the attitudes of officials, and of TANU leaders and members, will be even more important. For the really vital element in Decentralization is that we have to drop our present apparent urge to control everything from the centre. At the centre we can prod, urge and help, but not control. Ultimately, people can only develop themselves.

Mistakes will certainly be made under this new system. But we will learn from them and we can correct them as we go along. Care is necessary, but a desperate fear of mistakes results only in stagnation.

These proposals in fact follow logically from the Arusha Declaration and from Mwongozo, and from the basic principles of ujamaa. For they imply putting trust in the people. And if we cannot do that, we have no claim to be socialists.

42

After the Pearce Commission

This Paper was published on 3 June 1972, immediately before the 1972 OAU Conference at Raḅat, Morocco. Although President Nyerere did not attend, the Paper was distributed to all delegates at the very beginning of the meeting by the Tanzanian Delegation.

In considering the policies to be adopted after the publication of the Pearce Commission Report, it is vital to remember our objective in relation to Southern Rhodesia. That objective is now, as it has always been, the attainment of independence for Zimbabwe on the basis of majority rule, and under conditions which allow the development of human dignity for all citizens and of equality between them all. That is the goal for Tanzania, as for the people of Rhodesia themselves. Further, we would prefer—and it is evident that they would prefer—to attain this goal by peaceful means.

The prime responsibility in this struggle for self-determination for Zimbabwe rests with the people of that country. The role of Tanzania, as of other free African states, is to support the Zimbabwean people by whatever means are within our power, but never under any circumstances to try to control either their struggle or the decisions they make in relation to it. The question at issue is freedom for the people of Zimbabwe. It can only be won by them, and the shape it takes is for them to determine.

The free nations of the world, and especially the free nations of Africa, nonetheless have an important role to play in the Zimbabwean struggle for freedom, and they are all affected by it. In legal terms Rhodesia is still a British colony. But its future is now a world issue, and especially an African issue. All those countries which have expressed a belief in the fundamental equality of man regardless of colour are involved, as are all those who claim freedom for themselves. For the right to freedom exists, and is indivisible. This is, and must be, acknowledged by all those African states whose freedom owes little or nothing to the economic or military power marshalled by their people. If we claim freedom for ourselves—and we do—and if for ourselves we reject domination by a racial minority —and we do—then we must take the same position in relation to Zimbabwe. We have to support the Rhodesian struggle for freedom on the basis of human equality. We are involved in its success, in the methods by which that struggle is won, and especially in the international consequences of that struggle.

It is for these reasons that Tanzania has always demanded that the independence of Southern Rhodesia should be acknowledged only after majority rule exists there. Recognizing the independence of Rhodesia before the majority of its people are in a position to control their own government would not be an act of anti-colonialism. It would be to perpetuate the worst kind of tyranny— the kind which is based on a man's race and colour.

The demand for NIBMAR is thus not an acquiescence in colonialism—it is a recognition that the only kind of independence which is meaningful is one which leaves a people in control of their own affairs. Independence based on the 'Five Principles' enunciated by successive British Governments would not leave Rhodesia in that position; it would leave the majority at the mercy of a racial minority. Not even Principle Five—the need for the British Parliament 'to be satisfied that any basis proposed for independence was acceptable to the people of Rhodesia as a whole'—meets this fundamental point. For to ask a people whether they agree to being ruled by a local minority is like asking a slave which master he agrees to have, when his demand is for the end of his slavery.

The settlement between Ian Smith and Sir Alec Douglas-Home was therefore of interest to Tanzania only in so far as it demonstrated the strength or weakness of the Smith régime after six years of illegal independence, and the intensity of the current British Government's commitment to its proclaimed belief in human equality and national freedom. The proposals showed the position very clearly. While Smith wanted an end to sanctions and the recognition of Rhodesia's independence by the major Western powers, he was still willing to make only face-saving gestures to achieve these ends.

The British Government, on the other hand, was willing to settle for face-saving camouflage, subject only to an appearance of African acquiescence in the betrayal of the Rhodesian people.

The Pearce Commission was expected to register the necessary acquiescence. Everything which was said and done by the British Government, by British business, and by the Smith régime after the 'settlement' and before the Pearce Commission arrived in Rhodesia, makes clear the confidence with which a 'yes' answer was expected. Indeed, even Tanzania under-estimated the political consciousness and political bravery of the people of Zimbabwe, and feared that the Pearce Commission might report a 'yes' answer.

But in fact, the African people seized the opportunity created by the intended facade of consultation and spoke clearly and unmistakably. They converted the facade into a reality by the sheer force of their united opposition to the proposed settlement as a basis for independence. Denied their old leadership, who remained in detention or in prison, the African people organized themselves to spread an understanding of the proposals and their meaning in the future. As a result the answer given to the Pearce Commissioners, by an overwhelming majority, was an African 'no'—the basis proposed for independence was not acceptable to them.

In the face of this answer, the Pearce Commission met its responsibilities and itself gave an honest answer to the questions which had been put before it. While their own feeling that the settlement should have been accepted comes through very clearly, the Commissioners made no attempt to hide or disguise the unpalatable truth—the Africans rejected the proposals as a basis for independence.

THE VALIDITY OF THE PEARCE COMMISSION REPORT

In considering the implications of this development, it is necessary to acknowledge that in one respect the job given to the Pearce Commissioners was a ridiculous one. The Commission was given two questions to answer: (a) Had the proposals been fully and properly explained to the population of Rhodesia? (b) Did the people of Rhodesia as a whole regard them as an acceptable basis for independence?

The first question is dealt with in the Report by an explanation of what was done to publicize the proposals and by discussion of the people's comments and response at meetings and in private interviews. The Commission concluded that the 'people of Rhodesia as a whole' did have a sufficient understanding of the proposals to give validity to their answer to the second question.

The main difficulty about getting an answer to the Commissioners' second question, however, was the question itself. For it was of the type: 'When did you stop beating your wife?' There was no possible straight and simple answer. This is best illustrated by the comment of Ian Smith, who is reported to have said if the Africans replied 'no' to the Commission, it would mean that they were satisfied with things as they are. In the event, the Africans took the question at its face value and said they were not satisfied with the proposals as a basis for independence. It is only because of the fullness of the Pearce Commission Report that their dissatisfaction with, and distrust of, the Smith régime is spelled out so that it becomes impossible to draw the conclusion which Ian Smith desired to draw.

But, be all that as it may, there is no doubt that the visit of the Pearce Commission, and its Report, have affected the Rhodesian situation and especially the world's view of it. The Report and the British Government's reaction to it must therefore be taken seriously.

In this connection it is necessary to acknowledge that every Commission of investigation or enquiry, anywhere in the world, has a built-in bias created by the education, life experience, and value system of the Commissioners The Pearce Commission was no exception to this rule, and indeed the Commission's realization of this is shown by the way in which the Report gives outline biographies of the Commissioners. Its members were uniformly white although they were operating in an area of racial conflict; they were men who had a good education, often in British public (i.e. private) schools. They were men who for reasons of family background, as well as intellectual ability, had no personal experience of long-term unemployment; the Commissioners were men who had often during extensive colonial service been 'masters' rather than 'servants'.

It is important to recognize this built-in bias when considering the conclusions of the Commission. For it means that the Commissioners would generally tend to be sympathetic with established authority rather than with those fundamentally critical of it or in opposition to it. And this is reflected in the Report, as for example in the Commission's failure to understand the seriousness of even an implied threat to the job of a man who has no other foreseeable means of livelihood. Their background—as well as the circumstances under which they were operating—explained also their great sensitivity to points raised by the Rhodesian authorities on grounds of law and order. The Report makes clear that the Commissioners altered their original plans on a number of occasions because of such arguments. For example, they gave up plans to hold public meetings in Salisbury and none was held; public meetings in other urban areas were sometimes postponed at the last minute at the request of the authorities (sometimes with disastrous results as at Umtali); prior announcements about the arrival of the Commissioners and their meeting places were frequently not made because of an alleged danger of unrest; some tribal Trust Lands were not visited; and a proposed public opinion survey was not made.

Yet there was another respect in which the background of the Commissioners made them insist on doing their job honestly and to the best of their ability. They rejected the original procedures suggested by the Rhodesian authorities because these could not have led to conclusions which would command 'respect in Britain and elsewhere'. Despite many difficulties they worked hard to obtain opinions from the widest possible cross section of the population and from practically all geographical areas. They made great efforts to circulate widely, and among ordinary people, the summary of the proposals which they had themselves prepared. And they refused to accept official hospitality and white Rhodesians' judgement as to whether the Africans had any opinions or what opinions they held. The Commission investigated things for itself.

In the event, the Commission expressed reservation about the understanding of the proposals, and about the opinions expressed, only in relation to two sections of the African population. First, they did not obtain as many opinions as they would have liked from domestic servants in Salisbury—who apparently comprise nearly 40 per cent of the adult African population of that city. House-to-house visits were obviously impossible and there were no public meetings. The Commission does not appear to have understood the suspicion, and possible lack of opportunity, which would undoubtedly have discouraged the majority of people in domestic service from expressing an opinion possibly contrary to that of their employers, when such opinions might become known to those employers.

Secondly, as regards the Africans employed on European farms or in the mines, the Report says:

> 'In general our Commissioners reported that the more remote the area and the smaller the concern, the more likely it was that the workers there would lack any depth of understanding of the issues involved, and that they would reflect the views put to them by their employers. Conversely, Africans at the larger or more accessible centres tended to support the nationalist viewpoint and reject the Proposals. . . . We therefore feel considerable doubt as to the acceptability or otherwise of the Proposals amongst this section of the population.' (para. 248)

THE CONCLUSIONS OF THE PEARCE COMMISSION REPORT

The total of the evidence marshalled by the Pearce Commission has, however, been incontrovertible. They held many meetings in the rural areas, they interviewed many individuals and any group which wished to see them, and they visited farms, factories and offices. The Commissioners also made impromptu stops and talked to bystanders at random, as well as making unannounced visits to places where people were gathered for social or work purposes.

The conclusions of the Commission were clearly stated:

> 'We believe that taking into account the explanation given by the Rhodesian authorities, the activities of those opposing or promoting the Proposals, the distribution of our simplified version of the Proposals and the explanations given by the Commission at meetings and over the radio, the great majority of those who gave us their opinions had a sufficient understanding of the content and implications of the Proposals to enable them to pass judgement on them. We are satisfied that the Proposals have been fully and properly explained to the population of Rhodesia.' (para. 419)

'We are satisfied on our evidence that the Proposals are

acceptable to the great majority of Europeans. We are equally satisfied, after considering all our evidence including that on intimidation, that the majority of Africans rejected the Proposals. In our opinion the people of Rhodesia as a whole do not regard the Proposals as acceptable as a basis for independence.' (para 420)

NOTHING IS SETTLED

The British Government has informed Commonwealth Governments that it accepts the conclusion of the Pearce Commission that the settlement proposals are not acceptable to the people of Rhodesia as a whole; the British Government also said that it will shape its future policy in the light of this conclusion. But obviously this does not 'solve' the Rhodesian issue. It merely means that the Smith régime continues in power in Rhodesia; that it continues to be regarded as illegal, to be without international recognition, and that sanctions against it continue.

But it would not be true to say that the situation has therefore returned to what it was previously. The power situation is the same; but the effect of the Commissioners' visit to Rhodesia, the African reaction to that visit, and the Report itself, can never be undone. It is the implications of these things which have to be considered in answering the question 'What now?'.

If no further external action is taken, the immediate result of the African 'no' is likely to be an intensification of oppression within Rhodesia, further development of the close link-up which now exists between South Africa and the Rhodesian authorities, and even more rapid steps towards apartheid in the colony itself. All these trends were present before the so-called agreement between Ian Smith and Sir Alec Douglas-Home. They would not have been precluded by the settlement if this had been accepted by the Africans; indeed they would have taken place in a more favourable international climate. But the real point is that the Pearce Commission Report gives a new opportunity for international action against the régime, as it shows the real meaning of the regime. It therefore gives a new, though faint, possibility of avoiding widespread violence in Rhodesia.

It is relevant to remember, for example, that when independence was first declared by Ian Smith, the South African Government was very slow in giving active support to the régime. Before committing itself deeply, the South African Government wanted to see what action Britain was intending to take. Its concern was to avoid jeopardizing South Africa's apparent immunity to hostile international action—which rests heavily on the legal sovereignty of South Africa, so that many nations are reluctant to create a precedent of 'interfering in the internal affairs of an independent nation'. Now we have a similar situation. South Africa is unlikely to reduce the assistance it is already giving (which is very considerable indeed); but it is likely to wait before going any further in order to see how the world reacts to the Africans' clear repudiation of their rulers.

Similarly, at least a few of the white people in Rhodesia may have been shaken by the African reaction to the proposals. For it is probable that some had been living under the illusion that 'their Africans were happy', or at least uninterested in government. Difficult as it was to maintain this sort of ignorance before the Pearce Commission, it is surely impossible now. But it has yet to be seen whether this will result in any appreciable alteration in the dominant attitude of the minority community. The evidence so far does not give cause for hope.

Yet it is presumably this factor to which Sir Alec Douglas-Home was referring when he spoke of the need for 'a time for reflection, particularly by Rhodesians'. For there is no possibility of the Africans changing their minds; the Pearce Commission Report makes it clear that there was no sign of any change in African opinion towards the end of their stay. Further, the reasons given by Africans for their opposition to the proposals stem from their deep frustration and humiliation at the kind of life which is imposed on them by the white minority government.

Nor is there the slightest chance of Ian Smith suddenly being converted to a belief in human equality and dignity. His reaction to the Report is evidence enough for that. And even if there were to be a second miracle on the road to Damascus, it would not help the situation; for in that event it is clear that Smith would immediately be removed from power.

In fact, a change in the situation can only come from a radical alteration in the power structure of Rhodesia. For this reason it is not enough for Sir Alec Douglas-Home to commend the view of those who he says are clearly intent upon furthering multi-racial co-operation, nor to express hopes for the 'way of compromise'. The possibility of compromise is clearly there—on the African side. The Pearce Commission Report makes clear that the vast majority of the Africans who discussed the future with the Commission were not demanding immediate adult suffrage or even immediate majority rule. They were simply saying that there must be no independence until these objectives were accepted and until the Africans had a degree of power which would effectively prevent any back-sliding—which, in practice, means no independence before majority rule. On the objectives themselves, compromise is clearly as unacceptable to the Africans of Rhodesia as it would be to the rest of Africa.

This means that the only chance for 'the way of compromise' is if the British Government acts to assert its authority, and thus to change the present Rhodesian power structure. Indeed, it is now only through actions by Britain and other world powers, that Rhodesia can be saved from a future of increasing violence as the Africans give up hope of external assistance and turn to the only course left open. For they do still hope. It may seem strange that, after everything which has happened in the last ten years, the Rhodesian Africans still look to Britain for assistance in their plight. To many African nationalists this lack of self-reliance may be appalling. But it stems from a realization of what the alternative would mean to all Rhodesian citizens. Guerilla war is brutal, horrible, and destructive to innocent and guilty, victim and oppressor alike. It is to be avoided if possible.

Yet such a war cannot be avoided by tricks. No new 'settlement', agreed between Smith and the British government, will circumvent its probability. For the Africans are now politically conscious and will not agree to any independence which fails to give them power over their own future. Nor will any new and different method of meeting the 'Fifth Principle' after any such future agreement avoid this horrible destiny. The Africans demand reality, not window-dressing, and Rhodesia will be saved from eventual war only if they obtain justice by other means.

SANCTIONS

It is early yet to say whether that is likely to happen. In presenting the Pearce Commission Report to Parliament, Sir Alec Douglas-Home has said that sanctions will be continued until it is possible to 'judge whether an opportunity for a satisfactory settlement will occur once again'. Leaving aside the obvious fact that the last proposed settlement was not satisfactory so that there is no question of an opportunity occurring 'again', his statement is a very unsatisfactory comment on current needs. The Rhodesian authorities have received a damaging blow to their self-confidence. The result will be an intensification of their effort to consolidate power; this must be matched by an intensification also of the effort to undermine the minority régime.

This can be done. Certainly sanctions have not brought down the Smith régime even after six years. Their effect has been weakened by the actions of South Africa and Portugal, and by evasions from other countries. Yet it was, and is, sanctions which make the Europeans long for a settlement. The Pearce Commission Report makes this quite clear and says 'the overall impression left was a deep desire for a settlement and less enthusiasm for the Proposals themselves'. (para. 288)

In fact while sanctions have not caused a failure of the rebellion, and are unlikely to do so, it is obvious that they are gradually undermining what is sometimes referred to as the 'Rhodesian way of life', but which is in fact, the minority way of life. The white Rhodesians' comfort, ease, security and future expectations are being destroyed, and they are being forced to realize that some change is inevitable.

Yet the real choice before the minority in power is a limited one. They can—and it appears that they will—try to move completely into an open apartheid system. The facts, however, are against them; the sort of 'peace' which South Africa maintains at huge expense is hardly possible for a country where the white minority makes up less than 5 per cent of the population as against 20 per cent in South Africa itself. To counteract this, the question of amalgamation into, or federation with, South Africa may be mooted; but it is highly unlikely that South Africa would welcome an addition of more than 5 million Africans and only 230,000 whites.

Nor can the Rhodesian whites rely upon Rhodesia's other white-dominated neighbour, Mozambique; the Portuguese are already in trouble from the freedom fighters operating there under the leadership of Frelimo, and are in no position to give any military or financial assistance to the minority régime of Rhodesia.

Sooner or later the Rhodesian minority will therefore be forced to face the true choice which lies before them. They will certainly wriggle for some time; but events will show that they can choose only between increasing unrest and violence leading to a real war of liberation by the African people, or a gradual move towards majority rule before independence. The great advantage of sanctions to those who prefer to avoid violence is that they keep open for longer the possibility of majority rule coming through peaceful change.

For foreign powers, sanctions have another advantage. They delay, even if they do not ultimately prevent, the polarization of the world over the Southern Africa situation. For, when Eastern and Western bloc countries both support sanctions against Rhodesia, a confrontation in that area is avoided. This is no small matter for world peace, or for African freedom. For at present, although Britain and other Western powers consistently claim to be opposed to racialism and apartheid, they show the greatest reluctance even to support effective criticism of South Africa; their actions are dominated by the fact that the home of apartheid is a legally independent sovereign state whose trade is valuable to them. The Western powers also refuse to exert effective pressure on Portugal despite their claim to be against colonialism. The communist powers—for ideological, historical and economic reasons—are less inhibited in their support for the African cause. The result is a potential field of international conflict, the implications of which must be clear to all.

Sanctions against Rhodesia, on the other hand, provide Western countries with a cheap way of lending—at least temporarily—some credibility to their proclaimed opposition to racialism and minority rule. The country is not legally independent, and its exports are unimportant to the trade of any country and are easily substitutable (except for Zambia). Indeed for some countries international sanctions have even resulted in an increase in their exports, as nations like Zambia have turned to others in an endeavour to overcome the economic inheritance which bound them to the Rhodesian economy. For example, the increase in British exports to Zambia, from 26.8 million kwacha in 1964 to K82 million in 1970, is due in no small part to Zambia's tremendous achievement in cutting its imports from Rhodesia from K61.7 million in 1964 (when Rhodesia was the largest source of Zambian imports) to K23.2 million in 1970.

Sanctions are in fact an essential weapon in the Rhodesian struggle. They must be continued for as long as necessary to force the Rhodesian minority into accepting two elementary facts of modern life—that 5 per cent of the people of any country cannot indefinitely enforce their will on the rest, and that the world rejects racial solutions to social problems. Further, it must be known that they will continue. The existence of reasonable hope that sanctions will be ended before the principle of NIBMAR is accepted simply undermines African belief in the possibility of a peaceful remedy to their ills, and reduces the chances of effective sanctions enforcement while they are supposedly being applied. It is not irrelevant that many 'binding' trade agreements and contracts were signed with foreign firms after the 'agreement' between Smith and Home was announced.

Even this is not enough. The enforcement of present sanctions must be greatly tightened up, and sanctions must be extended—none of which is impossible.

Tightening up can be achieved by three quite easy methods. Firstly, allegations of sanctions-breaking (such as those which Sir Alec Douglas-Home said he had referred to the United Nations Sanctions Committee) must be publicized immediately, so that every Government, and all workers who may be involved in moving Rhodesian goods, know what is being attempted and where. Secondly, the United Nations must agree that any cargoes from Rhodesia being exported contrary to sanctions will be seized by the country of destination or transit, and the return from the sale of these goods paid to the United Nations for use in humanitarian work among refugees from Southern Africa or in the liberated areas of Southern Africa. Thirdly, the countries of Africa should take all appropriate steps to 'reward their friends and damage their enemies'.

The first two steps are self-explanatory. They require an act of political will; after that, any complicated details (especially of point 2) can be worked out. The third point makes special demands upon African states, commensurate with their special interest in, and responsibility for, the total liberation of Africa and the end of racialism on our continent.

Every African state has specially close links with one or other of the major world powers—either because of their colonial history or for other reasons. And it is not true that these relationships are totally one-sided in their advantage. In the first place, the European nations which give aid solely for altruistic reasons are very few indeed; in the second place, trade only takes place if it is to the advantage of the stronger power—even when the weaker has no alternatives. Thus, each African nation has a lever which can, at the very least, be used to draw the attention of some foreign governments to strongly held African opinion. African countries which are members of the Commonwealth have an easy means of expressing their view to the Commonwealth governments; franc zone countries have similar access to the French Government. Japan has large trade interests in some parts of Africa; Liberia has a special relationship with the United States of America; West Germany is developing links with certain African states, as are the various countries of the Eastern bloc; and so on.

These special links do not mean that African countries should allow the other Governments with which they have diplomatic relations to believe that they are uninterested in this matter. Indeed supportive action by them is essential. But history and economics have their own logic; when Tanzania protests to France, the impact is much less than if the Ivory Coast does so; similarly, strong opinion expressed to Britain by Nigeria stands more chance of leading to action than a similar protest from, say, Rwanda. But in both the above examples a registration of opinion from all African countries would be the most effective of all.

Government-to-government pressure will be appropriate to deal with failures to enforce the United Nations Mandatory Sanctions by which all member nations are bound. But it is also possible for African states to take direct action against those firms and businesses which are taking part in sanctions-breaking. For when a firm is given a choice between trading with Rhodesia or trading with free African states, there will be few, if any, which make what is for Africa a wrong choice! Yet nor is such discrimination an impossible task for even the weakest of African states. There are certain countries, like Botswana Zambia and Malawi, which would be unable to survive if they applied sanctions in their fullest rigour—though two of them make very great and expensive efforts in this direction. But every nation can afford to discriminate between the firms it deals with; there are unlikely to be many difficulties in finding people anxious to supply the goods which used to be supplied by a sanctions-breaker! It is necessary that Africa should decide to exert this kind of direct business pressure—one of the few actions which are unlikely to have heavy political costs to us. For it would be difficult for other governments to protest discrimination against their citizens if the reason for that discrimination is that these are breaking United Nations' sanctions!

WHAT IS THE AIM?

The purpose of sanctions, of refusing international recognition to the Smith régime, and of other forms of pressure, is to prepare the ground for a real settlement in Rhodesia—that is, one which leads by peaceful means, or with the minimum of violence, towards independence on the basis of majority rule. The immediate objective is therefore negotiations between representatives of the African majority of Rhodesia; of the white minority which is now in power; and of either the British Government which is legally responsible for the situation in that colony, or some other body such as the United Nations. The purpose of such negotiations must be, and must be understood to be, the next steps towards majority rule. The question of independence for Rhodesia comes only after that, i.e. when majority rule has been obtained.

If such negotiations as these were held tomorrow, the whites would presumably be represented by Ian Smith and his colleagues, the Africans by Bishop Muzorewa, Joshua Nkomo and the Rev. Sithole, and the British Government by Sir Alec Douglas-Home. But it is not the names which are important; it is the representative character of the leaders which matters in such a Conference. Africa is not fighting for this individual or that, but for the African people of Rhodesia to have a chance to select their own leaders and to determine their own future.

Already the African National Council has suggested a Convention of representatives of different Rhodesian groups, and the British Foreign Secretary has indicated that any new initiative should come from the different races of Rhodesia acting in concert. Smith and his ruling Rhodesian Front have dismissed the ANC proposal with expressions of contempt, and are unlikely to allow any such Convention to take place without them. But an intensification of sanctions, and increasing danger from the freedom fighters of Southern Africa, combined with the expected growth in Rhodesia's economic difficulties, may eventually make the Rhodesian authorities more amenable to reason—though they will certainly not become willing for such talks unless pressure on them is increased.

The fact that the current ANC initiative will probably fail is thus an argument for further efforts, not an argument for an international 'washing of hands'. For no one can say when and how the breakthrough will come. It may come from international economic pressure, it may come from the psychological and other effects of Frelimo activity in the Tete Province of Mozambique; it may not occur until these things have been combined with an effective challenge from the freedom fighters of Rhodesia itself. But whether the period is long or short, the only hope is to work for this end. And the Africans, who—as has been said *ad infinitum*—are the first sufferers of sanctions because they are 'at the bottom of the heap', have now stated publicly that they are prepared to pay the price necessary for winning human dignity and justice.

One other thing is also clear. From everything which has been said and done by Rhodesian Africans and by free African states in the last decade, there can be no doubt but that the vast mass of the people of this continent, including those of Rhodesia, prefer to achieve the goal of independence under majority rule by peaceful means, even when this method means some delay in attainment. But unfortunately the principle of majority rule has itself not yet been accepted by those in power in Rhodesia any more than it has in Mozambique, Angola, Guinea Bissau or South Africa. And there is a limit to everyone's patience.

Free African states, organized in the OAU, therefore cannot, and must not, cease to support the Liberation Movement of

Rhodesia. Quite apart from everything else, its existence is in itself a form of pressure on the minority of that country. The Freedom Movement is, and will increasingly become, a reminder of the long-run alternative to a negotiated evolution to majority rule. And it may still turn out that violence is the only way by which Rhodesia will obtain true independence. There must be an increase in Africa's efforts in this respect, not a decrease.

CONCLUSION

The prime responsibility for the future freedom of Rhodesia lies with the people of Rhodesia. But the peoples and governments of free African states have an inescapable duty to assist them. There are six things which African states must do as a minimum:

(a) They must themselves participate in, and actively enforce the United Nations Mandatory Sanctions, and give maximum assistance to those neighbours of Rhodesia who have paid, and are still paying, most heavily for the sanctions policy.

(b) They must exert the maximum possible pressure to ensure that governments of other countries enforce sanctions; and each African state should concentrate its efforts on that foreign power with which it has special links.

(c) They must discriminate against those firms and businesses which are breaking sanctions or are otherwise assisting the economy of Rhodesia, so that such organizations are forced to make a choice in their trading and other activities.

(d) They must work in the United Nations to make international enforcement procedures more effective, particularly in relation to giving publicity about sanctions-breaking, and must work for an agreement to seize without compensation goods exported from Rhodesia, even if these are travelling under false documents.

(e) They must seek to get sanctions extended into the communications field and other areas still exempted.

(f) They must step up their support for the Liberation Movements of Southern Africa, including those of Rhodesia.

Certainly the prospects for the immediate future in Rhodesia are not good; but in the long run there is reason for optimism. For the Africans of Rhodesia are now more politically conscious than ever before, and have made clear their determination and ability to endure suffering and still seize every opportunity to make their voice heard. The people of Rhodesia, under the leadership of the ANC, or whatever replaces this if the ANC is banned, deserve Africa's support. They must receive it.

43

International Unity

During the dinner he gave in honour of President Nimeiry on 3 July 1972, President Nyerere paid tribute to his guest and especially for his achievement of peace with unity in the Sudan. He then urged the continued importance of African unity.

... It is not surprising that the necessary degree of African co-operation and unity is difficult to achieve. Leaving aside the internal difficulties which many African states experience, each of our independent nations has different economic and social circumstances to contend with, and we none of us can afford to ignore our peoples' immediate need for progress in order to concentrate on the fundamental long-term need for unity. Further, different African states have adopted different ideological approaches to the common problem of poverty and backwardness; some of us are non-aligned —with different interpretations of what that means!—and a few have defence agreements with great powers; some of us are at least potentially rich, others appear to be without great natural resources. Indeed, when one considers all these and any other differences, the amazing thing about African unity is the degree of co-operation and unity which has already been achieved. We get discouraged because our aspirations outrun our achievements. But we need to remember a few facts of world history! For Europe's present progress towards unification comes after centuries of detructive wars; Latin America has less unity than Africa, although its nations achieved their independence some 150 years ago; even the United States of America found unity difficult to achieve, although all the then 13 colonies were inhabited by peoples of common stock and common history who had fought a war of independence together. Mr. President, in the light of these things, it seems to me that Africa has no reason for despair, and much reason for hope.

Do not let me be misunderstood. We have not achieved enough. For the technology of the modern world makes unity more urgent and more important than it has ever been in the past. The African people will continue to be ignored or exploited unless we make much faster progress towards unity than we have been doing. But I believe this is beginning to be recognized, at least in relation to certain issues. The Rabat Meeting of the OAU showed a new seriousness, and a unanimity we have not before seen, on many questions concerning our continent. This was particularly true as regards the need for action to liberate Southern Africa from the oppression of colonialism and racialism. . . .

44

All Men are Equal

In August 1972, General Amin in Uganda followed up his order expelling British citizens of Asian descent by a statement that Uganda citizens of similar descent would also have to leave. During a previously scheduled function at Chang'ombe Teachers' College, Dar es Salaam, on 21 August, President Nyerere addressed himself to this question of citizenship and man's common humanity. (Later General Amin 'investigated' the citizenship of the Asians, and a few hundred were allowed to remain, but were subjected to discriminatory residence regulations.) The President was speaking extempore in Swahili: what follows is therefore a translation made and recorded during the speech.

... We must learn two things from history. The first is a new refusal to be pushed around any more. We must mean this—not just say it. And we must demonstrate this determination by actions. There is no difficulty about meaning the determination to change if we know Africa's history. But do we act as if we know what this means? If an outsider says—Africa has recognized its past humiliation and degradation, let me see what they are doing now—will that visitor find actions always consistent with the words?

The second thing we have to learn is that there is a world movement now against being pushed around, and against pushing others around. Some people determine that they will not be the victims of oppression, and then begin to oppress others. In Guyana only the other day people from all over the world met at the Non-Aligned Conference and expressed solidarity with Africa's struggle against colonialism and racialism in Southern Africa. The Indians were there, the Koreans, the Pakistanis, people from the Carribean and Latin America; all of us were united on this issue as well as the Vietnamese issue.

Sometimes it is necessary to remind ourselves of these things. There is a world-wide movement now—even within the imperialist countries it exists—to put an end to the exploitation of man by man. This movement will succeed. Eventually, imperialism and racialism will become merely a chapter in the history of man—we shall hear about it in museums.

Humanity has already passed through many phases since man began his evolutionary journey. And nature shows us that not all life evolves in the same way. The chimpanzees—to whom once we were very near—got on to the wrong evolutionary path and they got stuck. And there were other species which became extinct; their teeth were so big, or their bodies so heavy, that they could not adapt to changing circumstances and they died out.

I am convinced that, in the history of the human race, imperialists and racialists will also become extinct. They are now very powerful. But they are a very primitive animal. The only difference between them and these other extinct creatures is that their teeth and claws are more elaborate and cause much greater harm—we can see this even now in the terrible use of napalm in Vietnam. But a failure to co-operate together is a mark of bestiality, it is not a characteristic of humanity.

Imperialists and racialists will go. Vorster, and all like him, will come to an end. Every racialist in the world is an animal of some kind or other, and all are kinds that have no future. Eventually they will become extinct.

Africa must refuse to be humiliated, exploited, and pushed around. And with the same determination we must refuse to humiliate, exploit, or push others around. We must act, not just say words.

In Munich now there are athletes who are refusing to play in the Olympics if the Rhodesians play. It is suggested that we should agree to play if the Rhodesians take British passports. But this is nonsense. We are not quarrelling about passports but about the things which are going on in Rhodesia. The Rhodesians are forcibly moving the Tangwena tribe, because their traditional land is now wanted by a European—they are taking the Tangwena children as hostages. That is the sort of thing we are quarrelling about—not passports.

I am saying this deliberately. My friends in the United Kingdom have their citizens in East Africa—citizens with British passports.

The United Kingdom refusal to allow these passport holders to go to the United Kingdom whenever they want is discrimination. We have already pointed this out to the British. When Kenya received its independence, the British Government made elaborate and expensive arrangements to allow their white citizens to go to Britain if they wanted. To do anything else with brown citizens is discrimination.

If a country expects other people to respect its passports, then it must itself respect them. Citizenship must be respected without discrimination, or it will be met with disrespect without discrimination.

General Amin has recently said to Britain, 'Take your citizens'. But in this quarrel between two countries a lot of people are liable to get badly hurt—people, not animals. But Amin says, 'They are your citizens'. Now he is saying 'All Asians must go'—including the Uganda citizens. How can you argue this? If you argue—as you can correctly argue in logic—that he has a right to demand that all British passport holders should leave Uganda because they hold British passports, how can you argue the second thing also?

What does it mean, to say to a large group of people 'From today—or tomorrow, or next week—you citizens are no longer citizens'? It means that they are people in the world who have no state, nor country; no place where they have a right to live.

Physically what do you do with such people? If you give them thirty days to get out—or any other period—what do you do when it is expired? Where are they supposed to go—to the moon? Suppose we in Tanzania were to decide to get rid of some of our citizens, what do we do? We herd them to the border with Kenya, and Kenya says, 'No, they are not our citizens.' Uganda, Malawi, Zambia, Zaire, Burundi and Rwanda, all say this. What do we do? Do we kill them? That is what Hitler did in Europe in the 1930s and 1940s. He said that all Germany's troubles were caused by the Jews; and he killed all those who could not escape from the country. He killed six million Jews—put them in gas chambers and used their bodies for fertilizer and their hair for stuffing. This was people, not chimpanzees. Is this what you do?

Sometimes we in Africa adopt the attitude that we have suffered so long it will be good for other people to suffer and see what it is like. But it is necessary to remember that we are talking about people.

The first statement of the TANU Creed says 'All men are equal, and Africa is one'. And the very first part is that 'All human beings are equal'. This being so we have to accept that the exploitation, the humiliation, the suffering, of all men—wherever it takes place—means the exploitation, humiliation, and suffering of mankind. All men are reduced by it.

There is one further thing we must recognize. When there is trouble, tyranny, or discrimination in one country of Europe, Asia, or Latin America, only that country is held responsible for it. Somehow it is different in Africa! All African countries are liable to be asked questions about what the governments or régimes of other free African states are doing.

But this has its advantages too. For as the first statement in the Creed says, Africa is one. It is better that we face the problems of Africa as Africa. For our history of being pushed around is an African history, and our strength to stop this is an African strength. Just now in Munich all Africa is united—but now we are hurting ourselves even there.

To learn history properly is to overcome all the primitive evils of imperialism and racialism.

45

A Call to European Socialists

In the November 1972 issue of Third World, *published by the International Committee of the Fabian Society of Britain, President Nyerere challenged European socialists to apply their socialism to international economic issues. The article was translated and published in socialist party newspapers and journals in the Scandinavian countries and West Germany.*

. . . 'To him that hath shall be given' is a law of capitalist and international economics; wealth produces wealth, and poverty, poverty. Further, the poverty of the poor is a function of the wealth of the rich. Each time he buys a loaf of bread a starving man contributes to the wealth of a baker who already lives in luxury.

Within their separate nations, socialists have formulated their philosophy and their policies in answer to these facts of capitalism. Internationally, however, it appears that socialists in the rich countries are hardly conscious of capitalism's effects. Yet the evils are the same, and the results to the poor are the same, as within a national economy.

Thus, Tanzania and other Third World countries are producers of primary commodities, and have an agricultural economy with very little industrialization. Even now Tanzania's industrial sector accounts for no more than 10 per cent of our monetary national income, and we produce no sophisticated development goods. All things like tractors, machines, and even lorries, have to be imported; and to pay for them we have to export our cotton, sisal, coffee, pyrethrum and such like goods.

As the world is at present organized, this means that on the world market we sell cheap and buy dear. For the prices of the machines,

technology, skill and freight transportation which we have to purchase are determined by the living standards in the rich countries
who produce these things. And the prices of our sisal, cotton,
coffee, cocoa, and so on, are also determined by the extent and the
intensity of demand in the rich countries. The net result is that the
prices of our imports go up continually and our export prices remain
almost the same or even go down.

For the poor nations are now in the position of a worker in
nineteenth century Europe. In order to live he had to sell his labour
at whatever price he could obtain for it. With his wages he bought
goods at prices fixed by members of the employing class in their
own interests. The only difference between the two situations is
that the beneficiaries in the international situation now are the
national economies of the rich nations—which includes the working
class of those nations. And the disagreements about division of
the spoils, which used to exist between members of the capitalist
class in the nineteenth century, are now represented by disagree-
ment about division of the spoils between workers and capitalists
in the rich economies. The meaning of this conflict to the poor of
the world can be illustrated by one very simple statistic: while
as late as 1965 (that is after a major fall in sisal prices) Tanzania
could buy a tractor with 5.3 tons of cotton or 17.3 tons of sisal,
by early 1972 an equivalent tractor cost 8 tons of cotton or 42 tons
of sisal!

It is in this sort of context that the developing countries are
condemned for their failure to achieve a breakthrough from the
vicious circle of their poverty. It is in this context that they are
expected to be 'grateful' for 'aid'! And it is in this context that
Tanzania, at least, is not grateful for 'aid'—especially when this is
defined as including private investment and commercial credits
which are never so defined when they are exchanged between the
developed countries themselves.

Charity—however well meaning—is no way out of the present
appalling poverty in the world. The poverty of the underdeveloped
world is as much a function of the world economic organization
as it is of anything else. And that cannot be changed by a developing
country's commitment to socialism. Such a country will remain
a victim of international capitalist economics, just as much as if its
people acquiesced in the grossest inequality within their nation.

Their society may become an egalitarian one, but it will be an equality of poverty both absolutely and relatively to the rest of the world. European socialists might note that in such a case, the poverty of that socialist country will be used as an argument against socialism itself!

Socialists in the developed countries have to face up to the implications of the exploitative international economic system. At present they are the beneficiaries of it—their nations are, and therefore a great deal of the wealth about whose distribution they quarrel with their own capitalists. And they have two choices open to them. They can support the continued exploitation of the world's poor by their national economies. Or they can act as socialists, and co-operate in the necessary reorganization of the structure of world trade, at the same time as they give interim, but genuine, assistance to the poor nations on the basis of national equality.

Yet the choice is really only a temporary one, for the poor of the world are becoming aware both of their poverty and the reasons for it. And as this happens they are becoming angry, and determined upon change. In the long term, therefore, the real choice facing socialists in the developed world is the gradual build up of an international class war—with all that this involves—or the development of real and equal partnership between the rich and the poor of the world for the common benefit of humanity. This is, in fact, the same choice which faces individual socialists within each nation—a choice between an economic revolution effected in an orderly and planned manner, or violent revolution with different members of the society pitted against one another in a destructive war.

There is some time for this choice, but it is getting short. Already people in the Third World are beginning to talk of the need of a 'trade union' of the poor nations. Slowly, haltingly, and very painfully, they are working towards co-operation in united opposition to the rich and powerful nations of the world. The 'Group of 77' at UNCTAD is just one sign of this; there are others.

No one imagines that this 'Trade Union of the Poor' is going to be quickly or easily organized. It requires a degree of unity and temporary sacrifice which is difficult to organize or maintain— just as it was difficult for a starving worker to stand fast with his comrades when the first trade unions were being organized in Europe. Up to now only the oil producing countries have achieved even the degree of unity which enables them to growl in unison at the oil consumers. But that is a foretaste of medicine which will get nastier the more of it has to be taken!

Socialists in Europe must think about their proper socialist reaction to the demand of the world's poor for justice, and to the steps which will be taken by Third World nations to achieve it. Are they going to react with 'sanctions' against any developing country which moves towards socialism by nationalizing its mineral resources and then demanding a fair price for them? Are they going to cut off 'aid', or access to capital, for a developing country which takes over its own financial institutions, or which refuses to acquiesce in international agreements reached by others contrary to its interests? Or are they going to assist a developing socialist country by an increase in grants, soft loans, and technical assistance of the type required, at the same time as negotiating fair and long-term trade and monetary agreements with it? In particular, are they going to work for a world order in which the struggle for existence does not end up in the liquidation of the poor?

The present international economic jungle cannot be replaced by equitable arrangements for international contact and exchange through the action of any particular state, whether from the developed or underdeveloped worlds. But this is no excuse for inaction; each socialist party, and each socialist government can contribute towards the necessary movement.

In international organizations socialist governments can support measures which increase the power and strength of the poor nations, or which give these the favourable treatment necessary if they are to have a chance of overcoming their present poverty. Domestically, socialist governments of Europe can stop the present tariff discrimination and restrictive quota systems which operate against the primary commodities and simple manufactures exported by the poor nations. They can increase genuine aid—that is grants and soft loans without strings—to developing nations. They can act so as to prevent the poor nations being forced to accept the burdens of redistributive struggles within the rich nations—so that, for example, the demands of dockers or seamen for a higher wage are met from within the rich society and not by increased freight charges levied on the poor nations.

In other words, socialist governments of Europe, and socialist parties of Europe, have to carry over into the international arena that struggle for equality which they have conducted and are conducting within their own nations. And they have to accept that internationally their nations are the rich and the exploiters—and act accordingly. Only if this is done will they be distinguishable by us from the capitalist parties and governments which make no pretence at believing in human equality.

I believe that such attitudes and actions could be adopted by the socialists of Europe. It is true that socialist parties in democratic states have to win votes from non-socialists as well as socialists. But they are themselves a contributory factor to the environment in which they attempt to do so. The persistence and intensity with which they conduct socialist education between elections is a factor in the freedom they win for themselves once they have won the elections—and may even contribute to the winning of them!

To the masses in the poor countries, capitalism is an evil. They will not tolerate its injustices for ever. Whether the change they rightly demand will come through violence or not may well depend upon socialists of the rich countries.

46

The Rational Choice

At the last minute, President Nyerere was unable to undertake his scheduled state visit to the Sudan at the end of December 1972. His speech for a gathering of intellectuals and leaders of the Sudanese Socialist Union had, however, been prepared. It was therefore read to the gathering on 2 January 1973 by Vice-President Jumbe who went to Sudan on behalf of the President.

My job today is to give a starting point for discussion and thought. And my subject is an examination of the alternative economic and social systems which are open to Third World countries.

In order to keep this discussion within reasonable bounds I must make certain assumptions. It is important that these should be clear before I begin; for if the assumptions are not shared, then much of what I say will be irrelevant.

Fortunately, my assumptions are not very controversial—at least within Africa.

THE ASSUMPTIONS

My first assumption is that any discussion about the appropriate economic and social organization must, for the time being at least, be conducted within each nation state, and the decision must be made exclusively by the people of that nation. Thus, it is the people of Tanzania as a whole, or the Sudan as a whole, who will decide the path for their country. Tanzania cannot decide for the Sudan, nor vice versa—and I hope that nothing I say today will be understood to imply otherwise! The fact that, for example, Zanzibar within the United Republic of Tanzania, and the Southern Provinces within Sudan, have autonomy in certain matters means that in these respects the smaller units will be the unit of choice rather than the nation as a whole.

Secondly, I take it to be axiomatic that all the peoples of the Third World desire to govern themselves, and want their country to be completely independent from external control. This does not rule out the possibility of political or economic links between two or more countries; nor does it exclude a possible voluntary merger of sovereignties, provided that these things are agreed upon after discussions based on the equality of all participants.

Thirdly, I shall assume that, to everyone in the Third World, the present degree of poverty, and the general lack of economic development, is completely unacceptable. We have to increase our production of wealth so that we may increase the level of our collective and individual consumption.

My fourth and final assumption is that our struggles for independence were national struggles, involving the rights of all the inhabitants. We were not aiming to replace our alien rulers by local privileged *élites*, but to create societies which ensure human dignity and self-respect for all. The concomitant of that is that every individual has the right to the maximum economic and political freedom which is compatible with equal freedom for all others; and that neither well fed slavery nor the necessity to beg for subsistence are acceptable human conditions.

I have said that these assumptions are not very controversial within Africa. It is equally true that they do not represent the present situation. They represent aspirations rather than facts. That is obvious from an examination of world affairs, or from the briefest visit to any of our rural areas—or even to those urban areas where our unskilled labourers live.

Yet because these stated assumptions are also a list of our fundamental aspirations, they must be the basis for our choice of policies. If a policy militates against the achievement of these conditions, then its acceptability must be questioned. Even more, if a social and economic system is incompatible with these goals, then it must be rejected.

THE CHOICE

In the modern world there are two basic systems of economic and social organization—capitalism and socialism. There are variations within these broad classifications, like welfare capitalism or humanistic socialism; but the broad distinction between the two systems remains, and our first choice has to be between them.

Remnants of feudalism and of primitive communalism do, of course, still exist in the world; but neither of these are viable systems when challenged by the organized technology of the twentieth century. Sometimes, as in Japan, these old systems influence the organization of capitalism for a while; but the influences are subordinate to the logic of the later organization, and will eventually be completely eradicated. For, in the last resort, anything which detracts from the profit of an individual capitalist enterprise will be abandoned by that enterprise; and anything which militates against the efficiency of the capitalist system will be uprooted.

Primitive communalism is equally doomed. The moment the first enamel pot, or factory woven cloth, is imported into a self-sufficient communal society, the economic and social structure of that society receives its death blow. Afterwards it is merely a question of time, and of whether the members of that community will be participants or victims in the new economic order.

Thus the choice for new nations lies effectively between socialism and capitalism. It is not a completely free choice, for all of us inherited certain patterns of trade, and have been to a greater or lesser extent indoctrinated by the value systems of our colonial master. Further, the great powers continue to regard us as being within the sphere of influence of one or other of them—which usually demonstrates its displeasure if we refuse to conform to the expected pattern of behaviour. But ultimately, if we so determine, and if we are prepared to overcome our recent past and the difficulties which others may place in our way, we can move towards the growth of one system or the other within our society.

Yet having said that, I now propose to argue that there is no real choice. In practice Third World nations cannot become developed capitalist societies without surrendering the reality of their freedom and without accepting a degree of inequality between their citizens which would deny the moral validity of our independence struggle.

I will argue that our present poverty and national weakness make socialism the only rational choice for us.

CAPITALISM AND INDEPENDENCE

Under a capitalist system the purpose of production and distribution is the making of profit for those who own the means of production and exchange. The need for goods is subsidiary to the profit involved in making them. Therefore the owner of the machines and equipment used in production—that is, he who provides the money for these things—is the one who determines whether there shall be any production, and of what kind, and in what quantity. Neither the men who provide the labour for the production, nor the men who need the goods which could be produced, have any say in these decisions. Under capitalism, money is King. He who owns wealth owns also power. He has power over all the workers who he can employ or not, and power over the governments which he can paralyse by withholding vital production, or sabotage by the manipulation of men and machines.

That has always been the essence of capitalism. But there is a further relevant fact in these decades of the twentieth century. That is that this power is now concentrated in very few hands. For whereas one hundred years ago a quite small amount of money sufficed to establish an industrial or commercial enterprise, modern technology now precludes this in all important areas of production. Thus, for example, Henry Ford could begin his manufacture of cars in a bicycle repair shop, and build up his capacity bit by bit. But now, in the 1970s, anyone who decides to begin making vehicles must be prepared to make a multi-million dollar investment before the first one rolls off the assembly line. Mass production techniques make small units uneconomic—they go bankrupt in an attempt to compete with the giants, or else sell out to a larger business. Therefore, instead of having a very large number of small capitalists, we have a very small number of large capitalists. 'Small men' exist; but they initiate an insignificant proportion of the total wealth produced, and usually confine their attention to the luxury trades.

This development is part of the dynamic of capitalism—for capitalism is very dynamic. It is a fighting system. Each capitalist enterprise survives by successfully fighting other capitalist enterprises. And the capitalist system as a whole survives by expansion, that is, by extending its area of operations and in the process eradicating all restraints upon it, and all weaker systems of society.

Consider now what this means for the new nations of the Third World.

According to capitalist theory, if we choose capitalism our citizens would be free to establish capitalist enterprises, and these Tanzanian or Sudanese capitalists would compete—that is, would fight—all other capitalist enterprises, including the foreign ones. In practice, however, two questions immediately arise. First, where in our lands are those citizens who have sufficient capital to establish modern industries; and second, how would our infant industries fight other capitalist enterprises?

I believe the answer to these questions is clear in all Third World countries. For Tanzania is no exception in not having within its borders the kind of wealth which is necessary to establish modern industrial units. As a general rule no individual, or group of individuals, from within any of our nations has the capacity to establish even a large modern textile mill, much less to operate a diamond mine, put up a steel mill, or run a large-scale commercial enterprise. That amount of money, and that kind of expertise, just do not exist. Certainly, the most which could be done by Tanzanians is the establishment of little workshops, which either assemble imported components, or which undertake simple processing of locally produced crops. Our citizens can establish small retail shops; wholesaling on any economic scale is likely to demand more resources than they have.

When Britain experienced its industrial revolution at the end of the eighteenth century, that was enough. It is not enough now! How could these little Tanzanian capitalists compete with I.C.I., Ford, Nippon Enterprises, and the other big multi-national corporations—or even with Walls Food Products? The answer is simple: they could not! The best they could do would be to become agents of these international capitalist concerns. And this would not bring progress in the attack on our underdevelopment; for the result would not be modern factories producing necessities, but local agents importing and processing those things—and only those things—which were profitable to both the local agents and the overseas enterprise.

In fact, Third World capitalism would have no choice except to co-operate with external capitalism, as a very junior partner. Otherwise it would be strangled at birth. You cannot develop capitalism in our countries without foreign capitalists, their money and their management expertise. And these foreign capitalists will invest in Third World countries only if, when, and to the extent that, they are convinced that to do so would be more profitable to them than any other investment. Development through capitalism therefore means that we Third World nations have to meet conditions laid down by others—by capitalists of other countries. And if we agreed to their conditions we should have to continue to be guided by them or face the threat of the new enterprises being run down, of money and skills being withdrawn, and of other economic sanctions being applied against us.

In fact, a reliance upon capitalist development means that we give to others the power to make vital decisions about our economy. The kind of economic production we shall undertake; the location of factories, offices and stores; the amount of employment available in any area; and even the kind of taxation system we adopt; all these matters will be determined by outsiders.

It is claimed that this would be a temporary phenomenon, as foreign capitalist investment in a Third World country would be a catalyst for local capitalist enterprise. To some extent this is true; small local businesses may grow up in the shadow of a major, foreign-owned, factory. But all such businesses would have the purpose of providing service to the workers of the big industry, or of making small components for it. They would therefore be absolutely dependent upon it, flourishing when it expanded and collapsing if it closed down. Local businesses would thus be the puppets, not the enemies of the foreign enterprise—the subsidiaries, not the competitors. They would be forced to identify themselves with all demands made by the foreign capitalists. The loss of real national self-determination would therefore be increased—not decreased; for the foreign owners would have secured a local political base to back up their economic power.

This is very easy to understand. If the Government for example, proposes to lay down new minimum wages, or to raise revenue from a tariff on goods of interest to the factory, the big employer may say—politely or otherwise—that in such a case they will close their factory. They can point out that this will not only result in a loss of livelihood for all those directly employed; it will also force into bankruptcy a number of ancillary units. Of course, the independent government can still go ahead with its proposals; but it will then have to deal with the consequences—and they are not likely to be pleasant either for that government or the people it wishes to serve.

Nor is this all. Foreign policy questions will also be affected by reliance upon foreign capitalists for economic development. It is true that American, British, or Japanese capitalists have no patriotic loyalty to their country of origin. But they do have loyalty to their largest investments—and these are unlikely to be inside any one underdeveloped country! Therefore, a poor nation's quarrel with one of the imperialist countries about, for example, its support for Zionist expansionism, or for South Africa, Rhodesia, or Portuguese colonialism, can easily lead to the withdrawal of capitalist expansion plans, or even to the contraction and eventual closing of established enterprises.

What I am saying is that, given the present inequalities between nations, capitalist development is incompatible with full national independence for Third World countries. For such development will be foreign owned, and foreign controlled; local capitalists will be subsidiary, and will remain subsidiary.

There can be no question about this—the foreign domination is permanent, not temporary. It is the big enterprise which will make the large profits and have large monies available for the next investment. The small ones will remain small—or be bought out! For confirmation of this fact, and its meaning, it is only necessary to look at what has happened within the major capitalist countries. One sees that medium size enterprises gobble up small ones, and are themselves gobbled up by large ones. Finally, the giants fight among themselves for ultimate supremacy. In the end the rich governments of the big capitalist countries find their own freedom of action is restricted by the economic power of the capitalist giants. Even if they are elected to fight capitalism, they find it necessary to ensure the raw materials, and the profitability, of the big corporations, or face mass unemployment and major economic crises.

The fact that a number of competing big capitalist institutions may invest in a particular developing country—perhaps from different foreign bases—does not invalidate this simplified analysis. As a general rule the meaning is that the poor country has given several hostages to fortune instead of one. In theory it can endeavour to play one enterprise off against another; but in practice it is much more likely to discover that its economic destiny has been determined by enterprise conflicts which originate outside its own borders, and about which it knows nothing! A 'take-over bid', or a rationalization scheme, or a new cartel arrangement, can undo years of local negotiation, and the independent government may well hear about the prospect only if one giant or the other hopes to use it in order to get better terms for its own shareholders!

CAPITALISM AND THE NATURE OF SOCIETY

This inevitable loss of real national freedom is, however, only one of those results of capitalism which I believe to be incompatible with the national purposes of all Third World governments. For capitalism does not only imply a fight between capitalists, with the developing nations' capitalists inevitably being worsted. It also involves a permanent fight between capitalists on one side and workers on the other.

This is a very important matter for us, coming as most of the African Third World countries do, out of primitive communalism into the modern world. For it means a new factor of national division at a time when all of us are still fighting to overcome the divisive forces of tribalism, religion, and race. It also means that the fruits of independence will be denied to the mass of the people who worked for it, or in whose name it was demanded.

There is no escaping this effect of capitalism. For the purpose of capitalist enterprise is the making of profit. To do this, the capitalist must keep his costs of production as low as possible, and get the maximum return from the sale of the products. In other words, he must pay the lowest wages for which he can get workers, and charge the maximum price at which he can sell the goods produced. A permanent conflict of interest between the worker and the employer inevitably follows. The former want to get high wages so as to live decently—and perhaps buy some of the goods they work to produce. The latter needs to pay low wages so as to maximize his profit, that is, the return on the money he has invested.

Thus capitalism automatically brings with it the development of two classes of people: a small group whose ownership of the means of production brings them wealth, power and privilege; and a very much larger group whose work provides that wealth and privilege. The one benefits by exploiting the other, and a failure in the attempt to exploit leads to a breakdown of the whole system with a consequent end to all production! The exploitation of the masses is, in fact, the basis on which capitalism has won the accolade for having solved the problem of production. There is no other basis on which it can operate. For if the workers ever succeeded in obtaining the full benefits of their industry, then the capitalist would receive no profit and would close down the enterprise!

What this means for the masses of the people in the Third World countries should be obvious. Their conditions of employment, and their return from employment, will be just sufficient to maintain the labour supply. Further, if the nation is dependent upon capitalist investment for all its desired economic expansion, the workers will have to be prevented from organizing themselves to fight for their rights. For an effective trade union struggle might lead the employer to argue once again that his factory has become uneconomic. The resultant threat of a close down may well prompt the government to intervene on the side of the employers in order to safeguard the economic growth rate and its own miserably small, but vital, tax revenue.

Development through capitalism is thus basically incompatible with the fourth aspiration I listed—that of human dignity and self-respect for all, with equal freedom for all inhabitants of the society. For capitalism means that the masses will work, and a few people—who may not labour at all—will benefit from that work. The few will sit down to a banquet, and the masses will eat whatever is left over.

This has a further implication. With a capitalist system the production of goods, measured statistically, may well go up considerably; if it happens to possess certain mineral resources, the Third World country may even find itself high on the list of 'successful states' as regards the growth rate of its gross national product. But the mass of the people, who produce the goods which are measured, will be without sufficient money to buy the things they need for a decent life. Their demand will exist, but it will not be effective. Consequently, the production of basic necessities—decent houses, food, and nice clothes—will be limited; such production would be less profitable to the capitalist investor than the provision of 'luxury goods'. It was no accident, for example, that one of the early post-independence investments in Tanzania was a drive-in cinema. Much more profit could be made from using cement that way than in producing worker's houses!

For on top of everything else, the choice of capitalism as the road to development means a particular kind of production, and a particular kind of social organization. Rural water supplies will have a low priority, regardless of the fact that they are needed for the health of the people. The importation, and perhaps even the production, of air conditioners, of private cars, and of other 'consumer durables' will have a high priority. The former brings no profit; the latter do.

To see the real meaning of this we can once again look at the developed capitalist societies. Then we can see the malnutrition among the people of the Appalachian mountains and of Harlem contrasted with the gadgetry of suburban America; or in Britain we can see the problem of homelessness while colour television sets are produced endlessly; and in the same societies we can observe the small resources devoted to things like education and health for the people as compared with those spent to satisfy the inessential desires of the minority.

THE ALTERNATIVE OF SOCIALISM

To argue, as I have been doing, that capitalism is incompatible with the aspirations of the Third World does not mean that the alternative of socialism is an easy one, nor that success under it is automatic. But socialism can be compatible with our aspirations; by adopting socialist policies it is possible for us to maintain our independence and develop towards human dignity for all our people.

The vital point is that the basis of socialist organization is the meeting of people's needs, not the making of profit. The decision to devote the nation's resources to the production of one thing rather than another is made in the light of what is needed, not what is most profitable. Furthermore, such decisions are made by the people through their responsible institutions—their own government, their own industrial corporations, their own commercial institutions. They are not made by a small group of capitalists, either local or foreign—and the question of foreign domination through economic ownership is thus excluded. Further the workers of the nation can receive—directly or indirectly—the full fruits of their industry; there is no group of private owners which constantly appropriates a large proportion of the wealth produced.

None of this means that great inequalities within the society, or the exploitation of groups, or even the seizure of power and privilege by a small minority, is automatically ruled out in a society which opts for socialism. Looking around the world we can see so-called socialist countries where all these things happen. But my point is that such things mark a failure to implement socialism; they are not inherent in it in the way that they are inherent in capitalism.

The major argument used against socialism for the developing world is, in fact, that it will not work, and that all socialist states are poor states because of their socialism. Without speaking for as long again as I have already spoken—which I do not propose to do—it is not possible to refute this argument in any detail. There are, however, three very fundamental points which I would ask you to consider in this respect.

The first is that to measure a country's wealth by its gross national product is to measure things, not satisfactions. An increase in the sale of heroin, in a country where this is legal, would be recorded as an increase in its national wealth; if human well-being was the unit of measurement, such an increase of sales would be a negative factor. Similarly, the spread of good health through the eradication of endemic diseases may, or may not, be recorded as an increase in statistical national wealth; it is certainly better for the people if it has happened!

My second point is that a successful harlot, or favoured slave, may be better off materially than a woman who refuses to sell her body, or a man to sell his freedom. We do not regard the condition of the harlot or slave as being consequently enviable—unless, of course, we are starving, and even then we recognize the possible amelioration in our circumstances as being uncertain and insecure.

Thirdly, I do not accept that the so-called unworkability of socialism has been proved. Capitalism has been developing for about two centuries. The first national commitment to socialism was made in 1917, by a backward and feudal nation devastated by war, which has subsequently suffered greatly from further civil and international conflict. Even so, few people would deny the material transformation which has been effected in the USSR during the past fifty-five years. And in fact, despite the major criticisms which can be made of all the socialist countries, it is difficult to argue that their peoples are worse off than the late capitalist starters—countries like Greece, or Spain, or Turkey, for example. On the contrary, they are clearly better off in the vital matters of health, education, and the security of their food and shelter. Whether or not they have the same number of television sets seems to me to be much less important!

CONCLUSION

It cannot be denied that many difficulties face a Third World country which chooses the socialist alternative of development. Not least among these are its own past, the dynamism of capitalist initiative techniques, and the gambler instinct which every human being seems to possess, so that we all hope we shall be among the privileged not the exploited! But I believe that we can choose the socialist path, and that by so doing we can develop ourselves in freedom, and towards those conditions which allow dignity and self-respect for every one of our citizens.

I believe that this prospect must be pursued, with vigour and determination. We shall not create socialist societies overnight; because we have to start from where we are, we shall have to make compromises with capitalist money and skill, and we shall have to take risks in our development. But I am convinced that Third World countries have the power to transform themselves, over time, into socialist societies in which their peoples can live in harmony and co-operation as they work together for their common benefit.

Index